the ULTIMATE GUIDE TO HOMESCHOOLING

the ULTIMATE GUIDE TO HOMESCHOOLING

by

Debra Bell

Tommy NELSON

Thomas Nelson, Inc.

Nashville • London • Vancouver

THE ULTIMATE GUIDE TO HOMESCHOOLING

Managing Editor: Laura Minchew
Project Editor: Beverly Phillips
Copyeditor: Sue Ann Jones
Design/Layout: Kelli Hagen
Icons/Illustrations: Dan Clayton

Unless otherwise indicated, Scripture quotations used in this book are from the New American Standard Bible (NASB), © 1960, 1962, 1963, 1968, 1971, 1972, 1973, 1975, 1977 by the Lockman Foundation. Used by permission.

Scriptures indicated AMP are from the Amplified Bible: Old Testament, copyright © 1962, 1964 by Zondervan Publishing House; and from the Amplified New Testament, copyright © 1958 by the Lockman Foundation. Used by permission.

Library of Congress Cataloging-in-Publication Data

Bell, Debra, 1955–
    The ultimate guide to homeschooling / by Debra Bell.
        p. cm. —
    Includes bibliographical references.
    ISBN 0-8499-3988-7
    1. Home schooling—United States—Handbooks, manuals, etc.   2. Homeschooling—United States—Curricula—Handbooks, manuals, etc.   I. Title.   II. Series.
LC40.B45 1997
649'.68—dc20   96-38912
                                                                                                    CIP

Printed in the United States of America.

97 98 99 00 01 02 03 QBP 9 8 7 6 5 4 3

To my dad and mom, Bill and Jean Joseph,

educators who always did what was in their power to do to help kids.
I know this isn't exactly what you envisioned when you told me to
teach, but you've both been good sports about it!

And to Kermit,

who knows me better than anyone else and still agrees to live with me.
What a feat! I can't imagine a better husband or father for our kids.
I love you!

Contents

● ●

Acknowledgments

• •

Love and kisses—don't grimace, boys—to Mike, Gabe, Katie, and Kristen for hanging in there throughout this project. You make us so proud. And yes, you can have the computer now.

Special appreciation and love to my in-laws, Marlin and Louise Bell. Thanks for all you do for us.

A golf cart full of thanks to our friend, author Sigmund Brouwer, for his vision and direction on this project and a host of others yet unfounded. Just let me catch my breath before you think of something else to do, Sigmund!

To the staff of the Home School Resource Center and Young Writers' Institute: Barb, Melanie, Nancy, and Tina. You are phenomenal! Thanks for looking out for me, organizing what I start, making sure I pay my taxes, and continuing to come to work, even when the load is far more than expected.

To my support team: the moms of the Learning Center homeschool co-op. What creative and committed teachers you are! Your love, prayers, tolerance, passion for the Lord, laughter, coffeecake—they humble me and spur me on.

Tips for Using This Book

Icons

These graphics alert you to important stuff you may want to know:

 Indicates addresses throughout the book where you can get more information about the cool stuff I've just mentioned.

 For the self-educating do-it-yourselfer. If you want to know more about the subject being discussed, here's suggested reading to get you started.

 If you're wired, you'll find what you're looking for at this Web site.

 From the Bell files. Stories not quite as scary as the *X Files* but good enough to keep you from nodding off, I trust.

 Voices of experience. Thought you'd like to read more than just my opinion for four hundred—odd pages, so I got my friends and acquaintances around the country to chip in with their experiences as well.

 At the risk of sounding like an infomercial, this icon indicates that resources tagged with an asterisk in the adjoining text are available from our family business:

Home School Resource Center
1425 E. Chocolate Avenue
Hershey, PA 17033

Write or call 717-533-1669 or 1-800-937-6311 to receive a catalog, or visit our Web site:
http://www.hsrc.com

Resource Guide

At the end of the book, this one-stop reference guide will get you plugged in to the homeschool community. Only the best organizations, suppliers, products, competitions, and other resources have been included here, and they're all organized for you in one convenient place.

Underlined Text

JUMP to the Resource Guide for sources of products and organizations <u>underlined in the text</u>. Sorry this doesn't work with the click of your mouse—maybe next edition.

Bold Text

Recommended book titles and resources appear in **bold type**. These are products or sources that have worked well for our family or for other homeschooling families, and we feel confident in recommending them.

Introduction

· ·

Detours Ahead!

I am reputed to have a terrible sense of direction. I maintain, however, it is a matter of perspective. Because of this quirk in my synapses, my children have unintentionally visited New Jersey and Ohio when we were aiming for someplace here in our home state of Pennsylvania. Others might have been frustrated that their intended destination had been delayed. But we chose to enjoy the unexpected pleasure of visiting a state we'd never been through before—even if it wasn't Hawaii.

The latter is my approach to life and to homeschooling.

Both have been filled with unexpected detours and unintended delays—often caused by my own human failings. Praise be to God and the unfathomable riches of His grace—the foundation upon which I have purposed to build my life! I'm not surprised or discouraged by these errors. I know my Redeemer lives, and He is able to "undo" exceedingly abundantly beyond all that I can ask or imagine, to paraphrase the apostle Paul.

A Long and Winding Road

If you are currently homeschooling or intending to homeschool your kids, then start with these givens: You're going to make mistakes. You're going to change your mind about resources and direction. Some days you'll get frustrated, feel like quitting, and wonder if all this effort is making any difference at all. In fact, all the evidence before you may suggest you've only made things worse!

I want to help you minimize those moments. That's the intent of this book. This is a "live-from-the-trenches" report, including:

- ✔ lots of stories
- ✔ practical tips
- ✔ concrete strategies
- ✔ recommended resources
- ✔ and more

The Ultimate Destination

But that's not the foundation for successful homeschooling, nor is it the source of joy that will keep you motivated. Those are only found in the grace of God.

So add one more thing to that list of givens: God doesn't expect you to get it right the first time. He wants you to enjoy the process—wrong turns and all.

Why? Because our *only* destination in life is really a journey of discovery—a discovery of who He truly is: merciful and sovereign over all.

> What we call *the process* God calls *the end.*
> —Oswald Chambers

A Graceful Finish

This is my prayer: May God's grace permeate these pages and my words. While I'd like you to think I've got it all together here, I know that dishonesty does nothing to help you successfully homeschool your children. All I'd have to do to dispel that myth is describe what my house looks like right now. Here it is algebraically:

$$\textbf{wildest imaginations}^{10} = \textbf{x}$$

This book is merely a distillation of our homeschooling adventure, an adventure I can honestly say has been a true journey of joy thus far. In these pages you'll find the successes and all the picture-perfect moments—but you'll also know the misfires and wrong turns, the limitations of our abilities, and the consequences of our failings. Above all, I pray you'll see throughout this book a testimony of the redeeming grace of God, which is equally available to all (even to *your* family) and is the *only* place to start and end the journey of life—and homeschooling.

Meet the ~~Wife~~ *Husband* and Kids

My intent in this book is to intersperse all kinds of impressive research, profound wisdom, and compelling arguments for homeschooling with vignettes from the real lives of homeschool families. Since my own kids and hubby have signed off on being featured in many of these tales, I'll take a few moments to introduce everyone to you now and give their vital statistics at the time of printing:

Kermit: "The Dad" and everyone's favorite playmate. Named after Teddy Roosevelt's son. (I'm sure you were wondering.) In college he was the only student carrying a briefcase. Today he's a systems analyst. Pennsylvania Dutch.

Gabe: Fourteen. Older than his brother by seven minutes (one of the first things he will want you to know), Gabe likes to read, write, and talk. Main interest: sports. Main ambition: to play football for Penn State. Mother's ambition: something a bit more certain, say, Rhodes Scholar.

Mike: Also fourteen. Mike claims he is the polite one. Evidence: He let his brother go first. Math whiz. Very dry wit. Main interests: sports and contemporary Christian music. Main ambition: ditto Penn State football.

Katie: Eleven. Very confident despite having identical twin brothers who dominate the landscape (and the refrigerator). Main interests: quilting, writing, and Bible study.

Kristen: Eight. She says the thing that makes her special is having brothers who are popular (we're working on her identity). Likes to sing, listen to books-on-tape, and socialize.

Supporting Cast

Cindy McKeown: Cindy has been a Titus 2 woman in my life since the earliest days of my marriage. (She insists that I make it clear she is not that much older than I am—I just married later.) She has four kids ages nineteen, seventeen, fifteen, and ten and has been my collaborator on a number of misadventures. She is my traveling companion—required by Kermit because of my *supposed* lack of direction.

Currently, Cindy is the director of Creative Home Educators' Support Services (CHESS), a hybrid of private schooling and homeschooling. Homeschooled students meet one day a week for CHESS classes in the core subject areas. I teach the junior and senior high English courses at CHESS.

Marie Gamon: Marie also has four kids, ages eighteen, sixteen, twelve, and ten. The Gamons and McKeowns co-own a vintage Victorian duplex. They do have distinct living quarters, but connecting doors in the attic and secret passageways in the cellar make it impossible to keep the kids separated. I tell them they are the last living Christian commune.

In addition, Marie's husband, John, a former science teacher, is a church pastor. Their home life is an eclectic mix of intellectuals who drop in to discuss Bonhoeffer and New Testament Greek and down-and-outers John has met at the corner mini-market and brought home for a sandwich and a cup of coffee. Needless to say, we love hanging out with these folks.

The Fruit

> I would never homeschool my kids.
> —Debby Bell, 1980

Fourteen years ago, when the first woman at our church began to homeschool, I wrote her off as being a bit eccentric (she also had her babies at home and did once-a-month cooking).

But when, the following year, my two closest friends, Cindy McKeown and Marie Gamon, likewise withdrew their children from a private school and took up homeschooling, I was on my knees in a panic, begging, "Oh please, please, Lord, don't let this be a trend! Let this be another silly, short-lived fad Christians get suckered into, like prayer plants!"

I had just given birth to twins (in a hospital—with drugs), and my goal in life was to survive till they were five and I could send them to school. (I was also hoping to comb my hair and take a shower then.) Having just finished the graduate work necessary for my permanent certification in teaching as well, I took offense at my friends' boldness to undertake my profession—without degrees!

But fruit is fruit and deserves an honest examination. I quelled my panic and waited for the results.

"Congratulations, Mrs. Bell! Your Test Is Positive"

Well, the results are in, and I couldn't argue with the evidence: Cindy and Marie's kids love to learn, they've scored well on the standardized tests I've given them over the years, and they are consistently motivated to do their best in their studies.

Further, these kids love the Lord, are kind to their younger siblings, enjoy and respect their parents, and are funny and fascinating to know.

Cindy's oldest, Nate, is now a pre-med student at a prestigious college. Marie's oldest, Tom, graduated from high school last year with SAT scores near 1300 and is planning a career in video production.

Guess Who Signs Up

In short, by the time my twins, Mike and Gabe, were five I had concluded that Cindy and Marie's kids were the way I wanted my own to turn out—and I had to admit homeschooling was a major contributor. (I'd also figured out how to get showering into the schedule as well.)

Ten years later, my enthusiasm has not been dampened.

Guess Who Opens a Recruitment Office

I have not only seen the positive results in my own children but in hundreds of students I've worked with since 1988.[1] Among those students are National Merit scholars, winners of national and international competitions, teens who have started and established their own businesses before leaving high school, and those who have distinguished themselves at college.

But homeschooling is not only a forum for intellectually talented kids to achieve their fullest. I've seen equal success with kids otherwise labeled delayed, dyslexic, ADHD (attention deficit hyperactive disorder), or whatever other term is in vogue for shifting blame for why kids fail away from the system.

It's All in the Family

Ultimately, though, my greatest enthusiasm comes from observing the quality of family life I see among homeschoolers. It is a powerful opportunity to integrate our children's spiritual, intellectual, and character development in a natural and nurturing setting. It's a proactive stand against a disintegrating culture that splinters families apart and exalts self-absorbed individualism.

Despite my reluctant beginnings, homeschooling has become my *joie de vivre*.

I was not only there the day each of my children walked, I was also there the day each began to read. Together we've spent the day learning triangular navigation while sailing the Chesapeake Bay. Together we've explored the battlefields of the Revolutionary and Civil Wars. And together we've shared the books that color their childhood: *The Cay, Shiloh, The Giver, To Kill a Mockingbird*, and others.

It is the fabric of our family life. We enjoy learning. We enjoy each other. I don't have perfect kids, and I certainly am a very imperfect mom, but I believe homeschooling has allowed Kermit and me to maximize the time we have to prepare our kids for adulthood—and I'm grateful for that and want to add my voice of encouragement to others who consider traveling this road.

A Blessing, Not a Cross

If God is calling your family to homeschool, it's not a cross to bear—it's a manifold blessing, one I look forward to helping you realize.

The Big Picture

Obviously, homeschooling can no longer be viewed as a short-lived fad. Recent findings by the <u>National Home Education Research Institute</u> (NHERI) show more than a 15 percent increase annually in the homeschool population. That has certainly proven true here in Pennsylvania. Nine years ago we were the only homeschooling family in our mid-size school district; today more than fifty students are home-educated. Last year there were thirteen thousand registered homeschoolers in our state, fifteen thousand listed in North Carolina, and a reported ninety thousand in Texas.

Conservative estimates put it nationally at close to one million. (It is difficult to compile an accurate count since many states do not have a registration requirement for homeschoolers.)

Why is this happening?

Techno-Revolution Meets Parental Choice

The growing homeschooling movement may be fueled by the collapse of our country's Judeo-Christian underpinnings that places conservative and Christian families increasingly at odds with our culture.

The bureaucratic quagmire of our public schools, as well as the demands of the National Education Association, leave parental concerns far down the list of considerations.

While these and other factors have provided the motivation for many families to exit the system, the technological revolution is providing the means. Online classes, university-size libraries compressed to a couple of CD-ROMs, interactive software, and internet connections to the far corners of the world have opened up new vistas of learning—and the homeschool community is among the first in line at these doors.

Even for those still plodding through life without e-mail, the proliferation of video courses, audiotapes, satellite schools, and hybrid organizations (like CHESS) that combine home and private schooling all enable an ever-increasing number of families to believe they can undertake home education without having to shoulder the responsibility alone.

While full-time homeschooling may never be mainstream, it is the radical edge of the parental-choice movement, which, coupled with the technological revolution, will eventually force our mass-production approach to education to give way to one that is individualized, flexible, and respectful of the diverse needs of families.

There's Something Happenin' Here

In the spiritual realm, I believe something far more profound is at work. While I never want to be interpreted as believing homeschooling is the only appropriate choice for

Christians, I do believe it is an example of the creative solutions God can be counted on to supply when we feel outmaneuvered by cultural forces. Like manna in the desert, homeschooling is a defense against the relentless and pernicious assault upon traditional family life. More than that, it is a training ground from which future redemptive leadership can come forth.

I don't know about you, but something in my heart of hearts tells me it is more than coincidental that the homeschool movement has been birthed into a generation run amuck with legalized abortion. As in the time of Moses and in the time of Christ as well, the wholesale slaughter of innocence has provoked a mighty response from God.

Crime, drug abuse, and teenage suicide can overwhelm many of us with fear for our kids. Homeschooling is a tactical step to insulate them from these harsher realities. But that's not the whole picture.

Converging Forces

God is more than protecting; He is preparing. At its fullest potential, homeschooling affords us the concentrated time we need to cultivate our children's talents and hone their skills, plus instill in them a passion for impacting their generation with the gospel.

New and innovative strategies for world evangelism, the resurgent prayer movement, the massive response to groups like Promise Keepers, and homeschooling make for an interesting discussion when viewed together as God's intervention into the affairs of His children.

Meditate on the potential of these movements then read Bill Gates's book *The Road Ahead* (Penguin, 1995) and see what future opportunities the technological revolution will make possible. Just as the Roman roads and Gutenberg's printing press facilitated mass evangelization, so will the information highway once again enable the gospel to blanket the ends of the earth.

As I meditate on the future convergence of these vastly different forces, I feel certain God's intent in calling our family to home-educate is a small part of His compassionate and prophetic response to the decadent times in which we live.

Our Pioneer Days Are Over

Ten years ago this would have been a thin book. The choices and opportunities for homeschoolers were few and far between. Pulling together a support group might have meant traveling a couple of hours to find the nearest homeschooling neighbor. Curriculum sources were limited to a few Christian school suppliers. And national organizations could be counted on one hand. But our pioneer days are over.

Warning! Information Overload Ahead

The problem now is too much choice. What curriculum do I buy? Which support group do I join? What educational philosophy should I adopt? Without direction you'll soon be trapped in a maze of confusion.

That's the purpose of this book. I want to give you a framework for your decision-making.

Right This Way

This is your access guide, a navigational chart to all the best destinations and opportunities you won't want to miss as well as all the pitfalls and danger points you need to avoid to realize the full potential home education has to offer. If you're game, then come on board. The first leg of the journey's about to begin.

Bon voyage! Toodleloo! It's time to leave the dock.

PART 1

Homeschooling: Is It for You?

In This Section

- Determining Your Destination
- The Advantages of Homeschooling
- The Challenges of Homeschooling
- Do I Have Time to Homeschool?
- Single Parents, Special Needs, Careers, and Other FAQs
- Six Ingredients of a Successful Homeschool
- But I Don't *Want* to Homeschool!
- Family Worksheet

1

Determining Your Destination

. . . .

How do you decide which educational choice is right for your family? It all depends on where you're headed.

Working backward is a nifty math strategy my kids have learned to use—I find it's a pretty useful approach to life as well. So the first step is deciding where you want to be when you complete your last step in the homeschooling journey. In other words, step one is to determine your destination.

Where Are You Going?

Where's your family headed? What goals do you desire to see your children reach while they are under your care?

If you haven't thought this out before, now's the time to do so. This little exercise will become an important reference point when you lose your focus in the future. It will also give you confidence that you have made a wise (logical and prayerful) decision and not a foolish (whimsical and presumptuous) one. Then you'll have the faith you need to press through the tough times (which are guaranteed to come).

Prayerfully consider the goals you desire your children to reach while they're under your care. Write them down. Share them with your kids.

Here's the list Kermit and I made a number of years ago:

> **Targets We Are Aiming to Hit While Our Children Are Under Our Care**
>
> 1. We want our children to love to learn.
> 2. We want our children to have a marketable set of skills.
> 3. We want our children to accurately understand the Christian faith and enjoy a vital relationship with the Lord.
> 4. We want our children to articulate with integrity the Christian faith to a lost and dying world in a way that is both culturally relevant and persuasive.

We certainly have other goals, values, and interests that are very important to us, but these are the biggies. These make the emphasis in our home just a bit different from the emphasis in another family's home.

When it came time, then, to decide how to school our kids, we looked at all the realistic options available to us:

- homeschooling
- local public school
- private schools in our area

We listed the advantages and disadvantages of each in terms of achieving our family goals. Then we chose the one we found to be the best fit for reaching them.

Over the years as our children have grown, we've reevaluated our targets and examined our options. Thus far, we've home-educated all four of our kids from the beginning, but we are open to God having different plans for each of them.

 Here are other targets gleaned from families I know and admire for the quality of their family life:

- spiritual growth
- preparation for missions
- academic excellence
- classical education[1]
- vocational training
- service in the church
- musical or athletic endeavors
- community or civic involvement
- friendship evangelism
- hospitality
- leadership
- urban or social outreach
- communication skills

These targets were specified by families with children in public, private, and home schools. (Many of them have exercised more than one option over the years to best facilitate each child's growth.) But in all cases, first determining the family's unique goals helped them discern their best schooling choice.

A Vision Corrals Our Impulses

This short list has served me well over the years. One of my favorite proverbs says, "Where there is no vision . . . the people perish" (Prov. 29:18 AMP). The New American Standard version says, "Where there is no vision, the people are unrestrained."

Do you know what it is to be unrestrained? I do.

When I don't have a clearly delineated vision guiding my decision-making, my life becomes chaotic. I waste time looking at all my options and heading down paths with no destination in mind. I meander aimlessly and accomplish nothing. I become "double-minded" and "unstable in all my ways" (see James 1:8), rethinking decisions over and over again and growing weary and discouraged.

The goals I've listed corral me in. They are the parameters I need for assessing my options—and not just which educational choice to pick, but also:

- what curriculum to follow
- what courses to teach
- what activities to engage in

A Vision Fuels Our Motivation

Further, these goals get me refocused when I am discouraged by the day-to-day grind. They are the source of my motivation. I would have skipped labor during the birth of my children if there had been a way (I asked)—but I chose to go through it time and again because I had a vision of the joy at the end of the journey.

The same holds true in choosing to homeschool (some parallels to labor can be drawn, I must admit). But the picture I envision of my children grown, loving to learn, and serving the Lord from the sincerity of their hearts fuels my motivation. And that energizes me daily to do what I can to make that vision a reality.

Okay, One More Time, Class

Have you written down your destination yet? You can't skip this part and hope to succeed. This isn't a self-help strategy—it's a biblical principle.

Throughout history God has consistently given a vision to His people: the promise of a coming Messiah, the hope of Christ's return, our future perfection in Christ, the list goes on. Why? So we will continue to be motivated and disciplined to press on. Consider this wisdom:

> Record the vision
> And inscribe it on tablets,
> *That the one who reads it may run.*
> —Hab. 2:2 (emphasis mine)

> Run in such a way that you may win. . . .
> Therefore I run in such a way, *as not without aim:*
> I box in such a way, *as not beating the air.*
> —1 Cor. 9:24, 26 (emphasis mine)

I can't emphasize enough the importance of a family vision to guide you through the parenting years. I'll be bringing it up again. I can't let you finish this book without reminding you quite a few times about the benefits of a guiding vision for your family life.

That's another useful teaching strategy—repetition.

The Advantages of Homeschooling

Here Comes the Sales Pitch!

Okay, here's the pitch—my best sales job on why *you* should homeschool. Keep in mind I was voted most outstanding cheerleader in high school, and I've been rooting for my team—whatever team that's been—ever since. However, this isn't a snow job. It's an exercise in conviction-building—an important ingredient of a successful homeschool.

I want to provide you with well-formed, rock-solid reasons for choosing the road less traveled (although it's getting busier every day). Your kids need to know these reasons as well, and your mother-in-law does too, I'm sure. Besides, during the difficult times you will draw faith from reviewing these reasons and be ready to make a persuasive defense should the media come calling.

Now, to be honest, after we've covered the major rewards I'll also list the drawbacks you need to consider as well. Then, like the wise man Luke described (see Luke 14:28ff), you can sit down and count the cost before undertaking the task.

 If you would like to compare my list of pluses with the advantages others have found in public and private education, I recommend the book *Schooling Choices* by H. Wayne House (Multnomah, 1988).

Now, onward. Here's what we saw that tipped the scale in favor of home-educating our brood:

Advantage #1: Transference of Our Family Values

Passing on our faith and our values to our children is our sacred trust. As someone who takes a pretty lighthearted approach to life, nothing sobers me more than the weight of this responsibility. Kermit and I endeavor to make all our parenting decisions in light of the impact our choices will have on our children's budding relationship with the Lord.

15

I find it ironic that here we finally are in the high school years of our sons' lives, and instead of being consumed by the academic demands of the curriculum (as I thought I would be), I am more than ever focused on their spiritual development—giving this far more weight in our decision-making than any academic considerations.

Academics Are Ephemeral

Worse-case scenario: My children don't understand physics, calculus, or Shakespeare or speak French as I would like them to by the time they leave home—what has been lost? Nothing of eternal value. Nothing that can't be picked up later.

But if we don't ardently pursue the cultivation of their relationship with the Lord—what has been sacrificed? An opportunity we as parents will never have again. Their hearts are malleable; their minds are impressionable. I want the best shot I've got to demonstrate to our kids the importance and impact of the faith that unites Kermit and me.

Maximum-Strength Parenting

Homeschooling maximizes parental influence and lengthens that window of opportunity. It also gives us the greatest control over who else will influence our kids and shape their beliefs.

The studies cited in *What Works: Research About Teaching and Learning* (U.S. Department of Education, 1986) found that values are most likely transferred when taught in an environment that supports them. Parents, teachers, and peer groups must all validate the beliefs being espoused.

If we teach our children that sex before marriage is wrong, that parents have the right and responsibility before God to hold authority in their lives, or that the Bible is inerrant and absolute, but we simultaneously place them in an environment every day that does not support these beliefs, we've seriously eroded the chances that these values will be embraced.

The homeschool community is certainly not a monolith of Christian virtue, but it has been effortless for us to find peers and other adults who also embrace the values we treasure and seek to impart. And we've been able to surround our children with them.

Positive Peer Pressure

I am most grateful for the influence on my children of older teens, like Cindy and Marie's kids, who have only grown bolder in their faith during these typically turbulent years and are not ashamed to seek out their parents' counsel or publicly express respect for them.

I choked back emotion during one of my first sessions with my senior high composition class at Creative Home Educators' Support Services (CHESS) this year. I have twenty-one students, ages fifteen through seventeen. In getting acquainted, I found two-thirds of them have already been on cross-cultural or overseas missions trips. I was moved by the ease with which many of them shared their faith as well as their desire to give themselves wholeheartedly to God's will for their lives. They spoke earnestly even though they were in a setting where most of them had never met before.

I've been teaching kids for years, in a variety of settings. This kind of candid discussion is pretty unusual, from my experience at least. I'm humbled that God has given me the opportunity to work with kids with such mature focus.

The Apron Strings Must Be Cut

There certainly will come a time when we, as parents, must pass the baton and watch our children run their leg of the journey alone. For Kermit and me, parenting is all about preparing our kids to make an impact in their generation. We aren't isolationists here. It's God's intention that our children integrate their lives with others outside our system of belief. But before they go, they need a faith that's rooted and mature, not one that will quickly shrivel in the face of opposition. So how do we best prepare them?

I think of the concentrated and intensive training of an Olympic contender who sets aside all other distractions—and I see a correlation to the opportunity homeschooling gives parents to coach their kids in the fundamentals of our faith.

Homeschooling does not guarantee a child's salvation. Only the grace of God does. But it's an option with impressive results.

If you have an authentic, active faith to pass on, if your life's been changed by the power of the gospel, if your home is a model of commitment and love, then homeschooling may just be the strategy to best deploy to your kids what God has done in your life.

Advantage #2: Character First

Closely tied to passing on our faith is our responsibility as parents to shape our children's character. It wasn't until I met Christians in college whose lives were consistent with the faith they espoused that I took a serious look at the claims of Christ.

The integrity of our character is what counts with unbelievers. It's what counts with God as well. Without it, we bring shame to the gospel of Christ.

I love to learn. I love intellectual pursuit. That bias will certainly bleed through these pages. I want to foster in my children the pleasure that comes from academic achievement. But—and that's a big "but"—character is paramount. When our kids ultimately stand before the throne of grace, they won't be bringing their transcripts and SAT scores with them. It will be their hearts the Lord will examine.

Homeschooling gives us the potential to stay on top of the condition of our child's heart daily. Within the dynamic of one-on-one instruction we are acutely aware of the bad attitudes or actions that erupt. And we can close our books and deal with the more important issues at hand.

There are many advantages to the CHESS classes Cindy has arranged, but this is not one of them. In the context of a classroom, I don't have close examination of my children's lives or the time to stop and deal with the character issues that arise.

Homeschooling does give me that time. I need to make sure I seize the opportunity.

Advantage #3: A Tailor-Made Education

Jeremy sat in my tenth-grade English class, struggling to construct a complete sentence while the others worked steadily on their five-paragraph compositions. Though I gave him far more attention than the rest, I couldn't do the one thing he needed most—the only thing that would have enabled him to eventually construct a five-paragraph composition with ease—slow down the curriculum. Jeremy needed to start at his level of success and move forward only as he mastered the necessary skills. But in fairness to the others I couldn't wait for Jeremy. His confidence and mastery of the English language continued to languish. Later that year he dropped out.

Lisa, on the other hand, stared out the window. Her five paragraphs had been effortlessly produced in the first ten minutes of the allotted time. The previous week she had shown me a remarkable short story she had written outside of class. She was, of course, identified as gifted. That entitled her to a forty-minute "pullout program" once a week. She wasn't particularly interested in the focus of that class, and she especially resented being required to make up any assignments missed while attending it. Eventually she convinced her parents to pull her out of the gifted track. And despite my scintillating personality, she sat in my English class, bored and under-challenged.

An Inner Timetable

Children are unique. They aren't computers who can be programmed or synchronized. Each one has an inner timetable designed by God that should be honored. Some babies walk at nine months, some at sixteen. Some kids read at four, some at ten. As adults, these early differences are usually indistinguishable.

Schools place kids on an artificial timetable. If you're seven it's time to read. If you don't, you're labeled "delayed." Fifth grade, first semester: time to memorize the state capitals.

We've created a linear and arbitrary scope and sequence, and we expect kids to fall in sync with it.

The Ebb and Flow of Growth

But kids are not machines, or blank minds, as French philosopher Jean Jacques Rousseau thought. They don't learn in sequential, evenly measured steps. Their intellectual growth ebbs and flows.

In less than nine months one year, my twins grew six inches and put on twenty pounds. That's how they mature intellectually as well—swinging between stages of dormancy and growth. In a six-week period, my daughter Katie jumped directly from struggling with her easiest readers to *The Boxcar Children* chapter books, skipping all the levels in between. Suddenly everything clicked for her. And I didn't hold her back by insisting she continue to work through her reading program in a systematic, sequential fashion. I capitalized on the growth spurt.

Readiness

Before your child is going to read *War and Peace*, solve a problem algebraically, or write a ten-page research paper successfully, he must master the prior skills necessary. Homeschooling gives you the opportunity to start your studies in every subject at the level of your child's success without labeling him "delayed" or "accelerated" as if there were a scientific standard we are measuring his progress against.

There needn't be any sense of falling behind or rushing to catch up. Your scope and sequence are cued to your child.

Interests-Based Learning

At age eight, Gabe became fascinated with flight. I didn't say, "Well, be patient there, buddy; in fifth grade your science text will cover the physics of flight." No, we capitalized on the opportunity to study something *when he was motivated to learn about it.* We checked out a stack of books at the library. We designed paper airplanes and recorded their flight. Kermit bought Estes rockets and set up a launch pad in the backyard (attracting all kinds of additional students). And a pilot at Kermit's office answered Gabe's questions. In third grade, this kid knew more about the physics of flight than most high school graduates.

And it's a good thing we captured the moment: By the time Gabe was in fifth grade, his interests had turned to rocks.

Immediate Feedback

My goal as an English teacher was to return all compositions within five days. I had to really press in to wade through thirty-five compositions—but even so, most teenagers' lives were eons beyond that assignment in a week's time. My comments went largely unnoticed. And the grade was already recorded. What difference did my feedback make anyway?

The best time to capitalize upon mistakes is when they are made, not two weeks later when the test is returned.

As soon as my own kids get headed down the wrong track, I can adjust their thinking. If Kristen forgets to carry her tens to the next column, I can catch her error before she completes the entire page incorrectly and reinforces her mistakes.

And we don't have to settle for just a passing grade. We can continue to work with the assignment until it's right.

I circle the wrong answers on my children's math tests and have them rework the problems. My sons self-check and self-correct their algebra. Then they explain the errors they discover to me.

In our house, mistakes are powerful teaching tools, not at all a measurement of failure.

Shifting Gears

Home education allows you to change immediately to better methods and materials. If what you're doing isn't working, stop and adjust. You don't have to wait for board approval or acquisition of funds (well, maybe).

 One must navigate a ream of red tape to change course in a traditional setting. In the early seventies the latest educational fad was mini-courses. English 10, 11, and 12 were replaced with scores of electives such as science fiction, media production, and independent reading. For my father, the director of guidance at a public high school, it was a scheduling nightmare. And very quickly, the research began to show this idea a resounding failure. The program was too splintered, and kids were missing basic skills in composition and literature. My own husband graduated from high school without ever reading one of Shakespeare's plays (a deficit that causes me far greater concern than it ever has him). It took more than a decade to weed mini-courses out of the schedule.

 The first reading program I tried with the twins spent far too much time on phonetics drills and far too little time on real reading. They were rapidly getting discouraged. I analyzed the problem, sold the program, and switched to a whole-language approach in less than a week. (Lest you are concerned, intensive phonetics is just what the woman I sold it to was looking for, and real books were what my kids craved.)

I Prefer a Custom Fit

No other option offers you the opportunity to customize your child's education to fit her readiness, interests, and abilities. Modifications are easy. Feedback is immediate. Results:

Kid reaches her maximum potential. Kid loves to learn. (Mike wants to cut in here to say he doesn't love algebra. But it comes under the marketable-skills category, so we keep it on the schedule.)

Advantage #4: Academic Excellence

For a myriad of reasons, academic standards in our educational system have plummeted. Despite recent reports of modest gains, American students still lag far behind their European and Asian counterparts.

Charles Sykes, a respected education journalist, reports these findings in his book *Dumbing Down Our Kids: Why American Children Feel Good About Themselves But Can't Read, Write, Or Add* (St. Martins, 1995):

- More than a decade after *A Nation at Risk* drew attention to the nation's educational mediocrity, the reading proficiency of nine- and thirteen-year-olds has declined even further.[1]

- Although the United States is among the countries expending the highest proportion of their gross national product on education, our elementary school and secondary school students *never place above the median* in comparative studies (with Asian and European students) of academic achievement.[2]

- The National Education Commission on Time and Learning found that most American students spend only about 41 percent of their school day on basic academics.[3]

- American students spend only 1,460 hours on subjects like math, science, and history during their four years of high school. Meanwhile, their counterparts in Japan spend 3,170 hours on basic subjects, students in France spend 3,280 hours on academics, and students in Germany, 3,528 hours studying such subjects— nearly three times the hours devoted to those core subjects in American schools.[4]

- According to the National Research Council, *average* students in other industrialized countries are as proficient in mathematics as America's *best* students. Further, when the very best American students—the top 1 percent—are measured against the best students of other countries, America's best and brightest finish at the bottom.[5]

Though critics argue that compulsory-attendance laws, working mothers, and the impact of television in this country explain the scores, Sykes points out these fallacies: Compulsory education for elementary school is worldwide, and the same discrepancies still show up at that level in student achievement. In many countries, a greater number of women are working outside the home than in the United States, and believe it or not, Japanese students on average watch more television daily than their American counterparts.[6]

Where's the Curriculum?

Sykes's book and others like it (see also *The Closing of the American Mind* by Alan Bloom [Simon and Schuster, 1987] and *Cultural Literacy* by E. D. Hirsch Jr. [Houghton Mifflin, 1987]) contend that our failure is rooted in the loss of a core curriculum. While European and Asian school systems focus heavily on academics and leave other arenas to the province of the family, American schools are saddled with politically correct agendas; faddish, untested reforms; and responsibility for salvaging societal problems:

> Schools have been asked to assume (and have asked to assume) extraordinary burdens; they are expected not to merely educate children but to deal with and help resolve society's race problems, to eradicate poverty, to be on the front lines of economic competitiveness, environmentalism, AIDS, multiculturalism, child abuse, drug addiction, sexual harassment, to mediate our ambivalence about family life and sexuality, and to provide children with a moral compass.[7]

No wonder many teachers complain that they don't have time to teach!

Homeschooling streamlines the educational process. High standards of academic excellence, accelerated learning, and a return to core studies in math, science, history, and literature are quickly and easily facilitated.

Full Exploration and Mastery

Homeschooling allows time for full exploration and mastery of the material. It's not once over lightly and quickly forgotten. *Okay class, it's second semester, seventh grade, time for our two-week study of the Roman Empire.* That was it, never to be mentioned again. *Okay kids, that was your chance to try that chemistry experiment. Sorry it didn't work for most of you, but the supplies have been consumed. Next week we move on to electrolysis. We have to complete this textbook by the end of the year.*

One summer, Gabe took a writing workshop through a local "College for Kids" program. It was his first experience in a traditional setting, and his comments during the week were insightful. He worked hurriedly one evening to complete the next day's assignment.

"You know, Mom," he said, "I know now why kids don't do their best in school. I'm just writing this poem to get it done. I don't have enough time to make it good, and I wasn't really interested in the topic in the first place."

When we rush kids through material, it is lost. That's why there is so much repetition in textbooks year after year. But even that redundancy often fails to lodge the material in a child's brain. If we do not s-l-o-w down the program to allow kids to delve deeply into the material and interact with it in a variety of contexts, it cannot be transferred from short-term to long-term memory.

Smarting Us Up

Homeschooling affords you the time you need to set and achieve high academic standards. No grading on a curve necessary. Set an objective standard and measure your child's success against that. If he doesn't hit the mark, reward his improvement and set a goal to come closer next time. With time on your side, you need not feel any pressure to lower the bar.

Many families introduce concepts to their kids years earlier than is traditionally accepted in a standard curriculum. And it's not that these kids are unusually bright—it has more to do with their personal drive and their parents' high expectations for their children's achievement.

Care to hazard a guess as to the sources of each of these vocabulary lists?

List 1	*List 2*
aggression	inimitable
divergent	epistolary
prestigious	assailed
bizarre	invidious
cogent	assiduous
propagate	appendages
ambiguous	sagacity
exonerated	pecuniary

SOURCES:

List 1: SAT I (revised) Practice Test

List 2: Fourth-grade *McGuffey Reader*, in use during the late 1800s (after compulsory education was mandated). An 1897 fifth-grade reader we purchased at a library sale includes the same literary selections I studied in my undergraduate American literature courses.

Authentic Experiences

Homeschooling also affords the opportunity to involve your kids with material and activities that are relevant and applicable to real life. Parents have full control of the content; we can use that advantage to our kids' benefit.

Homeschooling is far more than school-at-home. If you only recreate an institutionalized setting around your kitchen table, you've lost much of the opportunity homeschooling affords.

Do you remember wondering in school, *When will I ever use this?* or *Why do I need to know this?* Do you ever ask those questions when you must acquire new skills or knowledge for a job? No. That's because you are learning material in the context in which it is used. The immediate relevance to the tasks at hand is obvious. And we are motivated to learn because the learning is purposeful.

Many homeschoolers believe they must follow a state-prescribed scope and sequence. But while many state laws dictate the subjects that must be studied, none dictate the content or the methods. So visits to workplaces, historic sites, laboratories, musical performances, and dramatic productions; long-term, purposeful projects; apprenticeships; interviews with those in the field of study; and a spontaneous response to opportunities that arise can all be done as frequently as you wish.

As a classroom teacher, I took one field trip a year. The paperwork required, the sheer size of the group, and the students' attitudes that this was more a release from confinement than a learning adventure made it an exhausting effort. But arranging the same kind of opportunity for just my four kids is a frequent occurrence.

Entering the Twenty-First Century

We're in the midst of a technological revolution that will dramatically change every aspect of our lives. Our kids need to be equipped now to participate in the future. The job market of tomorrow is a lush opportunity for creative, independent thinkers with well-honed problem-solving skills and an entrepreneurial drive.

"Time on task," my father always says, is the only thing, research consistently shows, that determines kids' proficiency in a skill. Want better writers? They need to write—not to fill out worksheets, answer quick true-and-false tests, or do grammar exercises. The more they write, the better their writing skills. Want readers? Give them time to read, not crowd the schedule with special assemblies and then load them up with so much homework that reading a book for pleasure or enlightenment is out of the question. (A consistent comment I hear from parents whose home-educated kids have transitioned to a traditional setting is that they no longer have time to read!)

You want your kids prepared for the job market of the future, no matter how it shakes out? Then here's the short list of necessary proficiencies:

- ✔ research skills
- ✔ communication skills
- ✔ technical skills

If you will merely design a program that gives your kids lots of opportunities to hone these skills, they will be equipped to compete.

Advantage #5: Nurturing Environment

I'll Take Hothouse Tomatoes

Today's kids enter the rat race at the earliest possible moment. Infant daycare, highly structured preschools, and daily schedules beginning early in the morning and ending late at night are far too common. Dr. David Elkind, a highly respected child psychologist at Tufts University, has authored a number of disturbing books drawn from his practice. He noted adult diseases appearing in children at earlier and earlier ages including heart disease, hypertension, mental illnesses, eating disorders, and suicide. He's concluded that the hurried, harried lifestyle we've created is the root cause.

Tightly packed schedules and overly structured lives leave kids with no personal space, no control, and no time. Gone are the lazy, carefree days of childhood spent on a backyard tire swing or scouring the creeks for crayfish.

Some onlookers think homeschooling is time consuming—but kids in a traditional setting often complete two hours of homework most evenings after spending up to seven hours in school each day and then riding up to an hour to get home on a bus. Crammed into this already-tight schedule are ballet lessons, sports, and church activities. To top it off, vacations must be taken at the height of the season with two million other families. (Give me the beach in September—that's a vacation.)

Change agents crying for a longer school year, more hours in every day, and more home-work are only inviting further disaster in children's lives, I believe. (Better reforms center around streamlining the curriculum and maximizing kids' time in the classroom. See Theodore Sizer and the Coalition for Essential Schools movement if you'd like to know where I'd throw my hat.[8])

What attracted me to homeschooling was the opportunity to recapture childhood for my kids. After reading Dr. Elkind's *The Hurried Child* I vowed to not let the forces of our culture's whirlwind lifestyle drag us into its vortex.

I want a childhood for our kids that allows lots of time for play in the backyard, rainy afternoons in a cozy chair with a book, and building secret hideouts in the woods.

For details about Dr. Elkind's research and his suggestions for rearing relaxed, well-adjusted children, see his books *The Hurried Child: Growing Up Too Fast Too Soon* (Addison-Wesley, 1981) and *Miseducation: Preschoolers at Risk* (Knopf, 1987).

Confident to Learn

Homeschooling has also given us the safeguards to protect our children's self-esteem and confidence to learn. Comparison is a natural inclination of children. But for the ones who lag behind or don't fit into the constantly changing standards of peer acceptance, a belief in their own inabilities quickly becomes a downward spiral. And without faith in themselves, kids just don't do well in their studies—or in life.

I'm sure you've collected labels about your own abilities to learn: "I'm smart," "I'm dumb," "I don't do well on tests," "I can't speak in front of a group," "I'm good at math," etc. Aren't these labels rooted in your own school experience? And don't we then set limits for ourselves because of them?

I know otherwise rational adults who have had successful careers, recognized leadership in the community, financial security, even high grades in college and graduate school and who still view themselves as "unintelligent" because of the standardized tests they took in grade school.

Labels are extraordinarily powerful, especially on young children. As adults, we have the maturity to keep others' categorical statements about us in perspective. But it's different for kids. The comments of adults and peers in their lives will have a profound impact upon their self-image.

 Cindy McKeown's son, Joey, is a high school sophomore with impressive drive. In ninth grade, he read Steve Covey's *The Seven Habits of Highly Effective People* (Simon and Schuster, 1989) and set about getting organized. He got a job and used his wages to purchase Covey's expensive organizer. He then scripted out his goals for his high school years. Among many other ventures, he is currently interning at Pennsylvania Family Institute, a pro-family watchdog in our state capital. He is a recognized leader among his peers and scores quite high now on the standardized tests I administer. As a freshman, he had one of the top scores in a very difficult English course I taught at CHESS, which included tenth- through twelfth-graders as well.

But in grade school, Joey read late and lagged behind his peers in many areas. He had difficulty with math and didn't test particularly well. Cindy used many nontraditional strategies with Joey all through elementary school to give him a basis for abstract thinking. But above all, she didn't rush him or suggest he was lazy and falling behind. Her family doctor, who was not particularly pro-homeschooling, told her it was wise of her to home-educate Joey. He predicted that in a traditional setting Joey would quickly get lost in the shuffle.

While Cindy and her husband, Cliff, once worried privately that they might not be pushing their laid-back son enough, their current concern is whether they should try to restrain his boundless energy and ambitious goals.

I share Joey's story only because he is not an unusual situation. Had I the space, I could tell you of numerous children I have observed closely from grade school to graduation. I did not expect to find what I did: early test scores are not certain predictors of later achievement.

I wonder if the growth I have seen in these kids would have been possible had they been labeled delayed and tracked early in grade school. And what would the comments of their peers have done to their confidence to learn?

Advantage #6: Flexibility and Choice

If you ask Mike or Gabe why they like being home-educated, their answer will fall under this heading. They love the freedom to pursue their own interests, to control their time, to stay up late reading, to not be bogged down with homework after supper, to choose and change the direction of their education.

We spent two years on colonial American history because we wanted to. Mike and Gabe started algebra in sixth grade because they were ready. Katie read _The Adventures of Huckleberry Finn_, unabridged, in fourth. We can stay up late to catch a meteor shower or the final game of the World Series and then sleep in. When the _Concorde_, the world's fastest jet, landed at Harrisburg International Airport, word spread like wildfire through the homeschool phone chains—moms declared a field trip and drove their kids over to watch it take off.

One morning the papers ran a story on Mel Fisher, the man whose family had recovered the sunken treasure of the Spanish galleon _Atocha_. Mr. Fisher was appearing in Harrisburg that day with two million dollars' worth of recovered treasure to sell. We had just watched the _Reading Rainbow_ segment on the _Atocha_ and had read a book about it together. We put away our work, headed to Harrisburg, and had one of the most educational days of the year. Since mine were the only kids in the store (everyone else was actually there to consider buying this stuff), we got a lot of attention. Mr. Fisher was fascinated by our mode of education and the knowledge the kids demonstrated about his ten-year search. He allowed them each to handle gold bullion, emeralds, and pieces of eight.

No other option can give you the flexibility you need to seize these opportunities.

Before You Sign, Read the Fine Print

While these are a few of the benefits we've found, it's important you know they aren't guaranteed. Homeschooling affords us some wonderful opportunities to shape our children's lives and to tailor their education to their unique specifications. But that doesn't mean it isn't without its drawbacks. Homeschooling is and always will be a tradeoff.

It's time to count the cost before making that final decision.

3

The Challenges of Homeschooling

. . . .

When I was nine I got braces. The dental assistant who put the plaster of Paris in my mouth to make the mold said, "This is going to taste great, just like oatmeal." Well, I loved oatmeal as a kid, and I eagerly bit down on the mash she had scooped into my mouth. To this day I remember my disillusionment and astonishment that she had lied to me. (I believe that woman later wrote the book *Childbirth Without Pain*.)

And that is why I'm going to tell you the downside of homeschooling. I don't want any angry letters accusing me of an inflated sales pitch.

If you don't take the time to sit down and count the cost, as well as to lay a solid foundation in the grace of God before you begin to homeschool, you'll spend much of your time dealing with double-mindedness instead of seizing the opportunity at hand.

Frustration, discouragement, ambivalence: These are common emotions you will live with if you choose to homeschool. My friend Peggy calls homeschooling "the crucible of my life." It not only constantly brings to the surface her children's character flaws but her own as well. And she can't put off dealing with them.

It's very common for the conversations in the mothers lounge at the Learning Center homeschool co-op to center around the challenges and discouragement of homeschooling. Not only do our children need these bimonthly group experiences, but we moms need the support and reenvisioning that comes from upholding one another.

Some of the difficulties I want to address can be minimized with the strategies presented in this book. But others are inherent in the choice and must be weighed before you decide.

The Cost to the Homeschooling Parent

Challenge #1: Time

No matter how you approach it, homeschooling is a tremendous investment of time and energy. It's not another interest to fit into an already busy schedule. It's a way of life.

Other Demands upon Our Time

Other family members may have needs that require a competing time commitment. Perhaps you are caring for an elderly parent or a child with special needs. Perhaps you are working and do not have the option of quitting or scaling back your hours. In these situations, you may not have the time to give that homeschooling requires.

 My friend Barb is deeply committed to the principles of homeschooling. However, her third child, Anna, has had some learning delays, and she needs a lot of one-on-one attention in order to move forward. The time Barb was investing in Anna was leaving her older children without enough direction. After a particularly dissatisfying homeschooling year (when her oldest son, Adam, had most of his schoolwork "artisti-cally" rearranged by Anna), Barb and her husband, Steve, reluctantly visited a publicly funded intermediate unit classroom that serves their public school district—and were pleasantly surprised. The teacher was supportive of Barb's commitment to homeschooling, and Barb continues to work with Anna at home, but having Anna also enrolled several days a week in this therapy program has given Barb the time she needs for her other kids as well.

On the other hand, another friend with a special-needs child chose in the end to enroll her two older children in school as part of the solution to the time commitment her youngest daughter needs.

Even without extenuating circumstances, homeschooling is, in the end, primarily a time commitment. The time you might have given to a career or ministry gets diverted here. For women who have worked solely at home or who have children that have not yet been to school, the transition to homeschooling is usually not as big an adjustment as it is for the woman who must leave the work force or pull her children out of a traditional setting. If you are in the latter situation, then you need to be realistic about the adjustment and sense of restraint the transition to homeschooling will bring into your life.

Prep Time

While the actual time devoted to homeschooling your kids is far less than the time they would spend in school each day, you still have lots of things to do to prepare for that instructional time. To maximize the opportunities homeschooling affords, you need to be self-educating and constantly fine-tuning your program. In later chapters I'll give you strategies for raising an independent learner as well as motivating the reluctant one. But in the end, kids can't teach themselves. You need to provide daily accountability, direction, and tutoring.

My first year as a classroom teacher was very difficult because I had to create the courses I was teaching. But the years following were much less time consuming because I often taught the same courses over again. That's not true in homeschooling. Every year there's a different schedule. Every year there's new coursework to oversee. And even though Katie and Kristen are following behind the boys, in tailoring the program to their needs and interests, I'm doing a lot of new things with them as well.

But What about Me?

Depending upon our temperaments, never having a break from the kids or time to ourselves can be a difficult demand. I don't think homeschooling needs to be as restrictive as many people imagine in order to succeed. But the amount of time you can carve away from your responsibilities is certainly limited, and we have to be creative about finding moments of relaxation.

Once I spent a few days with a college roommate whose two children were doing well in public school. She hadn't yet returned to the work force, and her weekly schedule included aerobic classes, women's Bible study, and lunch with friends. Her house was neat as a pin and beautifully decorated. I returned home grumpy and envious.

I find I need to keep blinders on to maintain my contentment in homeschooling. Now that my children are older, I really do enjoy their company and don't think much about the limits of my life. But when they were little, it didn't come quite so naturally—by a long shot. I needed to stay fixed on the conviction that this was God's will for my life and He had designed the limits of my freedom, not just for my children's good, but for my own good as well. I can't let myself look at the "freedom" I think other women have and get resentful. But it's not always easy.

A Question That Needs an Honest Answer

Before you choose to homeschool, answer these questions:

- ✔ Am I able and willing to devote the time necessary to do this right?
- ✔ Will I have enthusiasm for teaching my children and be dedicated to seeking out opportunities and strategies for maximizing this opportunity?

If your answer is no, your children will probably be better served in a classroom setting with a teacher who is enthused about teaching and creative in his or her approach.

Many parents who want the benefits of an environment that reflects their value system but can't give the time necessary to teach the academics invest their energy in setting up a private school for their kids; classical schools, charter schools, parent-run schools, and hybrids of private and homeschooling like Creative Home Educators' Support Services (CHESS) are springing up all over the country. And in many places, it's still possible for parents to have a positive impact on their public schools through involvement in parent organizations, or booster clubs or by serving on their school board.

Challenge #2: Unrealistic Expectations

When we make the choice to homeschool, it's with the expectation of results commensurate with the sacrifices we are about to make. Or at the very least, we want enough evidence to prove our skeptics wrong. And we want it soon.

Many of us enter homeschooling anticipating immediate success. A spouse or relative may be adding pressure to that anticipation as well. With the prevalent hard sell of homeschooling and with all the glowing reports of individual students' successes, it's very easy to set unrealistic expectations for ourselves and for our children.

I think the homeschool moms of the Learning Center homeschool co-op I direct are the absolute cream of the crop. They are creative, diligent, and fervent in their faith. As we gathered to open our school year with prayer, I was surprised to hear how discouraged and wrought with guilt most of the moms were. They were very conscious of all they were not getting done in their homes and homeschools. They were worried that they were not doing something right with one or more of their kids. And they were sure they were the only one failing in this way. By the time it was my turn to share, I was feeling very guilty about not feeling guilty! And by golly, I then found it easy to make a list of all I was falling short on as well.

From my travels I've heard the same angst in many, many mothers' voices.

There Are Always Trade-Offs

Homeschooling is a trade-off. There are always going to be things that are not done or not done well. Howard Richman, a homeschool evaluator and researcher in Pennsylvania, evaluates more than five hundred homeschooled children every year. His cumulative research is very impressive. High SAT scores, high achievement scores, post-graduate success. But in his analysis of individual homeschool programs, what he consistently sees are strengths and weaknesses in every home. We do some things very well (usually homeschoolers raise very literate kids), but we sacrifice time in other areas to do so (say, in my case, science).

I minimize the impact of my weaknesses by involving my children in many cooperative learning experiences where they have other teachers who offset my shortcomings. But time restraints still prevent us from doing everything as well as I can envision. I have to be at peace with the gap between the ideal and the reality.

Homeschooling Is Not a Cure-All

Another frequent assumption is that homeschooling will remove our children's character flaws, rescue them from academic failure, or miraculously cure family problems. But the converse is true: Homeschooling will exacerbate these situations. These issues typically must be addressed at a more fundamental level. Homeschooling is an educational choice, not a biblical solution for fractures in our family life.

At the end of Part 1 of this book, I ask you to evaluate the health of your family relationships before beginning to homeschool. It's important that you have a realistic picture here and that you have a plan for dealing with these weaknesses if you want to minimize, not maximize, the stress homeschooling can bring.

I have seen numerous families undertake homeschooling as a last-ditch effort to prevent a rebellious teenager from dropping out of school. Unfortunately the issues that led to this impasse sprouted long ago. Homeschooling may be a good option for cutting off negative influences aggravating the situation, but "tough love" and biblical counseling are more likely to make the real difference in this child's life.

Fruit Takes Time, Faith, and Effort

When you consider homeschooling, you must recognize that the fruit you hope to realize will likely take longer and be harder to grow than you anticipate. In many cases you must merely live in faith for the future results. I watched Cindy spend most of her homeschooling years with Nate, her oldest, very ambivalent about the choice she had made. Then, shortly after his freshman year of college, Nate told his parents how grateful he was to have been homeschooled and how well prepared he felt he had been for college life. It's hard to quantify how much his comments meant to Cindy or how challenging the wait had been to hear them.

Challenge #3: Limits on Your Family's Impact

Homeschooling can limit your family's impact and outreach in your community. School forms a natural vehicle for getting to know other families and opening opportunities to share our faith and lives. Christian teachers, students, and parents whose character squares with the values they espouse can make a real difference in other children's lives and better their schools and community through their service.

For ten years, Kermit and I served on the board of a pregnancy care center we founded. Today this center operates three offices and reaches more than a thousand women annually. We loved being a part of a ministry that's making a tangible difference, coupling the gospel with meeting legitimate needs in our community. And we loved the people we labored with. Stepping down from active involvement there was one of the most difficult decisions I've had to make. But it was necessary if I was going to homeschool my children with integrity.

The center has likewise lost many volunteers because they have chosen to homeschool their children. It has created a dilemma that has been difficult to resolve.

A Source of Tension

Churches can feel this same tension. Many needs that were once met by the women of the church now go unmet because moms are reentering the workforce or homeschooling.

It's become a sore point in the church. It's a challenge to not become critical of the homeschool movement when the obvious impact these strong Christian families could be having is shifted away from legitimate needs.

Creative Solutions

This is a drawback I believe can be minimized. Many homeschool families I know with older children have found ways to reach out to others as part of their homeschool programs. The flexibility that homeschooling affords makes short-term missions trips a real possibility. Our co-op has done a number of service projects and put on an after-school program at the city mission. It's not always easy to facilitate these opportunities, but homeschool families who make outreach a priority find creative ways to serve in their churches and communities.

The Cost to the Homeschooled Child

It's hard to beat the one-on-one instruction homeschooling can provide for a child. But even with all its benefits, I find there are some drawbacks for our children that need to be considered, especially as they grow older.

Challenge #1: Limits of the Teacher

> **A pupil is not above his teacher.**
> —Matt. 10:24

Our children will benefit from our strengths and be limited by our weaknesses if we do not offset them. My kids are fluid writers. Gabe has been published and paid twice. In fifth grade he and Mike generated more than twenty thousand original words for school assignments. Katie routinely writes ten-page stories. They all read avidly and wish they were getting speaking engagements instead of their mother. Obviously they've benefited from the strength of my background. But they've suffered for my limits as well.

Katie attended her first Young Writers' Institute with Sigmund Brouwer in third grade. I was watching the children complete an assignment for Sigmund when I noticed all the other children (thirty-four of them to be exact) were composing their stories in cursive. Katie was laboriously printing hers. I suddenly realized I had completely forgotten to teach my daughter cursive handwriting! It just never entered my brain. I was almost hyperventilating over the panic attack that ensued—if I could forget cursive, what other venal or mortal oversight was I capable of? Would my daughter ever recover? What doors were now swinging shut because of her mother's incompetency?

Of course I overreacted, and Katie survived. Handwriting isn't a life-and-death skill, but this experience illustrated for me the impact the limits of my abilities or initiative can have on my children.

We Need Others' Involvement

I disagree with homeschooling families that isolate their kids. It's not healthy, and the children will not have the opportunity to hone their skills and character as they rub shoulders with others with different strengths and weaknesses.

A church is not healthy without every member contributing his or her gifts and talents to church life. A homeschool isn't healthy either if we misconstrue Scripture to mean parents are to be the *only* influence or teachers in our children's lives.

It is so important that we recognize our limitations and seek out opportunities for our kids to offset those limitations.

Challenge #2: Lack of Recognition

Many of the homeschooled kids I've evaluated have had tremendous academic and artistic achievements—but often these accomplishments are unrecognized. While the local papers feature pictures of school happenings and recognition of individual students, the homeschool community is mostly overlooked.

Several of the homeschooled students I've worked with have now transitioned into a public high school and have done exceptionally well. It is gratifying for me to see all the awards they've garnered. Frankly, they've found the accolades pretty motivational, too.

Appropriate recognition is an important source of motivation for adults and children. And local homeschool communities are beginning to find creative ways to recognize the accomplishments of students—awards banquets, exhibits at conventions, juried science and history fairs, graduation ceremonies. I'd like to see us go further by inviting the local media to these events. The local newspaper is not purposefully overlooking the homeschooled kids; it just doesn't have a clue as to what we are doing. It's our job to educate them.

Challenge #3: Lack of Competition

I've changed my views on competition over the years, and it's come from observing my identical twin sons. I've had to conclude that the natural competitiveness between them has been to their benefit.

When the first one began to read, the other was motivated to work harder at his own reading. When Michael works ahead in algebra, Gabe complains but buckles down and catches up. When one can beat the other racing or throwing a ball, the other works harder to exceed the standard. Once he does, then his brother stretches himself even further to surpass his twin's accomplishments once again.

Now, before you imagine a cutthroat environment at our house, let me assure you they haven't risked their relationship over this. They are best friends and have agreed on their own never to compete against each other publicly. (For example, rather than wrestle each other in a tournament, they ask the referee to flip a coin to determine the winner.)

Competition can be an important motivational tool, especially for older students. I've worked with quite a few families who found that a traditional setting was better suited for their teenagers (usually boys) because they needed an element of competition to be motivated to learn.

The CHESS classes Cindy McKeown has organized have demonstrated to me the benefits of competition in a carefully controlled environment. In this setting, the kids admire the students who do their best. My three oldest kids invest a lot more time on assignments for their classes there than on assignments they do at home because they know their projects are going to be displayed alongside those produced by their peers. They don't want to be embarrassed.

Challenge #4: Lack of Accountability

I've edited this section out of the book several times because I know I am going to take flak for it from my good friends who believe the state usurps parental authority when it requires any level of accountability from homeschoolers. Philosophically, I don't disagree with those who dislike this government oversight, but I am also a pragmatist.

In many places it is easy to home-educate without much outside accountability or government regulations. I'm not advocating tougher laws, but I do see a drawback that can work against our children's best interests if we allow it to.

Real change or progress in life is difficult to bring about without some level of accountability. That's why the Bible says, "confess your sins to one another" (James 5:16), and it's why accountability groups like Weight Watchers and Alcoholics Anonymous work.

At least in my own life, where I lack accountability I typically lack discipline. I do a much better job homeschooling my children now than I did prior to the enactment of our state law that requires an annual review of our program. I have gained valuable insights from my evaluator (chosen by my husband and me, not by the state), and my kids really look forward to sharing their schoolwork each June with her. The families I evaluate have often commented on the helpfulness of an outside review as well.

Without some kind of accountability, it is easy to slide year after year toward an undisciplined lifestyle. Are our kids learning to meet deadlines and to complete a course of study, sticking to it even when they are tired or disinterested in the material? A traditional setting does provide this framework. I personally find that framework too restrictive, but some framework is still beneficial.

If you home-educate in a state where little accountability is required, consider building accountability into your program. Deadlines, goals for the year in the core subject areas, and an annual day of sharing your work with others in your homeschool support group (especially for your older students) can only improve your program. We want our kids to cultivate a disciplined lifestyle, and that doesn't come from only doing those things they feel like doing.

Challenge #5: Exclusion from Scholastic Sports

Almost any opportunity available to conventionally schooled students is now open to kids who are homeschooled—except for scholastic sports. Academic competitions, such as <u>**Knowledge Open**</u>, <u>**Global Challenge**</u>, <u>**MathCounts**</u>, and <u>**Odyssey of the Mind**</u>, have adjusted their requirements to accept homeschoolers. Extracurricular activities in music, drama, dance, etc., can all be found at a competitive level outside of your local school district. But the athletic competition that will open doors to college-level play or scholarships often is not. And this has been a frequent reason for homeschooled students to enroll in a traditional setting.

A Confession

For some of you a passionate devotion to competitive sports is hard to comprehend. Kermit and I did not set out to raise athletes. It doesn't rank high on our list of targets in and of itself. We saw our recreation league's sports program as an arena for integrating our lives with those in our community. (See Target #4, page 11) So we innocently signed our sons up for T-ball when they were five. One thing led to another, and before I knew it I'd spent equivalent to a year of my life watching Mike and Gabe play baseball and my daughters play softball—and that's just the summer.

My children play competitive sports year-round—we have training videos, they go to camps, and we have a room-size wrestling mat in our basement and a mini weightroom. We have a shelf lined with athletic trophies and only two scrawny academic ones— though they are front and center. It's completely out of balance, and I can't think of anything I get more pleasure from than watching my kids and their friends play (and win!) competitively.

There. I've confessed. And as a result some of you are now planning to return this book to the point of purchase. For what it's worth, I have a hard time identifying with folks who are passionately devoted to . . . (never mind).

To say I was worried about what we were going to do when my sons no longer had access to competitive sports is an understatement. We've played on homeschool volleyball teams and basketball teams. Those are pretty easy to pull together, but Mike and Gabe wrestle and play football. I like a challenge, but there is no way I'm going to pull together a homeschooled wrestling team and then find a league to play in, at least not in this century.

So, two years before their teams were scheduled to come under the jurisdiction of the school district, I started a dialogue with my school board. In the end they extended to the homeschool community not only access to sports but also access to all extracurricular activities and secondary classes. (In chapter 29 I'll tell you how this came about.)

This is currently an issue heating up in the homeschool community. Several states have already legislated access to scholastic sports for homeschoolers, and around the country many homeschool families have a cooperative relationship with their school district. But those open doors have all come about through hard work.

And in most places the doors remain closed.

In homeschooling you don't waste time. That was an extreme adjustment for me in public school. For example, at home I could combine subjects; a science report could count for English and science. In public school you have to do a lot more to demonstrate your understanding of a subject—in homeschooling your mom knows what you know. We have to take a lot of quizzes just so the teacher can determine if we read the assignment. In homeschooling you can work more efficiently—you don't have twenty minutes for homeroom. Also, at school at least ten minutes of every class is taken up just getting kids in order. I find the other kids very distracting.

In homeschooling I could pursue my own interests. If I saw something on TV that interested me, I could go and find out more about it. After I saw the movie Apollo 13, *I got real interested in space, but it was not what we were studying in science at school.*

The advantage of public school, though, is the teachers are specialized in their area. I really like that I can talk to my science teacher. He knows so much. I think I am pushed harder in school. I have deadlines to meet. That has helped me to learn that the world functions in an orderly fashion. I've also learned how to speak in front of a large group. I have to do that a lot. I think school has given me more special opportunities. This year we had a Civil War reenactment, and another time a Holocaust survivor came and spoke—and sports, I couldn't have played organized football at home.

—Joel Martin, age fourteen

(Home-educated through seventh grade, now in a public high school.)

Do I Have Time to Homeschool?

A woman called my friend Cheri Moore at her homeschool supply store in Virginia Beach. "I'm going to homeschool my daughter," she said. "Tell me what I need to buy for a third grader."

"Well," Cheri replied, "it's not as easy as that. I would need some more information: What's your daughter's learning style? What goals do you have? What philosophy of education are you building upon?"

"I don't have time for all that," the woman answered. "Just tell me what I need to buy."

"If you don't have time for that," Cheri countered, "you don't have time to homeschool."

How much time does it take to homeschool? The answer has a number of contributing factors.

Getting Started

Your first year will be your hardest, Marie Gamon told me.

I didn't see how that was possible, considering we were just talking kindergarten here and not high school physics. But she was right—all because I had a lot to learn and needed to commit the time to that.

Preparing to begin homeschooling is your biggest time commitment. And one you must make if you are serious about doing a responsible job. If you don't have time to clear your schedule for a season and focus on educating yourself, then please don't undertake the education of your children.

A responsible parent will do several of the following *prior to* starting to homeschool:

✔ Read lots of books related to homeschooling and educating children.
My list:

> *For the Children's Sake,* Susan Schaeffer Macaulay (Crossway, 1984).*
>
> *The Christian Home School,* Gregg Harris (<u>Noble Publishing,</u> 1996).*
>
> *The Big Book of Home Learning,* vol. 1, Mary Pride (Crossway, 1996).*
>
> *The Three R's at Home,* Susan and Howard Richman (<u>Pennsylvania Homeschoolers,</u> 1988).*
>
> *Homeschooling: A Patchwork of Days,* Nancy Lande (WindyCreek Press, 1996).*

✔ Attend a homeschooling seminar on getting started.
✔ Attend a state convention and curriculum fair.
✔ Spend the day with a homeschooling family or co-op.
✔ Attend a support group meeting.
✔ Write to request a variety of catalogs from homeschool suppliers.
✔ Subscribe to a state newsletter and other homeschool periodicals.
My list:

> <u>*Practical Homeschooling*</u>
>
> <u>*Pennsylvania Homeschoolers Newsletter*</u>

You Have to Be a Reader

Here's a sample of my reading list from the summer prior to the twins beginning school (most of these are out-of-print but may be available through your public library):

> *Teach Your Own,* John Holt (Dell, 1982).
>
> *How to Tutor,* Samuel Blumenfeld (Paradigm, 1986).
>
> *The New Illiterates,* Samuel Blumenfeld (Paradigm, 1988).
>
> *A Nation at Risk* (The National Commission on Excellence in Education, 1983).
>
> *The Parents' Guide to Raising Children Who Love to Learn,* Children's Television Workshop (Prentice Hall, 1994).

If you don't have time to read, you don't have time to homeschool. Just to drive home this point, here's a sample of Cindy McKeown's recent reading list (after twelve years of homeschooling):

> *The Creative Mind,* Margaret A. Boden (Basic Books, 1992).
>
> *Time Management for Unmanageable People,* Ann McGee-Cooper (Bantam, 1994). This book helped Cindy get her kids organized.
>
> *The Art of Thinking,* Vincent Ruggiero (HarperCollins, 1995).

Raising Self-Reliant Children in a Self-Indulgent World, H. Stephen Glenn
    and Jane Nelson, Ed. D. (Prima Publishing, 1989).

Toxic Psychiatry, Peter Breggin (St. Martins, 1994).

The Seven Habits of Highly Effective People, Stephen Covey
    (Simon & Schuster, 1989).

Killing the Spirit: Higher Education, Page Smith (Penguin, 1991).

Cindy also enjoys reading a healthy dose of books by P. G. Wodehouse and Dorothy Sayers. She considers these her "stress-busters."

Point: If you're not self-educating, how will you reproduce that in your kids? If you don't have the time to *prepare* to homeschool, how will you have the time *to* homeschool?

A Typical School Day

Most homeschoolers will tell you there isn't such a thing as a "typical" day. Nancy Lande has compiled a charming collection of "A Day at Our House" anecdotes in her book *Homeschooling: A Patchwork of Days** (WindyCreek Press, 1996) just to illustrate this point.

It's a Lifestyle

Homeschooling is better described as a lifestyle—a complete integration of family life and learning. When school starts and stops is a nebulous line at best in most homes. Does going to the library after supper count? Or how about slowing down the car to watch a pair of whooping cranes alight beside a stream? Reading together at bedtime? Watching a Ken Burns documentary on the history of baseball? Staying up late to see the Hyakutake comet?

Could You Be More Specific, Please?

That may sound lyrical and enticing, but that doesn't help you make a decision, does it? What you really want to know is, *How much time—max—must I carve out of my schedule to devote solely to teaching a child to read, helping with assignments, organizing science experiments, grading papers, going to the library, testing, completing a textbook, and so forth?*

So, here's a rough generalization of school life, timewise, for you number crunchers. But you've missed the point if you don't grab the binoculars when a downy woodpecker shows up after regular school hours.

The hard-core work of **kindergarten** can be compressed into a thirty-minute daily schedule.

First through third grade: One to two hours of structured learning each day.

Fourth and fifth grades: three to four hours.

Sixth grade and up: Somewhere between sixth grade and eighth grade, many kids move away from hands-on, concrete learning (which takes a lot more time for Mom to set up) and begin to acquire the majority of their content knowledge from their own independent reading. Projects, field trips, and other concrete methods are still an important component, but if you've done your job well, the kids are now initiating these learning activities without much oversight from you.

Junior high and beyond: For the serious student, these years begin early in the morning and end around midafternoon. My sons' math lessons easily take sixty to ninety minutes a day. They practice piano a minimum of thirty minutes and read more than two hours as well as complete writing and research projects. They also do chores.

My involvement is pretty minimal. They are setting their own goals or completing assignments for Creative Home Educators' Support Services (CHESS) or the Learning Center homeschool co-op. I troubleshoot where necessary or meet with them for scheduled tutorials that they have requested.

My time of direct instruction is much more committed to Kristen.

Time's Up! We Must Call for Your Answer

So do you have the time to homeschool? The answer probably lies within the context of this larger question: How much other stuff do you have on your list of responsibilities that cannot be integrated into your homeschool life? A job outside the home? An elderly parent who needs constant care? Ministry responsibilities that don't include your kids? The most successful homeschools have a pretty short list in this regard.

Single Parents, Special Needs, Careers, and Other FAQs*

· ·

FAQ #1. *What If I'm a Single Parent?*

A growing number of single parents are making homeschooling work for their families, but it is not an easy task to accomplish. It requires a great deal of resourcefulness and initiative.

The Issue Is Work

The greatest tension exists when the homeschooling parent must work to support the family. It can succeed when the single parent works at home, works part-time, or has flex hours. It doesn't work when the children—including teenagers—are left alone during the school day or when a full-time job outside the home is necessary. In the latter situation, there just is not enough accountability or adult involvement with the kids.[1] I strongly believe in training our kids to be independent learners—but they still need the adults in their lives to be available and focused on their learning.

My office manager, Barb, is a single mom I greatly admire. She has three school-age children and began homeschooling her seventh-grade daughter this year solely because Erin pleaded with her to do so.

 Barb has a network of support that is a crucial component for the single parent. Erin is able to use an upstairs room at our store and is taking most of her core classes through Creative Home Educators' Support Services (CHESS) as well as enrichment classes at the Learning Center homeschool co-op. The number of subjects Barb needs to cover with

---

* That's Internet-ese for "frequently asked questions."

43

Erin on her own is minimal. Barb also has a computer and lots of software and self-instructional materials for Erin to use. Don't get the impression here that Barb is living on a comfortable income. She is not—she is sacrificing dearly to get creative resources into the hands of her children.

Despite the wide array of opportunities and support available to her, Barb was very thoughtful about this decision. She already finds the responsibility of being a single parent pretty overwhelming. Homeschooling has not reduced that feeling.

On the plus side, Barb loves to learn, has always supplemented her kids' education a lot at home, and is very attracted to the homeschool community she has come to know through working for the Home School Resource Center. And she has found an unexpected camaraderie among homeschoolers that she had little time for before; she's also enjoyed a great deal of support for her effort. For a single parent, I think she has many things leaning her way.

FAQ #2. *What If I Have a Special-Needs Child?*

No matter what area of difficulty your child faces, an individualized program and one-on-one instruction is the optimum learning environment. I have seen great success—actually remarkable improvement—with children challenged with a wide array of disabilities.

A study by Dr. Steven Duvall compared learning-disabled students in public school special education programs and those who were home-educated. Higher rates of "time on task" and greater academic gains were made by those who were homeschooled. Dr. Duvall concluded, "Parents, even without special education training, provided powerful instructional environments at home."[2]

The Success Factor

The common factors in these successful situations are:

- ✔ Parents who are self-educating about the specific challenge their child is facing.
- ✔ Support from a network of resource people in the community. Some of these are professionally qualified; others are simply warm and nurturing individuals from within the church or homeschool community.

Here are recommended sources of support for parents who are homeschooling special-needs children:

Home School Legal Defense Association (HSLDA)
P. O. Box 159
Paeonian Springs, VA 22129
540-338-5600

NATHHAN
National Challenged Homeschoolers Associated Network
5383 Alpine Road SE
Olalla, WA 98359
206-857-4257
e-mail: NATHANEWS@aol.com

Home Schooling Children with Special Needs, Sharon Hensley
(<u>Noble Publishing</u>, 1996).*

*In Their Own Way: Discovering and Encouraging Your Child's Personal
Learning Style,* Thomas Armstrong (Putnam, 1988).*

Learning in Spite of Labels, and other titles, Joyce Hertzog
(<u>Greenleaf Press</u>, 1994).*

Strategies for Struggling Learners, Dr. Joe Sutton
(<u>Exceptional Diagnostics</u>, 1995).*

Testing

If you suspect that your child has a learning disability, the staff at NATHHAN recommends you use a private testing service, such as Dr. Sutton's. NATHHAN can help you find a certified test administrator in your region as well as connect you to families homeschooling children challenged in the same area as yours.

Public Services

You may wish to avail yourself of public school services that are free of charge, but don't walk into the situation naive. Be prepared to speak intelligently about your child's needs and communicate graciously but clearly your intent to take an active role in the decision-making process. I've known a number of parents whose children were identified as special-needs through the local school system, and they had a difficult time retaining control of the situation. There's a lot of money flowing into the special-needs end of public education and a lot of incentive to get as many kids as possible into the system.

Be Advised before You Sign

If you wish to leave open your option to homeschool your special-needs child, then you should seek advice from Home School Legal Defense Association (p. 44) before you sign any papers indicating your agreement with the diagnosis of your child. In a number of states, the formal identification of a child as handicapped or special needs places him or her under separate legal regulations. This will then give you access to publicly funded services, but it can also make you legally bound to requirements you may wish to avoid.

FAQ #3. *What about My Career?*

Something has to give—you can't do it all. Believe me, if that were possible I would have figured out how because I love to "do"—anything and everything. Saying no is my biggest challenge; keeping things simple is a close second.

If you choose to homeschool, it has to be far higher on your list of priorities than your career. Ideally, the main teaching parent is not working outside the home, especially when the children are younger. But as that is often not the case, here's the way I have seen the two mix successfully.

Home Is Where the Work Is

Entrepreneurialism runs deep throughout the homeschool community. The same philosophical underpinnings that support home education have also led many to take charge of their careers. And as with education, technology is making it possible to base our work lives at home.

 A home-based career can integrate well with your child's education. Choose one that has inherent educational value: Wendy O'Donovan is a single mother who works for her extended family's geranium nursery that specializes in scientific research, with clients around the world. While acknowledging that it hasn't been easy, Wendy is enthusiastic about the fascinating business and research opportunities her children have been able to have.

 Stephen and Naomi Strunk are parents of seven children and the owners of **Creative Kids Learning Company**, a homeschool supply business. Each child has responsibility. Elizabeth (sixteen) is in charge of billing and graphic design, Hannah (fourteen) does sales, Lydia (eleven) is a clerk at smaller events and does all pricing and phone calling, Ezra (nine) and Benjamin (nine) are stock boys and work with the children at "Kamp K-NEX," a program the Strunks developed for local Christian schools, and even Suzanna (nine), who has Downs syndrome, helps with mailing and labeling. Prior to graduation Amanda (nineteen) worked hand-in-hand with her mother in overseeing daily operations.

Look for similar opportunities that will enable your children to be integrally involved with the business while acquiring a marketable skill and a specialized base of knowledge.

I know homeschooling families who have mixed education and occupation in the following areas: construction, horticulture, bulk-food co-ops, bread-making, private practice of medicine and psychology, writing, computer consulting, homeschool supplies, private instruction in music and art, animal-breeding, and legal services.

At Our House . . .

Kermit's career as a systems analyst had been very stable throughout most of our married life, so it was easy to take his job for granted. However, downsizing and reengineering—euphemisms for the disintegration of corporate America and job security—caused us to take a more serious look at my little side venture—**the Home School Resource Center**.

We realized my "not-for-much-profit, home-based business" was possibly God's provision for our family in uncertain times. Our catalog of "resources for creative homeschooling" kept growing to keep up with the mushrooming ranks of homeschoolers in our area. Even the local school administrators were sending families to us. When the business threatened to consume all of our living space, we took the big step of moving it out of our house.

We now operate a homeschool supply store and mail-order catalog from a business location in Hershey, where the **Young Writers' Institute** administrative offices are also located. We have been able to hire staff to manage the day-to-day operations.

I still maintain an office in an extra bedroom of our home and only need to spend several afternoons a week in the store. The rest of the time the staff communicates with me by fax and e-mail.

Reality Check

Just so you don't imagine this as a wildly profitable plan and launch your own venture with unrealistic expectations, let me add that we draw little income from the business. We see this as an investment for the future (we hope there's a payoff) and a training ground for our kids. They have the benefit of comparing the pluses and minuses of being in business for yourself with working for a Fortune 500 company (which Kermit does). It should make their future career choices far more informed than ours were.

A lot of what is currently being published about home-based businesses underestimates the time and costs involved and overinflates financial rewards. (Sorry to burst your bubble.)

These books are the best I've read for giving realistic advice:

> *Homemade Business: A Woman's Step-by-Step Guide to Earning Money at Home,* Donna Partow (Focus on the Family Publishing, 1992).
>
> *The Bootstrap Entrepreneur: Everything You Really Need to Know about Starting Your Own Business,* Steven Bursten (Thomas Nelson Publishing, 1993).
>
> *The Small Business Survival Guide: How to Manage Your Cash, Profits, and Taxes,* Robert E. Fluery (Sourcebooks Trade, 1992).
>
> *The E Myth Revisited: Why Most Small Businesses Don't Work and What to Do about It,* Michael Gerber (Harper Business, 1995).

FAQ #4. Can I Teach More Than One Child at Once?

Yes, you can teach more than one child at a time, but it's like juggling. It will take a bit of practice to keep all the balls rotating in the air. There are a couple of basic strategies to employ to manage this feat:

1. Choose multilevel resources that enable you to present the same subject to all or several of your kids at once. My children are five years apart in age. I can group Katie and the boys together for quite a few activities or let Mike and Gabe work independently and group Katie and Kristen. The subjects we've most frequently combined have been history, art, science, and English.

   Cindy McKeown and Marie Gamon have grouped their kids together for lots of subjects throughout the years. Marie will teach art to the younger children while Cindy has the older ones for science next door. Even though there is a span of four years between Marie's oldest teen and Cindy's youngest teen, they've been able to have the four of them do the same science and use the same math tutor simultaneously. Once we get the idea out of our heads that there is a linear progression of subject matter we must follow, we are free to do biology one year with kids in ninth through twelfth grades or colonial American history with children in second through fifth.

2. Recognize that your job is not so much to teach your children as it is to facilitate educational opportunities and undergird their independent learning. At this moment, Mike, Gabe, and Katie function fairly independently while I work one-on-one with Kristen, who can't remember all those wonderful units of study we did when she was two years old. My older three check in with me on an "as needed basis," and I hold them accountable to accomplish their weekly goals by reviewing their completed work.

  As you read through the practical tips that follow, you should get a clearer picture of homeschool life. As I tell the perplexed folks who frequently ask me how I do this, homeschooling is more like tutoring than teaching. If you have a picture in your mind of your children sitting in desks with you at the front of the class presenting all the lessons in lecture form, we've got to tune you to another station.

FAQ #5. But What about Socialization?

Of course this section wouldn't be complete without addressing the number-one FAQ posed to homeschoolers. Some folks seem to expect our kids to be as clueless in social situations as the *Beverly Hillbillies*. But if you spend even a little bit of time among homeschoolers you'll realize this is a nonissue.

First, let's define our terms. Make a list of what you mean by *socialization*. Here's mine:

- ✔ Kid can work cooperatively with other people, including those from different backgrounds and beliefs.
- ✔ Kid is not socially awkward in group situations.
- ✔ Kid can work out differences with others.
- ✔ Kid understands appropriate behavior in social situations.

Now let me ask you this: Where did you learn appropriate social behavior? School? Where did you learn to appreciate folks who dress differently, act differently, think differently? School? Where did you learn proper etiquette? High school cafeteria? Get the point?

Homeschooled kids can learn in a much broader context of social experiences than they would in school. Typically it is an age-integrated environment. They are frequently in group settings with adults, senior citizens, toddlers, and peers. There is none of this silliness about sixth graders not talking to fifth graders or big brothers not talking to younger sisters. There is no pecking order to fall in line with or acceptance measured by the clothes you wear or the dares you take.

My kids often find the social mores of their public school friends very perplexing. On one baseball team the twelve-year-olds relegated the eleven-year-olds to the end of the bench the entire season. One friend was astonished when Mike acknowledged his sister as she walked by him at the community pool. Once some players thought the backfield should shave their heads prior to an important game. Gabe, the quarterback, couldn't figure out what strategic advantage this would give them. He left his hair intact.

Here's one anecdote from a Learning Center co-op mom who began homeschooling reluctantly after watching her bright son lose his vitality in a private school setting:

Jeffrey was excelling academically in a Christian school but hurting in his heart. The cruel comments from classmates, being picked last for a sports team, and never feeling accepted by his peers was a daily happening. Every night John and I prayed with him, encouraged him, and told him he is special, but every day he came home defeated. Despite many misconceptions about homeschooling, we began praying for wisdom.

Two years later we began homeschooling and joined the Learning Center. We were received with open arms and hearts. Jeffrey now felt comfortable with friends of all ages. Maybe homeschoolers are so accepting of children who are a "little different" because they are a minority themselves. The good news is that Jeffrey is more secure and happy with who God has made him.

I see homeschooling as an environment to give my children wings. We were paying for Jeffrey to receive a wonderful education, but he could never reach his full potential when he felt so worthless.

—Beverly, mother of three

This is the kind of basic human decency I can count on finding among our homeschool community—and that, to me, is the essence of what is typically meant by socialization.

But you don't have to take my word for it . . .

Research Conclusions

Research focused on the social and emotional adjustment of homeschoolers has indicated:

✔ Home-educated children have significantly lower problem-behavior scores than their conventionally educated agemates (Shyers, 1992).

✔ Home-educated students have higher self-concepts than agemates in public school (Shyers, 1992, and Taylor, 1986).

✔ The social and emotional adjustment of home-educated students is comparable to private-schooled agemates. But home-educated students are less peer dependent (Delahooke, 1986).

✔ Home-educated students are just as involved in out-of-school and extracurricular activities that predict leadership in adulthood as are those in the comparison private school (that was comprised of students more involved than those in public schools) (Montgomery, 1989).[3]

FAQ #6. *But Am I Qualified to Teach My Children?*

Maybe you're with me so far, but you've got one hang-up. You seriously doubt your ability to teach your own children. After all, you didn't do so well in school yourself. Or perhaps you're so highly educated you think of teaching as an exacting science, like medicine.

Teaching Is an Acquired Skill

But teaching is an art, not a science. If you love your kids and are motivated to help them learn, you can acquire the skills you need.

Ask the best teachers you know what factor they most credit with their success. It won't be their degree or certification; it will be their on-the-job training.

❧ The large body of research that exists shows little empirical evidence that teacher certification impacts student outcomes. Private school students routinely outscore public-educated counterparts on standardized achievement tests, and teachers without certification are prevalent in private schools.

❧ All researched comparisons of homeschooled students' achievement scores show significantly above-average achievement as a group. In 1995, Riverside Publishing Company announced that of the sixteen thousand home-educated students tested with the Iowa Test of Basic Skills, the mean score in reading was in the 77 percentile, and the mean score in mathematics was in the 73 percentile.

Of the thirty moms in the Learning Center, I am the only certified teacher; three others have degrees in education. But you wouldn't be able to pick us out based on an observation of the classes taught. The moms at the Learning Center, like so many other homeschooling moms I know, are not hindered by their lack of professional training. These are _their_ kids they are teaching, and they are highly motivated to do their best.

The homeschool parents I know are continuously reading, networking, and weighing different strategies for becoming better teachers. It's the most stimulating professional environment I've been in.

If You've Potty-Trained, You're Qualified

Any child you've potty trained, you can certainly teach to read. And any child you've taught to read, you can certainly teach to learn on his own. And once you've taught a child to learn on his own, your job is just to facilitate that learning: scouring out resources, experiences, mentors, etc., that will support the child's own endeavors.

This is not to say without qualification that all parents are their children's best teacher. There are certain prerequisites that have been proven to make a difference.

Let's look now at the real recipe for success in homeschooling.

Six Ingredients
of a Successful Homeschool

 Marlene is unexpectedly pregnant—again. Today she's having a hard time getting started. From the bed, she listens to Timmy and James arguing in the kitchen. In the background, the television blares. She rolls over and sighs deeply. She hears the school bus pull up to the corner and swing open its doors. What she'd give to have her kids on it—especially the two-year-old. But no such luck. Marlene's homeschooling.

She can tell you a spiritualized story of how she arrived at this decision—but the bottom line is her pastor homeschools and she is eager for his respect.

Allen, her husband, left early this morning. He's out looking for work. It's a second marriage for both of them, and in the past seven years, he's been unemployed three times. Just not much of a market any more for printers. He really didn't want Marlene to homeschool; he wanted her to get a job. But that wasn't in her theology.

Her oldest, Robby, sticks his head in the room. He's a bright kid. He likes to read, and he likes to play soccer. "Uh, Mom, what should I be doing for school?"

Marlene has borrowed books for the year from her school district. And she found some workbooks and readers at the library sale, all for five dollars. She tells a great story of how the Holy Spirit guided her to this overlooked pile of material.

"Can't you just read the next chapters in science till I get up?" Her voice has an edge.

"That science book is really boring, Mom. I was wondering if I could finish the woodworking project Dad and I started."

"Rob, you know you aren't allowed to handle the tools alone. Listen, get Timmy and James breakfast while I get dressed."

Sometime after nine, Marlene makes an appearance. Robby, seated at the table, is just beginning to find his place in the science book. James and Timmy are watching "Shining Time Station."

The phone rings. Marlene's voice brightens as she talks to a young mother from church. Her friend is having problems with a toddler, and Marlene is full of advice.

Robby stares at the pages of his textbook and intermittently checks the clock. The little guys spill into the kitchen. Marlene periodically covers the phone and tells them to be quiet. Each time, her voice raises another notch.

Timmy has a fork. He aims for James but misses and sticks his mother. Marlene screams. She manages to hang up the phone before she vents her anger on everyone in sight.

Robby sighs, picks up his books, and heads for his bedroom.

After lunch, Marlene leaves for a weekly Bible study, and Robby's left in charge. At four o'clock, Robby thinks of his friends at school just heading out to the soccer fields. He misses the team, and he misses his friends. He misses English class. He even misses grouchy Mr. Whittler who gave him in-school suspension last year. He sure wishes God hadn't told his mom to homeschool.

Recipe for Success

It's been my experience that families who elect to home-educate meet with varying degrees of success. But that success has little to do with teaching certificates or college degrees. Rather, it has a lot to do with Christian character.

This recipe for success is not meant to discourage you. If your family is unable to meet one of these prerequisites but is willing to seek change, you're on the right road.

If you can't or won't add one of these ingredients to your homeschool, it still may be the *best* option you have. But, honestly, you will not be able to give your children the education they deserve, and you are going to be frustrated and stressed.

Is She Happy?

Probably the *key factor* in those homes that have happy, motivated children who are achieving at the level of their potential is *Mom's attitude.* Is she happy? Are we having fun yet? Does she enjoy homeschooling and maintain relatively consistent enthusiasm? Or does she have a pinched look on her face most of the time?

Here are the factors I find affect her outlook:

Ingredient #1: Family Relationships Are Healthy

Common Vision

Start with your spouse. Do the two of you have a common vision and goals? If you applied the principles of chapter 1 to your marriage would your list of targets have any overlap?

When Kermit and I first married, we were still two very independent people with divergent plans for our lives. Our views on money, church, a woman's role, and the proper way to fold a towel (just to name the biggies) were often at odds. Now, a decade and a half later, by the grace of God (and what can feel like sheer force of will) we're both headed in the same direction and very happy to be doing so. How that happened is another story, and I know many of you can relate to that scenario. (Towels should be folded in thirds and stacked with the folded side out, by the way.)

It is very typical for one partner to have more of a vision for homeschooling than the other at first. It can take time to balance this out. But here are the necessary components in marriage for surviving the rocky first years of homeschooling:

1. Quick Resolution of Conflict

You resolve conflict quickly. Notice, I didn't say you don't have any conflict. The crux is, you know *how* to resolve it. In our house that means not letting issues fester, demonstrating humility and forgiveness, communicating constructively, and asking for outside help from spiritually mature friends when necessary.

2. Dad's Attitude

Dad is supportive of homeschooling. I believe this factor, much more than Dad's *direct involvement* in homeschooling, determines success.

The worst thing a husband can say to his wife is, "All right, I'll give you a year, and we'll see how you do." It is very unfair to put this kind of pressure on your wife. The first year of homeschooling is the toughest. In the best of situations, there are going to be mistakes, discouragement, and self-doubt throughout. To add to that the stress of having to get this right the first time or she's pulled from the game is a setup for failure from the start.

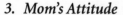

3. Mom's Attitude

Wives, on the other hand, need to be realistic about their husband's involvement. I've attended seminars and read books where the father's role in homeschooling is presented as something akin to the principal of the school: Dad should be directly involved in setting curriculum, reviewing work, and spending time daily instructing his children. As I look around the auditorium where this is being said, I see the fathers slowly sinking down in their seats under the pressure of one more thing on their plates.

It Looks Different at Every House

When our kids were younger, Kermit read aloud to them nearly every day and looked at their daily work. It was easy to use vacation days for special things. But he is now mid-career, and his responsibilities on the job have expanded. His work week is much longer, and he is overseeing our family business as well.

One day, I realized I knew countless home-educating families in the same situation. I'm grateful Kermit is gainfully employed. I'm happy that the free time he does have is devoted to his kids—but he wants to play ball or take the girls to the Fun Fort, not review papers or teach a course.

And he has always been willing to take over responsibilities at home so I can get away to plan or just have a break.

Some fathers do teach—but it's because they have an interest, not an obligation. John Gamon teaches science to his kids. He has a lab set up in the basement. Pickling there are fetal pigs and cows' eyes. He loves it. I know several homes where the father is the primary teacher. And I've seen many fathers' involvement increase as the kids enter their teen years. In general, they seem more comfortable with the material at that level. The point is there's a principle but not a pattern that must be adhered to.

It's a Joint Decision

Homeschooling needs to be a joint decision. Both spouses should be able to say, "We're going to try this for a year and give it our best shot. Then we'll reevaluate the situation." During the year, Dad needs to be committed to tangibly encouraging and supporting his wife.

Predetermine Responsibilities

Talk through with your spouse what responsibilities each of you will assume to contribute to the integrity and success of your homeschool. The job description for both of you will shift and change over the years, so don't expect this to be a once-and-done discussion.

If the primary teacher—usually Mom—starts showing signs of stress and exhaustion during the year, it's a good bet the other partner needs to either provide some R & R (a weekend away works wonders) or shift some responsibility onto his or her plate for a season.

Check Out the Kids

After assessing your marriage, be honest about your relationship with each of your children.

Kids need two things in order to learn well:

> ✔ a secure environment, free from stress and fear
> ✔ praise and encouragement from someone they trust

Is your child motivated by your praise and still interested in your approval? Do you have an effective plan for dealing with discipline problems?

Say It Again, Sam

If you have a strong-willed child or a dysfunctional relationship with your spouse, homeschooling is only going to accentuate these problems, not solve them. I know too many families who thought homeschooling was the solution. It isn't. These problems must be worked on at a deeper, more fundamental level. In some cases, you need outside help.

Meaningful Church Involvement

I am very grateful to be involved in a church where the pastoral staff and small-group leaders are available to constructively guide us through the challenges of marriage and parenting. I cannot overemphasize how crucial a role this has played in the success of our family life. It is that support, not homeschooling, that I credit with the fruit in my children and my marriage.

Marlene eventually put her children back in public school, and she and her husband sought pastoral help for their marriage. They aren't homeschooling today, but their home is much stabler. Robby is playing soccer, and his confidence in God's loving care in his life has grown.

If you need some sound advice in the parenting realm, here are the books that have had the greatest impact in our home:

> _Raising Children Who Hunger for God,_ Benny and Sheree Phillips
> (Chosen Books, 1991).*

Walking with the Wise (devotional for parents and teens), Benny and Sheree Phillips (<u>PDI Publications</u>, 1994).*

Shepherding a Child's Heart, Tedd Tripp (Shepherd Press, 1995).*

Ingredient #2: Your Home Is Educationally Stimulating

A quick tour of my home tells people a lot about me. I'm not very committed to laundry, or dusting, or even interior decorating. But my commitment to reading and learning, I hope, is evident. Books, magazines, projects, computers, music, etc., dominate the landscape. There are bookshelves in every room.

My downfall is any bookstore. My husband and I have a sick codependent relationship. He's not to be trusted near one either. Our family business is really an elaborate scheme I hatched to make sure I could get books any time I craved one. My heart sinks if the UPS truck passes my house without stopping. My library fines are so hefty they've mentioned naming me a major donor. Our kids are infected as well.

If your home does not reflect your commitment to education, your kids will clearly get the message that it isn't important. Your kids deserve to be taught by someone who loves to learn.

Is school time a pressured thing you rush to get through? Have you committed the finances to provide educational materials? I know what it is to live on a restricted budget. But I am committed to buying the best material I can afford.

When a parent's initial question is, "How cheaply can this be done?" I know their kids are going to be short-changed.

I know many, many families who are homeschooling on a limited budget, but the best of these are getting to the library regularly, setting aside funds for the used-curriculum sale, and praying in faith for the provisions to come in. There is serious personal sacrifice going on to see that the kids have access to quality materials.

Ingredient #3: You Have a Biblical Conviction That God Has Called You to Homeschool

Our initial decision to home-educate has to be more substantive than, "Gee, that's a neat idea. I think I'll try that," or acquiescence to the subtle pressure (real or perceived) that it is more "spiritual" to homeschool.

Our conviction must be borne out of prayer, study of God's Word, and godly counsel. It is imperative that we take the time we need to hear God personally. These convictions are the foundation for appropriating the faith and grace we need to complete the task. Otherwise, when discouragement and disillusionment hit, we will dig a deeper hole by questioning if we should be doing this in the first place. Constant doubts such as, *Am I really the best teacher for my children? Am I cheating them out of fun and opportunities? Is this going to be worth it in the end?* will wear us out.

The writer of James said a double-minded man is unstable in all his ways. Without this bedrock of faith that God said, "Do it!" we're in for some rough seas. Firmly rooted convictions will be the source of endurance for the course.

Read Gregg Harris's book *The Christian Home School** if you want a persuasive, biblical argument for homeschooling to help you build convictions.

Ingredient #4: You Have Initiative and Discipline

To homeschool successfully we don't need degrees or loads of creativity and talent, but we do need some measure of maturity in our character. We need "get up and go" and the ability to restrain ourselves when discipline is required.

There's a Learning Curve

If you are new to homeschooling then the hard part is now. You have to invest a lot of time in reading, preparing, figuring out what methods work best, and learning to manage your time.

Every new venture requires an initial outlay of time and training. I could not live without a computer. It is such a timesaver. But I spent hours reading, being frustrated, crying "Honey, help!" and learning in order to reap those benefits.

Just Say No

We need to be able to say no to other opportunities—and to be at peace when others don't understand why we do. Two things I've had to discipline myself to do are to go to bed on time and to not answer the phone. I return the calls I can in the afternoon. Some I just can't respond to. Sometimes people are angry and disappointed with me, but there's peace in our day now.

Hobbies, friendships, ministries, jobs—many things may have to be sacrificed in order to homeschool with integrity. It all comes back to this vision that provides us with parameters for evaluating all the choices before us. Homeschooling successfully requires us to take radical control of our schedules. If you don't, you'll never hit the target.

Ingredient #5: There Is a Support System Available to You

Your support system may be formal or informal, but it needs to be made up of tangible people, not a state newsletter or a homeschooling magazine. You need folks who are standing with you and committed to helping you through. The more multilayered this support system is, the quicker you will surmount discouragement.

I am blessed beyond measure that my church, my relatives, and my friends support the choice we've made and are available to pick me up when I am down.

My network has not always been so thick—neither my parents nor my in-laws supported our choice at first. My friends were threatened by our decision. And I've talked to many homeschool families in churches where they are isolated, even outrightly opposed by the leadership.

You need support. Get out of bad situations if you can. Find a church that is standing with families who make this choice, and find friends who homeschool. The relatives I guess you have to keep, but I've seen lots of grandparents change their minds once they see the fruit in their grandkids' lives. (They are only reacting out of love and concern, so don't be too hard on them.)

Some folks are going to call you a separatist—but your first priority when starting out is to lay a firm foundation. Get your house in order first. In the early years we immersed ourselves in the homeschool community. We talked about it nonstop and felt most attracted to others with our perspective. It was a necessary season of our life. It demanded our intense focus.

Today, our lives are much more balanced. Our family has many close friends who do not homeschool. We have other circles of interest we move in. We can only do this and remain effective at home because a solid foundation of support is in place.

Ingredient #6: You Are Willing to Seek Help

Homeschooling should not be done in isolation. It's not healthy for you or for your children. Without the input of others, you won't have a balanced perspective of things. Even though I have a teaching certificate and a lot of experience working with kids, I still need and pursue the input of others. I go to seminars, I read books, and I talk to parents further down the road than we are.

If you are a learner, you will always be looking and listening for better ways to fine-tune your program.

When you are discouraged or unmotivated, humble yourself and talk to someone with strengths in your area of weakness. The Bible says if we don't solicit the wise counsel of others we are proud and God will oppose our ways. Find a mature Christian woman who is obviously succeeding with her children and ask her advice. Be willing to serve her in return for her time. Annually attend seminars, listen to tapes, and read books, all with an attitude to learn. This is the fastest way to become qualified to teach your children.

But I Don't *Want* to Homeschool!

Okay, maybe after all this, we've gotten to the bottom of things. You really don't want to homeschool—but you're reading this book because you have this niggling feeling that maybe you *should* homeschool. Let me see if I can help you out there as well.

I didn't want to homeschool. I am pretty career-minded. I was willing to stay home with my kids until they were school age (and feel pretty smug about it), but then I was planning to get back to my real life.

I'll tell you something else. I didn't want to become a Christian either.

A campus missionary presented the gospel to me in a compelling, logical manner (à la Josh McDowell). I realized it was true—I was a sinner— I needed a Savior—but I sure didn't want to give up the lifestyle I was leading. What did I do? I knew it would be foolish of me not to become a Christian, but I certainly wasn't as happy about it as all the other folks in the room were. Talk about hubris!

But for the compelling grace of God in my life, I might have tragically let my feelings be my guide—and certainly modern society supports that kind of emotion-based decision-making.

How do I "feel" about being a Christian now? The joy is inexpressible. How do I "feel" about homeschooling? Well, I *could* describe that. Most days I love it. Some days, I sure don't. But I was there the day each one of my children learned to read, I was there the day Katie piloted a Pungy Schooner into port, and I was there the day we all sat in the living room listening to the closing chapter of *The Cay* on tape, our eyes glistening. And nothing beats the satisfaction I find in seeing all four of my kids with their noses in a book.

Right at the beginning of recorded history, God gives us a very important principle for living. He challenges Cain: "Why are you downcast? If you do right, would not your countenance be lifted up?" (Gen. 4:6). Paraphrased, the point is this: If we do what is right, our feelings will change. The Bible's way is not "feel your way to a new way of acting" but rather "act your way to a new way of feeling."

God's ways are not burdensome. He said, "Blessed are those who hear my commands and obey them" (Luke 11:28). We have a promise that obedience brings joy. But first things first. Forget about how you are feeling about homeschooling. Concentrate on determining God's will for your kids' lives (and feelings are not where we check to discern this), then draw faith from His promise that obedience to His will will produce joy in your life. We often look at the future calling God may have for us and imagine ourselves miserably obeying. That indicates a faulty view of who God is.

So exercise faith and draw hope from the promises of His Word.

I was recently asked if I liked homeschooling my four children. My usual response would have been, "Yes, it's great!"

But in recent years our oldest son has become a teenager, and I've come to admit to myself that no, I really don't like homeschooling my four children very much. Over the past decade I've taught three, almost four kids how to read; confronted innumerable personal weaknesses and sinful behavior in my children and myself; failed countless times to do what I planned in a school year; viewed good and bad test scores; and been discouraged and overwhelmed more times than I like to remember.

So my answer this time was, "Well . . . I like the fruit." I love what I am seeing in my children, especially my fourteen-year-old son. We simply do not have the same struggles that other parents of teens I know have, and I'm convinced that the reason is that my son is not being socialized and civilized by his peers.

I recently drove Stephen to a student meeting at our local college. When we got there, I nearly asked him if he wanted me to go in with him but quickly decided against it. I thought he would object. But when he mentioned that he was unsure where to go, I volunteered to go with him.

"If you don't mind . . . ," I said.

"No, I don't mind," he said sincerely.

I realized that he had no clue that boys his age don't like to be seen with their mothers, especially when meeting a college friend.

I love homeschooling because of episodes like this one that confirm to me we're on the right path for our family. I don't like the process much at all. I can talk big with my homeschooling friends, but when it comes right down to it, there are many days when I feel like a total failure. But I see things in my children that great schools and great programs could never produce, and I'm encouraged to keep going. I can't quit now. I'm not willing to give up what we've gained.

I don't expect that it will be clear sailing the whole way to adulthood. I can't do what only the Holy Spirit can do. But I can at least work hard in the garden He's given me to tend; I can keep the fence mended and the gate fixed and try to preserve the fruit we've already harvested. Do I like homeschooling? No, not really; but I love the fruit!

—Kristi, mother of four

Family Worksheet

· ·

Homeschooling: Is It for Your Family?

Here's the exit interview before we close out Part 1. Use it as a tool to help you and your spouse make a wise decision about homeschooling.

1. Evaluate your relationship with your spouse.

_____ **Excellent.** You have a common vision and goals. You are able to move quickly to resolve conflicts that arise.

_____ **Good.** You communicate well about your differences in vision and goals. You seek out wise counsel to resolve conflicts when necessary.

_____ **Fair.** You are both Christians. You eventually make peace about your differences. You rarely lose control of your emotions when you experience conflict. You do not seek help in resolving conflict.

_____ **Poor.** You disagree strongly about your vision and goals. You have a great deal of conflict, and you resolve it in a destructive way.

2. Evaluate your relationship with each of your children.

_____ **Excellent.** This child is highly motivated by your praise and has a strong desire to obey his or her parents.

_____ **Good.** This child can be motivated by your praise, and you are making steady progress in his or her willingness to obey you.

_____ **Fair.** This child is challenging, and you are often overwhelmed by him or her. You and your spouse do not have an agreed-upon plan for training the child. You do believe that God can sustain you.

_____ **Poor.** This child is wearing the pants, and you gave up long ago. You feel like a failure as a parent. You aren't getting help, and you have no hope that things are going to change.

3. Evaluate the atmosphere in your home. Check all that apply.

<u>Positive</u>   <u>Negative</u>

____ peaceful   ____ stressful

____ secure   ____ insecure

____ fun   ____ somber

____ hospitable   ____ isolated

____ spontaneous   ____ rigid

____ stable   ____ unstable

____ organized   ____ chaotic

____ encouraging   ____ discouraging

4. List all other responsibilities and commitments you and your spouse have beyond maintaining your home and caring for your children.

<u>EMPLOYMENT</u>   <u>CHURCH</u>   <u>VOLUNTEERING</u>   <u>HOBBIES</u>

5. What plans do you have for limiting other responsibilities and commitments in order to homeschool with integrity?

6. Evaluate your home as an educationally stimulating environment.

   a. How often do you use the library? _____

   b. How many hours a week is your television on? _____

   c. How many books are in your home? _____

   d. What types of presents do you usually buy your children? _____

e. What magazines do you subscribe to? _____

f. What interests do you share with your children? _____

g. What kinds of topics do you discuss as a family? _____

h. Are pencils, paper, and art supplies readily available to your children? _____

i. Do your children have an adequate place to play outside? _____

7. Can you commit a minimum of four hundred dollars per year to home-educating?

8. Rate yourself on initiative by asking yourself these questions and circling one of the words that follow. Are you a learner? How many books a year do you read? Do you enjoy tackling new projects?

   Excellent   Very Good   Good   Fair   Poor

9. Rate yourself on discipline. Do you finish a job? Can you set goals and achieve them? Do you get up and go to bed on time? Do you fulfill your obligations?

   Excellent   Very Good   Good   Fair   Poor

10. What are your reasons for homeschooling? Is this a biblical conviction?

11. How supportive of homeschooling is the father?

   ____Very supportive   ____Supportive   ____Neutral   ____Not supportive

12. What role will the father be able to play in your homeschool?

13. What support system is available to you? Your husband? Your family? Your church? A homeschool support group? A friendly teacher? A Christian school? A library? An educational consultant?

14. Are you willing to go to seminars, attend support group meetings, read books, etc., in order to always be improving your teaching skills and your homeschool?

15. Evaluate your willingness to seek help.

    ____ I readily seek help from others who have a strength in the area I am struggling with.

    ____ On occasion I do seek outside help if things get pretty bad.

    ____ I prefer to make things work on my own.

16. Are you willing to comply with the laws governing homeschooling in your state?

    ____ I am committed to fulfilling my legal responsibilities with excellence.

    ____ I will do what needs to be done to comply with the laws.

    ____ Frankly, I'm overwhelmed by the laws, but I'll try to comply.

    ____ I do not believe I have a biblical responsibility to comply with these laws.

17. Having prayerfully weighed the cost of homeschooling, are you prepared to commit yourself to home educating for *one year* before reevaluating your decision?

PART 2

Choosing a Curriculum

In This Section

8

How Do I Decide?

• •

Just tell me *what* to buy! That's the $64,000 question. Use to be pretty simple (and pretty dull). Ten years ago there wasn't much curricula to choose from. You just ordered textbooks from a school supplier who was willing to sell to homeschoolers, sometimes disguising your homeschool with a school-sounding name in order to do so.

Every time I ordered from one publisher, I endured the sales rep telling me why she did not approve of homeschoolers—and what a passing fad it was.

You're a Niche Market

Now homeschool conventions attract thousands of parents and hundreds of vendors. Some of the most traditional suppliers have added *"Great for homeschooling!"* to their splashy ads. Companies like Scholastic have hired a homeschooling consultant to help them better target their products. Homeschooling is going mainstream. It's a hot new niche market, and lots of businesses want your dollars. One analyst found $200 million is spent annually by homeschoolers on educational supplies.[1]

This all adds up to choice—lots of it. Not only are there scores of printed materials to help you teach every subject area, but there are software and video programs to consider as well.

All this is good news (even if you find it overwhelming). You have the opportunity to design a program that uniquely fits your child and your family. It's individualized, not institutionalized learning. And that allows you to produce kids who can learn at their fullest potential and enjoy it.

Prepackaged Programs

You can save yourself a lot of time wading through all these choices by settling on a traditional curriculum designed for Christian or public school use. This way you get all the material you could ever possibly want for every school subject. And no one says you have to buy it all. Another option is to purchase just a portion of a program for the subjects you feel most insecure handling alone.

Here are the advantages of prepackaged curricula:

1. The work's been done for you. The teacher's manuals lay out daily lessons and assignments. Textbooks and workbooks contain all the reading material and paperwork the student needs to complete for the year. You save time planning and organizing.
2. You have greater peace of mind. A common concern of parents is forgetting something. If you use a complete line from one supplier year after year, you know they've seen to it that nothing is left out.
3. If you think your child may return to a traditional setting, you've followed the standard scope and sequence.
4. The material is covered in a logical fashion.

Many of us feel most comfortable choosing this option when we begin to homeschool. We want to keep things simple until we get our feet wet. Taking responsibility for designing our own program can just be too drastic a step to add to the first years of homeschooling. Textbooks, workbooks, and teacher's manuals look familiar and make sense. They give us a framework to follow, and that feels secure.

Given my bottom-line indicator of a successful homeschool (Mom is happy), this may be reason enough to choose a traditional program at first.

I Recommend

Now, in a minute I'm going to reveal my true colors on this subject, so you may want to find a less biased source of advice. But for what it is worth, if I were going to use traditional materials in my program, I would look at the curricula from <u>Bob Jones University Press</u> first.

Why I Like Bob Jones University

BJU values academic excellence and the arts. (It has a fabulous American art collection on campus and a world renown drama and music department.) It has an outstanding group of professors and researchers in the field of education writing its curricula. And these folks are frequently available to talk with you by phone or at the curriculum fairs around the country. Further, most of the BJU material has been recently revised to include higher-level thinking and assignments that require the student to interact with the material on a more thoughtful level.

The teacher's manuals are especially well done. Marie Gamon has used much of the BJU program, and she has her children use the teacher's text for the higher-level courses instead of the student's. This way they get the information BJU has provided for the classroom lectures.

The controversial beliefs and practices that the media have highlighted at BJU are never mentioned in any of the materials I've seen (though I do know homeschoolers who do not do business with BJU as a matter of principle). I know Christian families across the theological spectrum who are using their materials and are happy with them.

Here is BJU's address as well as the sources of additional traditional materials that are popular among homeschoolers.

Bob Jones University Press
Greenville, SC 29614
800-845-5731
http://www.bju.edu/press/home.html

A Beka Book Publications
Box 18000
Pensacola, FL 32532
800-874-2352

Alpha Omega
300 North McKemy
Candler, AZ 85226-2618
800-622-3070

Christian Liberty Press
502 W. Euclid Avenue
Arlington Heights, IL 60004
800-259-8736

Modern Curriculum Press
P. O. Box 2649
Columbus, OH 43216
800-321-3106

Grade Levels Vary

You will find there is little standardization about grade level among textbook suppliers. Some material is very academically accelerated (A Beka for instance), and some is academically delayed. (If it is inexpensive, cheaply produced, and requires students to only fill in the blanks, it's suspect.)

Lay grade-level material from several companies side by side before making your purchase. This will make it easier for you to see the differences.

Make Your Own Curriculum

Quick, name your favorite textbook from school. How about your favorite worksheet? Drawing a blank? Why am I not surprised?

Well, how about your favorite books from childhood? (*Little Women, Huckleberry Finn, To Kill a Mockingbird* . . . what's on your list?) Or your favorite projects? (A short story in fourth, my leaf collection in fifth, a relief map of Egypt in seventh.) Wouldn't you prefer to draw these last two questions in a game of *Outburst*?

If we can't even remember the textbooks and worksheets of childhood, how much better can we remember what we learned from them?

I still remember where the Nile River flows through Egypt, the placement of the pyramids, the elaborate irrigation system of that ancient civilization. And I can identify quite a few trees by their leaves. I still have that short story locked in a trunk of mementos—but I seemed to have misplaced those worksheets.

So how come we're using textbooks to teach? And am I about to suggest you skip these lovely childhood treasures in your home-education program? (Skip is best; minimize their use is better.) And if that is where I'm headed, what in the world would you replace them with?

The Truth about Textbooks

Textbooks are our answer to how to package a wealth of information for mass distribution. We've got to teach everyone the same thing so we can administer a standardized test to compare their achievement at the end. This keeps everyone inching along that linear (and arbitrary) scope and sequence I mentioned in chapter 2.

We don't have time to individualize the curriculum to suit each child's needs, interests, and learning style. And we certainly don't have the time to do individual assessment of each kid. Thus the birth of the testing industry.

Besides that, the foremost concern I had as a classroom teacher was crowd control. How do I keep all these kids busy and out of trouble for the next forty minutes? Standardization is the key. *Everyone turn to page 41 of your textbook. Everyone fill out this worksheet for class tomorrow.*

Institutionalized versus Individualized Methods

Look at the chart below. This is a comparison of traditional teaching methods that we endure in many classrooms and the individualized methods you now have available to you in home education. Which one looks more inviting, motivating, and effective?

Institutionalized	_Individualized_
grades	mastery
standardized tests	evaluation of all work
sitting at desks/raising hands	freedom to move and contribute
textbooks, workbooks, worksheets	children's literature
	long-term projects
segmented subjects	integrated learning
sequential learning	teachable moments
component teaching	using in context
scope and sequence	readiness and interests
state-mandated objectives	God-given directives

The model on the left has already fallen out of favor in many innovative classrooms because the benefits of an individualized program, or at least one that is more hands-on and creative, is substantially supported in the research. Unfortunately, this market trend has caused some suppliers to pursue the homeschool market as a naive dumping ground for their outdated product.

What in the World Do I Use, Then?

So if I'm suggesting you abandon the standard grade-level curriculum route, with what, pray tell, you ask, do I suggest you replace it? Any number of inviting, creative, and inexpensive resources are available from homeschool suppliers—and better yet your local public library. You just have to take the time to pull it together.

Here's how to decide exactly what you are looking for and then where to find it.

It's That Vision Thing Again

Remember? You need a framework for making decisions. Time to march off to your state curriculum fair or sit down with your pile of homeschool supply catalogs (see the Resource Guide for sources) with the list of targets you're aiming to hit firmly in hand.

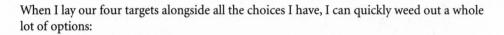

When I lay our four targets alongside all the choices I have, I can quickly weed out a whole lot of options:

- ✔ This resource is so boring and uninviting, it does nothing to cultivate a love for learning in my kid. How the author managed to stay awake throughout its development is beyond me. In the incinerator.

- ✔ This resource covers material that is no longer relevant to the changing job market or takes precious time away from those areas of the curriculum that are. I don't have time for this subject. To the recycling bin.

- ✔ The world view inherent in this product is an inaccurate representation of the Christian faith I wish to transfer to my kids. (This is not to say we do not use material from secular publishers; we do. I'm more likely to pass up resources with shoddy theology or a propaganda purpose, i.e., "Learn to Read with Captain Planet, Caretaker of the Earth.") Down the disposal.

- ✔ This item is counterproductive to equipping my kids to impact their generation with the gospel (judgmental attitude toward unbelievers, an isolationist or ethnocentristic view). Not on our list.

Your Turn

Now it's your turn. I know being the responsible student you are, you completed your assignment from chapter 1 before moving on. Weed out the "not-on-your-life" products based on your vision for your family life—by now you should have quite a few copies lying around the house . . . I knew I could trust you.

That's done. But you still have lots of stuff left to consider. Here's the next terminator of choices:

Hone your list down to resources that match these three:

1. Your child: His or her interests, learning style, and level of mastery.
2. You: Your time constraints, other responsibilities to consider, and preferred teaching style.
3. Budget: Unfortunately.

Mom Counts, Too

Let's talk about the teacher before we look at choosing curriculum to fit your child and budget. As I've mentioned, a successful homeschool condenses down to Mom being happy. If you don't ultimately choose resources and curricula you enjoy or feel comfortable with, you'll find homeschooling quickly becomes a drudgery. We want to keep that spring in your step.

Even though you've cleared your schedule of all nonessential responsibilities, there's still plenty that needs to get done—new babies, other children, church, or part-time work can all be on your list.

What's the Big Picture of Your Life?

When you look at potential curricula, keep the big picture in mind. Having an active toddler in the house seriously limits not only the types of resources you purchase but also the amount of direct teaching time you can put in. Video courses or software programs that simulate subjects like chemistry might be the solution for your older kids during those years. Math curricula that require you to present the lesson will probably not work if you have four other children to teach at different grade levels. And then, you also have a preferred teaching style (you should be able to recognize this when we look at learning styles).

I like to pull resources together and create my own curriculum. Following someone else's program takes a lot of the fun out of it for me. But other women hate the pressure of doing things this way. It saps them of energy. They are much better off finding an inviting, pre-designed program that fits their kids without the responsibility of deciding what to do.

Profile Your Child

Areas of Interest

Now let's look at each child you'll be teaching.

What are his or her areas of interest? You'll want to integrate these into the curriculum wherever possible, especially at points where some extra motivation is needed. If he loves baseball and can't sit still to read, then a series of sports biographies and fiction by Matt Christopher are what you'll use. If she loves cooking and helping you run the home but can't make sense of the arithmetic problems on the paper, you'll use couponing, budgeting, **Grocery Cart Math*** (Common Sense Press), and other household responsibilities either to reinforce your math program or to replace it.

Levels of Mastery

Curricula can be divided into two categories: skill areas and content areas.

Is This a Content Area? . . .

American history, biology, and classical literature are content areas. Your job is to choose *creative* and *motivating* resources that help your kids *acquire a base of knowledge* in these subjects. This can happen through a wide variety of methods and does not need to be learned in a sequential, systematic style (random and chaotic is also an option).

Or a Skill Area?

Skill areas, on the other hand, are subjects like handwriting, arithmetic, composition, spelling, and reading. Most kids (emphasis on *most*, not *all*) more easily acquire these when presented in a *sequential, systematic fashion* with lots of *practice in a variety of different contexts.*

Example: Reading

- Daily systematic phonics-based reading program
- Reading real books, not just basals (readers with a controlled vocabulary)
- Playing word games with magnetic letters and other concrete models
- Writing on a word processor and other creative projects that require the use of words (cards, signs, original stories, etc.)
- Reading signs on the road, cereal boxes, directions, and other contexts from daily life
- Being read to daily

Start at the Child's Level of Success

You'll want to determine each child's level of mastery in key skill areas. That's where you start—regardless of his or her grade.

This will be disconcerting for those of you with kids you think of as being delayed. Lots of us undertake homeschooling as a means of bringing our kids up to snuff. Now that's not a bad goal. I want to encourage academic excellence. But the quickest method is to start the curriculum at your child's level of success in each skill area. And that pretty much shoots the idea of buying the complete line of third-grade materials from A Beka for your eight-year-old.

Think this through with me. Say you had never learned to drive (which may be true for some of us, even if we do have a license). How successful would you be if your instructor started with parallel parking when you can't even start the car? How frustrated would you be if he insisted you start there because the course manual says students your age should be ready to parallel park? What is the fastest and most motivational route to pursue? When you can't even start the car, you aren't going to parallel park, are you?

As long as your ten-year-old cannot recall the sounds of the short vowels or how to blend triple consonants, he isn't going to understand his fifth-grade reader—no matter how much labor you invest. In fact, the opposite results occur. The kid is further demoralized by his failure. There won't be any aspect of reading he feels successful about. And he'll soon find ways to avoid it altogether. The good news is, there are age-appropriate materials available such as the **Winning Tutoring Kit** (<u>**International Learning Systems**</u>) to use with a ten-year-old boy who cannot blend triple consonants.

What can the child already do well? Is his cursive handwriting legible and uniform? No need to keep that on the schedule, even if there are two more levels in the series you are using. Can he consistently carry when adding double-digit numbers but often gets confused when borrowing to solve a subtraction problem? His math program should give him plenty of practice with borrowing and move him into triple-digit addition and higher.

It will probably be easier for you to determine levels of mastery in your preschoolers than in an older child you may be pulling out of a traditional setting.

Placement Test Services

If you have a college degree you can order the Iowa Test of Basic Skills from Bob Jones University and administer it to your child. The scoring report you receive back will give you a skill-by-skill analysis of your child's performance. This can then be used to determine what skills need to be reinforced and what skills have been mastered. (I explain how to read this report—called a criterion-skills analysis—in chapter 35.)

Here's the source of another placement test that does not require the parent to have a college degree:

Hewitt Homeschooling Resources
P. O. Box 9, 2103 B Street
Washougal, WA 98671-0009
360-835-8708   Fax: 360-835-8697

Once you have a profile of each child's areas of interest and levels of mastery, next look for resources that teach to these areas using a method that honors each kid's preferred learning style. I'll show you how to determine that in just a moment.

This Process Eventually Becomes Intuitive

This process might seem a bit complicated at first. But it's really just a step-by-step analysis of what many parents will be able to intuitively discern about their kids. Once you get comfortable homeschooling, you'll quickly recognize what resources will be successful and which ones just won't work. There's nothing like experience. But in the meantime, I want you to have the tools to begin a program that maximizes the advantages of homeschooling.

9

Determining Your Child's Learning Style

Learning Styles

About ten years ago, I set out to learn everything I could about learning styles. I ended up with a lot of academic research and clinical tests for figuring these out. Most of the material centered around the theory of learning modalities: auditory, visual, tactile, and kinesthetic. While I understand that research supports this theory, I found this information rather unhelpful. I couldn't determine which sense was dominant in myself, let alone in my own children. Do I learn better through hearing or seeing? Doing or touching? I still don't know.

Enter Dr. Golay

Then I came across the work of Dr. Keith Golay and found it a breeze not only to recognize my own preferences but also to plug the scores of students I had taught into his model.

The difference is this: Golay's work is based upon personality types, or temperaments. You may be familiar with the personality model used by Florence Littauer and Tim LaHaye; Golay uses a different model but the same principle. His work is based upon the temperament theory of David Keirsey, who grouped people into four general personality types.[1]

The Dionysian temperament: This fellow is fiercely independent and spontaneous. He lives in the "here and now" and derives self-worth from his ability to act swiftly with precision. Golay calls the Dionsyian's learning style actual-spontaneous.

The Epimethean temperament: The strongest motivator in this personality type is duty. Her foremost concern is fulfilling her responsibilitis. She does this by establishing,

81

nurturing, and maintaining social order and organization in her life and community. The Epimethean does all things in moderation and is conservative and predictable. Golay calls the Epimethean's learning style actual-routine.

The Promethean temperament: The goal of the Promethean is to be competent. He does this by acquiring knowledge and exercising great patience and tenacity in delaying action until a rational, pragmatic, and carefully calculated conclusion can be drawn. He gives little credence to his emotions or desires. This is Golay's conceptual-specific learner.

The Apollonian temperament: For the Apollonian, life's goal is a quest for her unique identity and purpose. She is motivated to make a difference or leave her mark. The Apollonian is highly relational and gifted in leadership. Golay calls this the conceptual-global learner.

Golay's research tacks along these lines: If there are certain temperament types that we can generally group people into, then it stands to reason that each temperament has its preferred way of learning.

While I'm skeptical of Greek philosophy (which is the root of our interest in temperaments) I think there is a correlation between temperament theory and biblical teaching on spiritual gifts. Bill Hybels and Bill Gothard have both developed materials to help believers discern these areas of our lives. The key to recognition is locked in our personality type.

So I gave Dr. Golay's model consideration and have found it very helpful in our own program and in scores of others.[2]

Ground Rules

Here are a few parameters to keep in mind as we work through these profiles:

1. This is not a scientific model. Don't panic if you can't fit yourself or one of your children perfectly into one of the profiles.

    Here is the principle: Use your child's personal preferences, the characteristics on the surface of his life, as clues to how he learns best. Use this empirical evidence when selecting resources and teaching methods.

    I often ask parents what their child chooses to do in his spare time as a helpful clue to his learning style. Does she play alone or set out to find the neighborhood kids? Does he build with Legos or read a book? These all say something about how your kid is wired to learn.

2. Typically, learning styles do not solidify until ages nine or ten. Almost all five-year-olds learn better when material is presented through a hands-on experience.

    So follow the principle above: Use your kid's characteristics as the indicators of his preferred method of learning. As he matures, be ready to adjust your methods to accommodate his preferences.

3. Within every learning style you will find children of varying intelligence, skill, and talents. These need to be factored into the program you design. And remember that one type of learner is not generally more intelligent than another. It can be easy to underestimate the intelligence of the active learner (Profile 1) and overestimate the intelligence of the focused learner (Profile 3). These are stereotypical assumptions, and we need to guard against them.

4. And finally, Dr. Golay believes that temperament governs behavior. As a Christian, I believe temperament *influences* behavior. We have a fallen nature. Through the power of the cross we now have access to the grace of God that enables us to overcome sin in our lives. Thus, an important distinction needs to be made: Each of the following learners has inherent character weaknesses. I am not encouraging parents to accommodate these weaknesses but rather to work to help your children overcome them through grace.

The Actual-Spontaneous Learner

"I Dare You to Teach Me"

You've heard of the *Accidental Tourist*? Well, meet the Accidental Learner. It's never his intended purpose to acquire a useful base of knowledge; it just sort of happens "accidentally" as he motors happily through life leaving a trail of broken parts in his wake. *Ouch! This stove is hot! Maybe I should figure out how to turn off those red lights before dismantling the burners. I think the same thing happened last time I did this.*

This guy believes the world was meant to be taken apart, and he's the man for the job.

Dr. Golay calls this child the actual-spontaneous learner (ASL). His learning is involuntary and, without training, is limited to a concrete level of thinking. He is impulsive, adventuresome, and better suited for the Wild, Wild West than today's confining world. Driving wagon trains, tracking gunslingers, blazing the Oregon Trail—that's the kind of mettle you find in this six-packing, nerves-of-steel human bulldozer.

You want me to sit where? For how long? And fill out all these pages! . . . Make me!

ASL's Indicators:

— impulsive   — thrives on variety and adventure
— autonomous   — competitive
— distractable   — quick
— flexible   — inventive
— short attention span   — outgoing
— risk taker   — defiant when boundaries
— constant motion   are imposed

> ### *Some Strong Dislikes:*
>
> — structure   — reading or seatwork
> — routine   — convention
> — sitting still   — delayed gratification
>
> ### *Weaknesses*
>
> — study skills
> — long-range planning
> — planning and organization

An Overview

This kid is controlled by his impulses. Doing is his thing. Forethought is not. He lives for the moment. Any learning that occurs is an unintentional by-product of his actions.

While it is not in the research, I'm sure there is a high correlation between the ASL and the kid with at least one broken bone by age eight.

The ASL does not grow up to teach in academia or contribute to analytical geometry. He wants to deal with the actual, concrete world and has little time for theories and abstractions.

Dr. Golay quotes Charles Lindbergh, a classic ASL, as saying he couldn't understand why anyone should "spend hours of life on formula, semicolons, and on crazy English." He could sit and concentrate for so long "and then, willy-nilly, my body stands up and walks away."[3]

It goes without saying, this guy is the least suited for the traditional classroom and formal learning experiences. He won't sit still for lectures, repetition, or drill. Material requiring concentration or seatwork quickly frustrates him. He does not organize or plan ahead. He cannot sustain a project or assignment over an extended period of time.

He wants to be unrestrained by structure, routine, or authority. He loves games and enjoys being in a group but is competitive and often takes charge. Other kids enjoy him for his antics and sense of fun. In a highly structured environment with strong authority he can quickly become a behavior problem, causing disruptions and acting defiantly.

Here we have Dr. Dobson's strong-willed child, and among teachers, psychologists, and exhausted parents, he is quickly labeled hyperactive and often medicated. Without consideration for this child's learning style, he will likely become a dropout.

That's the bad news.

Wait! There's Hope

Here's the good news. This little guy is just who you need to get the job done when the situation calls for quick wits and resourcefulness. He often has the ability to act swiftly with precision. He's Huck Finn improvising a plan that saves Jim's life or Jim Lovell patching together an air filter that rescues the Apollo 13 mission.

He's Jacques Cousteau, Henry Ford, Wilbur Wright, or Daniel Boone, taking risks and opening up new frontiers.

He's adept at manipulating, constructing, and performing. In an environment that allows for his interests, he excels in areas requiring invention, physical dexterity, resourcefulness, and courage. He will respond well to any subject presented in such a way that he is free to move and act.

Case in Point

As a teacher I had my share of ASLs in my classroom. These are not the children whose names and faces you forget! A group home for troubled boys was located in our district, and in my English classes I had several of these guys who had been labeled incorrigible by the court. I really had problems if I required excessive seatwork from them. They would become disruptive, put on a show, or get the other kids all keyed up. Each year, though, I taught a unit in which the class members videotaped a play they had produced. It took about five weeks of practicing, designing costumes, organizing the set, training the camera crew, editing, and then showing each production. This was always my most successful experience with my actual-spontaneous learners. They loved it, and I loved working with them on it. Unfortunately, it was a very noisy and confusing project, and we frequently got in trouble for disrupting other classes.

A conventional school setting is just not the place for an ASL to thrive. The order necessary and the constant distraction of a large group is just too much out of synch with the ASL's need for flexibility and limited stimulation.

Many parents who would not have otherwise considered homeschooling are now doing so because they have this type of learner in their home. Either out of pity for the classroom teacher or because they recognize their child was never wired to succeed in a traditional setting, they have undertaken his education. And I praise them for doing so.

More than any other child, this one needs to be homeschooled.

A Success Story

Our neighbor Anthony is a classic ASL. Until fourth grade he was in a variety of school settings: public, private, and special classes for kids with learning disabilities. This kid is the Energizer Bunny. The same age but half the size of Mike and Gabe, he physically exhausts them. After a ten-mile bike hike, A. D., as he is affectionately called, will jump off and challenge them to basketball. We were the first family to invite him to spend the night—and I found out why. He was still going strong at 11:00 P.M., and by six the next morning, I peered bleary-eyed outside to see him zipping around on his bike, frustrated that he couldn't rouse Mike and Gabe from bed. I wondered if his parents had just had their first good night's rest since his birth.

A few years ago A. D.'s parents came over to talk about homeschooling him. They were pretty unsure about undertaking this challenge, but it seemed like the only option left. A. D. was now spending an hour each way on a school bus to attend a Christian school that used a traditional curriculum and ran a very regimented program. He was coming home with two hours of homework every night. This was a nightmare for him and very demoralizing. He was falling further and further behind. But his behavior was so erratic and defiant, his folks were afraid they weren't up for the task. I wasn't very confident either.

Well, three years later—this has been a real homeschool success story. A. D. is still a white tornado. But his ability to respond to parental authority has dramatically improved, and so has his school success. His mom has organized lots of field trips with other homeschoolers and runs a program that relies heavily on the computer—which A. D. loves. She also allows plenty of opportunities for A. D. to go outside during the day and run off pent-up energy. Most days he is able to stay focused till 3:00 P.M., when he is free to come over to our house and get the boys.

Designing a Program for Your Actual-Spontaneous Learner

The first step in designing a program for your AS learner is to accept him as God has made him. I am not asking you to acquiesce to his defiant nature or to give up on his character deficiencies. This kid needs strong parenting (see Benny and Sheree Phillips's *Raising Children Who Hunger for God** and Tedd Tripp's *Shepherding a Child's Heart** for help). But I am asking you to stop wishing he would turn into someone else's child or be recast from another mold. The only way the ASL will ever be the kind of kid who can sit passively for hours doing seatwork and compliantly follow routine structure is if you break his spirit. And that is too high a cost for a little peace and quiet.

But don't despair. In most situations the behavior of your ASL will dramatically improve once an educational program is in place to accommodate how he learns. A lot of his frustration and defiance is rooted in years of being a square peg hammered relentlessly into a round hole.

He Needs Quiet

First, set up an environment that is quiet and clear of distractions—this will help him stay more focused on his schoolwork. Other kids, the phone, television, pets, etc., will all get him off task if they are within his range of vision. Once Mike and Gabe show up on the basketball court outside his window, A. D. is unable to concentrate on his work. They have agreed to stay off the court until he is free to play.

He Needs to Move

Establish a daily routine that delays the activities and subjects he likes best until the afternoon as a reward for staying on task during the morning. Give him short breaks after each subject has been completed—this may be as frequently as every fifteen minutes for young AS learners. Let him do something physical at this time—go outside, exercise, do chores, etc.

And be tolerant of his need to move around, lie on the floor, or fidget when studying. This is the kid who taps his pencil or wiggles his feet. It may drive you nuts; but if you demand that he stop, all his energy will be focused on doing just that. He won't have anything left to concentrate on the material you want him to learn. Be flexible; tolerate the nonessential stuff. Fight the battles that really matter.

He Needs Rewards

Set short, achievable goals and immediately reward good attitudes and acceptable work. Incentive charts, stickers, or a special treat can all be motivational. But don't expect him to be affected by delayed gratification, i.e., you'll buy him a bike for Christmas if he does well first semester. When the twins were younger I'd let them run down to the corner store for a pack of baseball cards if they had accomplished their morning goals.

Don't Wimp Out

Even though he doesn't like it, this child needs strong leadership, a daily routine, and clear boundaries. A chaotic, random approach to teaching him will only exacerbate his impulsiveness. To keep his frustration level low spice up the routine regularly with variety: field trips, special projects, cooperative classes. Introduce an element of competition where possible. A lot of computer software, such as **Math Blaster** (<u>Davidson</u>), has a game-like format that rewards kids for improving their scores in skill areas.

Success by Increments

To improve his behavior and performance, set short goals starting at his level of success and incrementally increase these. If he can't stay on task for twenty math exercises, start with five. Then break and switch to reading. Then return to do five more math problems. Switch to another subject, and keep returning till the page for the day is done. After a week of success, extend the math exercises at one sitting to seven or eight. Repeat the steps above. Eventually he should be able to do the entire page in one sitting. The key is incremental steps toward the goal.

Don't avoid situations where your AS learner must obey authority or cooperate. He needs to learn to control his impulses. Just expose him to these situations in short doses and gradually increase. When he becomes disruptive or takes charge in a group, isolate him. His desire to be with his peers should motivate him to control his behavior.

Think Concrete

When looking at resources, choose as many as possible that are activity-based. Your AS learner needs to physically handle the material he's learning and be able to manipulate it in a variety of contexts to understand it. A reading program such as **Sing, Spell, Read and Write** (International Learning Systems)* is the only kind that has a chance of capturing his interest. It is multisensory and includes a measure of competition. Math manipulatives are absolutely essential (see the mathematics section in chapter 21 for details on manipulatives) as are physical demonstrations in science and history.

This learner needs help to think conceptually. Design concrete models to demonstrate abstractions: Use styrofoam balls for a unit on the solar system, relief maps he can run his hands over for geography, pennies and dimes to explain decimals, a cherry pie to demonstrate fractions. He should have plenty of time to mess around with these, then, as a way of building a concrete base for higher level thinking.

This route may seem too time-consuming, but it is the shortest path to understanding in the end. A more traditional approach will only lead to frustration, resistance, and a loss of confidence on the part of your AS learner. Without his motivation and cooperation, be prepared for daily battles over doing school.

Take a look at the <u>KONOS</u> curriculum as an excellent example of the kind of program designed to enable this kind of learner to thrive.

Think Sports

One final suggestion. This learner frequently is gifted in areas that require physical dexterity, primarily athletics. I've seen many ASLs thrive in an organized sports program. This is an acceptable release of their energy; it is often one place in which they can excel and feel good about their achievements, it gives them a much needed focus in life, and it teaches them to control their impulsive behavior because they are highly motivated to play.

The Actual-Routine Learner

"Teacher, May I Help You?"

Whereas the ASL is every teacher's challenge, this learner is every teacher's joy. Here we have the cooperative child who is motivated by a desire to win the approval of her parents and teachers. She is responsible, studious, and nurturing. In a group of children, she is the one earnestly listening to the teacher or helping the ASL find his place on the page.

Dr. Golay calls her the actual-routine learner (ARL), and she does best in a quiet, well-organized, and structured environment.

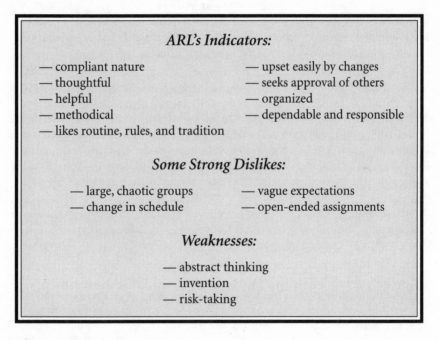

ARL's Indicators:

— compliant nature
— thoughtful
— helpful
— methodical
— likes routine, rules, and tradition

— upset easily by changes
— seeks approval of others
— organized
— dependable and responsible

Some Strong Dislikes:

— large, chaotic groups
— change in schedule

— vague expectations
— open-ended assignments

Weaknesses:

— abstract thinking
— invention
— risk-taking

An Overview

This learner is most concerned with understanding and meeting expectations. She will ask for clarification frequently in an effort to avoid making a mistake. Hearing lots of questions from the routine learner is a good indicator that she is stressed and insecure about the learning environment.

The actual-routine learner assimilates information by identifying and memorizing facts and procedures. She needs material presented in a sequential, step-by-step manner. She likes assignments with clearly defined instructions and expectations. She is most comfortable with traditional teaching methods: written assignments, repetition, drill, bookwork, workbook learning.

While she works hard to master subskills, her weakness is in seeing the big picture—understanding principles, concepts, and abstractions. She will do fine with her punctuation exercises in her language arts book but won't recognize when a semicolon is needed in her own writing. It will be important for you to design a program that will help her move to a higher level of understanding in her studies.

The actual-routine learner does not do well if she is expected to handle open-ended assignments or to chose her own activities. She does not like role-playing, estimating, predicting, or other exercises that require spontaneity, creativity, or extrapolation. To do an AR learner in, just assign an impromptu speech.

She needs a learning environment with clear leadership and recognized rules. She respects authority and expects others to as well. She will quickly bring to your attention any infraction of the rules by others. *Teacher! Teacher! Sammy's not doing what he's supposed to. Mom, you told Melissa to leave the baby alone, and she isn't obeying!*

If the routine or schedule changes, this learner becomes insecure and distressed.

In hindsight I can see now that my ARLs were distressed with me as a classroom teacher. I love creativity and spontaneity. I used lots of open-ended assignments, and I graded more highly those students who used them as a springboard for their own creative ideas. As a teacher and as a homeschooler my ultimate goal has always been to help children become independent learners. The AR learner resists this more than any other type.

This is the kid who says *"Just tell me what I need to do to get an A,"* or the homeschool mom who appeals, *"Just tell me exactly what I need to buy. All these choices are very overwhelming, and I'm afraid I'll make a mistake."*

We've Got One at Our House

My son, Mike, has strong ARL tendencies. He has forced me to be more organized than I prefer. When we first started homeschooling he wanted me to set up a schedule of classes and follow it every day. He especially wanted recess. Why? The neighborhood kids had told him that was the best part of school.

At ten o'clock each morning he would head outside and swing for fifteen minutes. I found this very curious because this kid had long ago lost interest in the swing set. When I asked him why he was so hot on swinging, he said the neighbors had told him that's what you do at recess. He was determined to do his part to make sure our homeschool was legitimate.

At fourteen, Mike amazes me with his incredible self-discipline and commitment to imposing order on our chaotic lifestyle. During the school year, Mike is the first one up in the morning. He gave up on me long ago and has taken matters into his own hands. He has maintained the same daily schedule for quite a few years. Math at 6:30 every morning. (He is frustrated when I ask him to work cooperatively with his brother, the later sleeper, because it messes up his schedule.)

He's created an exercise chart on the computer that incrementally increases every day. He'll go for months without missing his routine and is disconcerted when I throw in a kink that interferes with it. For this reason he wasn't sure he wanted to go on a family vacation to Canada! In the end he smuggled his weights along in his suitcase.

He does not procrastinate but starts cracking on assignments as soon as they are given, creating checklists and deadlines and carefully reviewing the instructions throughout. At our cooperative classes, his favorite teachers are those who give clear directions and run an orderly class.

Designing a Program for Your Routine Learner

This learner needs well-organized, sequential lessons presented in incremental steps. Look for resources with clear directions and standards of evaluations. Make sure your expectations are clearly articulated as you launch into a subject of study.

Materials developed for classroom use are easily adapted to this kind of learner. However, look over a sample lesson. How many concepts are presented per lesson? Does the math workbook jump around between concepts, i.e., are multiplication and division problems intermingled? This learner is the one who will have the most difficulty switching gears. She likes to travel the well-worn rut in the road.

Saxon math and **Professor Phonics** are examples of the kind of resources the routine learner will be comfortable with. Each lesson has one clear goal, and the skills incrementally progress along a very linear scope and sequence.

Think Concepts

The ARL will naturally divide big projects into smaller steps and segment out subjects for study. This is an effective tool for accomplishing goals, but it's important to make sure your AR learner doesn't lose sight of the larger picture. She may have memorized the dates of the Civil War battles, states of the Union and Confederacy, etc., but does she understand how economics, politics, scientific inventions, and religious movements converged to create this cataclysmic moment of our history?

Don't just settle for correct answers on a multiple choice test; essay tests are a much better method for assessing the AR learner's understanding of the larger concepts.

Move Her Toward Independence

Because this child is typically very compliant and satisfied with a steady dose of seatwork, it can be easy to not stretch her beyond her boundaries or place her in situations where she must learn to think creatively and take risks. This is a disservice in the end.

This child needs to be equipped to act when independence is given. She must learn to make decisions and act spontaneously. Otherwise, you end up with an adult who's rendered immobile by decision-making. She needs to be equipped to handle new situations and evaluate choices with confidence. That only comes from repeated opportunities to do so.

Tap Her Creativity

Encourage your routine learner to invent and take risks. Reward her for creativity and trying new ventures: food, a sport, an academic competition, a creative story. Build open-ended assignments into your program. Teach her to handle these in a step-by-step fashion.

Case in Point

Once I asked a group of kids to take turns assuming the role of a character they invented on the spot. Some of the kids could slip into a role and fabricate a personality almost endlessly (we'll meet that kind of learner at the end of this discussion). But not my routine learners. They were frozen to the stage, stressed by a situation that had no wrong answers.

I joined one little girl who was near tears on the stage. Step by step, I took her through the process. Is your character male or female? I asked. Give her a name. Tell us where she lives. What does she look like? She relaxed as she found she could create answers to these simple questions and was pleased when she realized she had entertained the group for almost five minutes.

Use Her Nurturing Nature to Her Advantage

This learner has an innate drive to be helpful. Teaching other children is an effective strategy, then, with this learner. It will appeal to her nurturing nature and has the added plus of reinforcing her own learning in the areas she is presenting.

The Conceptual-Specific Learner

"Frankly, Mother, I Prefer to Do It Myself"

Good news. This next student will learn despite you! Bad news. He's going to exhaust you with his intensity and questions.

This learner has an insatiable appetite for knowledge. He wants to be able to understand, explain, predict, and control realities. He seeks to understand principles and to use them in structuring his cognitive and intellectual world. The absent-minded professor, Mr. Spock, and the mad scientist are all caricatures of this personality. Dr. Golay calls him the conceptual-specific learner (CSL), and he is not interested in isolated facts and information but in the theories and principles behind them.

CSL's Indicators:

— serious-minded
— inquisitive
— satisfied being alone
— focused interest
— prizes intellectual achievement
— strong powers of concentration

— collector (rocks, stamps, specimens)
— must be reminded to eat, change his clothes, comb his hair
— easily frustrated
— perfectionist
— detail-oriented

Some Strong Dislikes:

— wasted time
— menial assignments

Weaknesses:

— social skills
— accepting his own limitations
— awareness of others' needs

An Overview

This learner loves problem-solving, research, experimentation, and intellectual inquiry. He is a creative thinker and chooses scientific investigation as a leisure activity. He will focus on one task for long periods of time and can tune out all distractions.

One mom of a CSL I evaluate was perplexed by her son's habit of curling up for the evening with a volume of the *Encyclopedia Brittanica*.

I recently read Bill Gates's book *The Road Ahead* and was struck by his intense focus and vision at an early age. At sixteen he and his eventual cofounder of Microsoft, Paul Allen, were spending all their free time hacking around on computers, programming them to the edge of their abilities (this was back in the sixties, when just booking computer time was a challenge). Gates dropped out of Harvard the day the first programmable microprocessor was released. He knew this seemingly insignificant announcement from Intel would revolutionize the computer industry, and he and Paul had predetermined to position themselves to capitalize on it. He was nineteen. Obviously Gates, now the richest man in the United States, has more foresight than the rest of us.

This learner has a serious nature and is happy that way. He finds great self-satisfaction in his own achievements and doesn't need the approval from others that the AR learner seeks.

His difficulties lie in accepting his own limitations. He becomes very distressed if he cannot succeed in solving a problem or attaining his goals. He will need your help and encouragement in keeping his shortcomings in perspective.

He will pay close attention to a teacher's presentation as long as it is not repetitious or routine. He becomes very frustrated with any hindrances to his own intellectual growth, such as being forced to work through material again that he has already mastered. He is often not a fluent writer and doesn't like to take the time to communicate what he already believes he understands.

This learner enjoys working independently or in a tutorial relationship with a competent teacher. But he does not do well in a situation where he must work with those not as interested in intellectual inquiry. I like to organize kids into cooperative groups. You can spot the conceptual-global learners right away then—they are the kids still working alone.

These kids don't grow up to join organizations; they don't thrive in a business environment that emphasizes team-building. These are the adults who tinker in the garage every weekend or work long hours in a research and development lab.

The CSL is very objective in his decision-making and has a difficult time expressing emotion or understanding others' emotional responses. He typically relates to peers in an instructional, not personal, manner. For this reason he is often the odd man out socially.

The CSL gravitates toward careers in the sciences, engineering, technology, mathematics, and research and development.

Case in Point

At one point in my teaching career, I developed and taught an honors English program for gifted and highly motivated students. I am reminded here of George, a remarkably gifted student but one who had little interest in my classes, which predominantly involved discussing in a subjective way the literature we were studying. What were the ideas and opinions the kids had formulated after reading a work? How did they see these ideas influencing their lives? Every day we would discuss such things, just for the sake of sharing our reactions. Well, this just wasn't for George and others like him. The CSL values facts and imperial knowledge, not knowledge that is personal in nature.

Probably the most rapport I ever had with George came when I asked him to teach me to play chess. (The reason I asked was I was about to marry Kermit, who loves chess. This should have been a big clue . . . Guess what kind of learner I married!)

Designing a Program for Your CSL Learner

This student can be satisfied with materials created for classroom use, if you must go this route, but don't hand him inferior stuff. He doesn't need to be entertained, but he needs to be challenged. Make sure the activities and assignments do more than just measure memorization of material.

Allow Acceleration

Don't hesitate to let him jump several levels in subject areas of great interest and strength. In many cases, a college textbook may be a better investment. My friend Susan Richman's son, Jacob, is intensely focused in math and computer science. He scored a 5 on the Advanced Placement Calculus Exam in ninth grade and an 800 in mathematics on the SATs in tenth. (Those are perfect scores, folks!) He has competed on the international level in mathematics and programming. This is only possible because his parents let him work with advanced math years earlier than traditionally accepted. He was free to whiz through lessons or skip entire sections until he hit his level of competency.

And obviously his abilities in programming would never have come to the surface had he not had a computer.

Prepare to Spend Some Bucks

This is not, then, a cheap child to homeschool. He needs raw data and supplies for his investigations. You can save money by skipping the textbooks and using nonfiction from the library. Invest what you can in those items that best support his inquiry: lab equipment, computer (with Internet access), tools, etc. Don't even bother with resources for areas with no apparent difficulties.

Think Mentors

Most of the CS learners I have worked with have had mentors in their fields of interest. This has usually been a formalized relationship on the high school level. One student I evaluated, Scott, has been mentored in computer science for several years by a man in our church who works in artificial intelligence research. The mentor even arranged for Scott to have a summer internship (usually reserved for college students) in the R & D department of his company.

Cindy McKeown's son Daniel has a focused interest in film production. She arranged for him to spend a summer working at a video production company in D.C. The apprenticeship solidified Daniel's determination to pursue this as a course of study in college and also gave him valuable experience that has led to other work experiences.

While a tutor may seem too big a step for an elementary student, participation in an organization or club for his area of interest is a way to cultivate informal mentoring. My sons' friend Christopher loves rocks. By fourth grade he had an extensive rock museum in his basement with everything neatly displayed and identified. He spent every dollar he earned on specimens and books about rocks. His parents were very perplexed by this fixation but supported his interest by taking Chris to rock and mineral shows and connecting him up with local geologists.

Work on Interpersonal Skills

The CSL does need to hone his social skills. And as with the other learners' weaknesses, this is best done in a step-by-step fashion. He needs to be made aware of his perceived insensitivity to others. Training in proper etiquette and polite conversation will help. "Here's how you show interest in others, son. Ask about their hobbies and family, etc." Then role-play a conversation.

Have your CSL serve in the children's program at church, babysit, or volunteer for a local ministry to thrust him into situations where he will need to cultivate his people skills and develop some empathy.

At Our House

Kermit has many CS characteristics. He is pragmatic and objective in his decision-making. In college, his friends called him "The Professor"—unlike the rest of us, he had come to study. He was usually either in class or in the library. (Two places I rarely visited; thus we did not meet till after graduation.)

Like many men, he thinks whenever I tell him I have a problem I'm asking for a logical solution to it. Are you kidding? I enjoy the drama of my pain! I just want him to listen and empathize with my emotions. I've finally taught him to say, "I understand, Honey" on cue. He still jokingly parrots this phrase when I unload.

The Conceptual-Global Learner

"Hey, Everybody, Look at Me!"

Have you been most curious to discover what kind of learner you are as you've been reading this section? That's a strong indication you'll fit this last profile.

Dr. Golay calls this final type the conceptual-global learner (CGL). She is first and foremost people-oriented. It is in her nature to look for the potential in others and to help bring out these possibilities. For this reason, she is often a leader who inspires others through her abilities to speak and write fluently. This learner loves group situations, especially when that group is her audience.

CGL's Indicators:

— creative
— early reader
— outgoing
— ambitious
— dramatic
— perceptive

— popular with adults
    and peers
— forgetful
— broad array of interests
— not competitive
— careless

Some Strong Dislikes:

— unresolved conflict
— dry lectures

— routine assignments
— not having choices

Weaknesses:

— study skills
— technical details

— organization
— spelling

An Overview

In contrast to the CSL's specific focus, this learner has a wide breadth of interests, often finding it difficult to narrow her pursuits to a few areas. This learner has the longest entry in the yearbook and keeps her parents hopping as they try to keep track of all the social engagements she has scheduled.

The CGL is visionary and thinks about the future, but unlike the focused learner who thinks about the possibilities of principles applied to, say, problem-solving, the CGL focuses on the possibilities in people. She is fascinated by others' beliefs and attitudes: what they think, what they want, how they feel, how they respond.

She enjoys learning about ideas and values and tends to look at herself more subjectively than objectively. She is the student most interested in searching for the significance of things and personalizing their meaning. She is motivated to make a difference in the world, to search for her unique contribution to history.

She is creative and flexible but not detail-oriented or technical. Rather, this learner will act on hunches and impressions to form broad conclusions. This is the kid who takes a quick look at his or her math homework and says, "Oh, I know how to do this" then proceeds to fill out the whole thing incorrectly.

CGLs are generally high-achievers and do well academically. But they often set high standards for themselves. Their creations and work are an extension of themselves and are strongly tied to their sense of self-worth. Therefore, failure or rejection of their work is often interpreted as failure or rejection of themselves.

The CGL loves functioning in a group. She is a communicator and performer. She needs to be known, recognized, and acknowledged by others, especially her teacher. Yet she demands individuality and autonomy and the opportunity to act and express herself creatively.

She does not show the competitive nature of the AS learner in a group. Friendship and cooperation are important to her. She empathizes strongly with others and does not do well in a competitive environment where ruthlessness and conflict are uncontrolled. She is usually well liked and sought after by her peers and enjoyed by adults.

The CSL typically gravitates toward the language arts, performing arts such as music and drama, psychology, counseling, the ministry, and social services.

The CG learner's greatest area of academic weakness is in attention to details.

C'est Moi

It may be obvious by now that I am a conceptual-global learner. The inherent biases of my temperament will bleed through these pages: my passion for a guiding vision, my commitment to individualizing each child's program, and my belief that every student has a unique destiny we as parents should be set on discovering and cultivating.

Recognizing my learning style has made me a much better teacher for my children and my students at Creative Home Educators' Support Services (CHESS). I've made a lot of adjustments to my presentations because I'm conscious of the different kinds of learners in our family and in my classes.

Designing a Program for Your Global Learner

Dr. Golay recommends an individualized and personalized approach with this student. She will be interactive and enthusiastic as long as there is opportunity for her input and creative response. Thus a discussion group will be more motivating than a lecture and a project more than a test.

Because of her interest in people, choose resources that focus on how individuals or people groups have been impacted by the areas of study. Study scientists behind the theories or how inventions changed people's lives. In history, biographies and historical fiction will have great appeal. *The Guides to Famous Men of . . .* (Greece, Rome, Middle Ages, etc.) (<u>Greenleaf Press</u>)* and *History Through Literature* unit studies (<u>Beautiful Feet Books</u>)* are the types of curricula that the CGL enjoys most.

For technical material, introduce the people behind the information. My kids have enjoyed **Mathematicians Are People, Too** (<u>Dale Seymour</u>, 1995)* and other such titles that give background information on inventors, scientists, and mathematicians.

Because she thinks globally, a unit study approach that integrates subjects such as science, history, and literature around a common theme, Japanese culture, for example, will appeal to her interest in understanding how events, ideas, and inventions affect the people of that time and place.

Think Groups

Group activities are a must. And as you have probably gathered, we are certainly involved in our share. Katie and Gabe are predominantly CG learners. They both thrive in the humanities.

Katie was speaking in sentences at age two and reading avidly by age six. She is frequently chosen for the lead in the plays our co-op produces and is always organizing some kind of activity for the betterment of her friends.

Gabe's first response to a suggested activity is, "Can we invite some other kids to come along, Mom?" He spends days on his creative projects for CHESS and then forgets them at home the day they're due. (Mike, on the other hand, is a pain to live with while trying to complete a creative assignment but submits it ahead of time—and also tells Gabe where he has left his.)

Even though all my kids enjoy our cooperative activities, these two (and their mom) both "light up" in a group situation.

Details, Details

This learner needs help in paying attention to details. She is forgetful and careless in her errors. I know I have this flaw, so I have taken steps to compensate for it. I always use a spell-checker or a dictionary and an organizer to keep track of my commitments. My husband has pretty much given up on getting me to balance the checkbook, though.

Don't yell at your CGL for being a bit ditzy. Give her the strategies to compensate for her lack of attention to detail:

- Recognize her tendency to be careless
- Re-read directions, write down assignments
- Encourage her to have someone edit her work
- Show her how to create organizational systems

Smarter Kids by Lawrence Green (Body Press, 1987) is a book, not about raising your child's IQ, but rather about helping your otherwise-intelligent learner develop study habits and organizational skills that maximize her potential. Check it out.

I've Got a Zillion Kids. I Can't Possibly Accommodate Them All in Every Area and Stay Sane!

That's right. Even those of us with fewer than a zillion cannot put together a program that is individualized to the fullest potential. It's a balancing act, and there are trade-offs in every area. My husband is strongly conceptual-specific; Mike is a mix of that and the ARL; Gabe, Katie, and I all approach material globally; and my Kristen, though not hyperactive, is predominantly a concrete-spontaneous learner as of this writing. ("Kristen, focus . . . focus" is my constant refrain). What an eclectic mix.

Our group activities appeal to everyone, but for different reasons. Gabe and Katie enjoy class discussions. Mike likes best his teachers who are most organized. Kristen loves to socialize. The computer is also an essential tool: Mike does research on the Internet. Gabe and Katie wouldn't do near as much writing without word processing. Kristen likes the educational games.

With the exception of Kristen, my kids have the freedom and responsibility to select their resources and set up their daily schedule. Other than the times we gather for books we are reading aloud or projects we are completing together, Mike, Gabe, and Katie are achieving their weekly goals their way. I'm the one who has had to be most accommodating. For Mike's sake, I'm more organized than I prefer to be, and because it's preparing my sons for future employment, I've had to wade through my share of technical material that's of little interest to me personally.

Choose material for science that is hands-on for your actual-concrete learner, and then meet bi-monthly with a unit study co-op to keep your global learner motivated. Buy a sequential reading program to use with all your kids if you are an ARL and need the security of a well-organized system.

The goal is to keep the family frustration level low and the motivation high. Have your children use the resources and subjects they find least appealing at the beginning of the day. Save the fun stuff for the afternoon as a motivator for keeping on task earlier.

For more information about learning styles, here are the best sources:

> ***The Christian Home Educators' Curriculum Manual,*** vol. 1 (elementary) and vol. 2 (junior/senior high), Cathy Duffy (<u>Home Run Enterprises</u>, 1997).* This is an indispensable resource that, among other things, evaluates curricula according to the type of learner (using Golay's model) it is best suited for.
> ***Awakening Your Child's Natural Genius,*** Thomas Armstrong (Putnam, 1991).*
> ***Every Child Can Succeed,*** Cynthia Ulrich Tobias (Focus on the Family Publishing, 1996).*

In Their Own Way: Discovering and Encouraging Your Child's Personal Learning Style, Thomas Armstrong (Putnam, 1988).*
The Way They Learn: How to Discover and Teach to Your Child's Strengths, Cynthia Ulrich Tobias (Focus on the Family Publishing, 1994).*

The Last Hurdle

Now we know what kind of resources we're looking for to suit each of our children as well as what Mom, the teacher, needs to feel comfortable. But there's one more factor we've got to consider—the budgetary constraints we all must live with. I've seen lots of resources I know all my kids would love and I would find easy to use, but Kermit would need a third job for us to afford them. And he's not offering. We all have only so many homeschool dollars to commit. The final chapter in this part of the book will tell you how to make the most of them.

Homeschooling on a Shoestring

10

First, let's clarify what kind of shoestring we are talking about here. If your kids are wearing Air Jordan Nikes with glow-in-the-dark sixty-inch laces, you can skip this section. On the other hand, if your kids' shoelaces are held together with knots and retipped with candle wax, then I've got some advice you'll find helpful.

Time Is Money

Here's what you lose when economy drives the decision about which homeschool curriculum to buy. You trade time for money. Inexpensive resources leave a lot of work for the teacher. You get to prepare the lesson plans, make the games, cut out the shapes, and gather the materials (beans, buttons for counters, etc.).

When you buy software, textbooks, and expensive reading programs or video courses, you are paying for someone else's time. So don't just look at the price tag without answering the question "Will I have the time to use this?"

I invest money where I don't have the time and skimp on resources where I do. In my case, I very rarely buy composition or literature study aids. This is my forte and love. I enjoy inventing writing exercises and discussion questions for our language arts program. But math is another story. I've got lots of dollars invested there: software programs, textbooks, testing materials, mathematical games, videos. I feel very incompetent at this end of the curriculum and am willing to pay for someone else's planning and expertise.

 Here are two examples of beginning reading programs at opposite ends of the price range. **Sing, Spell, Read and Write** (<u>International Learning Systems</u>)* retails for $175. For that you get master teacher Sue Dixon on video plus workbooks, lesson plans, games, audiotapes, readers—everything but the kitchen sink. Plus, all but the workbooks can be reused with your other children. Or for $24 you can buy <u>Alphaphonics</u>, a reading program designed by Samuel Blumenfeld that's condensed to one 168-page book. Until recently it did not have any support material other than a brief instructional paragraph for the tutor that accompanied each lesson. The phonics approach is excellent. (I like it better than **Sing, Spell, Read and Write.** On page 198 I explain why.) But you will need to spend a lot of time finding readers for this program and developing practice work, games, and whatever else it takes to flesh out the lessons for your kids. I used **Alphaphonics** but switched to **Sing, Spell, Read and Write** when I realized I no longer had the time for all the preparation **Alphaphonics** required.

Think Multilevel and Reusable

Discounting video schools and satellite links, the most expensive route you can choose is a grade-specific line of textbooks with support materials from a publisher that markets its products primarily to public schools (where your tax dollars are consumed by inflated prices).

Resources developed for individualized instruction or the homeschool community can often be used by more than one child and span a number of grade levels. This not only saves on your budget but also allows you the time-saving strategy of teaching several children using the same material. The <u>**KONOS**</u> curriculum is an excellent example of this. It is a collection of unit studies appropriate for all elementary grades that uses children's literature and trade books (nonfiction) typically available at your local library. The reading is augmented with hands-on activities in all subject areas. You will get years of use from even one volume of KONOS. But the trade-off is time—you'll spend hours gathering resources and preparing your activities. (That's why the most successful use of KONOS I've seen has been among families who form a KONOS co-op and spread out the teaching load.)

Jan Van Cleave's science books* (Wiley) are another fine example of a lot of bang for the buck. Books in her science exploration series, such as *Microscopes, Molecules,* and *Weather,* retail for $9.95 and were written for home use. Each book contains thirty experiments that can be pulled off with stuff around the house. They illustrate a central scientific principle and work well for all grades through junior high. At the end of each lesson is a section marked "Check It Out" that poses a science question your older students can research at the library (or on the Internet). Using just the *Molecules* book and a few PBS videos, we met with another family for a weekly science lab that lasted most of the school year and included kids in third through seventh grades. Not a bad return for less than ten dollars!

Shop Used

Many support groups hold an annual used-curriculum sale. Cindy McKeown holds one each spring to benefit Creative Home Educators' Support Services (CHESS), the family school she directs. This is scheduled right before our state convention to allow families to pick up what they can buy used before shopping for new stuff two weeks later. And in some areas, you'll find a homeschool family running a used-curriculum supply business. Some supply businesses that are set up to sell mail order are listed in the Resource Guide.

Ask for Donations

Other sources of used materials include your local library, Christian or public schools, and colleges. Be bold. Call them up and ask if they have any materials they would be interested in selling or donating to your homeschool support group (more likely than to an individual). You'll be surprised how many will.

Homeschool Discounters

<u>Great Christian Books</u> is the Wal-Mart of homeschooling. If it's popular with homeschoolers, they've got it. They've recently started a publishing division, as well, that has released a number of titles for the homeschooling market.

Great Christian Books
229 South Bridge Street
Elkton, MD 21922-8000
(800) 775-5422

http://www.GreatChristianBooks.com

Check the Resource Guide for other sources of discount suppliers as well.

A Tempest in a Teacup

Let me throw in this note, though. I shop at GCB and Wal-Mart. But just as Wal-Mart has driven out the small, independent family businesses wherever it has moved in, homeschool discounters threaten to do the same. There are many fine homeschooling families around the country who have invested years building a business that supplies homeschoolers with resources—often when no one else was interested in doing so. Now that we are talking big bucks, it's easy for outfits to merely duplicate what others have done and beat them by cutting prices. It's called capitalism, and the consumer wins. I wouldn't change the system; if our particular family business can't find ways to stay competitive, we need to pick up our ball and go home.

Rule of thumb, though: Do business with those companies you want to see stay in business. Folks like <u>Greenleaf Press</u>, <u>Elijah Company</u>, and <u>Lifetime Books and Gifts</u> cannot discount and support their families. But they publish very helpful catalogs and exhaust themselves over the phone and at curriculum fairs dispensing advice from their wealth of experience. If we don't want to lose their contribution to the homeschool community, then we need to do business with them.

Other Strategies

1. Set up your homeschool co-op or support group as a nonprofit organization. Then you can solicit donations in goods and services from individuals and businesses.

2. Pool your orders to qualify for bulk rates. The **Home School Resource Center** and **God's World Publications**, for example, have much lower rates for bigger orders.

3. Split the purchase of big-ticket items with another family. Just work out the details for sharing these resources ahead of time. I purchased KONOS, vol. 1, and a friend purchased KONOS, vol. 2. After two years of use, we switched volumes.

4. Buy items with a resell value among homeschoolers. **Saxon math; Sing, Spell, Read and Write; A Beka and Bob Jones University** textbooks can all be resold for close to two-thirds of their original purchase value. Keep these in mint condition to get the best price.

5. Attend annual library and book sales.

6. Take advantage of community programs and field trips that are low-cost. Many parks and historic sites offer free admission and also publish literature filled with lots of educational information.

7. Check out *Free Stuff for Kids* (Simon and Schuster, 1997)* and *Free Things for Teachers* by Susan Osborn (Berkley Publishing, 1993)*. These books list sources of free or almost-free educational materials.

8. Susan Richman, editor of *Pennsylvania Homeschoolers* newsletter (well worth the subscription cost for homeschoolers anywhere), writes a regular column describing sources of free educational resources and opportunities.

9. While we are on it, Pennsylvania Homeschoolers also carries modestly priced resources you will not find elsewhere. *Figure It Out* is a year's worth of challenging math problems that costs just three dollars for the student workbook. The Richmans also have the rights to rent, at a modest price, video courses from the **Annenberg School** (one of the most prestigious in the nation). These high school/college level classes include French, Spanish, algebra I, physics, and chemistry, among others.

10. The best tip I have for the resourceful homeschooler is *use the library*—and that's such a biggie, it warrants a chapter of its own.

Using the Library

The local public library, one of the few institutions I do not mind supporting with my tax dollars, is the best friend of the resourceful homeschooler as well as a creative one.

Find the friendliest library in your area and travel there regularly. If it's a bit of a hike, turn it into a school day by organizing research projects for your kids to complete while there.

Interlibrary Loan

Most libraries now participate in an interlibrary loan program. This allows you to request books from any participating library in the United States. There is rarely a title, including Christian and obscure works, that I cannot find in some public or university library system in the country. I frequently use this option to review a book or resource I am thinking about buying. If your library does not have the title you are looking for, ask your librarian to help you submit an interlibrary loan request. Your library will then order the book for you from a library that has the book.

Some Are Even Wired

I can also access my library's database from my modem at no charge. Here I can see how many overdue books I currently have and determine if my tab has exceeded six figures yet, as well as reserve and request books from anywhere in the country. What a convenience! If your library doesn't have this service, ask if any of the other ones in your local dialing area do and sign up for it. (Did I mention you'll need a computer first?)

A Little Courtesy Goes a Long Way

One library in our area is particularly friendly to homeschoolers—and as such has become an informal waterhole for us. The staff has gone so far as to purchase resources from a wish list we compiled. This is likely when you go out of your way to serve your local library (volunteering to reshelve books, for example) and manage your children's behavior while there.

They've Got the Very Best at an Unbeatable Price

This all leads to a bigger point: Your local public library is where you'll find the creative and motivating resources you need to individualize your program. The core of our studies for years have been made up of children's literature and trade books (nonfiction) we've checked out from our library.

Books Kids Love

One of our targeted goals, you'll recall, is to raise children who love to learn. I want to put in their hands resources developed by folks with the same creative drive and passion for learning we're desiring to cultivate in them. These folks are not writing textbooks—which are subject to an array of artistic restraints—they are working where they have freedom to delve deeply into their subject and convey the essence of the material that so fascinates them.

As an example of this difference, compare these two presentations of the same Revolutionary battle:

> The fighting that had begun in New England spread to New York, New Jersey and other colonies. In December 1776, Washington and his army had to leave New Jersey. They crossed the Delaware River to Pennsylvania. On Christmas night the Americans recrossed the Delaware and attacked a camp of **Hessians** (hesh enz) at Trenton, New Jersey. The Hessians were soldiers from Germany who were hired to fight for the British. The American army captured 900 Hessians. This battle, known as the battle of Trenton, was the first great victory for the Americans in the war.
>
> —fifth-grade social studies textbook

What drama! What pathos! Don't stop reading, Mom. *NOT!*

There wouldn't be any connection between why United States students can't remember the decade in which the Civil War was fought and the vivid and compelling writing in their textbooks, now would there?

 Here's how Joy Hakim describes the same event in her **History of Us** (Oxford University Press, 1993)* series:

> Howe thought Washington and his army were done for and could be finished off in springtime. . . . But George Washington was no quitter. On Christmas Eve of 1776, in bitter cold, Washington got the Massachusetts fishermen to ferry his men across the Delaware River from Pennsylvania back to New Jersey. The river was clogged with huge chunks of ice. You had to be crazy, or coolly courageous, to go out into that dangerous water. While the Massachusetts boatmen were getting the army across, the Hessians, on the other side—at Trenton, New Jersey—were celebrating

Christmas by getting drunk. Before the Germans could focus their eyes, the Americans captured 900 of them.

— Joy Hakim, _From Colony to Country_

Hakim was compelled to write her ten-book series of American history after seeing the insipid and dumbed down textbooks her oldest daughter was required to read in school. Her enthusiasm for her subject is infectious. My daughter Katie chose to continue reading through the series even during our summer break.

These Books Draw Us In

Why do you remember those favorite books from childhood? Because they were about people you came to care about. Children's literature and quality nonfiction, as well, employ the elements of good fiction. Their descriptive writing, vivid settings, realistic characters, and detailed action help us vicariously experience the drama ourselves.

One of the first books I read aloud with my kids was _Sign of the Beaver_* by Elizabeth George Speare (Houghton Mifflin, 1983). It is the story of ten-year-old Matt, who must survive alone on the frontier of Maine during the winter of 1721. Had he not been befriended by a young Indian brave who taught him to track and trap, he would never have made it. We can remember all the details of the harsh conditions colonists faced, the tensions between European and Native American cultures, and the historic events of the time because we cared about Matt and these realistic details impacted his life. That's just not true of material learned from a textbook. It is a sterile and impersonal presentation of fact upon fact upon irrelevant fact.

Why I Love Homeschooling

People ask me how I can enjoy homeschooling. The crux is right here. I love these books. I love the creative resources we are using. Learning is fascinating when you are using materials created by folks who were fascinated with the subject themselves and want to light that spark of interest in their readers. I frequently read ahead in the books we're reading aloud to our kids. So does Kermit. Can't say I've ever been tempted to read ahead in a textbook, though.

More Advantages

1. Children's literature and trade books have the additional advantage of being specifically targeted to your child's interests and reading level. Here's an example:

Interest: Ben Franklin
  Reading level: Second grade. Choice: _Benjamin Franklin: A Man with Many Jobs_ by Carole Greene (Childrens, 1988).*

Reading level: Fourth grade. Choice: *Benjamin Franklin: Young Printer* by Augusta Stevenson (Macmillan, 1986).*

Reading level: Junior high. Choice: *Poor Richard* by James Daugherty (Viking, 1941).

Reading level: High school. Choice: *The Autobiography of Benjamin Franklin* (Penguin Classics, 1986).

Gabe was reading about George Washington a few years back. His specific interest, though, was his presidency—typically not covered at all in traditional history books. We found the perfect fit, *George and Martha Washington at Home in New York* by Beatrice Seigel (Simon and Schuster, 1989), and we also learned the nation's capital was originally located in New York City.

2. Children's literature is easily adapted to multilevel teaching. Many of the books suggested on the resource list that begins on page 111 can be used with all your elementary-age children. And many are appropriate on higher levels as well.

Here's a sample of the books I used with my kids for a unit of study centered around colonial America:

Witch of Blackbird Pond, Elizabeth George Speare (Dell, 1996, or Houghton Mifflin, 1958).*

Sign of the Beaver, Elizabeth George Speare (Houghton Mifflin, 1983).*

Calico Captive, Elizabeth George Speare (Bantam, 1973).*

A Lion to Guard Us, Clyde Robert Bulla (HarperCollins, 1989).*

Life in Colonial America series, James Knight (Troll).*

Colonial Living, Edward Tunis (World Publishing, 1957).

Cities of the Revolution series (Children's Press).

Childhood of Famous Americans biographies (Macmillan).*

Can't You Make Them Behave, King George? (Putnam, 1996) and others by Jean Fritz.*

Steven Caney's Kids' America (Workman, 1978).*

If You Were There series (Scholastic).*

Colonial Craftsmen series, Leonard Fisher (Franklin Watts).

3. Children's literature is integrated. That means the information is set in the full context of meaning. The Eyewitness book *Ancient Egypt* covers the history, geography, art, science, and chief players. When learned in this way, kids have a much easier time visualizing the implications of the information and understanding the concepts and principles rather than just memorizing facts that seem divorced from a meaningful context.

Here's Where I Start

This is where I always start when I set out to choose curriculum materials. I head to my local library. There I will find the resources that offer the greatest selection of choices for kids of all learning styles, readiness, and interests at the lowest price (usually free). If I am looking for resources to use consistently throughout the year, I review my options here first and then purchase the ones that fit best. But during my kids' elementary education almost everything we did in history, literature, science, art, music, and geography came from books at our library.

I thought you might be interested in seeing some of the titles we've used:

Top 150 Titles Available at Your Local Library

These titles are recommended on their artistic merit and adaptability to a home-education program. Our family has not found them offensive to our Christian world view, but they are secular and may not all be suitable for your family.

- 🐭 "Young adult" denotes language or situations that require parental guidance.
- 🐭 Authors in bold are key writers in this subject area.
- 🐭 OP: out of print but still available in better libraries.

Art and Architecture

Arnosky, Jim. *Drawing from Nature,* and others (Lothrop, Lee and Shepard, 1982). Use this with older children and *Come Out, Muskrats* (1989), with your little ones.

Bjork, Christina. *Linnea in Monet's Garden* (R & S Books, 1987). A charming trip through Monet's life guided by a European "Ramona." Grade level: 2–5.

Brooks, Mona. *Drawing with Children* (Tarcher, 1996). Buy this one. Grade level: K–6.

Brown, Marc, and Luarene Brown. *Visiting the Art Museum* (Dutton, 1986). Before you go to a museum, share this book. Grade level: 2–3.

Globok, Shirley. *The Art of Colonial America,* and others (Macmillan, 1970). Integrate Globok's books into your history program. OP. Grade level: all.

Goldstein, Ernest. *Winslow Homer: The Gulf Stream,* and others (Garrard, 1982). From the "Let's Get Lost in a Painting" series. Learn to look at art in general as Goldstein draws your attention to the specific points of each masterpiece in this series. Grade level: 3–up.

Isaacson, Philip. *Round Buildings, Square Buildings and Buildings that Wiggle Like a Fish* (Knopf, 1988). A lawyer wrote this fascinating pictorial history of world architecture. Delicious writing. Grade level: 3–up.

Kohl, Mary Ann. *Mudworks: Creative Clay, Dough and Modeling Experiences,* and others (Bright Ring, 1989). Wonderful art projects for K–6. Recipes for every kind of goo you can think of. Grade level: elementary.

Macaulay, David. *Cathedral,* and others (Houghton Mifflin, 1973). With meticulously drawn sketches, Macaulay shows us the process required to build the great churches of Europe. Grade level: 3–up.

Milord, Susan. *Adventures in Art* (Williamson, 1990). Activities and tidbits of art history. My art program came from here. Grade level: 2–8.

Nakano, Dokuohtei. *Easy Origami* (Viking, 1985). This *Reading Rainbow* selection is the best one available for beginning folders. Grade level: K–6.

Parish, Peggy. *Let's Be Indians* (Harper and Row, 1962) and other Ready-to-Read Handbook titles. Grade level: 1–3.

Raboff, Ernest. *Michelangelo Buonarroti* (Doubleday, 1969). Included in the Art for Children series. All titles are very worthwhile. Full-color reproductions in each. OP. Grade level: K–6.

Shachtman, Tom. *The President Builds a House* (Simon and Schuster, 1989). Photo essay about Jimmy Carter's work for Habitat for Humanity. Very moving.

Venezia, Mike. *Van Gogh* (Childrens, 1988). Getting to Know the World's Greatest Artists is a humorous and colorful new series for beginning readers. Grade level: 2–4.

Yenawine, Philip. *Colors,* and others in this series from the Museum of Modern Art (1991). Grade level: 2–up.

History/Geography—American

Alcott, Louisa M. *Little Women* (Grosset and Dunlap, 1947). Civil War era. Grade level: 5–up.

Armstrong, Jennifer. *Steal Away* (Orchard, 1992). Two friends escape to the North. Grade level: young adult.

Avi. *The True Confessions of Charlotte Doyle* (Orchard, 1990). We like the history titles Avi wrote during his earlier years. Grade level: 4–up.

Benchley, Nathaniel. *Sam the Minuteman* (Harper and Row, 1969). From the I Can Read series. There are other good history titles in the series as well. Grade level: 1–3.

Blos, Joan. *A Gathering of Days* (Scribner, 1979). New England in the 1830s. Grade level: 4–up.

Brink, Carol Ryrie. *Caddie Woodlawn* (Macmillan, 1935). The Midwest in the 1860s. Grade level: 4–up.

Bulla, Clyde. *Squanto, Friend of the Pilgrims* (Scholastic, 1990), *Pocahontas and the Strangers* (Scholastic, 1987), and many others. Grade level: 2–4.

Caney, Steven. *Steven Caney's Kids' America* (Workman, 1978). Instructions for recreating colonial crafts intermingled with Americana folklore. Grade level: K–8.

Collier, Christopher, and James Collier. *My Brother Sam Is Dead* (Simon and Schuster, 1984). Some may find the earthy language and realistic descriptions in their books offensive, but the Collier brothers are unmatched in the authentic historic details of their fiction. Grade level: young adult.

Dalgliesh, Alice. *The Courage of Sarah Noble* (Scribner, 1954), *The Fourth of July Story* (Scribner, 1956), and others. Grade level: 2–4.

D'Aulaire, Ingri, and Edgar D'Aulaire. *Benjamin Franklin* (Doubleday, 1950), *Abraham Lincoln* (Doubleday, 1957), and many other biographies of early American leaders. Grade level: 2–4.

Daugherty, James. *Poor Richard* (Viking, 1941), and others. OP. Grade level: 5–8.

DeAngeli, Marguerite. *Thee, Hannah!* (Doubleday, 1940), *Yonie Wondernose* (Doubleday,

1944). DeAngeli may be the Pennsylvania Dutch country's most distinguished author. OP. Grade level: 2–4.

Donnelly, Judy. *Who Shot the President? The Death of John F. Kennedy* (Random House, 1988). A Step into Reading book, part of a highly recommended series. Grade level: K–3.

Edmonds, Walter. *The Matchlock Gun* (Putnam, 1941). The true tale of a boy's courage in the face of an Indian attack. Grade level: 2–4.

Fisher, Leonard. *The Blacksmiths* (Franklin Watts, 1976). From the Colonial American Craftsmen series, includes *The Doctors, The Papermakers,* and *The Cabinetmakers.* Excellent wood engravings. OP. Grade level: all.

Forbes, Esther. *Johnny Tremain* (Houghton Mifflin, 1960). Compare this book with modern author Avi's *The Fighting Ground.* Grade level: 5–up.

Foster, Genevieve. *1620: Year of the Pilgrim.* A favorite author here. This title provides an overview of world history the year the Pilgrims landed; one of many world history books by this author. Her titles are being brought back into print by Beautiful Feet Books. Grade level: 3–8.

Freeman, Russell. *Lincoln: A Photobiography* (Clarion, 1987). The first nonfiction book to win the Newbery Award. A superb storyteller writing in the nonfiction genre. If you like Ken Burns's documentaries, you'll like Russell Freeman's writing. Grade level: 4–up.

Fritz, Jean. *And Then What Happened, Paul Revere?* (Coward, 1973), *The Cabin Faced West* (Puffin, 1987), and many others. Don't miss this author! Grade level: 3–8.

Greene, Carol. *Benjamin Franklin: A Man with Many Jobs* (Childrens, 1988). A Rookie Biography book, a fine series for emerging readers. Lots of historic detail, illustrations, and photographs. Grade level: 1–3.

Hall, Donald. *Ox-cart Man* (Viking, 1979). Caldecott Medal. Grade level: K–2.

Henry, Marguerite. *Justin Morgan Had a Horse* (Rand McNally, 1954), *Benjamin West and His Cat Grimalkin* (Bobbs-Merrill, 1947). This beloved writer of horse stories also tells history in these. Grade level: 2–5.

Holling, Holling C. *Paddle-to-the-Sea* (Houghton Mifflin, 1941), and many others. A unique blend of geography and history. Grade level: 3–6.

Hunt, Irene. *Across Five Aprils* (Berkely Books, 1964). A Newbery Honor book set during the Civil War. Grade level: 5–up.

Keith, Harold. *Rifles for Watie* (Crowell, 1957). Newbery Award winner. Grade level: 5–up.

Kellogg, Steven. *Johnny Appleseed* (Morrow, 1988). This outstanding illustrator has told an entertaining tale for the 4–7 age group. Grade level: K–2.

Knight, James. Adventures in Colonial America series (Troll, 1982). Grade level: 2–5.

Latham, Jean Lee. *Carry On, Mr. Bowditch* (Houghton Mifflin, 1955). Lots of science and mathematics here. Grade level: 2–5.

Lenski, Lois. *Strawberry Girl* (Lippincott, 1945). Lenski writes stories set in various regions of the United States. Grade level: 2–5.

Levine, Ellen. *If You Traveled on the Underground Railroad* (Scholastic, 1993). From the unique series by Scholastic. Grade level: 1–4.

Loeper, John. *Going to School in 1776* (Atheneum, 1973), *Going to School in 1886* (Atheneum, 1984). Grade level: 3–6.

MacLachlan, Patricia. *Sarah, Plain and Tall* (Harper and Row, 1985). Newbery Award and Scott O'Dell Award. A simple story, but the writer's lyrical style and characterization are flawless. Grade level: 3–7.

Monjo, F. N. *The Drinking Gourd* (HarperCollins, 1993). Another I Can Read book about the underground railroad. Monjo has mastered the art of fine writing with a controlled vocabulary. Grade level: 1–3.

O'Dell, Scott. *Streams to the River, River to the Sea* (Houghton Mifflin, 1986), and many others. This book follows the trail of Lewis & Clark. Don't miss this important author. Grade level: 4–8.

Perl, Lila. *Slumps, Grunts and Snickerdoodles: What Colonial America Ate and Why* (Seabury, 1975). Great recipes with historical notes. Grade level: elementary.

Roop, Peter, and Connie Roop. *Keep the Lights Burning, Abbie* (Carolrhoda, 1985). Maine, 1856. Grade level: 2–4.

Siegel, Beatrice. *George and Martha Washington at Home in New York* (Four Winds Press, 1989). Grade level: 4–7.

Speare, Elizabeth George. *The Sign of the Beaver* (Houghton Mifflin, 1983), and others. Winner of the Scott O'Dell Award. Grade level: 3–7.

Steele, William O. *Perilous Road* (Harcourt Brace, 1990). A Civil War story. Also see *The Buffalo Knife,* and others for a vivid portrayal of wilderness life. Grade level: 4–8.

Tunis, Edwin. *Frontier Living* (World Publishing, 1961), *Indians* (World Publishing, 1959), and many others. OP. Grade level: 5–up.

Turner, Ann. *Grasshopper Summer* (Macmillan, 1989). Eighteenth-century prairie life. Grade level: 3–6.

Twain, Mark. *Huckleberry Finn,* and others. Grade level: 5–up.

Waters, Kate. *Sarah Morton's Day: A Day in the Life of a Pilgrim Girl.* A pictorial tour of Plimoth Plantation, a living history museum in Plymouth, Massachusetts. Grade level: 1–4.

Wilder, Laura Ingalls. Little House on the Prairie books. Grade level: 2–5.

History/Geography—Other Lands

Ballard, Robert. *The Lost Wreck of the Isis* (Scholastic, 1990). A Time Quest book. Nonfiction that reads like high adventure. Grade level: 3–6.

Ceserani, Gian Paolo. *Marco Polo* (Putnam, 1982). Grade level: 3–6.

Colum, Padraic. *The Children's Homer* (1918, Macmillan, 1948), *Children of Odin,* and *The Golden Fleece.* Best source of ancient mythology for elementary students. Grade level: 4–8.

DeAngeli, Marguerite. *The Door in the Wall* (Doubleday, 1949). Medieval life. Grade level: 4–6.

de Jenkins, Lyll Becerra. *The Honorable Prison* (Puffin, 1989). Modern-day South America. Grade level: 5–8.

Grun, Bernard. *The Timetables of History* (Simon and Schuster, 1991). Reference tool.

Holman, Felice. *The Wild Children* (Puffin, 1985). Russia in the 1920s. Grade level: 5–8.

Hunter, Nigel. *The Expeditions of Cortes* (Brookwright, 1990). One from the Great Journeys series. Grade level: 3–6.

James, Simon. *Ancient Rome* (Knopf, 1990). An Eyewitness Book. All are highly recommended. Grade level: all.

Krumgold, Joseph. *And Now Miguel* (Crowell, 1953). Newbery Award. Grade level: 4–6.

O'Dell, Scott. *The Hawk That Dare Not Hunt by Day* (Bob Jones University, 1975). The story of William Tyndale. Grade level: 4–8.

McGraw, Eloise. *The Golden Goblet* (Puffin, 1986). Ancient Egypt. All of this author's books are the finest of historical fiction. Grade level: 4–8.

Patterson, Katherine. *Rebels of the Heavenly Kingdom* (Dutton, 1983). One of my favorite authors. This story is set in China in the 1850s. Grade level: 4–8.

Pyle, Howard. *The Merry Adventures of Robin Hood* (Grosset and Dunlap, 1952). Grade level: 5–up.

Ryan, Peter. *Explorers and Mapmakers* (Lodestar, 1990). From the Time Detectives series. Grade level: 3–6.

Speare, Elizabeth George. *The Bronze Bow* (Houghton Mifflin, 1961). Palestine at the time of Christ. Grade level: 5–8.

Sperry, Armstrong. *Call It Courage* (Collier, 1971). A South Seas Island boy must conquer his fear of the sea. Grade level: 3–6.

Stevenson, Robert Louis. *The Black Arrow,* illustrated by N. C. Wyeth (Scribner, 1944). The Wars of the Roses come to life in this master storyteller's hands. Grade level: 5–up.

Sutcliff, Rosemary. *Flame-Colored Taffeta* (Farrar, 1986), and others. Rich, detailed writings of English history. Grade level: 5–8.

Wright, David, and Jill Wright. *The Facts on File Children's Atlas* (Facts on File, 1993). Best atlas for the elementary level. Grade level: 2–6.

Mathematics

Anno, Mitsumasa. *Anno's Math Games* (Philome, 1991), and many more. There is no one like Anno! Don't miss this inventive and brilliant author/illustrator. Grade level: 2–5.

Asimov, Isaac. *How Did We Find Out about Numbers?* (Walker, 1973). This leading science writer has authored scores of nonfiction titles for kids. Grade level: 2–4.

Burns, Marilyn. *The I Hate Mathematics! Book* (Little, Brown, 1975), and *The Book of Think* (Little, Brown, 1976). Both from the Brown Paper School book series, all of which are worth your attention. Grade level: 3–8.

Dennis, Richard. *Fractions Are Parts of Things* (Crowell, 1971). From the Young Math Book series, which teaches mathematical concepts through hands-on activities. Grade level: 1–3.

Froman, Robert. *Less Than Nothing Is Really Something* (Crowell, 1973). Introduction to negative numbers. Grade level: 1–4.

Gardner, Martin. *Aha! Aha! Insight* (Scientific America, 1978), *Aha! Gotcha* (Scientific America, 1978), and many more. Grade level: 5–up.

Ipsen, D. C. *Archimedes: Greatest Scientist of the Ancient World* (Enslow, 1988). Grade level: 5–up.

Maybury, Richard. *Whatever Happened to Penny Candy?* (Bluestocking, 1993). The best introduction to economics for young people. Grade level: 6–up.

Sitomer, Mindel, and Harry Sitomer. *Zero Is Not Nothing* (Crowell, 1978). Another Young Math Book. Grade level: 1–3.

Schwartz, David, and Steven Kellogg, illustrator. *How Much Is a Million?* (Lothrop, Lee, and Shepard, 1989), and *If You Made a Million* (Lothrop, Lee, and Shepard, 1985). Lots of fun! Grade level: K–3.

Wyler, Rose, and Gerald Ames. *It's All Done with Numbers* (Doubleday, 1979). "Magic" tricks that are performed with mathematics. Grade level: 2–5.

Science

Allison, Linda. *Blood and Guts: A Working Guide to Your Own Insides* (Little, Brown, 1976). Another excellent Brown Paper School Book author. Grade level: 3–8.

Berger, Melvin. *Quasars, Pulsars and Black Holes in Space* (Putnam, 1977), and others. Grade level: 4–up.

Beshore, George. *Science in Early Islamic Culture* (Franklin Watts, 1988). From a series that covers technological achievements of other cultures in other times. Grade level: 5–up.

Bourgeois, Paulette. *The Amazing Dirt Book* (Addison-Wesley, 1990). Activities for the grades 2–5 group.

Caney, Steven. *Steven Caney's Invention Book,* and others. Workman Publishing has many titles that are great for home schooling. Grade level: 2–6.

Cobb, Vickie. *Bet You Can't: Science Impossibilities to Fool You* (Workman, 1985), and lots of others. Grade level: 4–8.

Cole, Joanna. *The Magic School Bus Inside the Earth,* (Scholastic, 1987) and others. All the titles in this series are wonderful—humorous with lots of detail. Grade level: K–3.

Durrell, Gerald. *Amateur Naturalist* (Knopf, 1986). Comprehensive, illustrated guide to collecting specimens from five environments. Grade level: 5–up.

Epstein, Sam, and Beryl Epstein. *Dr. Beaumont and the Man with a Hole in His Stomach* (Coward, 1978). Don't miss this bizarre but true story from the 1820s. Grade level: 3–6.

Gallant, Roy. *National Geographic Picture Atlas of Our Universe* (National Geographic, 1986). *National Geographic* has done a few reference books for children, and they are superb. Grade level: 5–up.

Gardner, Robert. *The Whale Watchers' Guide* (J. Messner, 1984). From a prolific science writer. Grade level: 4–6.

Grey, Vivian. *The Chemist Who Lost His Head: The Story of Antoine LaVoisier* (Coward, 1982). Founder of the metric system. Grade level: 4–up.

Johnston, Tom. *Energy: Making It Work* (G. Stevens, 1988). Good activities to do at home from the Science in Action series. Grade level: 3–6.

Krupp, E. C. *The Big Dipper and You* (Morrow, 1989). A historical and scientific introduction to the night sky. Richly illustrated. Grade level: 2–4.

Lewis, James. *Rub-a-Dub-Dub Science in the Tub* (Meadowbrook, 1989). For the two- to five-year-old set. Grade level: Pre-K–2.

Macaulay, David. *The Way Things Work* (Houghton Mifflin, 1988). Like Anno, Macaulay is in a class by himself. Grade level: all.

Milton, Joyce. *Whales: The Gentle Giants* (Random House, 1989). From the Step into Reading series. Use this series to teach your child to read. It is great! Grade level: 1–3.

Ontario Science Center. *Scienceworks* and *Sportworks* (Addison-Wesley, 1984). If you can't visit this outstanding hands-on museum, at least get their books. Grade level: elementary.

Provensen, Alice, and Martin Provensen. *The Glorious Flight* (Viking, 1983). A Caldecott winner. Grade level: 1–3.

Quackenbush, Robert. *Ahoy! Ahoy! Are You There? A Story of Alexander Graham Bell* (Prentice Hall, 1981). From a beginning-reader series that introduces kids to famous inventors. Grade level: 2–4.

Rey, H. A. *The Stars: A New Way to See Them* (Houghton Mifflin, 1976). Surprise, surprise! Curious George's creator also liked astronomy. Grade level: 1–3.

Simon, Seymour. *The Moon* (Four Winds Press, 1984), and many others. Clear, crisp writing and full-color NASA pictures make this series unbeatable. Grade level: 4–8.

Stein, Sara. *The Science Book* (Workman, 1979). Stein is an evolutionist, but this book has lots of great information in a highly readable form. Grade level: 3–6.

Sussman, Susan, and Robert James. *Big Friend, Little Friend: A Book about Symbiosis* (Houghton Mifflin, 1989). Grade level: 1–3.

Thompson, C. E. *Glow-in-the-Dark Constellations: A Field Guide for Young Stargazers* (Grosset and Dunlap, 1989). Grade level: 3–6.

VanCleave, Janice Pratt. *Chemistry for Every Kid* (Wiley, 1989), and *Biology for Every Kid* (Wiley, 1990). Each of these books has 101 easy experiments. Grade level: 4–8.

Walpole, Brenda. *175 Science Experiments to Amuse and Amaze Your Friends* (Random House, 1988). This book lives up to its title. Grade level: 4–8.

Williams, J. Alan. *The Inter-planetary Toy Book* (Collier, 1985). Use easy-to-get supplies to create space adventures. Grade level: 3–6.

Wyler, Rose. *What Happens If?* (Walker, 1974). We did every experiment in this book. Everything you need is on hand! My kind of science book. Grade level: 2–5.

Yolen, Jane, and John Schoenherr. *Owl Moon.* Caldecott Medal. Primarily listed here to draw your attention to Schoenherr, a naturalist/author/illustrator. Grade level: K–2.

Zubrowski, Bernie. *Bubbles* (Little, Brown, 1979). A Children's Museum Activity Book. Others in the series are good, too. Grade level: 2–5.

Music

Athey, Margaret, and Gwen Hotchkiss. *Complete Handbook of Music Games and Activities for Early Childhood* (Parker, 1982). A complete curriculum for K–3 within these pages.

Fox, Dan. *Go In and Out the Window: An Illustrated Songbook for Young People.* Published by the Metropolitan Museum of Art (1987), this book integrates folk music and historical artifacts.

Langstaff, John, and Nancy Langstaff. *Jim Along, Josie: A Collection of Folk Songs and Singing Games for Young Children* (Harcourt Brace, 1970). Introduce your children to Langstaff's recordings of American folk songs, too.

Rosenberg, Jane. *Sing Me a Story: The Metropolitan Opera's Book of Opera Stories for Children* (Thames and Hudson, 1989). Adults will find this a welcome source of explanation, too.

Ventura, Piero. *Great Composers* (Putnam, 1989). Check out all of Ventura's books! They cover a wide spectrum of subjects. Grade level: elementary.

Wiseman, Ann. *Making Musical Things* (Scribner, 1979). Another *Reading Rainbow* selection. Kids can really make these very ingenious folk instruments. I used this to teach a music class to early-elementary students at our co-op. Grade level: K–4.

Language Arts and Reference

Heller, Ruth. *A Cache of Jewels and Other Collective Nouns* (Putnam, 1987). This lavish *Reading Rainbow* selection is one of a series on parts of speech.
Grade level: elementary.

Hirsch, E. D. *First Dictionary of Cultural Literacy* (Houghton Mifflin, 1989). This makes interesting reading. Grade level: 1–3.

Kohl, Herbert. *A Book of Puzzlements: Play and Invention with Language* (Schocken Books, 1981). If you want some quickie games to play with your kids, here's a big book of ideas. Grade level: 4–8.

Macmillan Dictionary for Children. My favorite elementary dictionary.

Meadowbrook Press. *Free Stuff for Kids* (current edition). Lots of places to write for fun and educational things to receive by mail. Grade level: elementary.

Becoming a Connoisseur of Children's Literature

Children's publishing is enjoying unprecedented growth. The call for literacy, as well as the whole-language movement, is creating a huge demand. Publishers are pouring millions of dollars into the industry and attracting better and better writers to it. Kids' books are bigger, brighter, and filled with impressive photography and graphic punch. Sure, there's plenty being published purely for propaganda purposes, but those titles are easy to spot and avoid.

If you want to stay on top of the latest offerings or read reviews about the best books being released, here are sources to help you become an expert about children's literature:

Reference Tools at the Library

Books in Print. This massive set of indices allows you to locate a book by subject, title, or author.

The Children's Catalog. An annotated listing of recommended books organized by subject area.

Fiction Index. Use this to locate historical fiction set in a specific time period or locale.

Associations and Periodicals

Reading Rainbow
c/o GPN
P.O. Box 80669
Lincoln, NE 68501
800-228-4630
$3.00 for packet with info and
programming guide.

The Five Owls
2004 Sheridan Avenue South
Minneapolis, MN 55405
$18/year

International Reading Association
P.O. Box 8139
800 Barksdale Road
Newark, DE 19714
(publishes _The Reading Teacher_)

Scholastic Inc.
P.O. Box 7502
Jefferson City, MO 65102

Parents Choice Foundation
Box 185
Newton, MA 02168

Children's Book Council, Inc.
67 Irving Place
New York, NY 10003
(publishes _Horn_ magazine)

Books with Annotated Bibliographies

The New Read-Aloud Handbook, Jim Trelease (Penguin, 1989).
Books Children Love, Elizabeth Wilson (Crossway, 1987).*
Eyeopeners II, Beverly Kobrin (Scholastic, 1995).
America As Story, Elizabeth Howard (American Library Association, 1988).
Honey for a Child's Heart, Gladys Hunt (Zondervan, 1989).*
Let the Authors Speak: A Guide to Worthy Books Based on Historical Setting,
Carolyn Hatcher (Old Pinnacle Publishing).*
Read for Your Life, Gladys Hunt (Zondervan, 1992).* Reading for teens.
Books to Build On: A Grade-by-Grade Resource Guide for Parents and Teachers,
E. D. Hirsch Jr. (Delta, 1996). New titles.*

12

Surviving a Curriculum Fair

$\mathbf{N}$ow it's time to spend the money. What you can't find at your library, as well as resources that must be used longer than one month (or whatever your library's maximum lending time is), must be sought out and paid for.

And the best place to see all your options in the flesh is your state's curriculum fair.

These extravaganzas are not to be missed, especially if you are a new homeschooler. The chaos, the choices, the speakers, and the fellowship will rev your engines for this new venture—or run you quickly out of gas—depending on your temperament style.

Here are some tips for maximizing your time:

Making the Most of Your Day

At my first curriculum fair I couldn't stand not buying anything, everything. That's the first impulse you have to resist—the temptation to overbuy.

I frequently take books *off* the piles accumulated by Home School Resource Center customers—I tell them they are getting more than they'll ever use. It may not seem like the wisest business practice, but I know helping folks make choices they won't regret will lead to loyal customers in the long run.

Keep these strategies in mind:

- ❦ **Do your homework before you come.** Read reviews, request catalogs, make a list. What goals and objectives do you have for next year? What core curriculum do you know you need for sure? What other products sound the most promising? How much can you afford to spend right now? Your best prices are usually at the fair, so it is wise to be prepared to buy.

- **Set realistic goals.** Expect crowds and lines. Expect information overload and feelings of confusion. It's the nature of the beast. If you come pressured to accomplish too much, you'll be frustrated and probably make bad purchasing decisions.

- **Prioritize.** Come early and get your essential shopping out of the way. Attend the workshops highest on your list. If you tire out before you complete all you'd hoped to, at least the most important things are done. You can order the tapes from the workshops you missed and shop by mail at home.

- **Discuss your goals with your companion.** People attend a curriculum fair for three reasons: to browse, to attend workshops, and to buy. If you go to the curriculum fair with a friend, discuss your goals for the fair before you arrive. If your companion has different goals, both of you are going to feel disappointed. Separate to get the most done.

- **For new homeschoolers:** It's better to get an education before you start buying. Go to the workshops. Talk with distributors and veteran homeschoolers first. You can always buy later. Information is what you need now. Bring a roll of address labels and use these to quickly add your name to mailing lists. By the time the next fair rolls around, you'll have received plenty of catalogs to review before going.

- **Say thank you to the volunteer coordinators.** Hundreds of hours go into organizing a curriculum fair, and almost all the fairs are run by volunteers. These folks have sacrificed countless hours of family time to create this opportunity for you. They need to be appreciated.

Ten Questions to Ask before You Buy

1. **Is this product developed for homeschoolers? If not, is the product still designed for individualized instruction?** Homeschooling is more like tutoring than traditional schooling. Material intended for classroom or group instruction will have lots of stuff designed to keep everybody busy for a fifty-minute class period. You don't need to spend the extra money for a resource with heavy doses of busywork.

2. **Is this a product that other homeschoolers I know are using?** The most successful resources we've used are those recommended by other homeschoolers. Reviewers don't have time to use every product extensively before writing up their recommendations. And company representatives have a built-in bias.

3. **Is this product compatible with my child's learning style, readiness, and reading level?** You will find wide discrepancies among products labeled for a particular grade. You'll need to use the information provided about learning styles and readiness first and then check out the reading level. Generally the larger the print, the lower the reading level.

4.   Does this product require a lot of teacher preparation? If so, will I conceivably have time for that throughout the year? The more kids you are homeschooling the less time you can allocate to teacher preparation for individual subjects. If things never get fully used it is usually for this reason. Self-instructional materials or those with everything planned out seem to work best when teaching more than one child.

5.   Is this product consumable, or will I get years of use from it? This is an important consideration when evaluating the price. A CD-ROM program that contains an entire set of encyclopedias has a lot more return on the investment than a consumable reading program for the same amount of money.

6.   What about the artistic merit? Is the student text and material colorful and artistically appealing? Does the layout draw the child into the pages? Is the writing lively and specific? If this product is not inviting (especially a factor with younger children), what are you planning to do to engage your child's interest in the subject? Do you find this resource intellectually stimulating? If not, what attitude toward learning are you conveying to your kids?

7.   Are there activities for the child to work on that involve higher-level thinking skills and move him or her away from the text and out into the world? If there is only one correct answer to chapter questions, then the text is only measuring memorization. Assessment tools that require more thoughtful responses, either in the form of an essay or research project, require students to work with the material on a deeper level.

8.   Does the product have a resell value among homeschoolers? Especially important if this is a big-ticket item and you hope to recoup some of that investment someday.

9.   Does the material have a theological/philosophical slant that you can embrace? This should usually be evident in the introductory comments or the program overview. If not, ask the representatives. Some publishers believe learning is an avocation, and their materials are designed to cultivate this sense of wonder and joy. Others believe school is a child's job, and the material is designed to cultivate a work ethic. Many popular history resources targeted to homeschoolers hold to a providential theology (God's chosen destiny that once rested on the nation of Israel now rests on the United States). Where you fall in that debate will determine the appropriateness of, say, Peter Marshall's *Light and the Glory* (Revell, 1977), which is providential in view, for your program.

10. Is the program complete, or must I buy supplemental materials? One expensive reading program I bought did not have readers. Some math programs require an additional purchase of manipulatives. Is the teacher's manual additional? And is it really necessary? Find out where the answers to the student assignments are printed. Make sure you ask these questions before you buy so you can accurately evaluate the cost of the resource.

PART 3

Organization and Planning

In This Section

- Setting Up a Learning Environment
- Maintaining Control of Your Day

13

Setting Up a Learning Environment

. . . .

A local newspaper featured our homeschool one year. The picture that ran with the article showed my kids composting with earthworms in the middle of our kitchen. I didn't realize how strange this would appear till several neighbors teased me about our health habits. (If you are interested—*Worms Eat My Garbage* by Mary Appelhof, published by Flower Press in 1982, [John Holt Bookstore] will show you how to get started with this great science project. If you're squeamish, you don't have to maintain your worm farm in the kitchen.)

If you choose to homeschool, forget about being featured in *House Beautiful*. Creating a learning environment that invites invention, inquiry, and discovery is pretty much incompatible with clutter control. Most of the homeschooling houses I frequent have books, art projects, science apparatus, insect collections, etc., sharing space with all available seating. Good conversation is easily had, but standing-room-only is the standard.

What I can offer you here are suggestions for managing the mass and masses but *not* for passing a white-glove inspection.

Swimming in Stimuli

Far more important than the actual lessons you may organize to present to your children is the environment in which they learn. Think in terms of "immersion." You want your kids living and breathing in an environment that more than supports learning, it invites and stimulates their inquiry. Everywhere they turn as they move through their daily lives they should find the stuff for exploration at their fingertips.

Exploration

Long before you begin formal lessons in ANY subject area, your kids need a generous, leisurely time of informal exposure and investigation of the stuff they are going to be trained to use in a skillful way later.

If you want kids who read, immerse them in a print-rich environment. Put books and magazines in every room—some of my kids learned to read in the bathroom; we kept our Dr. Seuss collection in there.

If you want your kids to take an interest in science, they should be tripping over butterfly and insect collections, posters, magnifying glasses, binoculars, field guides, and other support material for scientific exploration at every turn.

 My favorite homeschooling household to visit is the home of Howard and Susan Richman, owners of <u>Pennsylvania Homeschoolers</u>. My kids voted it the top field trip one year. Instead of a house, imagine, if you will, a hands-on museum—or maybe the attic of a hands-on museum. The walls and ceilings of the Richmans' three-story farmhouse are papered with National Geographic maps. Computers (many assembled from spare parts), a bone museum, plant cuttings, musical instruments, drawings and art projects from every school year, science apparatus, and mathematical puzzles and games are spread through-out. Wasps' nests and origami projects suspend from the ceiling. Books, from very old to brand-new, rule the place. These tomes fill not only the makeshift bookcases and shelves, but rise in piles from the floor, sofa, and chairs. The Richmans' farmyard contains the same invitation to exploration.

The one thing missing—a television. (Well, there actually is a television but without reception—they use it for video instruction.)

The fruit of this environment: four kids who can't help but love to learn.

The Stuff You Need for the Elementary Levels

Here's a wish list for you to leave for Santa or the grandparents. Pass on faddish, plastic toys, and hold out for these old-fashioned and long-lasting favorites that require kids to use their imaginations. A lot of the educational resources sold at retail are very cheaply produced and will never outlast a passel of kids. I've included the source of durable goods that may cost a bit more but will last long enough to have on hand for your own grandkids.

Books—hardcover picture books and classics (illustrated)

Some of our favorites:

Goodnight Moon and *The Runaway Bunny,* Margaret Wise Brown (Harper and Row).
Eyewitness series (Knopf).
Bedtime Hugs for Little Ones, Gabriel Ferrer (Harvest House, 1988).
A Dangerous Journey, a retelling of *Pilgrim's Progress* by John Bunyan (Marshall Morgan and Scott, 1985).
St. George and the Dragon (a retelling), Margaret Hodges (Little Brown, 1984).

The Way Things Work, David Macaulay (Houghton Mifflin, 1988).
Curdie and the Princess, George MacDonald (Dell, 1986).
The Tale of Peter Rabbit, and others, Beatrix Potter (F. Warne).
The Cat in the Hat, and others, Dr. Seuss (Random House).
Titles illustrated by Michael Hague, Jan Brett, Ruth Heller, Eric Carle, and
     Tomie DePaoli.
<u>Usborne</u> books

Find more suggestions for enduring children's books you ought to own in:

Gladys Hunt, *Honey for a Child's Heart* (Zondervan, 1989).*
Beverly Kobrin, *EyeOpeners II* (Scholastic, 1995).*

Jim Trelease, *New Read-Aloud Handbook* (Penguin, 1989).*

Magazines:
   American Girl (800-845-0005)
   Clubhouse, Jr. (800-232-6459)
   Clubhouse (800-232-6459)
   Cobblestone (800-821-0115)
   Highlights for Children (800-253-8688)
   My Big Backyard (800-588-1650)
   National Geographic World (800-647-5463)
   Sports Illustrated for Kids (a super magazine for any kid but especially the
      reluctant reader) (800-331-4009)

For stimulating imaginative and educational play:

   art supplies
   basic sports equipment
   big pencils
   binoculars, magnifying glass, videoscope
   calculator (Texas Instruments are best.)
   computer
   Cuisenaire rods
   easel
   field guides (<u>Dorling Kindersley</u> and <u>Usborne</u> are recommended.)
   flags of the world
   jump rope
   kitchen utensils
   large analog clock (the kind with minute and second hands—look for this at a farm
      supply store)
   Lauri puzzles
   Legos
   magnetic numbers and letters, including lower case

maps, globe
puppets
Ravenburger puzzles
stamps
strategy games: checkers, chess, Abalone
tools
trunk of your old clothes for playing dress-up
wooden and plastic figurines
workbench

Materials for developing background knowledge and basic skills:

writing supplies
desk
postcard prints of famous art masterpieces
musical instruments

Music tapes:

Music Masters series*
Wee Sing series
Raffi
Sharon, Lois, and Bram
American folk songs
French and Spanish folk songs

Audiotapes:

Focus on the Family Odyssey audiotapes
Your Story Hour audiotapes (<u>Library & Educational Services</u>)

Recommended sources of durable toys and art supplies:

Dick Blick (arts and crafts supplies)
P. O. Box 1267
Galesburg, IL 61402-1267
800-723-2787

Discount School Supply
P. O. Box 7636
Spreckles, CA 93962-7636
800-627-2829
Fax: 800-879-3753

http://www.earlychildhood.com

Hearth Song
6519 N. Galena Road
P.O. Box 1773
Peoria, IL 61656-1773
800-325-2502

Miller Pads and Paper
2840 Neff Road
Boscobel, WI 53805
608-375-2181

Toys to Grow On
P. O. Box 17
Long Beach, CA 90801
800-874-4242

Make It Accessible

I erroneously tried to homeschool and keep all surfaces cleared at the same time. This is not possible. If you homeschool, it's hard to hide the evidence. Projects-in-progress cannot always be put neatly away at the end of the day.

I discouraged my kids' exploration by dragging home scores of books from the library and then shelving them neatly in the bookcase. Magazines were in dated order in the filing cabinet. Art supplies, science apparatus, and strategy games were packed away in their original boxes in cupboards with closed doors. My kids didn't touch them.

Then I tried an experiment. I took a few books off the shelf and set them on the coffee table. I left a crystal-growing kit on the kitchen table. I put the art easel up in the den. Guess what: My kids read those library books, took an interest in growing crystals, and started a major art project. Go figure.

Don't get the impression, though, that we let everything lie where it falls. I do require all entrances to be free and clear. And though I've had to lower my expectations dramatically and learn to live with things a bit disheveled around the edges, I still believe Mom's organizational skills are the key to getting it all done.

Organizing It All

Where, exactly, will you hold school? This was really a dilemma when we first started. We kept migrating around the house the first few weeks—the kitchen, the living room, the kids' bedrooms. I realized I needed to make a decision, set up our learning area, and stay put. We settled on the kitchen table.

A Schoolroom Is Nice

I know quite a few families who have a school room. It may be an extra bedroom or the basement. Lobbying heavily for our need for one of our own, I convinced my husband to build a new house a few years ago. But a month after we moved in, we were back where we started—at the kitchen table. This enables me to work on my household chores while overseeing the kids' studies.

But the Kitchen Will Have to Do

So we have a kitchen that looks pretty odd—I keep a bookcase in the corner with the resources that we use daily. We have maps and posters on the wall and art projects on the floor. We are continuously clearing the table for meals and then for school. I'm used to how it looks, but first-time visitors who don't know we homeschool usually look perplexed.

Hardware

You'll need a few items to create an organized learning space: For office supplies, we shop Sam's Club and Quill (800-789-1331). Shipping charges on furniture makes Quill an impractical choice for bigger ticket items. So we've bought most of our files, desks, storage cabinets, etc., from the local home office supplier, such as Office Max, which offers free delivery with a minimum order.

Setting Boundaries

At a seminar several years ago, I acquired an organizational strategy that has been my saving grace. I use baskets, plastic tubs, containers, filing cabinets, storage chests, and such to *create boundaries for stuff.* For example, our math manipulatives are in one color-coded tub, our art supplies in another. I use stacking trays on the school shelf to separate graphing, construction, and handwriting paper. And each child has his or her own supply box for pencils, calculator, scissors, ruler, and such. I even use containers inside closets and drawers to keep everything clearly visible and easy to return to its rightful place. In my best moments these are all clearly labeled, and everyone knows what goes where.

Every August when planning the next school year, I also dejunk the house and improve our organization. I buy a few more pieces of hardware to further help us manage the clutter.

Last summer our project was moving Mike and Gabe to a bigger bedroom downstairs (on the ground rule they cannot create a life of their own down there—we're still a family). We bought bunkbeds, shelving, a bookcase, and a desk in order to better organize a study area for their changing needs. (They sprang for the stereo system they say enhances their intellectual growth.) We can't make all the changes we'd like to make at once, but if I prioritize my list and chip away at it as we can, I can at least say things are more efficient than five years ago.

Filing Cabinet

I keep files in every subject area. I store in these files any pamphlets, magazine articles, field-trip ideas, teaching tips, etc., as I collect them. Then I pull a file as I am planning out a subject area for the year. It's one way to make sure all the good ideas I come across eventually get implemented into my program.

Your filing cabinets are going to get full if you homeschool long term. So get something durable. I recommend a four-drawer, commercial-grade file with high sides for hanging folders. The best buy is made by Anderson Hickey and available from Staples (800-333-3330. See items #614909 or #614958; these are significantly less expensive than anywhere else and just as sturdy).

Bookcases

I buy more every year and now have our books shelved similarly to the library system so my kids can quickly see what we have on hand for research projects. The one in the kitchen is for current school subjects, but we've lined a wall in the family room for our children's literature collection, and then of course there's the one in the living room, and some in all the bedrooms. There are none in the bathroom yet, but that's not a bad idea. Sauder is my favorite brand of ready-to-assemble furniture for quality, durability, and price (800-523-3987).

Organization = Time

You get the picture, I'm sure. You can come up with your own systems for keeping things available but properly stored. Just remember: The more organized you are the more time you will have. Any effort you invest in setting up and maintaining your learning environment will never be wasted.

Now on to the homeschool mom's greatest daily challenge . . .

14

Maintaining Control of Your Day

A Method to the Madness

"Order brings peace," a spiritual mentor told me shortly after my conversion. And though I can't quote you a biblical chapter and verse, it's a life principle I'm convinced is true.

If there ever was a house in need of order it was ours the weeks after we brought the twins home from the hospital. I couldn't believe the doctor had entrusted these babies to our care. They looked so fragile.

I needn't have worried. They may have been small, but Mike and Gabe had lungs of steel. And right away they started calling the shots. My salvation came from a book called *My First 300 Babies* by Gladys West Hendrick (Vision House). Unfortunately now out of print, it is the best gift to ever hand a new mother. It was written by a nanny who, if you could afford her, moved in for six weeks with the new parents and whipped into shape, not only that baby, but the husband, household, and anyone else in her range of vision. (All you La Leche League members are cringing, aren't you?) Had I only brought home one child from the hospital, I wouldn't have been willing to make the efforts her program demanded. But as wimpy new parents of a pair who had obviously organized a coup in utero, we were ready for desperate measures.

I read Hendrick's book and announced to the twins, "This is the end of life on your own terms." Gladys Hendrick's strategy is simple. Baby is put on a daily schedule divided into fifteen-minute increments. This is followed no matter what the baby does. 10:00 A.M.: bathtime, 10:15 singtime, 10:30 nap, 12:30 P.M.: afternoon feeding, 7:00 P.M.: bedtime, etc. I stuck to it—even awakening the boys if the schedule dictated and putting them to bed even when they weren't willing.

Did they complain? You bet. But a week later, they were synchronized and—here's the important part—contented. We were more flexible when Katie and Kristen came along, but the principle of maintaining a consistent routine and structure was still applied. I am convinced order brings peace—and produces contented, secure kids.

Of course, we are no longer controlling our children's lives in fifteen-minute intervals. In fact, Mike, Gabe, and Katie set their own routines—but that's the fruit. It is second nature to them to manage their time wisely and to structure their day and learning environment rather than take an undisciplined, chaotic approach to life.

Here are the strategies that will bring peace to your homeschool life by bringing order. They are simple and few. Complex systems that require too much time to maintain fail very quickly. These are the ones that have lasted at our house over the years.

Strategy #1: Long-Range Planning

A peaceful and well-managed homeschool begins with a commitment to plan. You can't invest too much time at this end of the spectrum. Long-range planning and weekly goal-setting will eliminate unnecessary day-to-day decision-making and give you confidence. It will also give your children direction—if you take the time to clue them in on things. (Something I must remind myself to do.)

Summertime Is Planning Time

Some families find homeschooling year round suits them. I've tried that but found we do best taking a summer break long enough to miss school. I use this time to regroup and do my long-range planning. After soliciting feedback from my kids, I scope out our year. First I focus on areas of weakness. I prioritize these and set goals for improvement. I'm never going to correct all of them in a year's time, but I am determined to keep chipping away at the list.

Add Faith

Don't let unmet goals discourage you. You'll get more accomplished in life by setting goals and not meeting all of them than by not setting goals at all.

Bring faith to your planning. Treat your goals as a prayer list. Sometimes I feel as though we aren't getting anywhere, or worse, we're moving backward. But when I look at my goals from previous years, I'm encouraged by the gains that have been made. Often God brings special opportunities our way that allow us to meet our goals in unexpected ways. Just putting the goals on the list makes me more conscious of God's commitment to our success and my awareness of His intercession on our behalf.

Foreign language has been a big flop at our house. Everything we try usually peters out by October. But I still put it on the list every year. Last year, a missionary on furlough from France began teaching at CHESS. When Cindy told me about her application to teach, I felt God had answered my personal prayer unexpectedly.

Write Objectives

After tackling our weaknesses, I then write out objectives for every subject for each child. I first began doing this because it is required by Pennsylvania law and these must be filed with our school district. The requirement is vague and could be done in a cursory manner, but I take the time to make it meaningful. I use this plan throughout the year as a yardstick for our progress.

Fortunately, our law doesn't require us to meet these objectives, so it is easy to adjust or change as the year progresses. Planning is the strategy that will help you hit those targets you are aiming at. But don't let it enslave you. Always be ready to adapt your program to the needs of your children.

At the end of each school year, I go into my objectives file on the computer and enter a brief paragraph indicating whether or not the objective was _met, partially met,_ or _not met_ and then detail evidence to support my evaluation. Again, this is not required by our law. I do it for my own benefit and accountability.

Here is my educational plan from Mike and Gabe's third-grade year, along with my end-of-the-year notes.

Educational Plan
1991–1992 School Term

Students: Gabriel Joseph Bell   Grade: 3rd
                    Michael Benjamin Bell

Academic Objectives (to include but not limited to the following):

English (to include spelling, reading, and writing):

Will continue daily, literature-based, sustained silent reading program (thirty to sixty minutes/day).
[End-of-year notes:] Michael and Gabriel continue to love reading and do so without encouragement. Typically we all read silently after lunch for at least an hour. This year they each read approximately sixty chapter books. They read well above grade level with good comprehension and speed. For example, Gabriel's favorite book, _A Father's Promise_, is the novel that concludes Bob Jones University's sixth-grade reading course. Michael has been reading those titles in the Chronicles of Narnia series. Both have really enjoyed the Childhood of Famous Americans series.

Will continue reading widely from various genres: nonfiction, fiction, biography, poetry, etc.
The boys willingly read biographies and historical fiction. I required them to read nonfiction titles as part of their Book-It goals this year. We read many nonfiction titles aloud, too, as part

---

of our unit studies. They also regularly read the *New International Version Adventure Bible*. We read some poetry about sports this year, but I intend to increase their exposure to verse.

Will continue to master library and research skills. Will write their first research paper. We use the library at least two times a month. Michael and Gabriel know well how the library is organized, and they can find books independently on topics of interest and for their research. They also use the library computer system without assistance to locate titles by subject and author and are then able to request the books through interlibrary loan.

The boys successfully wrote their first research paper. I feel the final draft of the paper could have been better, but the time involved in the science fair project and paper became overwhelming. I was very pleased with the amount of reading and research they did on their topics. They sent away for information, ordered titles through interlibrary loan, read their books, met to discuss their projects with me, and then logged their notes and rough drafts in their journals and on the computer.

Will improve rate, expression, and enjoyment of oral reading.
Mike and Gabe read aloud more frequently this year to me and to their sisters. Gabriel is particularly dramatic in his reading and enjoys entertaining his four-year-old sister with a good book.

Will improve recitation and memorization skills.
The boys portrayed several characters in a play our co-op produced, and they executed their lines flawlessly with good expression. Michael did especially well as the lead in *Ethan Allen and the Green Mountain Boys*, a character he was delighted to portray after reading a biography earlier in the year. They regularly memorized Scripture, also.

Will continue to use contextual clues and phonics skills to expand reading comprehension and vocabulary. An emphasis will be placed on learning vocabulary across the curriculum. Objective met. Vocabulary words were drawn primarily from the books we read together for history and science. They frequently ask me the meaning of words they run into while reading. I first ask for their ideas (which are usually close) and then precisely define it for them or refer them to the dictionary. We like to talk about words. (Or at least I do.)

Will continue to improve spelling through reading critically and editing their work. Objective met.

Will develop writer's voice through regular and sustained written composition.
I continue to be pleased with the writing that Michael and Gabriel do. They view themselves as writers. They did a wide variety of writing this year: science reports, history report, fiction, poetry, friendly letters, etc. They like to write letters and notes to friends. Their biggest frustration is in finding others who will write regularly to them. They prefer to use WordPerfect as opposed to longhand, and I do not blame them.

Will determine appropriate language, form, and content of written composition based upon analysis of audience and purpose.

Once again the boys participated in a writers group that I ran. We did several short lessons about the concerns of the writer. We've discussed these concerns at home mostly within the context of the letters they have written to friends and adults.

Will publish written compositions in a variety of forums.

Michael and Gabriel were regular contributors to *The Learning Center Rag*, a student-run newspaper at our co-op. They made and sent many cards. They have submitted work to a couple of contests but have not been published yet.

Will develop editing skills.

This objective was primarily met through the research paper they wrote and rewrote. They also jointly wrote a composition for a Mother's Day contest that went through many drafts (shown in the portfolio).

Will improve sentence structure, mechanics, punctuation, and word choice as dictated by the purpose of the written composition or oral communications.

Objective met. The *Daily Grams* for third and fourth grade also provided exercises in these areas.

Will respond critically to the written work-in-progress of others.

Objective met through the writers group they participated in and by reviewing each other's work.

Will develop listening skills through regular reading aloud.

Objective met.

Will begin to develop their ability to respond critically to literature.

Objective met. We read nonfiction and historical fiction this year for information, but I also drew the boys' attention to the writer behind the work. We informally discussed plot, conflict, tone, character development, and theme. They have very perceptive comments about why they do or do not like a particular book.

Arithmetic

Will continue to recognize the importance and applications of mathematics and mathematical reasoning in daily life.

Objective met. We seize opportunities to solve problems in daily life mathematically whenever possible, for example, determining the best buy, dividing items evenly between four children, scheduling our day, etc.

Will study the lives of famous mathematicians and their contributions.

Not met.

Will continue to improve and expand computer literacy and applications.
Met. Boys learned to use the formatting and editing features of WordPerfect 5.1. They use the computer as a learning tool whenever I allow it.

Will review finding the sum or difference of three-digit and two-digit numbers when renaming is necessary.
Objective met.

Will master the multiplication tables through 9x9=81 and division tables through 81÷9=9.
Objective met.

Will begin to compute multiplication and division of two- and three-digit numbers by a single-digit number.
Objective met and exceeded.

Will continue to use calculators effectively.
Objective partially met. I intend to use some additional resources next year to expand their use of the calculator.

Will continue to develop multiple-step problem-solving strategies.
Objective met, primarily through the *Figure It Out* workbook we used. The boys did not like this when we began it last year, but now they are feeling quite successful with it and enjoy the program.

Will continue to practice estimation skills with all problems.
This is practiced in Saxon math and in *Figure It Out.*

Will be able to identify order and place value of numbers through 1,000,000 and explore those beyond.
Objective met.

Will name, compare, and problem-solve with basic fractions.
Objective met in Saxon and in making recipes. We typically double or even triple recipes.

Will use money to explore concept of decimal numbers such as tenths and hundredths.
Objective met.

Will continue exploration of elementary geometry (polygons, angles, and parallel and perpendicular lines).
Objective met.

Will work problems involving various standards of measurement (standard, metric, Celsius, Fahrenheit, etc.).
Objective met.

Will continue to gather information from graphs, maps, charts, etc., as well as translate information into these forms.
Objective met.

Will continue to discover symmetry and patterns in mathematics.
Objective met, though it is their younger sister who loves this aspect of math and routinely points out patterns to them.

Science and Health

Will practice proper care of own body through diet, exercise, rest, and good hygiene.
Objective met. Both Michael and Gabriel excel in this area. They eat a balanced diet, exercise daily, rest well, and practice healthy hygiene.

Will be introduced to human reproduction, birth, and growth.
Objective met.

Will continue to study colonial craftsmen and methods of manufacturing goods.
Objective met, primarily through visit to Valley Forge and reading Leonard Fisher's Colonial Craftsmen series aloud.

Will study the history of science and the lives of famous scientists, especially during colonial America.
Objective met. We mainly focused on colonial medicine because Michael had a great interest in that. We studied key doctors, the history of surgical methods, and the problems of caring for the wounded in times of war. Some of the scientists we covered include Benjamin Rush, Dr. Warren, Ben Franklin, Clara Barton, Florence Nightingale, George Washington Carver, Orville and Wilbur Wright, the Mayo Brothers, Charles Goodyear, and Louis Pasteur.

Will study a science unit of weather, make weather instruments, and conduct numerous experiments related to this.
Objective met. We studied this a good portion of the year. Michael reported to us frequently about his research for his science project.

Will study creationism and evolution.
Objective met. A Bible scholar conducted classes at the science camp we participated in, and Michael and Gabriel attended a presentation at the Hershey Evangelical Free Church. We read selections from a number of resources when we have questions in this area.

Will write a science research paper.
Objective met. Michael wrote about measuring weather and Gabriel about the growing stages of the peanut.

Will participate in a science fair.
Objective met.

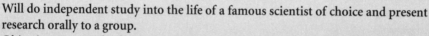

Will do independent study into the life of a famous scientist of choice and present research orally to a group.
Objective met. Michael reported on the Mayo Brothers and Gabriel on George Washington Carver.

History of the United States and Pennsylvania; Geography and Civics

Will continue to deepen understanding of God's design for the family.
Objective met through our discussions, primarily those following our regular Bible reading.

Will study colonial America, the American Revolution, and the formation of a new nation.
Objective met. This was our primary focus during the first semester. We read numerous books aloud and independently, and we listened to many tapes related to the topic. We also took field trips to Valley Forge and Philadelphia.

Will study geography within the context of colonial America.
Objective met. We used many maps during our studies. We also made our own maps.

Will study the history of types of government and the history of the political process in America.
Objective met.

Will study current events and the effect they have upon our nation, community, and personal lives.
Objective met. The boys both skim our daily newspaper (they devour the sports page) and listen to commentary on the radio. They read a bimonthly current-events paper. We discuss events a lot.

Will continue to learn about and practice community service.
Michael and Gabriel organized a youth group this year that raised money for Susquehanna Valley Pregnancy Center. They also helped to buy Thanksgiving turkeys for Bethesda Mission. We visited a nursing home. We value contributing to our community, and we discuss this value with them and strive to model it in our lives.

Our co-op also prepared care packages at Christmastime for Bethesda Mission and an orphanage in Romania.

Will study and appreciate people from different cultures in America and in the world.
Objective met. Michael and Gabriel have been exposed to the customs and foods of other cultures through a variety of ways. We've done formal studies and several special projects at the Learning Center; for example, we had a special presentation about Romania by a woman who lived there. We've studied our own Arabic and Pennsylvania Dutch backgrounds.

Will continue to take an interest in other people, to practice hospitality, and to improve social etiquette.
Objective met.

Physical Education

Will continue to value and demonstrate good sportsmanship.
Objective met. Several of their coaches have commented on Mike and Gabe's encouragement to other players. Kermit emphasizes this over athletic ability. And our main purpose in involving the boys in organized sports is to enjoy the social benefits and learn cooperation.

Will continue to enjoy and appreciate the benefits of team sports as well as personal fitness.
Michael and Gabriel exercise regularly. They worked toward the Presidential Fitness Challenge. Michael qualified for nationals, and Gabriel just missed (his "flexed arm hang" was a few seconds short). Michael and Gabriel were on soccer, wrestling, and baseball teams. They also are members at the community pool.

Will improve basic skills for soccer.
Objective met.

Will participate in an advanced swimming course.
Mike and Gabe passed the advanced beginners course.

Will improve wrestling skills and participate on a wrestling team.
Objective met.

Will improve strength, speed, and coordination.
Objective met.

Will participate in several track and field events.
Objective met. We participated in the homeschoolers track and field day at Messiah college. More than one hundred homeschooled students competed.

Will improve skills and knowledge of baseball.
Objective met. I even enjoy baseball now. We have a _Sports Illustrated_ video on baseball skills for kids, and that has helped a lot. Gabriel is doing well as a catcher for his team. Michael usually plays shortstop, but he is developing his pitching for next year. Both have been selected to play on the All Stars team this summer.

Safety Education

Will practice water safety.
Objective met.

Will practice bike safety.
Objective met.

Will demonstrate understanding of the dangers and prevention of fires.
Objective met. Attended a special presentation by the E-town Fire Department. We were interrupted by a fire alarm, and we had a real life demonstration on the value of preparedness.

Will demonstrate cooking safety.
Objective met. Michael and Gabriel enjoy cooking, and they made quite a number of recipes this year. At the beginning of the year we attended several 4-H cooking classes.

Will learn basic first aid.
Objective met. We held a special class at the Learning Center.

Music

Will continue to develop the ability to sing on pitch with good tone quality.
Objective met. My mother, a retired music teacher, gave the children some voice instruction over Christmas, and that helped a great deal. We sing a lot together, and the children sang with a children's choir several times this year.

Will continue to develop ability to hear and mimic rhythmic patterns.
Objective met.

Will continue to learn to follow a conductor's directions.
Objective met.

Will participate in regular group singing.
Objective met. Mike and Gabe love to sing.

Will recognize types of music (jazz, folk, classical, hymns, contemporary).
Partially met. Music is a big part of our family life, and we listen to a broad spectrum. They are beginning to recognize different styles.

Will study the lives of major composers, especially those who lived between 1492 and 1865, through their music and biographies.
Partially met. We've read a few biographies but have done nothing formal. They have been exposed to the works of the major composers through the tapes we listen to.

Will begin instruction in the piano. Formal lessons are desired if an appropriate and affordable teacher can be found.
Objective met. The boys studied with a talented music teacher this year and have done very well. They have progressed almost two levels. Plus, the opportunity to hear the other students (some of whom are quite advanced) sing and perform on piano at the recitals has exposed them to a diversity of styles.

Art

Will study the lives of famous painters, primarily during the period of 1492 through 1865, through their biographies and works.
Partially met. We read a few biographies and looked at a special exhibit of paintings from this era at the state museum. I also used several library books with reproductions in them from the colonial period.

Will experiment with a variety of media (clay, tempera, pottery, etc.).
Barely met. We did not get to several of the projects I had planned.

Will participate in a fine arts painting/drawing class.
Partially met. Mike and Gabe had a few lessons in the fall, but we just didn't have the time to continue. I did subscribe to *Spark!* magazine, and we did several lessons from this.

Will complete several craft projects of own choosing.
Objective met. Primary craft was the spinning, dying, and felting of wool. We also hand-dipped candles as well as made tin lanterns, an assemblage, and sand castings.

Will visit at least one art museum.
Visited the collection at the state museum.

Will participate in an art/music appreciation class.
Participated for two months during the fall semester.

Help with Objectives

Here are some sources of curriculum guidelines that are helpful in developing objectives. I refer to these often but view them merely as a checklist for ensuring I don't neglect an area Kermit and I think is worthwhile in achieving our targeted goals. My objectives for each child are still primarily based upon his or her needs, readiness, and interests.

Scope and Sequence

A scope and sequence is the order in which various skills and subtopics of the major subject areas (social studies, language arts, science, and mathematics) are presented to grades K–12. Your local school district should have one available to parents, or you can request a scope and sequence from publishers such as **Bob Jones University Press** or **Rod and Staff**. Another helpful publication is "Kindergarten Through Grade 12: A Typical Course of Study" available from **World Book, Inc.**

The state of Virginia has posted its standards of learning (SOL) for grades K–12 on the Internet. These are traditional academic goals, not loaded with political correctness. They also can provide a framework for planning your school year in each subject.

 http://www.pen.k12.va.us/go/Sols/home.shtml

Books with Curriculum Guides

I highly recommend E. D. Hirsch's Core Knowledge series, which now includes a book for every grade level, K–6, titled *What Your First Grader Needs to Know, What Your Second Grader Needs to Know,* and so forth (Bantam, 1991)*.

Also see . . .

Cultural Literacy: What Every American Needs to Know, E. D. Hirsch (Doubleday, 1987).*
This book is very helpful for high school.

And . . .

Teaching Children: A Curriculum Guide to What Children Need to Know at Every Level Through Sixth Grade, Diane Lopez (Crossway, 1988).*

Strategy #2: Weekly Planning

You aren't done yet. Planning is an ongoing discipline that allows you to maximize your time. Without it, you will waste time daily gathering resources, making decisions, and solving problems you didn't anticipate. Then you will feel frustrated and unsuccessful. Your children will sit around waiting for you to give direction, or more likely, they'll wander off. Carve two hours out of your schedule regularly to prepare for the coming school week.

Before my older children began managing their own time, I spent an afternoon every week at our local library working on our homeschool program. I used the time to anticipate problems and prepare for them, to gather books, and to script out my goals and schedule in my plan book.

Leaving the house was an essential part of being able to focus and get organized. And I deeply appreciated Kermit's commitment to seeing I had this time.

Remember: Time on task determines mastery of a skill or subject area. Plan so that your children can use their time wisely.

Your Schedule Will Be Uneven

When setting up your weekly schedule, don't shoot for even allotments of time across the board as they do in a traditional setting. This strategy does not help children achieve mastery in any area.

I look at the elementary years as one big chunk of time and the secondary years as another. Over the course of each I have goals I intend to meet, but within the context of each school year our program has strengths and weaknesses. As we take time to focus on certain subject areas, I will purposely neglect others. For example, we overdosed on American history four years—we love the field trips and the historical fiction that we can integrate into this subject area. Where was our program weaker as a result? Art and science. Then, last year, several classes in these areas were offered at Creative Home Educators' Support Services (CHESS) and the Learning Center homeschool co-op. I seized the opportunity to focus there and neglected history in order to do so.

Some families do science first semester and history second. We found science once a week, with at least two or more hours devoted to experiments and study, worked well for us. As a rule of thumb: *Skill areas* are mastered through practice. Handwriting, spelling, mathematics, reading, etc., should be on your daily schedule. But *content areas* such as literature, history, science, etc., are better learned through fewer sessions in larger chunks of time. These also require more setup time on your part; so doing that once a week or for one semester is often better time management.

Plan for Toddlers

The best-laid plans of homeschool moms can quickly be blown to smithereens by our little ones who have no commitment to all those objectives we've so carefully crafted. Don't forget to anticipate your younger children's needs as you script out your weekly schedule. See chapter 30 for suggestions for occupying and integrating your toddlers.

Strategy #3: Establish Policies and Procedures

My best household management tips come from the world of business. Where profit is the bottom line, efficiency is the key to maximum productivity. In my home, at the office, and at the co-op, I am a manager. I invest my time in developing organizational systems that allow everyone to know what his or her job is and how to do it without my constant oversight or direction. How does this translate into your home?

Make a Rut to Run In

Routines may get boring, but they still make things run smoothly. (If you can't take consistency, just cut a new rut periodically.)

What decisions do you currently make daily? Meals? Chores? School assignments? Who sits where in the car? (Are we the only family with this squabble?) Plan these out at least a week at a time, if not by the month.

During the school year, kids should have a set bedtime and rising time. You should, too. I begin losing control of my day the minute we sleep in. From there, maintain a loose routine for the day and week. Food is a pretty important motivator for my kids. I have minimum standards that must be reached before lunch and then before supper.

If I haven't lost control by sleeping in, I surely do when I answer the phone.

Just Say No!

Remember the anti-drug slogan from a few years back? I used to have it hanging on my phone. Not because I was tempted to substance abuse but because I was tempted to say yes to anything anyone asked of me. My goals for the day would quickly go by the wayside as I let the phone calls control my day.

Get an Answering Machine

I don't have enough internal discipline to say no to people, so my first strategy was to stop answering the phone. I didn't have the discipline to resist this either, so I bought an answering machine. But I still went running to hear who might be calling and frequently picked up.

My kids made me realize how intrusive they find the phone one summer while discussing ways to improve our next school year. Since then, I not only use an answering machine, but I've also turned all the phones in the house off so I don't even know when they ring. If someone wants to reach me, they have to send a fax or e-mail.

You probably have more self-control than that, but minimally, an answering machine will save you loads of time and prevent your day from slipping away from you with phone calls that turn into long conversations.

Strategy #4: Use Organizers

Pocket-Size

A personal organizer is an essential life-management tool. After reading Anne Ortlund's classic *Disciplines of the Beautiful Woman* (Word, 1977)*, I purchased an inexpensive three-ring binder that was small enough to fit into my purse. I divided the notebook with tabs that categorized my life: meals, husband, children, house, prayer, Bible study, calendar, and a daily "to do" list. Over the years, the divisions have changed a lot. (Kermit still hasn't recovered from the fact that his tab has been replaced.) But, the practice hasn't.

I've kept an organizer now for nearly twenty years. One homeschool student called it "my brain," and she is right. Without my organizer, I forget lots of commitments I've made and goals I've determined to reach. It's my peace of mind. Do intrusive thoughts often disrupt your concentration—usually during your quiet time? With my organizer beside me, I quickly jot them down and then forget them. Without it, I invest lots of time reminding myself over and over to remember to not forget to do whatever.

A few years ago, of course, the concept really caught on, and the market was flooded with trendy organizers for today's high-impact woman. My little black notebook looked pretty paltry next to them. I held a garage sale and squandered all the cash I earned on an updated deluxe model. But then I felt obligated to maintain all those sections—at least twenty of them. This became a major time commitment. Besides that, my new organizer was too big to fit in my purse. I kept forgetting to bring it with me. I started missing appointments because I was leaving "my brain" at home.

You guessed it. I sold my organizer at my next garage sale and purchased a little black notebook for $4.95 that fits in my purse. I'm functional again.

The essential premise is this: Use an organizer simple enough to take with you everywhere you go. Create a section for every area of your life that you currently need to manage. Include a monthly appointment calendar and a section for frequently used addresses. I've found an eighteen-month academic calendar is the best for my needs.

Every morning I make a list of what I need to do that day and record it in my organizer. I prioritize this and check things off as they are completed. It takes no more than ten minutes because it is an ingrained habit.

Central Calendar

Kermit and I were both good about maintaining our appointment books, but we started running into scheduling conflicts because we didn't know each other's commitments. And now my four kids all have outside commitments of their own. We keep a central calendar on the refrigerator and everyone keeps his or her appointments there as well.

It also helps my kids feel more in control of their lives. I'm a great one for planning things and not telling anyone else. As soon as I put up the new monthly calendar, my children hurry to see what's coming up and then to transfer that information to their own daily organizers.

Teacher's Plan Book

A teacher's plan book is the only other organizational tool I use regularly. Quite a few that are designed for homeschooling are on the market, but my favorite is **The Homeschool Journal***, published by <u>FERG N US Services</u>. It's the simplest, that's why, and the most easily adapted to different families' needs. Recently FERG N US released a plan book for students, and Katie, Mike, and Gabe now use this as their own daily logbook where they record their weekly academic goals.

Here are some other sources of good tips on organization and planning:

Disciplines of the Beautiful Woman, Anne Ortlund (Word, 1977).*

Is There Life After Housework? and other titles, Don Aslett (Writers Digest, 1992).

Once a Month Cooking, Mimi Wilson and Mary Lagerborg (Focus on the Family Publishing, 1993).

Confessions of an Organized Homemaker (contains a great chapter on "How to Organize Another Person!"), Deniece Schofield (Betterway Books, 1994).*

PART 4

Preventing Burnout

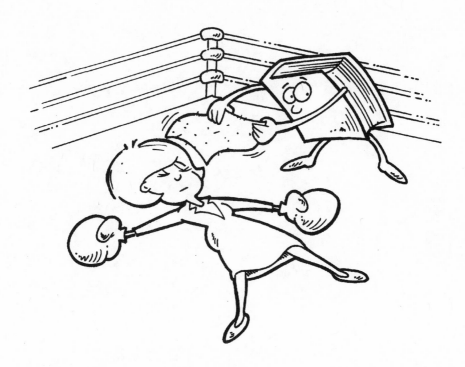

In This Section

- Burnout Buster #1: Raise an Independent Learner
- Burnout Buster #2: Raise Responsible Kids
- Burnout Buster #3: Fantastic Field Trips
- Burnout Buster #4: Share the Load
- Burnout Buster #5: Get Plugged In

15

Burnout Buster #1:
Raise an Independent Learner

• •

When it comes to the difference between surviving or thriving in homeschooling, raising an independent learner is the key. It's also in your child's best interest.

Kids learn best when they take responsibility for their learning.

Lessons from a Toddler

Think back to your children's early years. They were remarkably independent little learners, weren't they? They spent the entire day exploring and investigating on their own—especially what you didn't want them to! They didn't need you to motivate them or organize their exploration.

School Days

But look what happens when these highly motivated, independent learners are packed off to school at age five. We make them *dependent* upon the teacher for their learning. Now she decides what will be taught, what projects will be tackled, and what schedule will be followed.

By junior high, many of these energetic little grade school children have little motivation to initiate learning on their own, and the teachers have little discretion in selecting a curriculum that fits the needs and interests of each student.

Don't Repeat the Pattern

Unfortunately, we often repeat this same pattern in our home education programs. We wish our children would take more responsibility for their own learning, especially as they grow older. But we take our five-year-old independent learner and turn him into a dependent learner by following traditional teaching methods (refer back to the chart on page 75). And then we wish he would mysteriously turn back into a self-motivated student once again.

The solution? Don't make him a dependent learner in the first place. Here's how:

#1. *Give Him Control*

When the twins were nine and Katie was seven, I took steps to transfer responsibility for their learning from me to them. As is typical of my temperament, I make radical right turns in life, for which minor adjustments are then needed. The week I undertook to transfer this responsibility, I neglected to mention my plans to Kermit—integral to this story.

How Not to Start Out on the Right Foot

I met with each of my school-age kids separately for a Monday morning tutorial. Here I gave them a daily log in which they were to record the goals in each subject I wanted them to complete that week. It was up to them to manage their time as they chose.

I was surprised and offended when Mike asked, "What happens if we don't get done?"

Having not given any thought to this possibility, I hadn't considered any consequences. So I said the first thing that came to mind, "Well, you won't eat on Friday night till you are done."

"You can't do that," he replied. And the line was drawn in the sand.

Gabe and Katie liked this new idea, and they went happily along with it. But come Friday night, Mike had three long lessons of Saxon math uncompleted. I told him he could not have supper. Unfortunately, I was in the laundry room when Kermit arrived home from work, so Mike beat me to the door. Here he informed his father that I was forbidding him to have dinner just because he hadn't completed all his math that day. I heard Kermit say, "We'll see about this."

Hearing the tone in his voice, I knew I needed to talk fast. I asked Kermit to meet me in the bedroom for a private consultation and said, "Honey, I know I didn't tell you about this new plan I was using in school and I should have and I should have thought through the consequences more objectively, but I NEED TO WIN THIS ONE! If you don't back me, not only will Mike not think he has to get his schoolwork done, but everyone else will start revolting as well."

After reminding me (once again) to talk these major shifts in policy over with him ahead of time, he went downstairs and informed Mike he could not have dinner till the Saxon was done.

Mike is my most emotionally controlled child, or rather I thought he was. We just hadn't pushed the right button before. Apparently food is pretty high up on his list of basic needs. This kid sat in the family room trying to do all this math, wailing, while the rest of us tried to have a family dinner. Have you ever had one of those dinners at your house? Pretty soon I could see Katie's lower lip start to tremble, then Gabe's, and suddenly they were both sniveling in sympathy.

I was so relieved when Mike got his work done two hours later. I didn't even care if it was right; I made him a nice hot meal.

But, you know what? Come Monday morning Mike was the first one up and at work on his weekly assignments. And I've never had anyone not complete his or her goals since (with the exception of Kristen, whom we will talk about later, in the reluctant learner chapter).

I learned some other interesting things about my kids when we started this plan. They all chose to manage their time differently. Mike, probably because of this childhood trauma inflicted by his mother, would get up early and complete his assignments as quickly as possible with a goal to have Fridays free. Katie liked to do one subject a day—a week's worth of math on Monday, a week's worth of spelling the next, a week's worth of hand-writing the next, and so forth. I found this amusing, but it was her time and I wanted her to have control. Gabe, like his mother, works best under pressure. He ran a pretty light schedule on Mondays and Tuesdays. By Wednesday he'd show some signs of life, and Thursdays and Fridays were heavy-duty workdays with lots of accompanying groans—especially since Mike was in the backyard kicking the football.

How It Has Evolved

That was five years ago. The next thing I did was give Mike, Gabe, and Katie control of the curriculum. They began to determine what their weekly goals would be. At first I thought they might lower the standards and begin to underachieve. But actually, once they were in control of not only their time but also what they studied, they accomplished *more* than I would have expected.

I did have parameters. This is not a free-for-all. I required each of them always to be reading something, writing something, and researching something. They had to meet the requirements of the Pennsylvania law and show progress in every subject area; they couldn't just cut geography from the schedule. We did still meet regularly for reading aloud or group projects and activities I had arranged. And I've worked at building a vision in them for future opportunities, so they see the value of studying subjects that merely require discipline. (*"You want to grow up and play football for Penn State, don't you? You can't get in without at least two years of a foreign language." "Okay, Mom, you win; we'll sign up for French."*)

Joining Creative Home Educators' Support Services (CHESS) last year did change the complexion of our schedule once again. They are now getting assignments from their teachers and have given up a measure of control in their lives, which they don't necessarily like. The first year I made the mistake of signing them up for the courses I didn't want responsibility for at home. Because they never had any input into this decision, they complained a lot throughout the year about their classes. This year, I let them make all the choices. Mike and Gabe aren't entirely satisfied with their classes, so we're talking now about how they might want to choose differently next year. As much as possible, I want them to feel in control. I want them to see that it is their responsibility to learn, not my responsibility to teach. I want them to be setting their own future targets they want to hit and then taking responsibility for hitting them.

At this moment, Mike, Gabe, and Katie are fully responsible for their time and assignments. I help them when they ask. I hold them accountable where they need it. But they typically self-check and correct even their tests. I can trust them to do so, because they aren't doing this work to please me; they are doing it because they see their work as relevant to the goals they've set for themselves to achieve. They have ownership.

This strategy has also been God's provision for me. He could see the future. Right now Kristen needs a lot of one-on-one attention from me. If my older kids were likewise dependent, I would be overwhelmed with the responsibility.

#2. *Give Them Choice*

Allow your children to initiate projects and writings of their own choosing. We all have more motivation when it is our baby. Instead of relying on the assignments in your curriculum or topics in the composition book, give your children the guidelines and tools necessary, but let them choose what to make or write. Then you assist them in accomplishing their goals.

My ears perk up when one of my kids says, "Mom, you know what I'm really curious about? . . ." My next stop is the library to get a book or find a video to view. I want my kids to see that their participation really matters and that one reason we are home educating is so they can have a tailor-made education.

If your child is engaged in an intellectually stimulating activity such as staging a play, writing a letter, or building an invention, don't interrupt him for "school." Rather, use his expressed interest as a springboard for skills he needs to practice: Integrate handwriting with his letter writing or arithmetic with purchasing the materials for his invention. You don't want to stifle this independence; you will regret it later.

Let your children choose the books they read. If they get stuck in a genre, nudge them forward by requiring them to choose from a different category, such as Newbery Award winners or historical fiction. Be as broad in your requirements as you possibly can. Yes, require a science fair project, but let your child choose the area of interest. Allow your teens to participate in curriculum choices and courses of study. They should go to the fairs with you, attend workshops, and talk to vendors. If you give them choice, this will fuel their motivation.

#3. *Wait Till They Are Ready*

Do not start a subject of study or project until the child is ready to do the majority of the work. I've prematurely launched too many ventures that dissolved into my kids watching *me* paint the mural, organize the play, or make the recipe because I was too anxious and they weren't ready.

Kristen is taking an elementary French class at CHESS this year, and there is a lot of written work to complete. As one of the youngest members of the class, she just can't keep up. At first I let her dictate her answers to me, but as the work became more challenging even that didn't work. The day I found myself filling out her homework assignment while she was off playing somewhere else, I knew something was out of kilter. Kristen said she didn't want to drop the class because it was "cool" (the teacher uses a lot of French songs and audiotapes that Kristen enjoys); she just isn't ready for the amount of homework. Assured that she still had a strong interest here, I arranged with her teacher for Kristen just to "audit" the class. We'll save the written work for another year.

#4. *Let Them Do It*

Before you do anything for your child, ask yourself, "Could she do this herself?" If so, let her. For example, in states like ours parents must present a portfolio of their child's work at the end of the year for review. I know homeschool moms who spend days, even weeks, pulling these together. The kids should have responsibility for doing this. I've also seen moms, myself included, spend two hours making up a chapter test that takes a kid fifteen minutes to complete. When you see that kind of imbalance of time, you know you are creating a dependent learner. This is why I favor essay tests. It takes me fifteen minutes to design one. It takes the students forty minutes to an hour to complete it. The responsibility for demonstrating the learning is on the student, not the teacher. That's where it should be.

I taught *The Hawk That Dare Not Hunt By Day* by Scott O'Dell (Bob Jones University Press, 1975) a few years back to a literature group at the Learning Center homeschool co-op. This is a wonderful novel based upon the life of William Tyndale. When I began preparing for the class, I realized there were a lot of historical references in the book that I knew nothing about—Sir Thomas More, the Holy Roman Empire, Charles V, the black plague. I had never studied this period of English history, and I doubted most of the students had either. I realized we would need some background information before we could begin.

I was actually at the library, a pile of world history atlases spread before me, when I realized I was going about this all wrong. It was going to take me hours to prepare a forty-minute lecture on the historical backdrop for the novel. I put away the books, went home, created a list of all the historical references in the book, and passed out the list to the kids the first day of class. I told them we needed some background information before we could begin and I wanted each of them to choose a topic, research it, and report back to the class next time so we might better understand the storyline.

It went great. The kids got an education, and so did I, but with a lot shorter time commitment from me.

At the Learning Center, the kids write, cast, and direct our spring program. They run the lights, and they design and print the program. The moms comprise the stage crew. Our productions are not at all as polished as some of the teacher-run performances I've been in. But in which scenario do kids learn the most? You should see how thrilled the students are to have more than a hundred people attend an evening performance of a play they have written and produced. And while not polished, the opportunity motivates the kids to create the very best production they can.

#5. *Focus on the Skills for Independent Learning*

Most moms I talk to with a serious case of burnout are running a very demanding program and are burdened by the fear they will skip something.

Aghhh! I've Skipped Something!

Let's address this universal fear right now. You ARE going to skip something. Further, it will probably be something REALLY IMPORTANT. We're in the midst of an information explosion. Much of what we learn today will be irrelevant tomorrow. How will you figure out what will be applicable? You won't. Here's the solution:

Instead of wasting one sleepless moment worrying about "skipping something," all you have to do is teach your child HOW TO LEARN. If you'll just focus on the latter, then when your kid *inevitably* finds himself in a situation where he doesn't know how to do something, he is not rendered immobile . . . stunted for life . . . no longer employable . . . ultimately a panhandler on the corner . . . . a sign around his neck begging "Please feed me. My mother homeschooled me." . . . Your worse fear realized.

Reality Check

WAIT A MINUTE! Get a grip. You forget—your child has the skills of an independent learner! He heads right down to the local public library or jumps on the Internet, does a computer search, requests some books, and figures it out for himself—thus averting the major disaster in his life that you had envisioned.

How do you cultivate these skills? By building a program that allows plenty of opportunity for research that culminates in a paper or project that reflects what your child has discovered. Your job is to provide him with the tools necessary to complete his investigation: technology, books, trips to the library, time spent with an expert, etc., and then aid him in his investigation.

I often tell my kids, "It's your job to learn, not my job to teach." I am a facilitator, a mentor, a fellow lifelong learner, a guidance counselor, a coach—and only occasionally the teacher.

That Base of Knowledge Is Fluid

Our knowledge base is rapidly changing anyway. *Peak Learning* by Ronald Gross (Tarcher, 1991) points out that the average half-life for the information acquired in medical school (that is, the point at which 50 percent of the knowledge is outdated) is fifteen years. Do you want to choose a physician sixteen years past graduation who doesn't have the skills or motivation to learn independently?

It's the same with our children. To compete in the twenty-first century they need the skills of a lifelong learner. That's at the core of my husband's job. Most of his time is spent just trying to keep up with the latest technology so his company can stay current. He has frequently commented that it isn't that there aren't good jobs available; it's that there aren't any qualified applicants. His company is looking for folks who know how to learn.

Research skills

Teach your child to use the library. You can foster this by skipping the workbooks and assigning lots of research papers and research projects. This will give your kids a meaningful reason for familiarizing themselves with the atlases, indices, periodicals, and other reference tools there.

Teach your child to use the Internet. We'll talk specifically about this in chapter 28, but don't let your children leave school without equipping them to retrieve information quickly here as well.

Find an Expert

Reading isn't the only way a lifelong learner acquires knowledge. He is also a people-person who seizes the opportunity to draw upon the expertise and experience of the people he meets. My husband's the one who models this for our family. He has met the most fascinating folks on airplanes, in shopping malls, and at the beach just because he never hesitates to strike up a conversation. This is a very simple but effective method for gaining a firsthand education. I've read about China and Australia, but none of the books gave me the same perspective as the information Kermit gleaned from a young Chinese immigrant and an Australian businessman he sat next to on a plane.

We attended a Civil War reenactment at Gettysburg one summer. The battle was impressive, but our real education came from walking through the grounds and talking to the men and women encamped there. They put a human face to all the facts we had read about.

Along with your children, track down the resource people in your community with interesting hobbies or knowledge. Invite them to share with your group, or visit them as a family. At least for our children, I've noted how much they remember from the conversations we've had with the interesting people we have met.

Study Skills

When working with your child one-on-one, show him how to tutor himself. In helping Gabe get a grip on his algebra, I focused on explaining to him how *I prepare* to tutor him each day:

- ✔ I read the unit summary at the end so I know what the big picture is for every chapter.
- ✔ I reference unfamiliar terms in the index so I can understand each sentence.
- ✔ I replace the variables with real numbers and work several samples so I understand the equation.
- ✔ If I don't understand how they got the solution in the text, I don't assume it is a misprint (his strategy); I look at the part of the equation I didn't get and ask myself, *Now, where did they get that "4" from?* I look back over each step, *working backward* till I see where the sign changed from negative to positive, breaking it apart until I can see the solution.

These are study habits researchers have found successful students use. Your kids can find more study skill tips in these books:

The Everything Study Book, Steven Frank (Adams Publishing, 1996).*

What Smart Students Know, Adam Robinson (Crown Publishing, 1993).*

#6. *Take Time for Questions*

In Howard and Susan Richman's book, *The Three R's at Home*, Howard cites research that found 96 percent of the questions generated in a classroom are asked by the teacher. Another study showed teachers, on average, wait three seconds for a student response to a question. Is it a surprise, then, that another study found children typically stop asking questions in school by age seven? Compare that with the kinds of questions your four-year-old fires off to you all day, every day.

If we want our kids to take responsibility for their education and to stay actively engaged in the learning process, then we must value and solicit their questions.

If you don't know the answer, show them their questions are important by writing them down and then researching the answer together the next time you are at the library. Before you take a field trip, ask your children to have questions in mind to ask of the tour guide. Consciously model this strategy for them by asking questions yourself.

#7. *Use Discovery Learning*

Every professional educator worth his or her salt will tell you discovery learning is the best way for children to learn. Unfortunately, the classroom teacher does not have the time to allow each child to discover underlying principles and solutions on his own. But homeschoolers do!

Let your child uncover the connections himself. Bite your tongue when you think the answer to a problem should be obvious. A thought-provoking question is a better strategy.

Quite a few years ago I bought a software program called the *Alpine Tram Ride* that requires deductive reasoning to solve problems. Given the choice of twenty-five different animals, the player must determine which animals in which order are hidden behind the four tram doors. After the boys had gone to bed one night, I loaded the game and started playing it myself. Within a few minutes, I was able to strategically eliminate enough of the choices to solve the puzzle. So the next day I loaded the game for Mike and Gabe, and they began to play. Standing behind them, I felt my frustration begin to build as time after time they continued to randomly choose. I was just about ready to jump in and show them how to figure this game out when I thought, *Wait a minute, Deb. You paid good money for this program to teach them just that. Let them figure it out!* But I found watching excruciating. I had to leave the room and close the door behind me in order to restrain myself.

By the end of the week, my sons were calling me to come into the computer room. "Hey, Mom, let us show you how to play this game. See, we know it isn't the giraffe in this car; then it must be the lion in number three and. . . . Here, you try and we'll help you figure it out."

They were so proud of themselves for discovering the underlying strategies on their own. I can still remember the expression on their faces. And I almost shortchanged them. I almost missed an excellent opportunity to build confidence in their ability to learn.

When we give kids the time they need to figure things out, they take ownership in their learning. They feel successful. They feel confident. And then they are motivated to learn more.

Cultivate Confidence

In life, we invest time where we feel successful. We minimize our time in the areas where we don't. That's why your children's view of themselves as learners must be carefully cultivated. Give your children the time they need. Don't make them feel they are not figuring things out quickly enough. Make a big "to-do" about the special moments of discovery they have made on their own. You can then build upon this confidence in other areas that are more difficult for them to grasp.

#8. *Let the Child Teach*

In any given learning situation, it is the teacher who learns the most. Think about it. Those of us who are homeschooling know more about the Civil War, parts of speech, and converting decimals to fractions than we ever did in school because we've had responsibility for explaining this to our kids. So turn the tables and let your child do the teaching.

Managing a Passel of Kids

How do you teach multiples? Give your older kids some of the responsibility for teaching the younger ones. Katie has been helping Kristen learn to read. When Katie competed in **Math Olympiad**, Mike (the previous winner) showed her how to solve the problems. A teen in our group taught a chess class at the Learning Center. A friend's seventh-grade daughter taught health one year to her elementary-age brothers. The speeches and reports I assign for my kids and co-op students are for the purpose of educating the whole group, not for earning a grade from the teacher in the back of the room.

This is how moms who know nothing about a subject guide their children through a course of study in that area. The kids do the research, and mom gets an education along with everyone else in the family. My kids are thrilled when they know something I don't know (and this began occurring many moons ago). They enjoy telling me about their independent studies. My job is to be an interested audience.

#9. *Model Independent Learning Yourself*

Remember, "*a student is not above his teacher*" (Matt. 10:24). We need to model what we want our children to become. Our own attitude toward learning is the key influence on our children's view of education. If our children see us reading, investigating, and discussing new areas of inquiry as adults, they will come to value lifelong learning, too.

I credit my own parents with transferring a love for learning to me. I grew up in a home where everyone was always reading. (And where everyone always had an opinion as well!) When I stayed with my grandmother every summer, she was always reading—well into the middle of the night at times. When I catch the glow of a flashlight under blankets at night, I'm really thrilled my kids can't stand to put down that book. When Gabe told me he couldn't wait for football practice to be over so he could finish *Blood of Heaven* (Zondervan, 1996), a terrific read by our friend Bill Myers, I knew his priorities in life were still in place—and our family tradition had been passed on.

This chart is an over-simplification of our program, but it is representative of the skeleton upon which our daily activities hang.

Academic Achievement		
<u>Necessary skills</u>	<u>Key activities</u>	<u>Success demonstrated by</u>
Research skills	writing	papers
Communication skills	reading	projects
Technical skills	research	performances

16

Burnout Buster #2: Raise Responsible Kids

. . . .

I believe in moms at home, but not so everyone else can leave their dirty laundry on the floor, dishes in the sink, or projects on the table. We are there to train our children into responsible adults, not to burn out prematurely trying to homeschool and keep the house clean simultaneously. We must learn to do what any good manager does: delegate.

The Fine Art of Delegation

Quite a few years ago our church showed Benny and Sheree Phillips's parenting video series (<u>PDI Publications</u>). They are really the ones who inspired me to pass on household duties to my kids at an early age. They did an excellent job of laying out a step-by-step procedure for *gradually* transferring responsibilities onto the children. However, all I saw were eight-year-olds *and younger* who could do laundry, vacuum, clean the bathrooms, and make simple meals. I thought, *Hot diggity-dog, the Allied troops have landed! It's liberation day at my house!*

Mike and Gabe were five, Katie was three, and Kristen was just out of the oven. But I ran home, skipped all the procedures, and announced, "Effective immediately, household chores have been transferred to my subordinates! All right, troops, fall out!"

The boys immediately pushed a kitchen chair up to the washer and set the dials while perched on top of the machine. They were learning estimating skills in mathematics, so they practiced this with the laundry detergent, erring heavily on the more-than-enough side. I didn't know it at the time because I was upstairs hooking up the vacuum cleaner for Katie, who was trying hard not to cry. A week later, with all the whites now tinted pink, the vacuum clogged, and dirty dishes stacked in the cupboard, I reviewed my notes. Seems I had skipped basic training.

Here's the sequence of events to walk your children through in every area as you transfer responsibility for a chore, duty, or school assignment:

1. You show him how to do it.
2. You do it with him.
3. You watch him do it.
4. He does it alone.
5. He decides when it needs to be done.

Depending upon the degree of complexity involved, this procedure can take anywhere from one to six weeks, or more. Kermit began training Mike and Gabe to mow the lawn when they were nine. By age ten, they were skilled enough to do it alone, but he still required that he be home while they were mowing. This is no longer necessary. They not only have taken full responsibility for maintaining the yard, but neighbors, who've watched them work, have hired them as well.

I've shared this model with quite a few moms who just didn't feel they had the time to train their children completely. It was easier to keep doing it themselves or to transfer responsibility quickly and then get frustrated when things were not done well. I know sticking to this training model is a time commitment—but you will reap a terrific reward down the line. My kids are very self-reliant now, and they do their jobs WELL. There are household duties I never have to think about because one of my children has full responsibility for it.

We perpetuate our children's immaturity by continuing to take on tasks that should be their responsibility. If they are old enough to get their toys out of the toy box, they are old enough to put them back in. If they are old enough to sleep in a bed, they are old enough to pull up their covers neatly when they get out. If they are old enough to get food out of the refrigerator, they are old enough to clean up the table and put everything away.

You can facilitate this by simplifying your maintenance. That's why I've bought lots of sealable plastic tubs and labeled them. Everything has an assigned place. At one point I even had my pantry alphabetized (I'm not quite so compulsive anymore).

Invest time in determining the simplest procedure for completing a task, and then train your kids in that. (I've been a changed woman since we listened to *Cheaper by the Dozen* on audiotape [Bantam Audio]—listen yourself and find out why.)

It Builds Their Esteem

The Phillipses were so right when they said giving our kids responsibility would raise their self-esteem and make them feel like team members of the family. Sure, I met with resistance at first because we had not had this philosophy in place from the beginning. We had to retrain attitudes and sometimes apply biblical discipline. But I've found, not only in my own children but across the board with all the kids I've taught, that when they know you are not backing down and are committed to consistency, they will comply and even reach the point where they are obedient from the heart.

What about Compensation?

Well, yes, the pay helps, too.

We've never been convinced of the merits of an allowance. So kids learn to manage money—but money they haven't earned? To me, that isn't a practical preparation for real life.

We do pay our children wages, though. When they were younger, this was often not money. I had a compensation package in place that involved complicated charts, stickers, and graduated prizes—sort of an Amway-type model. "Clean this bathroom and win a trip to your vacation dreamland—Dairy Queen!" It's a lot simpler now that they understand the value of cash. Some chores have a set payment no matter who completes them, but Mike and Gabe typically get an hourly wage because they do so much around the house, including meal preparation, babysitting, laundry, major cleaning, and yardwork. This is a lot simpler to keep track of. Mike, Gabe, and Katie also receive an hourly wage for working regularly at the Home School Resource Center.

And they are learning to manage their money. We expect the boys and Katie to help pay for clothing, shoes, sports equipment, and other nonessential items. Our biggest area of emphasis is their savings account. And as a result of a stock market class they have been involved with, Mike and Gabe are now investing their earnings. They are better money managers than I was at twenty-five. (I'm sure Kermit will be editing that last sentence to say than I am now.)

Raising them to be responsible has been a key factor in preventing my burnout, but it's really for a greater reason than that. Raising them to be responsible is in their best interest. Having this character strength in an age of irresponsibility will make them successful in family life and the future job market.

Here are some other good resources for instilling responsibility in your children:

Raising Self-Reliant Children in a Self-Indulgent World, H. Stephen Glenn and Jane Nelson, Ed. D. (Prima, 1988).

The Choreganizer, Jennifer Steward (**Noble Publishing**). An excellent tool for assigning chores to your non-reading children.

The 21 Rules of This House, Gregg and Josh Harris (**Noble Publishing**).

Burnout Buster #3: Fantastic Field Trips

My kids get grumpy when our homeschool life gets too routine and too bookish. Their bad attitudes generally result in my discouragement. I don't like investing all this time and receiving nothing but complaints in return.

A quick home remedy for this situation is to do something fun. For us that means either reading a book aloud together or taking a field trip someplace new. Both of these remedies reinvigorate me because I want to do the things that make homeschooling unique—the flexibility, the hands-on learning, the firsthand experiences all motivate me. Recreating an environment that can just as easily be produced in a traditional classroom does nothing for my sense of achievement. It feels like wasted time.

Fantastic Field Trips

Many of our best moments in homeschooling have come during the field trips we've taken. The awe and enthusiasm on my kids' faces is a real burnout remedy for me.

But there's a right way and a wrong way to do this field trip thing. I've had quite a few that were so ill-planned and harried I collapsed in sheer exhaustion once I got back home. Here's a hassle-free guide to field trips that teach and refresh:

#1. Make Them an Extension of Subjects You've Already Studied at Home

The more background knowledge kids bring to the experience, the more they will get out of the trip. And vice versa. The more field trips you take, the more your kids will get out of their studies at home.

167

Prior to our visit to Williamsburg, Virginia, some years ago, we read books on colonial life, Patrick Henry, and the Revolutionary War events that occurred there. We also checked out a video of the site from the library. Without this, my children would have been quickly bored by the endless tour of houses. Instead, the kids excitedly ran toward the places they recognized and asked detailed questions of our tour guides. Mike impressed the senior citizens in our group (who had at first questioned why he wasn't in school) by being the only one to correctly identify for our guide the House of Burgesses and its purpose. "He's homeschooled," I whispered loudly.

I've found that site staff will go out of their way for kids who show any degree of interest and understanding. I took my children and several of their friends to visit a National Oceanic and Atmospheric Administration (NOAA) weather station after a unit of study. The meteorologists were surprised by the degree of background knowledge the kids had and waxed quite eloquent once they realized they had an engaged audience. They even entrusted the kids with some of the high-tech instruments—something they emphatically said they never did. When our co-op went sailing on the Chesapeake Bay through the Living Classroom Foundation, the crew kept us out an hour longer at no charge, just because the kids were asking such intelligent questions and the crew was having a ball with them.

#2. Bring Closure

Wrap up the trip with more reading and a family discussion. Ask your children what they enjoyed most, what was not as they had expected, and what they would like to know more about, etc., just to ensure that you wring all the learning potential possible out of the trip. (By golly, if we're going to spend the money, I'm going to make sure they never forget a thing!)

#3. Call Ahead and Ask for a Guide

My father originally taught history. Growing up I saw lots of monuments, museums, and historic sites that glazed my eyes over. After I married Kermit, I found out too late he was a history buff as well. Once again I found myself staring solemnly at battlefields and monuments, wondering how anyone found this interesting. Then another couple invited us to visit Gettysburg with a retired tour guide. I reluctantly tagged along.

We spent hours staring solemnly once again at battlefields and monuments, but this time I couldn't tear myself away. What a difference a guide makes! I was fascinated as this elderly gentleman recounted story after story of the human drama that occurred there. I even bought a stack of books so I could read more. Since then, I've loved going to Gettysburg. And I also arrange for a guide when possible for any field trip.

#4. Go in the Off Season

Visiting attractions during the off season may mean reduced staff or fewer artisans and interpreters at historic sites, but it still gives your kids greater access to the displays. We typically find the guides and curators will spend a lot more time talking with us when the site isn't busy.

I call ahead to find out the best time to come. And I always ask if any school groups are scheduled for the same time. We've had quite a few trips turn into useless ventures when a busload of poorly supervised schoolchildren, thrilled to be released from confinement, came tearing through the place. (And while we are on it, the benefit these kids get from racing through a hands-on museum pushing every button and pulling every lever is minimal. This doesn't make me a candidate for Mom of the Year with my children, but I require them to read the display before touching anything.)

We've found September to be a good time to still find the site at full staff but the number of school groups and summer tourists greatly reduced. You'll often find reduced-rate days during the fall lull. We visited the Carnegie Science Center in Pittsburgh (one of the top hands-on science museums in the United States) on a Monday in September for half price and were among a handful of visitors in the building. My kids spent hours at their favorite areas with no pressure from anyone to hurry up and move on.

#5. Keep the Tour Group Small

Field trips are a fun thing to do with one other family, but beyond that you start losing educational value. First, you have the administrative hassle. Once we planned to spend the day in our state capitol with friends, and we got separated at the beginning in a crowded parking garage. More time was spent riding up and down the elevators looking for each other while trying to keep the kids we had found corralled than at the sites.

If I wanted to further embarrass myself, I could tell you about the twenty-family field trip I tried to execute with everyone following me sixty miles to a rural site I had never been to before. (Did I mention that I lack a sense of direction?) Have you ever tried to have twelve vans—the vehicle of choice for homeschoolers—turn around on a farm lane? (By the end of the day we were getting pretty good at that maneuver.) I also learned some physics from an irritated mom. If the lead van does the speed limit (or, perhaps, just a tad more than the speed limit), everyone following must drive progressively faster. This mom, who was last, was going 80 miles per hour. Now, isn't that interesting?

The point? Keep the group small. Besides the administrative hassle, too many kids distract each other and they compete for time on the displays. When a site requires a minimum group size for a tour or class, I pass out maps to the families involved, then it's every van for himself. Otherwise we keep our field trips to eight kids or less.

#6. Make Sure It Is Age-Level Appropriate

I've taken my kids on one too many nature hikes or dragged them prematurely to sites that presented material too abstract or technical for their understanding. We visited the Corning Glass Center in Corning, New York, for our very first day of kindergarten back in 1988. I was enthralled by the research going on there in fiber optics and loved the antique glass collection, but my kids had more fun at the MacDonald's playland at lunch. It's still one of my favorite sites ever, but we need to go back now that my children are old enough to understand the technology discussed and maybe appreciate the artistry involved in spinning glass.

#7. Keep It Short

Most kids max out after two hours, even in a visually stimulating environment. If you've paid a hefty admissions price, it's easy to assume you'll be there dawn to dusk to get your money's worth, but most kids just can't focus that long—especially without food.

One strategy for museums and sites within your driving range is to purchase an annual membership and then visit the site several times during the year, each time focusing on a new aspect. I'm heading back to all the science museums and battlefields we visited in Pennsylvania several years ago because Kristen just wasn't old enough to benefit. And now my older children are ready to think through these experiences on a higher level as well.

#8. Give Guidance

A tour guide is not always possible, but you can provide this service with just a bit of preparation beforehand. I learned this from Kermit, a devoted reader of AAA travel guides. He always has interesting tidbits of information to pass along as we travel through cities.

You can extend your children's attention span by doing some reading beforehand and then giving direction to their learning while at the site. Point out areas of interest and guide them through the displays.

What Constitutes a Field Trip?

Any site can be turned into a "field experience" if you take the time to provide background knowledge, direct children's attention while at the site, and engage the staff in conversation. Help young children understand how their community works by visiting the fire department, city hall, the post office, and local businesses.

Visit engineering projects, medical centers, and research facilities to help your teens see abstractions in math and science concretely applied to life.

Wherever possible, I look for a way to give my kids field experience. When possible, I also spend time talking with the site staff about the background experiences the kids I am bringing have and suggest what we are most hoping to get out of our trip. This bit of investment goes a long way to better tailor the visit to the needs and interests of our group.

Bring the Field Trip to You

Sometimes it's easier to bring the field experience to your homeschool support group than to take the kids there. We've done this by inviting hobbyists and senior citizens with areas of interest and expertise to visit us. In many cases, these folks are delighted to be asked to share. My favorite has to be Pastor Holman, who was close to ninety when we met him. He is an amateur geologist, but all the science centers we've visited cannot compare with the samples he has collected from his missionary trips around the world. And he was very generous in allowing the children to handle his treasures.

Where to Find Field Trip Ideas

These resources can help you find fantastic field trip sites in your area:

The Yellow Pages Guide to Educational Field Trips, edited by Gregg Harris (<u>Noble Publishing</u>, 1995).

Travel magazines geared toward senior citizens have lots of interesting suggestions. Raid your parents' magazine rack, as I have.

AAA membership has been well worth the investment for our family. It offers lots of free maps and pamphlets we can study even if we don't go. And road service is indispensable for a mom alone on a trip with a carload of kids.

18

Burnout Buster #4: Share the Load

. . . .

Homeschooling shouldn't mean you are your children's only teacher. It just means you get to control who their teachers are: virtual or real.

Self-Instructional Resources

Mix into each child's program some resources that can be used independently. **GeoSafari***, software, video courses, and audiotapes are engaging and complete. If you need one-on-one instructional time with a child, have his or her siblings involved with a meaningful activity like these—not busywork.

Educational Television, an Oxymoron?

When my kids were younger, we even included one television show a day in their program. Some of the shows we've followed have been *Reading Rainbow, 3-2-1 Contact,* and *Square One.* This gave me a welcomed midmorning break. It's always best to watch television with your children, but I must admit I often used this time to get lunch started or catch up on the laundry.

You can also take a load off your shoulders by becoming a member of the class and watching documentaries together. Take notes and hold follow-up discussions. Being avid sports fans, our family enjoyed Ken Burns's documentary on baseball a few years ago. We extended the experience into a history unit with our follow-up reading and discussions. This year the girls, Kermit, and I watched Burns's new documentary, *The West,* and marveled at how history has changed since we were kids. (I think the cowboys and Indians stereotypes we were raised with *needed* some revision.)

One year I used the PBS show *Newton's Apple* several times a week for science. Checking these out on video from the library enabled us to stop the program when someone had a question or to rewatch certain parts to reinforce our understanding.

We lived without a television for several years at the beginning of our marriage. When we finally bought one we quite virtuously watched only PBS and Penn State football games— until last year. This can be viewed as an erosion of our values, depending upon which member of our marriage you talk to, but we now have (gasp!) cable. There is some excellent educational broadcasting available. I enjoy it (especially A & E's *Pride and Prejudice*). And my sons make sure they watch their quota a month to ensure that they can still keep ESPN—which is always on the verge of being unplugged. Educational television can ease the burden, if you can restrain yourself from otherwise wasting time in front of the tube—which we do find to be an issue.

Cooperative Activities

Pool your teaching talents with other homeschool families. In most regions of the country you'll find support groups already in place that offer enrichment classes, special activities, or field trips that are open to new homeschool families. If not, then start your own. (Remember, initiative is one of the successful homeschool ingredients.)

The Benefits to Kids

We have involved ourselves in a wide array of cooperative groups. My teaching style probably explains why we do more than our share. But I also believe strongly in the benefits of cooperative experiences. Your children will be challenged to grow in character and intellect as they interact with kids and adults who look at the material differently.

Besides that, becoming a team player is an important skill in the workplace and the church. Without this training, it is easy to produce selfish children who don't understand that God has given them gifts and talents to use for the mutual benefit of the body of Christ, not their own glory or self-gratification. (This is one reason I am hot on organized sports—with the right coach, kids learn that pooling their strengths and talents together for a common goal often results in success while an every-man-for-himself attitude and self-seeking glory invariably leads to defeat.)

One year we participated in the <u>Science-by-Mail</u> program. It is very worthwhile educationally. But the greatest area of growth came in my sons' character, not their science knowledge. I had two groups of kids working to solve the science challenge simultaneously. My guys were in a group with three of their friends—all terrific kids with a lot of intelligence and a lot of leadership. That was the problem. They were all used to being in charge and had very underdeveloped skills in teamwork. While Katie and her friends effortlessly organized themselves and set out to attack the science problem, I spent the majority of my time helping this group of guys come to a consensus of opinion.

When all was said and done, though, I was glad that I had put my sons in a situation where these character issues could come to the surface and I could help them deal with them while they were still under our supervision.

The Benefits for Mom

But let's focus on the benefits for Mom: You get to take entire subjects off your plate and put them onto someone else's. Art, physical education, science, chorus, weaving, sign language, health, and many more subjects have all been taught to my kids by other people who have far more knowledge and passion for the subject than I could ever muster.

You'll have adult conversation on a regular basis, too. I do love all the online opportunities my kids are just beginning to access, but it will never replace our cooperative learning. I need the encouragement and stimulation that comes from weekly interaction with other homeschooling families.

How to Organize Your Co-op for Success

Our homeschool co-op, the Learning Center, is now ten years old. It includes twenty-nine families and more than one hundred kids, including twenty-three teens. We meet twice a month on Fridays from 9:00 A.M. to 12:30 P.M. During that time we run three class periods. The younger grades take an art, gym, and unit study class; the older students sign up for a number of electives at the beginning of each semester.

I've advised a number of co-op leaders over the years and have unfortunately seen several groups disband, always for similar reasons. Here are some essential ingredients that will position your co-op for long-term survival and prevent leadership burnout.

#1. Clear, Recognized Leadership

The Learning Center was originally comprised of four families at my church. As other church members began homeschooling, they were invited to join. For a few years the co-op was small enough to be run by consensus. With a growth in membership, though, we inevitably hit an issue on which we could not agree. In our case it was balancing the needs of older students against those of younger ones. For other groups it has been such things as contemporary Christian music, the qualifications for membership, or managing children.

The issues are often different, but the problem is the same: How do you decide what to do when a consensus cannot be reached? In our case, we asked our pastors for help. For a number of reasons, they elected to disband the Learning Center as a ministry of our church and then turned the future of the co-op over to me, making it clear to all members that I was free to discontinue it completely or to reinvent it as I willed.

After some prayerful consideration, I held a meeting in which I presented the direction and organization of the co-op and invited previous members to rejoin. Everyone did. It may have seemed a little silly on the surface, but it was a crucial foundation to put in place.

Since then I have continued to lead the Learning Center. Last year I appointed two other women to serve on a leadership team with me. I realized I was often arbitrary in my decision-making (my big clue: people were mad at me). Adding others with complementing gifts and talents has formalized the process but resulted in more thoughtful and equitable decisions, which keeps members happier—or at least spreads the dissatisfaction around a bit more.

Input is solicited regularly from members through summer meetings and semester evaluation forms. I hold open discussions on important issues and strive to reach a consensus wherever possible. Where it's not, I take time to explain thoroughly the rationale for the direction we choose.

#2. A Commonly Held Vision

Every prospective member of the Learning Center receives a membership packet that clearly defines the targets we are aiming to hit. By now, you know how important I think a personal vision is. I also believe a common vision is the essential ingredient that holds any organization together, be it the family, the church, a nonprofit ministry, or a homeschool support group. People who aren't working toward the same goal cannot labor together. We can be friends, we can fellowship, but we can't pool our talents and build something successfully. A copy of our membership packet is provided in the appendix of the Resource Guide as a model to work from.

This packet also includes the qualifications and responsibilities of membership, the teaching philosophy we hold to, the types of classes we offer, and expected standards of children's behavior. When a family signs our membership contract, they should have a pretty good idea what they are getting involved with and be ready to contribute to that end.

#3. Shared Responsibility

From past experience, I knew I would burn out if I didn't delegate responsibilities among others. The Learning Center works because every mom is contributing her share to the pot. Moms teach or help two out of the three scheduled classes. Exceptions are granted for extenuating circumstances—a new baby, for instance—but we try to keep these to a minimum. There are other duties, too, that are divvied up as evenly as possible. I have an administrator who doesn't help with any classes at all but contributes more than her share of time by handling all the scheduling, the newsletter, and the arrangements with the church.

Don't accept anyone into membership who is not in a position to contribute to the workload (even our moms with extenuating circumstances find ways to help out). Stay small and only grow as you have interested families who come ready to contribute their gifts and talents. If you feel torn between this position and ministering to new or weaker families, then start a support group as well. But—and this is from a lot of experience— don't try to provide meaningful cooperative experiences for your kids and run a support group for needy families under the same umbrella; it is a conflicting vision and will not work.

#4.   Deal with Offenses Biblically and Quickly

Every ministry or organization I know of that has failed did so because of personal conflicts that arose and went unresolved. It's our adversary's most potent tactic.

Besides adding members with a common vision, add only those who understand how to handle personal conflicts and are committed to dealing with them appropriately.

I've delegated so much of my leadership responsibility at this point in the Learning Center that I now view dealing with relational rifts as my primary responsibility. Our co-op is providing some fantastic experiences for our children, and the friendships among the women are a crucial factor in their long-term survival in homeschooling. I know that personal conflict is the one area that could do it all in quickly. I keep this at the forefront with our members. If you are offended and cannot extend grace in the situation, then you must go to the person directly—_not after discussing it with several other people_. If you cannot resolve the situation, then you must involve me. Our goal is to keep the conflict as small as possible. That's why dealing quickly is essential. I've learned the hard way that things don't go away with time; they fester, get bigger, and ultimately pollute others.

The Benefits Are Worth It

You may be thinking that organizing a learning co-op sounds like more work than it is worth. Anything that lasts—your homeschool, your co-op, your Christian service—does so because the foundations are secure. And laying those foundations requires time. But once they are in place, things can run smoothly for a long, long time. A shoddy foundation requires continuous shoring up.

It is so worth it! The friendships we have through the Learning Center are a most valued possession. And many of our best opportunities have been only possible in this context.

19

Burnout Buster #5: Get Plugged In

Building a support team is the final strategy to keep burnout at bay. As I mentioned before, the more multilayered this is, the more quickly you will overcome moments of discouragement. So here's how to find the homeschool community locally, nationally, and virtually:

Locally

Use the Resource Guide to locate the homeschool organizations in your state. These folks will have information on support groups in your area. Evangelical churches, the public library, Christian bookstores, and your school district may also have a contact for local groups. Make sure you go to any conventions or seminars that are scheduled as well. These often have a new homeschoolers workshop track and will get you pointed in the right direction.

In most areas, you will find that a number of groups have been organized. Some of these may limit their membership. Don't be discouraged by this. Getting plugged in may take some time. Here are some tips for finding and joining the group that best suits your family.

What Kind of Group Are You Looking For?

You're looking for families with a faith and an educational philosophy that complement yours and with kids that you want your children to be influenced by. This is one of my favorite advantages of homeschooling. From their earliest years, my children have been surrounded by older kids I want them to emulate: kids who are not ashamed of their faith, kids who respect their parents, kids who aren't caught up in the latest fashion or jockeying

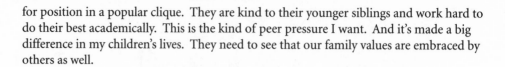

for position in a popular clique. They are kind to their younger siblings and work hard to do their best academically. This is the kind of peer pressure I want. And it's made a big difference in my children's lives. They need to see that our family values are embraced by others as well.

What Kind of Person Are Support Groups Looking For?

They are also looking for folks with a faith and an educational philosophy that are similar to theirs and with kids they want their children to be influenced by.

But more importantly, they are praying for folks who will come to give, not get.

 One reason I am writing this book is to give the harried local support group leader a tool to hand to the myriad of new homeschoolers who are calling her daily asking for her help. Homeschool moms are nurturers to a fault. With the burgeoning of the movement, most support group leaders I've met around the country are on the verge of collapse. They are struggling to meet their families' needs plus help out all the newbies in their locale.

Many needy families are trying out homeschooling as a last-ditch effort to salvage their family life or to get their kids through school. In one state, school officials are actually encouraging families with incorrigible kids to try homeschooling. Along with their expulsion notice is the phone number for the local homeschool leader. These poor women feel obligated to try to salvage the situation but invariably end up overwhelmed by the needs of the family. All of our families have blemishes, some a lot more than others. That doesn't disqualify us from homeschooling—but assuming others should take responsibility for our needs does.

Come with Your Sleeves Rolled Up

When you find a group you'd like to join, approach the leadership with an offer to help out. Certainly, you are looking for support and advice. I'm still looking for support and advice from the ladies in my support system. The balance is being sensitive to their other responsibilities and looking for opportunities to lighten their burdens, too, where you are able.

Watching children, preparing a meal for the freezer, doing a mailing, organizing a field trip—thoughtful gestures like these go far beyond the practicality of the service. If you bring a servant's heart to the homeschool community, a lot of special opportunities and friendships are going to open up, not only for you, but for your kids as well.

Nationally

There are a number of organizations, magazines, and newsletters that will keep you abreast of national trends and opportunities. In the Resource Guide you will find the addresses and phone numbers for those listed in this chapter as well as several others.

Here are the key contacts to keep you tied in with the homeschool network:

Home School Legal Defense Association

HSLDA has engineered much of the legal freedom homeschoolers now enjoy in all states. Its premier team of lawyers tirelessly presents a compelling defense for homeschooling families to legislators, school administrators, and media. Membership dues of one hundred dollars per year (less if you register under a recognized support group) will give you free legal aid should the need arise.

The HSLDA newsletter, _The Home School Court Report,_ which covers legal news around the country, is included with membership or can be subscribed to for fifteen dollars a year. HSLDA offers many other helpful resources as well.

Bob Jones University Press

The folks at Bob Jones University won my heart a long time ago. Despite the perceived threat homeschooling can be to the Christian school movement, BJU was one of the first to lend its wholehearted support and respect to homeschooling families. While other Christian publishers tried to set up requirements that pressed home-educating parents into their Christian-school mold, BJU adapted itself to the trend. It now holds a convention for home educators on its campus regularly and publishes the _Homeschool Helper_ newsletter for users of its products.

Practical Homeschooling

This is my favorite national magazine. Editors Bill and Mary Pride embody the pioneer spirit of the movement. They can be counted on to create and report on the latest innovations and opportunities available to homeschoolers. Articles representing a broad spectrum of educational philosophies are regularly featured as well as lots of product reviews and recommendations.

Teaching Home

The Teaching Home is the granddaddy of Christian homeschooling magazines. Each issue focuses on one theme such as teaching writing, special-needs children, homeschooling teens, etc., and back issues are available. Information on conventions and seminars around the country is given, plus newsletter inserts from participating states. _The Teaching Home_ is liberally sprinkled with spiritual encouragement as well.

Homeschooling Today

This is the magazine for lovers of unit studies and literature-based learning. An energetic and creative bunch of people are publishing _Homeschooling Today_ as well as creating products for the homeschool market that support this philosophy of education. A special

feature is a full-color reproduction of an art masterpiece in every issue with study notes by
David Quine of the <u>Cornerstone Curriculum Project</u>.

Virtually

A wealth of information and support is now available via the Internet and online services.
To get you started, here's a sampling of Web sites with lots of links to other sites of interest.
These include state and regional support group listings as well as event schedules and legal
information.

Homeschool World
http://www.home-school.com

Learn At Home
http://www.learnathome.com

Christian Interactive Network's Homeschool Forum
http://www.gocin.com/homeschool/

Online Friendships

If you can't find support locally, you and your kids can make connections here. It is easy to
strike up and maintain online friendships. It just takes minutes each morning to download your e-mail and type out a quick response. Plus you'll now have input from
homeschoolers all over the country. This will broaden your perspective and uncover lots
of new resources, ideas, and opportunities you may not be aware of locally.

But don't forget to train your children in discretion. They should not give away personal
information to strangers. Anything posted in a folder or on a bulletin board can be read by
anyone. E-mail cannot.

America Online

This online service (800-827-6364) is now offering unlimited access to the Internet and its
own sites for $19.95 per month. America Online runs homeschool-related bulletin boards
under Learning & Cultures/Educators' Network/Families Education/Home Schooling
Forum. My favorite area, though, is maintained by *Practical Homeschooling*. You can reach
this by selecting "Go To" then "Keyword." Then type in PHS. There you will find scores of
folder topics from state and regional information and subject area guides to advice for
teaching toddlers through teens.

Homeschool PC

To keep up on the latest virtual sites and sources available, subscribe to _Homeschool PC_ (800-346-6322), another venture by Bill and Mary Pride. This bimonthly magazine has all the cutting-edge places and opportunities awaiting you on the Net.

Well, the foundation's been laid. The framework's been constructed. It's now time to get down to the brass tacks. It's 8:00 A.M. Monday morning. The kids are seated 'round the table, wild with anticipation (at least on Day 1). _What in the world are you going to teach? When? And how?????????_

PART 5

What to Teach—When and How

In This Section

- ❦ Real Teachers Play Ball
- ❦ Subject-by-Subject Guidelines

20

Real Teachers Play Ball

· ·

This is an "amateur field guide" to teaching the core school subjects, and it comes more from experience, observation, and self-education than from my formal training.

In case you want to likewise be self-educating, here's how I've acquired my opinions of what I teach and how I do it:

#1. I Read Research and Professional Journals

I do my homework—but I don't just run head-long with what I find there. I've got some filters in place: I recognize that, first, I don't need to figure out how "most" children learn best; I need to figure out how *my* kid learns best. Even though 80 percent of the tested children learned successfully with a particular method, my kids could be in the other 20 percent. And second, the world view held by the folks behind the research may not be compatible with mine. Biases exist in the purest of studies.

But I still find a lot to think about in my reading. And it gives me the appropriate lingo to sling around when I talk with school officials. Here are some sources I regularly scan (most of these can be found at a university or city library):

Educational Leadership, published by the Association for Supervision and Curriculum Development, focuses on the latest innovations in education. Many applicable ideas for homeschool setting. Academic in tone.
> http://www.ascd.org

Learning Magazine focuses on creative teaching tips for elementary classrooms. Great ideas and resource suggestions. Easy reading.

The Reading Teacher focuses solely on the teaching of reading. Academic research is included, but you'll also find a lot of good book titles buried in these articles.

Phi Delta Kappan, journal of the professional fraternity of education. Not for the faint-hearted. Academic and policy centered. More targeted to school administrators, but you'll find an occasional article of interest to those in the trenches.

Heinemann Publishers
361 Hanover Street
Portsmouth, NH 03810
800-541-2086

Heinemann is a publisher of many helpful books for teachers based on the latest research and innovations in education.

#2. I Ask Myself, "What Skills in This Area Are Necessary in Adult Life?"

This might sound like a dumb idea, but I ask people with jobs in the field what skills they use, and then I make those the targets I try to hit in that subject area. *(Duh!)*

I was foolish enough to pose this question in an undergraduate course one time: "Exactly how might we teach transformational grammar in a high school English class, Professor Albert?"

"FOOL, YOU WOULD NEVER CAST THESE PEARLS BEFORE SWINE. TRANSFORMA-TIONAL GRAMMAR IS ONLY FOR THE ELITE!" He didn't exactly say it that way, but that's my "transformation" of what he did say, and in a deconstructionist's world, it's my word against his. Transformational grammar is, if you are interested (keeping in mind I was in a junior fog at the time), the psychoanalysis of the abusive childhoods of sentences. *Lie down here, Mr. Verb, while we write reams of paper on your deeply embedded intended meaning.*

But I digress . . .

#3. I Observe Kids

I've been teaching kids since 1977. From the classroom to Sunday school to the cooperative classes for homeschoolers, I've worked with kids of all ages in most subject areas. I pay attention to what works and what doesn't. When are they motivated? When are they bored? When did they get it? When were they confused? I'm more interested in figuring out how kids tick than in making them fit into my presupposed model.

I recommend that parents trust their "field experience" more than anything else, and maybe someday researchers will be interested in knowing what homeschool parents have figured out. (Actually there *is* a study posing this very question that's going on at Penn State as we speak.)

If you're with me, then, here's what I've observed and concluded:

Lessons from the Ball Field

> *Stand and Deliver,* a movie about teacher Jaime Escalante, is one worth seeing. Though others viewed the Latino students of Garfield Senior High as disadvantaged and limited in ability, his faith in them and his inspired teaching resulted in record numbers of students passing the grueling advanced placement calculus test.
>
> When Dr. Dobson asked Escalante to what he attributed his success in the classroom, he simply replied, "I'm just the coach."

Besides a long-held fascination with how children learn, I've always been interested in how to teach well. I enjoy reading about master teachers, admiring deeply Jamie Escalante, Marva Collins, and Guy Doud, but I found the most powerful model for the classroom in the least-expected place: the ball field.

What peaked my interest was the many active-spontaneous learners I recognized on my sons' baseball teams—and the fact that they were often the better players. Why were these kids intensely focused here and excelling, when I knew they were distracted and failing in school? And why did other players, like Mike and Gabe, invest significant time and energy—without prodding—into their athletic success? Why not the same commitment to their academic studies as well?

Certainly our culture's preoccupation with sports and hero worship of athletes are factors. If we'd likewise admire scholars and feature them every seven minutes on TV commercials, we'd see a marked improvement in kids' school performance. But I think there is a lot more to it than that—kids also give themselves wholeheartedly to athletic competitions that have not captured the public imagination and have no national heroes. My daughters play field hockey, not an event to pack a stadium by any stretch of the imagination. But those girls are working just as hard as their male counterparts who dream of the big leagues.

I'm convinced sports is a powerful model for the classroom. The teacher's the coach; the kids are the players. Our job is to prepare our teams through practice and drill to play regularly scheduled games where the rewards are worth the work.

How do you translate that into academic endeavors?

It means the work you have your kids engaged in during school is *purposeful and immediate,* not irrelevant and distant. When the kids ask, "When will we ever have to use this?" the answer should be "tomorrow."

Instead the kids hear, "Okay, kids, we will be studying algebra this year because a few of you will use it at your future job ten years from now. We will be studying French because it is a prerequisite for college admissions." And we wonder why they aren't motivated?

Now try this scenario: "Listen up kids, our MathCounts team needs to get ready for the competition in two months. We will compete against hundreds of students in the area at a local college and get our pictures in the paper if we win, plus trophies and prizes. Now let's drill on simplifying polynomials, and then we'll do a lightning round solving for x in less than ten seconds."

Or, "Katie, let's work on French words related to school so you can explain to your French-speaking pen-pal on the Internet what it is like being home-educated. We better practice conjugating the verbs 'to learn' and 'to study' so she won't tease you about your grammar."

In which scenario do you picture kids energized and motivated to complete their assignments?

What do you do while they're having all this fun? Coach—*from the sidelines.* Applaud their success, stretch their achievement, and *look for a field to play on* (i.e., find an authentic application of the skills they are learning).

Then get out of the way. Let the kids do the stuff. We adults have a very bad habit of seizing the learning opportunities away from children—"Here, Johnny, you don't want to do it that way. Let me show you the best way to build that bridge from toothpicks," or, "Okay, kids, we moms have organized a spring program. We'll be assigning you each a part." Who learns the most, the children above or the kid who figures out the best way to build a bridge by repeatedly experimenting and improving his design? Or how about the kids who actually write, direct, and cast the spring program?

 A speaker once asked a group of teachers at a conference I attended, "Are you 'the Sage on the Stage' or 'the Guide on the Side'?" I wanted to be the latter, but that was hard to pull off with a classroom of thirty-two students. Lecturing was the only way to cover all the ground I was required to cover in forty minutes. But not so at home.

Mary, here's how you do this; now you try. Okay, try that again. All right, let's put all the skills we've been practicing together and play the game: Write a short story for our family newspaper. We want the next issue to be ready for our Christmas mailing.

PLAY BALL!

Learn computer skills by creating a family homepage.

Learn economics by participating in <u>**SMG Stock Market Competition**</u> or starting a family business.

Learn civics by getting involved in a local campaign.

Learn science by setting up a backyard habitat or joining a conservation troop or an amateur astronomy club.

Learn geography by orienteering.

Learn to write by sending a letter to the editor.

As you review the chapters in this section and plan activities for your children in the core subject areas, always think in terms of *playing the game*. What skills do we need to practice for real life? What material do we need to cover that will enable my kids to complete this composition or project for this scheduled event?

If you find yourself fumbling around for an answer to the question, *"Why do we need to know this, Mom?"* it's time to rethink your approach.

Subject-by-Subject Guidelines

Your Framework

Make the overarching framework for your program this:

During the elementary years your goal is *breadth*. Give your kids broad exposure to all subject areas through reading, field trips, and opportunities. The purpose is to bring to the surface their areas of talents and interests. This is so you can begin to discern God's calling upon each of their lives.

Then, during the high school years, your goal should be *depth*. Let your kids invest significantly more time in those areas that are identified gifts and interests and less in those that seem unrelated to their future calling.

I don't believe God is going to tell us specifically that Mike is called to be an aerospace engineer—but I do have faith to believe He intends to reveal the areas of focus we should have during the high school years in order to maximize our time.

The traditional system does not allow for in-depth study and mastery, but kids are ready for this by the time they reach high school. Already, Mike allocates more time to mathematics than to the humanities. Along with a strong interest indicator, his test scores consistently indicate high aptitude in math. Katie believes God has called her to be a writer. While not shutting any other doors, we allow her to invest considerable time in this area and minimize her work elsewhere as she seeks to cultivate and discern God's intentions for this talent. (Gabe still has the broad-based interests typical of the conceptual-global learner. His greatest talent is providing a steady stream of color commentary during sporting events. How this skill will be used to further the kingdom is yet unclear.)

About This Section

After I determine what targets in each subject area I am preparing my children to hit in adult life, I work backward to determine the steps we need to get there.

This section is designed to help you do just that.

To keep things simple, I've broken down each area into three stages:

>   primary (preschool–second grade)
>   elementary (third–sixth)
>   secondary (junior high and up)

Children are going to progress through these stages at faster or slower rates, but in most cases this is the sequence of events they will follow as they move from readiness to mastery of a skill or content area.

I've suggested resources I and many other homeschoolers have found helpful. And—just a reminder—resources that are especially recommended are set in bold type. Take a look at these, but don't skip the guidelines in Part 2 before investing in the materials you believe best suited to the unique needs of your child. For a complete list and reviews of resources available to the homeschool market, check out these helpful guides:

The Big Book of Home Learning, volumes 1–3, Mary Pride (Crossway, 1996).*

Christian Home Educators' Curriculum Manual, Cathy Duffy (**Home Run Enterprises**, 1997). Elementary and secondary guides available.*

Reading

Where Are We Headed?

"Leaders are readers," Kermit commented in conversation shortly after we'd met. I thought, *Now here's a man with possibilities,* as I calculated my next move. Though not yet open to home education, I did know I would be miserable married to someone who was not self-educating or who held no vision for making an impact in his sphere of influence.

Seventeen years later, we're set on producing these same ambitions in our children as well, and reading is the prerequisite. If our kids do not read fluently, they will be limited in their spiritual growth, career choices, and social influence. It's another reason homeschooling is so attractive to us: In our program our children have all the time they want to read. There isn't any irrelevant busywork to compete with that time.

Reading is also the key to preventing homeschool burnout. Once you have an independent reader, you're one short step away from having an independent learner.

How Do We Get There?

Forests have been leveled churning out books and dissertations on how to teach children to read. Sometimes called "The Great Debate," it rivals only evolution and creationism in the emotions it stirs (and just edges out the PC versus Mac wars). The two opposing camps are those who advocate intensive phonics instruction and those who recommend a "whole-language" approach. Vocal Christians come down squarely in the phonics camp, elevating it almost to the level of Scripture.

Whole-language in its purest form advocates the use of real books (not "reader" textbooks) in the classroom and involving children in authentic purposes for reading and writing, for example, publishing a school newspaper, writing to a favorite author. It deemphasizes phonics and spelling instruction, instead believing children will acquire these skills intuitively in the course of their more holistic (and meaningful) language experiences.

Phonics is, of course, an essential tool for teaching children to *sound out* words, but it does not teach children to *comprehend* or to *construct* meaning—both things a child must do before he or she is *reading*.

Unfortunately, whole-language has unleashed parental concerns more by the misapplication of its tenets than by the foundational principles of the movement. The politically correct crowd will seize whatever educational reform is currently in vogue to foist their propaganda on schoolchildren.

I find I get myself in a lot less trouble if I say I advocate a "literature-based program" with a strong phonics base. How's that for straddling the fence? A lover of good books, I could never bear to hand my children a basal reader or boil the art of reading down to intensive phonics drills.

 If you'd like to learn more in this area, *Beginning to Read* by Marilyn Jager Adams (Bradford Books, 1990), is the major work that supports the position that the best reading programs combine phonics instruction with the use of real books and contextual reading.

Now, Back to Where You Live

But let's take this discussion down to ground zero. You have a child who needs to learn to read, and you haven't a clue where to begin. I didn't either. I was taught to read in a wacky, experimental program that made every word in our readers look like the pronunciation key in the dictionary. It was short-lived, to say the least, but may be the reason I am a poor speller.

Nevertheless, having emerged battle-worn but victorious from potty-training my children, I figured I could muster the faith to teach them to read. I read lots and lots of books on the subject—convinced by "experts" this was *one* task that *did* take a rocket scientist.

When I no longer knew which end was up, I had a thought: *You know, they said childbirth was very complicated, and it was pretty simple; they said parenting was complicated, and that's pretty simple, too. Complex reading theories must be just another setup to keep those "experts" employed.*

So I boiled all the theories down to three components that previous generations would have called plain old common sense:

✔ Kids need to be able to sound out words and understand their meaning.

✔ Kids need to be given books they want to read.

✔ Kids need to be taught by someone who loves to read.

That's the three-part program: basic phonics instruction, books kids are interested in reading, and parents who love to read. Sooner or later you'll produce a reader every time. Even if your child has a legitimate learning disability, any professionally designed program will feature one-on-one instruction using kid-engaging materials.

What to Do When in Reading

Primary Years:

Reading readiness includes letter and number recognition, being able to make consonant sounds, and having an ear for rhyme. Why rhyme? Readers ultimately decode new words by associating them with words they already know. A child meets the word "grouse" for the first time and realizes it looks similar to "house." A proficient reader will decode it by rhyming it, not attacking every letter individually. Dr. Seuss is the best author for encouraging a child to read by rhyming.

Reading readiness also includes lots of background knowledge. Research has shown that children who come to school with a breadth of experiences—they've traveled, attended plays and musical performances, visited historic sites and museums, and met a variety of people, etc.,—learn to read more quickly than children with limited exposure outside their home or community.

What is the connection? We think in pictures and construct meaning from the words we read through the images formed in our minds. If your child has visited a log cabin or a museum featuring artifacts from pioneer life, she will be able to imagine *and understand* more readily the stories Laura Ingalls Wilder writes about in her Little House series.

If you've never been around computers or used technology, a computer manual is difficult reading. Pick that same manual up after hacking around with your new system for a while, and a lot more of it will make sense. Give your child the same immersion into the world he'll be reading about.

Strategies:

❧ Read lots of poetry, nursery rhymes, and lyrical stories. Beatrice Potter and E. B. White are premier examples of writers for young children who use language beautifully.

❧ Run your finger under the words as you read aloud to teach left to right reading.

- Read aloud daily to your child from a wide, wide variety of genres: fairy tales, biographies, science series, realistic stories, Bible stories, etc.

- Seize every opportunity to expose your young children to the wider world in which we live. Explain what they are seeing.

- Play word games.

- Use magnetic letters or other concrete models to teach letter recognition and sounds. They're hard to find, but a set of lowercase letters is very useful. Use these to approximate the way words will look in print.

Elementary Years:

As soon as your child shows an interest in reading, begin phonics instruction. If he is young, move at his pace, stopping when he loses interest or shows frustration.

Discontinue phonics instruction as soon as your child is independently reading chapter books (for example, books such as *Boxcar Children* or *Childhood of Famous Americans*) and move into higher reading levels roughly every six months. If you stop formal phonics and your child levels off before reaching a fifth-grade reading level (see *Sign of the Beaver* by Elizabeth George Speare or *Caddie Woodlawn* by Carol Ryrie Brink as samples), then return to phonics instruction until he is progressing in his independent reading once again.

To continue plodding through a phonics program when your child has obviously "gotten it" actually discourages kids from reading. I've known several children who "unlocked the code" without any phonics instruction and read independently before kindergarten. In those rare cases you can give God the glory and just skip formal phonics instruction—they've figured it out intuitively. The children I know who did this continue to be voracious readers.

Katie, Mike, and Gabe needed six weeks of phonics instruction to take off independently. I didn't get much beyond beginning consonant blends (*br, sh, pl*, etc.) before they had wings. I returned briefly to practice syllabication with Mike when he got stuck (he'd decode the beginning and guess at the rest), but that was it for the others. Kristen, on the other hand, has needed a much longer time of phonics instruction running concurrently with her independent reading to help her break into higher levels.

A mother of identical twin girls told me one daughter learned to read almost solely with a whole-language approach while the other needed an intensive phonics course. The components are the same: real books plus a phonics base in a unique mix for each kid.

Strategies:

- Even within phonics instruction there are divergent camps. One teaches blending words left to right: "Bat" is taught as *ba - t*. Other words in that grouping would include "bag," "back," "ban." The other teaches word families: "bat" is taught as part of the "at" word family, with other members being "cat," "rat," "fat," etc. I prefer the second approach because it is based upon rhyming, the ultimate way we decode unknown words.

🐾 Reading is a skill. That means consistency yields fruit. Daily, progressive practice with the phonics-based program of your choice is the key to success.

Recommendations:

Sing, Spell, Read and Write (International Learning Systems).* It is multisensory, systematic, and not phonics overload—just thirty-six steps to independent reading. The readers are so well written, my kids have mistaken them for real stories and enjoyed them. It's a more expensive choice, $175, but with video instruction, audiotapes, workbooks, and games, there's little preparation on your part. However, there isn't much reinforcement work in SSR&W for the child who cannot master the lesson the first time around. That does leave the parent creating additional exercises.

At Last! A Reading Method for EVERY CHILD! by Mary Pecci (**Pecci Educational Publishers**, 1988)* and **Super Seatwork*** workbooks. This is the perfect fit for the budget-conscious homeschooler who doesn't mind pulling together the activities and games if she is just told what to make. It's also an excellent program for the child having difficulty reading, and it's what I am now using to give Kristen the reinforcement work lacking in SSR&W. Mary Pecci recommends the Life series readers published by Review & Herald (301-791-7000, ext. 2329).

Alphaphonics. This is the low-budget program but must be supplemented with books to read, games, and daily lessons designed by you. Alphaphonics, unlike SSR&W, does use the word families approach, and I have used it to supplement SSR&W. It is now available on CD-ROM as well (**4:20 Communications**).

> Steer clear of expensive reading programs that promise miracles in a short amount of time. Find out what program a homeschooler you respect has used, and bet on that before being seduced by multimillion-dollar advertising campaigns through the media.

Independent Reading

Concurrent with phonics instruction, hand your child books of interest that gently move him or her to higher and higher levels of independent reading.

Here is a sample list of books in ascending order of difficulty you might use to systematically move your child to full independence:

Bright and Early books by Dr. Seuss (Random House).

I Can Read It All By Myself Beginner Books by Dr. Seuss (Random House), such as:
> *Hop on Pop* (1963).
> *Green Eggs and Ham* (1960).
> *The Cat in the Hat* (1957).
> *The Cat in the Hat Came Back* (1958).

Ready! . . . Set! . . . Read! and *Ready! . . . Set! . . . Read!—and Laugh,* compiled by Joanne Cole and Stephanie Calmenson (Doubleday, 1995).

Step into Reading series, levels 1–4 (Random House)*, such as:
> *Happy Birthday, Thomas,* W. Awdry (1990).
> *The Bravest Dog Ever: The True Story of Balto,* Natalie Standiford (1989).

An **"I Can Read" Book** series, levels 1–3 (Harper and Row)*, such as:
> *Little Bear,* Else Holmelund Minarik (1957).
> *Frog and Toad Together,* Arnold Lobel (1972).
> *The Golly Sisters Go West,* Betsy Byars (1985).

Rookie Biographies (Children's Press)*, such as:
> *Ben Franklin: A Man with Many Jobs,* Carole Greene (1988).
> *Jackie Robinson, Baseball's First Black Major Leaguer,* Carole Greene (1990).

The **Boxcar Children** series by Gertrude Chandler (Warner).

The **Childhood of Famous Americans** series, especially those by Augusta Stevenson (MacMillan).*

Accidental Detectives series by Sigmund Brouwer (Victor).*

American Girl series (Pleasant Company).*

Once Upon America series (Penguin).*

Little House books by Laura Ingalls Wilder (Harper and Row).*

Scholastic biographies

Incredible Worlds of Wally McDoogle series by Bill Myers (Word).*

Caddie Woodlawn, Carol Ryrie Brink (Macmillan, 1935).*

Shiloh, Joyce Reynolds Naylor (Atheneum, 1991).*

Sign of the Beaver, Elizabeth George Speare (Houghton Mifflin, 1983).*

Sustained Silent Reading

We have also maintained for years what the schools call SSR—sustained, silent reading. This started out as ten minutes after lunch each day. Everyone, including Mom, must read—or take a nap if you are a nonreader (adds some extra motivation). When we first started, the twins would ask every few minutes if time was up yet. But I stuck to it, and pretty soon they were looking forward to their daily independent reading time. The ten minutes quickly stretched twenty and then to an hour. And now it is very common for Katie, Mike, and Gabe to spend two hours or more a day reading good books for pleasure. It's a habit.

Vary the Genre

Once your child is reading independently, don't let him get stuck in a particular genre such as Hardy Boys mysteries or Janette Oke romances. One mom I know prevented this by requiring her children to read one historical fiction, one Newbery Award winner, one Christian biography, one nonfiction, and one book for pleasure per month.

This Is a No-No!

Whatever you do, don't stoop to the level of R. L. Stine or the Babysitter Club series, thinking this will produce an intelligent reader. This formula fiction is as addictive as television and does nothing to whet kids' appetites for better fare—rather, it dulls their senses.

More strategies and suggested titles for growing a reader can be found in these highly recommended sources:

The Three R's at Home, Howard and Susan Richman (<u>**Pennsylvania Homeschoolers**</u>, 1988).*
The Three R's: Grades K–3, Ruth Beechick (Educational Services).*
Honey for a Child's Heart, Gladys Hunt (Zondervan, 1989).*

If you have an American Online account, you'll find wonderful suggestions and discussion in the *Practical Homeschooling* Library under Children's Literature. (Keyword: PHS).

Secondary:

The key here is *breadth.* Kids should now be gaining the majority of their knowledge in the content areas from their own independent reading. They should be reading widely across the disciplines to expand their comprehension and vocabulary. Many parents do not realize that the vocabulary sections of standardized tests and the college boards are drawn from science and social studies as well as literature. If your children are only reading fiction, they will not acquire the vocabulary skills they need.

A helpful tool is *Reading Lists for College-Bound Students** (Arco, 1990). This will prepare them for the SATs as well as the kind of reading they'll be expected to handle in college.

For pleasure reading, the very best suggestions can be found in *Read for Your Life** by Gladys Hunt (Zondervan, 1992). Written from a Christian perspective, the book is a guide to engaging and well-written fiction suitable for teens. Hunt includes a synopsis of the author's world view to help you with discernment.

Reading Critically

Teach your children to read critically and analyze literature by using the <u>**Progeny Press**</u> Bible-based Study Guides* or <u>**Common Sense Press's**</u> Reading Discovery Program*.

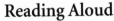

Reading Aloud

Final strategy for your independent readers: Read aloud. So many of us abandon this practice once our children have taken off on their own. But sharing a book is a wonderful way to bind your family together as well as to involve your kids in the better literature they might otherwise avoid. The McKeown and Gamon families gather once a week to read scenes from Shakespeare aloud. They've held Shakespeare parties and attended performances together. Their kids love the bard because he's been introduced in the context of family fun.

We're very fond of books on tape. Long-distance trips are eagerly anticipated if I take the time to order a special book to listen to on the way. And it's just the ticket for drawing a child into a book he might otherwise avoid.

Sources of books on tape:

Blackstone Audio
P. O. Box 969
Ashland, OR 97520
800-729-2665

Books-on-Tape
P. O. Box 7900
Newport Beach, CA 92658
800-626-3333

Listening Library
One Park Avenue
Old Greenwich, CT 06870-1727
800-243-4504

Recorded Books, Inc.
270 Skipjack Road
Prince Frederick, MD 20678
800-638-1304

Language Arts

Perhaps a definition is in order: *language arts* is the collective term used for composition, speech, reading or literature, spelling, vocabulary, and grammar.

Where Are We Headed?

If you recall the targets Kermit and I have set for our children's education, then it will come as no surprise that we have heavy doses of language arts in our program. Here is where our children hone the communication skills they need to confidently and competently articulate in speech and writing their faith and ideas.

My goal is that our kids will not shrink back from opportunities to influence but will pursue them. I know for them to do this they need to be confident in this area. So I make sure we practice and play the game often.

Influential leadership aside, communication skills are also at the top of nearly every job qualification list I checked into. The information age is for the articulate. Don't send your kids out the door without a strong grasp of the English language.

How Do We Get There?

Employ two key strategies in your program:

1. **Kids need to write and speak *regularly* for an audience, K–12.** The operative words are *regularly* and *for an audience*. Before your kids hit the self-conscious stage of adolescence, they must be confident speaking in front of a group and sharing their written work with others. This happens through regular practice.

2. **Language arts skills should be practiced in the context in which they are used.** That means we don't subdivide these six areas into separate subjects, i.e., spelling, vocabulary, grammar, etc., instead we integrate them into authentic assignments such as creating stories for a family newspaper or preparing a speech for the Thanksgiving performance. Research has shown that kids who read avidly and write regularly acquire competency in grammar, vocabulary, and spelling. The converse has also been shown: Kids who practice grammar, vocabulary, and spelling skills divorced from regular reading and composing don't.

What to Do When in Language Arts

Primary:

The first stories your child creates will be the pictures he draws. If encouraged, he will begin to experiment by adding letters to his pages. As he begins to acquire an understanding of phonics, he will approximate the spelling of words by approximating their sounds. Your child might produce "DRS" for "dress" or "YL" for "while." His vocabulary will expand or stagnate, depending upon the amount of "live language" he is exposed to and the level of its complexity. (Live language is conversation between family and friends and not speech overheard from radio or television.)

Strategies:

- Do not talk down to young children. Use English precisely, and speak in complete sentences. Engage your child in discussion about the pictures she is creating. Call these "stories."

- Your child will be ready to compose complex stories long before she is able to print them. Let her dictate these to you. I wrote down stories for my children even through third grade. By then they had keyboarding skills that could keep up with their thinking.

> Most primary curricula I have seen require far too much handwriting of young children. Fine motor skills do not develop as rapidly in children as their thinking skills. Don't limit your child's progress by requiring her to do all this writing. She can read, speak, and think far faster and deeper than she can print. So do some of the printing for her or do the required work orally. Better yet, see that she has a computer and a children's word processing program as early as possible.

- Some of our favorite mementos are the books my children created during their primary years. You can do this by folding several sheets of 8 1/2" by 11" paper in half. With a cross-stitch, sew along the folded edge with dental floss. Bind cardboard covers to the pages with packing tape.

- Occasionally provide an audience for your child's inventive play. Encourage her to perform a puppet show for you or act out a favorite Bible story. But don't take over. Children love to create secret worlds that are not populated by adults.

- Inventive play stimulates a child's mental development and creative thinking skills. Our children and their homeschooled friends engaged in this almost until adolescence. Elaborate battles between Narnia and the evil Calormenes raged back and forth for hours in the backyard while scores of stuffed animals were positioned to defend the bedrooms. Had they gone to school, I'm sure they would have been teased into stopping this. But I knew this was not immaturity on their part; rather, it was laying the groundwork for their future reading and writing skills.

- Don't start dumping money into resources yet. Delay structured learning and seatwork as long as possible. Young children may be anxious to "play school," but they are not really asking you to structure their time and require assignments of them. Rather, support their initiative in composing, inventing, and conversing.

A regular rereading of *For the Children's Sake,* Susan Schaeffer Macaulay (Crossway, 1984), will remind you of the benefits of a carefree and lingering time of childhood for your kids. Don't worry; the rat race will still be there when they must finally leave childhood behind.

Recommendations:

Write from the Start: Tapping Your Child's Natural Writing Ability by Donald Graves (NAL Penguin, 1987) is unfortunately out-of-print but still available through the library.

1-2-3 Reading and Writing by Jean Warren (Frank Schaeffer Publications)* is a collection of easy-to-do readiness exercises for primary level children.

Elementary:

By the time your child leaves his elementary years behind, his writing portfolio should include both creative and expository compositions. Within the context of regular writing, he should master the conventions of English in spelling, grammar, and punctuation.

Spelling will progress naturally and with practice from (wildly) inventive to standard.

The audiences with whom he shares his work should be varied and informal: his peers, his relatives, his family.

The child should have daily opportunities to speak and formulate his ideas into thoughtful responses.

Recommendations:

Great Source Books* publishes my favorite language arts curriculum, which includes the English handbooks *Writer's Express* (elementary), *WriteSource 2000* (middle school), and *Writer's Inc.* (high school). This series integrates what research has shown works best in teaching children to compose, think, and learn. The complete program for grades fourth through twelfth grades can be ordered from the Home School Resource Center.

Introduce parts of speech with these incredible feasts for the eyes written and illustrated by Ruth Heller (published by Putnam):

> *A Cache of Jewels and Other Collective Nouns**
> *Many Luscious Lollipops: A Book about Adjectives**
> *Kites Sail High: A Book about Verbs**
> *Up, Up and Away: A Book about Adverbs**
> *Merry-Go-Round: A Book about Nouns**
> *Behind the Mask: A Book about Prepositions**

Composition:

Kids can only write about what they know or have experienced. A wide breadth of studies and diverse experiences must precede composing. The topics they write about should be drawn from this.

Strategies:

- Kids need a regular time they can count on to write. Keep composing on the schedule, and it will eventually be a habit.

- Help your children discover what they want to write about and who their audience will be. Instead of specific assignments, I give my kids parameters for their writing, for example, a research paper on a topic of interest or a short piece of historical fiction. My job is to brainstorm with them to discover the topic they want to write about or to give ideas for getting unstuck while the piece is in progress.

Michael was a very reluctant writer when younger. I had asked him to keep a daily journal in third grade. But he was stubbornly stuck despite my continuous list of suggested topics. I knew to be motivated he needed an audience and a purpose for his writing that he cared about. I finally punched the right button:

Kermit is the storyteller in our family. He often sneaks into the children's bedrooms after hours and keeps them up late telling stories from his own childhood. My kids just love this, especially since the goal is to make sure Mom doesn't find out. I suggested to Mike that he record his daily life and the current events going on in the world so he could someday share them with his own kids the way his dad does. That did it. Mike filled his pages very quickly that year.

- Teach writing as a process of planning, composing, revising, and editing. A good piece will go through this cycle several times. This process is how real writers write; let your children mimic it.

- The goal is fluency. Many ideas should be started in their daily journals, but choose only a few to polish up and finish. These should be presented to an audience.

- One way to find an audience is to join a writers' group. These work best if they are small enough for all the children involved to share a portion of their work-in-progress each time the group gathers.

 Writer's Co-op Handbook* by Maggie Hogan (1996) will give you lots of strategies for organizing an effective writers club.

Young Writers' Institute

Several years ago I set out to impress my kids by arranging for their favorite author, Sigmund Brouwer, to do an author-signing for the Home School Resource Center. It ended up being a lot bigger deal than that. When I found out Sigmund is as motivated as I am to helping kids discover the pleasures of reading and writing, we created The Young Writers' Institute.

At these two-day events, kids have the opportunity to participate in workshops taught by some of their favorite authors, like Sigmund or Bill Myers (creator of the McGee and Me series), and Nancy Rue (Christian Heritage series).

These events not only get kids, especially boys, pumped about writing but show parents how real writers work and what they ought to do at home to keep the inspiration flowing.

Young Writers' Institutes are now scheduled in major cities around the United States and Canada. For more information contact **YWI, 1425 E. Chocolate Avenue, Hershey, PA 17033. Or call 717-520-1303.**

- When you or others respond to a child's writing, focus first on the content and last on the mechanics. The goal is to raise kids who have something worthwhile to say, not who have merely mastered the conventions of the English language.

- The success of a piece of writing should be measured by the degree to which it fulfills its intended purpose and reaches its intended audience. When the kids at our co-op created picture books to read aloud to the preschoolers, their success was measured by the interest shown by the little guys. When my secondary students write a research paper, their success is based upon the degree to which their research supports their thesis.

 In these books you'll find more terrific strategies for encouraging elementary students to write:

Write to Learn, Donald Murray (Holt, 1989).
Any Child Can Write, Harvey Weiner (Oxford University Press, 1990).*
Writing from Home, Susan Richman (<u>Pennsylvania Homeschoolers,</u> 1990).*

Speaking:

Discuss with your child the material he is studying. This will teach him to be an active thinker and to practice formulating his thoughts into articulate responses. Ask questions frequently. The burden for learning is on the student, not the teacher. Require your kids to interact with the material and to expect to talk about it.

Find increasingly larger and varied audiences for your kids—first family members and relatives, then retirement centers and peers. Formal performances such as recitals and plays should be annual events.

 The first time I taught a class of sophomores, I was so nervous I completed the forty-minute lesson in ten-minutes. I stood petrified with no clue what to do for a moment and then gave a study hall, which got my relationship with students off on the right foot. More than a thousand classes later, I never run out of things to say. Practice is what made the difference. I've made a fool of myself quite a few times, too, but I have so many positive experiences to offset those, it doesn't hinder my confidence one bit. That's the goal with your kids. Give them so much practice and so many opportunities their success rate far outweighs their sense of failure, especially when they are young.

I didn't participate in piano recitals until I was in junior high. Then I flubbed up and lost my confidence. After that I avoided the situation and even switched my major from music to English when I realized semester recitals would be a big part of my grade. I didn't want the same scenario for my kids. They've been in piano recitals twice a year since age eight and numerous plays and performances since age five. They probably suffer from overconfidence far more than underconfidence. But by the time they are adults I want them to be polished, articulate public speakers.

Spelling:

I write from the experience of a poor speller who still managed to become an English teacher. I had a lot of private theories about spelling that have been validated by Dr. Richard Gentry, himself a poor speller, who got back at the system by earning a doctorate in teaching spelling. His books *Spel . . . Is a Four-Letter Word** and *Teaching Kids to Spell** are highly recommended.

First, spelling is a visual perception problem, not a linguistic one. Hence, you can have kids who score very high in reading and vocabulary and bottom out in this area. I'm convinced natural spellers, like natural artists, can visualize correctly spelled words in their mind. At least that's what they tell me.

Despite having parents who are both poor spellers, Mike and Gabe have always spelled well. I've never used a spelling program with them. I've done nothing except encourage them as readers and writers. Katie, on the other hand, my most inventive child, has atrocious spelling. She didn't even attempt phonetic equivalency for years. I couldn't decipher her compositions, and she often couldn't either. Self-confident child that she is, we can tease her about this.

Her spelling is greatly improved now, at age eleven, because she has regularly used *Spell It Plus 3* (**Davidson**), a software program, and reads and writes all the time. The spell checker on the computer has helped her clean up her work before submission.

Strategies:

- 🐛 An effective spelling program is multi-strategy. That means you use a variety of methods and games for teaching kids to spell. Be concrete wherever possible: I used crossword puzzles, magnetic letters, Scrabble tiles, and word games like Boggle to help my kids better visualize standard spelling.

- 🐛 Don't limit your children to only writing what they can spell. Inventive spelling is okay. We don't prevent kids from playing baseball until they know all the rules and have mastered all the skills; rather, we use playing the game as the method for learning the rules and improving their skills. Encourage your children to self-correct. As Katie matured, she first learned to recognize misspelled words in her writing and then finally to spell them correctly.

Recommendations:

Choose a spelling program that groups spelling words according to a generalization, for example, *i before e except after c or when sounding like "a" as in neighbor and weigh.* Bob Jones University's spelling program does this, as does Kathryn Stout's **The Natural Speller** (**Design-a-Study**), but many other traditional programs group spelling words randomly.

Secondary:

It's time to prod Junior out of the nest. The tools he's acquired in speech, composition, spelling, vocabulary, etc., should now be used in a masterful way to accomplish real goals—academic, civic, employment, etc. The audience to whom he communicates his ideas orally and in writing must be to a growing degree beyond his family members.

Your student should be writing to learn across the curriculum. Creative writing should continue, but technical writing and research should be a weekly practice. Besides writing from his experience, a student should now be writing out of the knowledge base acquired from his reading. This must go beyond just the regurgitation of facts he's memorized to a thoughtful discussion of ideas and opinions he is now formulating.

An intuitive understanding of English grammar should be in place as a result of all the writing and reading done on the elementary level. It is now time for the college-bound student to learn the correct terminology for grammatical constructions, i.e., adverbial clauses, participial phrases, etc. This technical understanding of syntax will give him the tools he needs to better control his writing.

Recommendations:

The program I mentioned earlier, *Great Source Books* does the best job I know of teaching this technical understanding with direct application to purposeful writing. Another recommendation is *Easy Writing* (<u>ISHA Enterprises</u>)* by Wanda Phillips. You'll need to make sure the grammar exercises in this book are integrated with a composition program, but here you'll find plenty of practice worksheets to reinforce instruction in this area.

Strategies:

- To keep writing purposeful, serious students should be encouraged to enter some of the academic compositions listed in the Resource Guide—especially those that require a written project. Some support groups publish a newsletter or yearbook that is produced by high school students; this is another excellent way to involve kids in meaningful communications.

- Group activities that are discussion-based will give students an informal setting for testing ideas, modifying opinions, and improving communications. Make sure to place a high premium on class participation to nudge more reticent students into taking risks and learning to contribute.

- Either organize a semester course in public speaking or see that your child gives a formal speech or oral presentation at least once a year. Many students I evaluate have found a forum for doing this in 4-H.

Recommendations:

Increase vocabulary through systematic study in Greek and Latin roots. **Vocabulary from Classical Roots** (<u>Educators Publishing Service</u>)is one program that will help you do this.

WordSmart (800-858-9673) is the leading vocabulary builder in software. Visit their Web site at http://www.wordsmart.com and play their word challenge for fun and to learn more about this product.

Webster's New World Student Writing Handbook by Sharon Sorenson* (Macmillan, 1992) contains models and step-by-step instruction for composing all the types of writing secondary students are expected to do across the curriculum. This is a good high school and college reference tool.

Mathematics

Since I did not know this, I'll assume some of my readers do not either: *Arithmetic* refers to problem-solving using the basic operations of addition, subtraction, multiplication, and division when all the quantities are known. *Higher math* is what we use to solve problems with unknown quantities or variables, often represented by x's and y's. (For example, it takes arithmetic to balance my checkbook when the "debit" and "credit" columns all have known quantities written in; it takes higher math when various entries have been left blank ranging back to 1988 or filled with variables, such as an emphatic-looking ??? or !!!! left by Kermit.)

Where Are We Headed?

We need mathematics to solve problems and make decisions in life *logically* (as opposed to *intuitively,* my preferred method of reasoning—otherwise known by my husband as *randomly*).

The bigger the numbers, the more pieces that must be factored into the solution, the higher the math necessary. As science, engineering, and technology increasingly invades every aspect of our lives, more and more of us who've tried to avoid this will need to use higher-level math to make the decisions and perform the jobs required in our daily lives.

I thought this algebra, trigonometry, and calculus stuff was just for techies like Kermit, but as our modest-size business has grown, I've come to see my need for mathematical thinking. I can't yet solve the challenges of managing the Home School Resource Center mathematically; I can't even set up the problem! But I tell Kermit he should be encouraged that at least I now recognize that the decisions we need to make are essentially mathematical.

Your goals for your children in this area should be to equip them to be good stewards of their finances. Wisely budgeting for groceries, purchasing a home, investing for the future, etc., all require a strong grasp of basic arithmetic. At one time this might have been enough; but for them to compete in the future job market as well as make full use of the technological opportunities in their daily lives, they will need a better understanding of higher-level math than we have probably found necessary.

Further, if we teach mathematics as a method of thinking, we will have trained our children to make decisions and solve problems—even those not involving numerical operations—well.

How Do We Get There?

To be ready, then, to use mathematical skills in adult life, our kids must be taught to manipulate numbers and solve complex problems within the context of their real-life application. A *Newsweek* special issue on learning gave this insightful illustration:

> Most middle school kids are proficient enough to divide 1,128 by 36—at least with their calculators. But when a national assessment test asked American high school students to solve this problem: "An Army bus holds 36 soldiers. If 1,128 soldiers are being bused to their training site, how many buses are needed?" only 70 percent performed the correct operation—dividing 1,128 by 36 to arrive at 31 with a remainder of 12 (or 31 1/3). But worse, of those who got that far, only one in three went on to draw the conclusion 32 buses were needed. The rest, accustomed to the sterile, self-referential world of school math courses, did not stop to question an answer involving 1/3 of a bus.[1]

Kids need to see at every bend that arithmetic and mathematics are the tools that enable us to think through real-life problems to a logical conclusion. If I don't teach mathematics within the context, though, of solving authentic problems, my kids will end up trying to put 1,128 soldiers on 31 1/3 buses just as I certainly would have in high school.

What to Teach When in Mathematics

Primary:

As with every other area of study, we want to begin by immersing kids in an environment of numbers and mathematical concepts. We encourage them to mess around with these abstractions by playing games using concrete objects. We build a base for mathematical understanding by using mathematical terms while conversing with our children.

- ✔ *Johnny, please get me a couple of apples from the bin. I need to add two more apples to this recipe.*
- ✔ *Amy, please share two of your stuffed animals with Johnny. You will still have three left to play with.*
- ✔ *This recipe makes enough macaroni and cheese for four people. Because we have eight people in our family, we must double all the ingredients.*

Here are some of the mathematical concepts to talk about and illustrate during the primary years:

counting	shapes
measuring	size
date and time	matching
money	finding patterns
adding	doubling
taking away	dividing in half

Strategies:

- ❦ Concrete, concrete, concrete. Everything you do to get your child ready for formal instruction needs to be within the confines of a hands-on model. It's not time to be holding up flashcards and memorizing math facts yet—in fact, that's the very approach that gets children thinking mathematics exists only in an abstract realm and is not the outgrowth of our need to solve problems in daily life.

- ❦ You need lots of things to count and sort:

  - ✔ Have at least one hundred counters that are all the same: pennies, Popsicle sticks, etc.

  - ✔ Have another collection that is easy to sort into groups: colored poker chips, marbles, etc.

  - ✔ Have another collection that is diverse in shape, size, color, etc., for example, buttons.

Orally, give your child word problems to solve with these manipulatives.

When Michael was three, I created an ongoing tale of battle and valor for his wooden soldier collection. I would instruct him to bring me five soldiers from the playroom to reinforce the troops in the living room. I'd then ask him to take the seven fatally wounded men back to the playroom hospital. His next instruction would be to add six more reinforcements and let me know how many soldiers were now on the battlefield. The story became more and more complicated involving dividing the troops in half, dispatching them to different venues, doubling their numbers, etc. Create your own game. The strategy is to let your child hear the need for mathematical reasoning in the context of live language.

- ❦ Wonderful books are now being produced for children that cultivate math literacy within the context of story. Check out books by Stephen Kellogg, Anno, Tana Hoban, and Bruce McMillan from your library.

- ❦ Draw your young children into your daily mathematical decision-making. Discuss this with them as you prepare dinner, go to the grocery store, clip coupons, count change, or make a purchase. The point is not so much that they understand the concepts but that they begin to understand adults make mathematical decisions as a regular part of their lives.

- ❦ Hunt for patterns and symmetry in nature.

- ❦ Use jigsaw puzzles to help young children develop early problem-solving skills.

- ❦ Sort clothes, coins, buttons, and blocks into various categories, i.e., colors, shapes, value, etc.

- ❦ Teach fractions by dividing apples, pizzas, or desserts into equal parts.

- ❦ Learn children's counting rhymes and songs. Teach skip counting (2, 4, 6, 8, . . . 5, 10, 15, 20, 25, 30, 35 . . .).

- ❦ Even though we're almost all digital now, kids still need to tell time from a face clock. Purchase a big one at a farm supply center. When ready, use this, not just to teach telling time but also to teach fractions of an hour.

- ❦ Make or buy a blank calendar large enough for children to mark the days on.
- ❦ Hang an oversized thermometer outside a kitchen window and have your children track the daily temperature.
- ❦ Use a large scale for weighing. Purchase a balance scale as well to teach the concept of "equal." (This concrete image can later be used to teach older children to "balance" both sides of an algebraic equation.)
- ❦ Spend a day measuring the house. Use a ruler, yardstick, and Daddy's heavy-duty retractable measuring tape.

Recommendations:

1-2-3 Math by Jean Warren (Frank Shaeffer Publications)* will give you more readiness games to play with your primary-age children.

Math Safari (<u>Educational Insights</u>)* is an electronic game based upon the new math standards that drills kids in basic operations. It's a good tool for children who are ready for arithmetic but aren't ready for all the printing involved. Kristen finds this resource very motivational.

Elementary:

After a leisurely season of math fun and games, you are now ready to add to this strategy formal instruction in arithmetic. But just what that instruction should include is, as in reading, the subject of debate. The National Council of Teachers of Mathematics issued new standards for mathematics education in 1991. These have been widely adopted and are reflected in the most recent revisions of standardized tests. Among other things, the new standards heavily emphasize mathematical reasoning and communicating mathematically. This means kids are working on problems that are more complex and often in written form. And rather than teacher-directed instruction, the focus is on kids talking about the *processes* they have used in solving the problem.

Critics of these standards charge American kids are now doing even less drill work while Asian and European students widen their lead, and the misapplication of these standards is creating classrooms where no answer is ever wrong and all routes taken to solve a problem are equal in value.

It probably won't surprise you to learn that I once again straddle the fence on this debate, advocating instruction that includes:

- ✔ drill
- ✔ daily practice in basic arithmetic
- ✔ weekly word problem-solving
- ✔ lots of math projects and games
- ✔ regular doses of competition and group work

Strategies:

- Before kids move into higher mathematics, they should be able to rattle off their math facts without thought. This will enable them to move quickly to the more difficult reasoning aspects of the problems. Math facts are mastered through drill—give your kids timed tests, making it a game to improve their time. **Calculadders** (<u>**Providence Project**</u>) is one source of graduated and timed math drills.

- Use manipulatives to create concrete models of mathematical concepts and abstractions. We use **Cuisenaire rods*** daily. These rods are color-coded and graduated in size to represent the values 1–10. Deceptively simple and inexpensive, they are indispensable for illustrating addition, subtraction, multiplication, division, fractions, equivalencies, ratios, and more. I needed to do a bit of reading to learn how to use them, but once I understood the basic concepts it was easy to make them integral to our program. They are a regular part of the **Miquon Math** (<u>**Key Curriculum Press**</u>)* elementary program I used with Kristen and Katie, and I frequently get them out to help the boys visualize their algebra concepts as well.

- We carry the Cuisenaire rods required for the Miquon series, but a more extensive line, as well as support materials, can be ordered from **Addison-Wesley** (800-447-2226). Ask for the Cuisenaire catalog.

- A treasure trove of kid-enticing manipulatives and other mathematical tools can also be ordered from **Delta Education's** *Hands-On Math* catalog (800-442-5444).

- Have fun creating charts and graphs. Create surveys and analyze the data. Gabe got so interested in a project surveying his friends, he ended up simulating university-level research by collecting data from homeschooled kids across Pennsylvania, compiling his results, and "publishing" them in a ten-page report—when he was ten. It was later part of a story he sold to a regional magazine.

- Familiarize kids with the tools a mathematician has at his disposal, for example, calculators, weights and measures, charts, graphs, spreadsheets, etc. The best math calculators are made by **Texas Instruments,** available from Delta Education as well. We used the **TI-108** for early elementary (it has big keys for little fingers) and the **Math Explorer Plus** after that. (Kids will then need a graphing calculator in high school.) Once my kids understand conceptually the process by which an algorithm is solved, I allow them to use the calculator to solve or check their problems.

- Practice estimating the answer before solving a problem to foster mathematical reasoning. Ask kids if their answer makes sense as well to keep them focused on using logic.

- Let them earn money around the house and then develop responsibility for managing it wisely.

- Use strategy games: cards, dominoes, chess, <u>**Mancala,**</u> <u>**Twenty-Four,**</u> etc., to develop mathematical reasoning intuitively.

- Organize a <u>Math Olympiad</u> group. This is a super problem-solving competition for kids in fourth through sixth grades. My kids' math coach, Jane Rimmer, runs a Math Olympiad group and a <u>MathCounts</u> team for junior high kids as a class at CHESS and uses this as a vehicle for teaching kids a repertoire of problem-solving strategies. If that's the focus, your kids will greatly benefit, no matter how successful they ultimately are at the meets.

- Music is essentially mathematical in structure. Studying an instrument and chord theory will also develop your child's mathematical thinking.

Recommendations:

For developing mathematical reasoning and a concrete base, I recommend the following manipulative-based programs:

Miquon Math (<u>Key Curriculum Press</u>)* is an inexpensive K–3 program that uses Cuisenaire rods as integral to instruction. It is very strong in helping young children conceptualize the mathematics process.

<u>Math-U-See</u> is a manipulative-based program designed by math teacher and homeschooling father Steve Demme. It is more of an investment than Miquon, but that's because it includes very helpful instructional videos and manipulatives that can be cleverly interlocked à la Legos. A demonstration video can be rented for ten dollars, and that's all you'll need to be convinced this is an exceptional program.

For drill work and daily practice in basic arithmetic operations, the King of the Hill:

<u>Saxon Math</u>*: There is little to compete for ease of use and presentation with Saxon's middle elementary program.[2] This begins with Saxon 54 (indicates average fifth-grader, bright fourth; Saxon 65 means average sixth-grader, bright fifth, etc.). We use this through pre-algebra. Kids who use Saxon math often score markedly higher on those standardized tests that test traditional arithmetic skills. (It is, conversely, a disadvantage on tests modified to the new math standards.)

For developing a repertoire of problem-solving strategies:

Figure It Out: Levels 1–6 (roughly first through sixth) available from <u>Pennsylvania Homeschoolers</u>.

Math by Kids, Susan Richman. Available from <u>Pennsylvania Homeschoolers</u>.*

Creative Problem Solving in School Mathematics, George Lenchner. By the founder of <u>Math Olympiad</u> and can be ordered through them. Use as a supplement or core text for students fourth grade or older.

For fun and games:

Family Math (<u>Lawrence Institute of Science</u>).* Hands-on activities designed for parents to do at home with their children, K–8. Cindy used this as her core program one year to give Joey and Daniel a concrete foundation. Joey transitioned from this directly into Saxon 76.

I Hate Mathematics! Book (Little, Brown, 1975) and any others by Marilyn Burns.*
Burns is a leading educator in mathematics as well as a prolific writer. Read anything
you can get your hands on by her, and you'll have all the ideas you need for a top-flight
math program.

Secondary:

What course of study you follow in high school will be heavily influenced by the college
and career goals your child is considering. If your daughter's talking medicine, you need
three to four years of advanced mathematics; if your son is interested in starting his own
business, you need to fulfill the basic algebra and geometry requirement and then focus on
accounting and business math. So in this section, I'll limit myself to a general overview of
high school mathematics and try to get you pointed in the right direction for scouring out
your options.

The typical sequence of study at this level includes algebra 1 and geometry and then, for
the college-bound, algebra 2, and trigonometry and precalculus, usually integrated into an
advanced mathematics course. I also recommend squeezing in somewhere, through either
a course of study or work experience, consumer math, financial management and investment, and computer science. These later skills are much more integral to real life than the
trig will ever be.

Strategies:

- ❦ Expose your teen to as many occupations and fields of study as possible to help
  determine early on if he is headed for the sciences or humanities at college or to
  a vocational or technical-training school—or if he is headed directly to the
  workforce. Then you can hone in on the best sequence of mathematics to study
  during high school. Either visit places of employment or invite folks into your
  co-op to talk with the kids about their occupations.

- ❦ Use math tutors, video instruction, and software programs to cover the higher-
  level mathematics you are not up to.

- ❦ Expect your teens to earn and save money. If you require them to pay for all but
  their basic needs, you'll be able to mentor them in responsible money management while under your supervision.

- ❦ Continue to keep mathematics as concrete as possible and applied to authentic
  problem-solving. **When Are We Ever Gonna Have to Use This? (<u>Dale
  Seymour</u>)*** is an excellent supplement that gives kids real mathematical problems drawn from more than one hundred different occupations.

- ❦ Continue to emphasize the reasoning skills involved in mathematics. I've been
  told that the geometry kids need to master for the college boards can be covered
  in a half-year course and that the theorems and proofs we learned have little
  application anymore to business or science; but I want my kids to study them
  thoroughly for a greater reason:

Geometry is where I first learned the beauty and science of logical thinking—and that set me up for a coup de grace by C. S. Lewis, who proves in *Mere Christianity* that Christ is either who He says He is or a madman—equivalent to a poached egg.[3] Deftly maneuvered into this course by Lewis's deductive reasoning, I was left without a comfortable choice. There was no syllogism for Christ as a good teacher or moral person, no overlapping circles where I could occupy the middle ground. Having dutifully practiced those geometric proofs in high school, I knew a conclusion, and only one, could be drawn. I had no recourse but to convert.

Geometry is the same tool I intend to use to give my children a well-reasoned faith.

Recommendations:

Basic texts:

Saxon Math*: Algebra 1, algebra 2, advanced mathematics, calculus, and physics are the favored choices. The higher-level texts are challenging enough to prepare students for AP examinations. Some students find Saxon's repetitive presentation rather dry by this time; but for the homeschool mom, the lessons and step-by-step solutions manuals make it hard to pass up. This program also works well for tutoring. Saxon does little to demonstrate how this higher-level mathematics is applied, so you'll need to supplement through experience or other resources.

Elementary Algebra, Harold Jacobs* and *Geometry,* Harold Jacobs* (<u>W. H. Freeman</u>). We are using this for algebra because Mike and Gabe found Saxon just too boring. Without a solutions manual, I find it a challenge to keep up, but other than that, Jacobs's text has a lot more personality and creative problem-solving than Saxon. Because this is a possible area of future direction for Mike and Gabe, I feel the extra time on my part is well-spent.

Discovering Geometry: An Inductive Approach (<u>Key Curriculum Press</u>) This is a wonderfully creative text that will certainly spark an interest in all but the most math-resistant child. The drawback is the prep time you or a class instructor must invest. It's been designed for classroom use with lots of cooperative learning activities. If I were organizing a small group for geometry, this would be my text selection.

Advanced Algebra through Data Exploration: A Graphing Calculator Approach (<u>Key Curriculum Press</u>) has just been released and intends to teach algebra 2 in the context of real life application as well as adhere to the new math standards. A graphing calculator is used heavily in this course.

Keys to Algebra and *Keys to Geometry* (<u>Key Curriculum Press</u>)* For the student who just wants to get this requirement out of the way and is highly unlikely to pursue the math or sciences at college, then this simplified program is the most creative and least painful way to present the material. (This works well with accelerated elementary students who want a challenge too.)

Video courses worth considering are available from **Chalk Dust Company** (800-588-7564), **The Annenburg/CPB Collection** (800-LEARNER), and **The Teaching Company** (800-832-2412).

For financial management and applied math:

Get a Grip on Your Money, Larry Burkett (Focus on the Family Publishing, 1990). This is a course in money management designed to be taught as a six-week elective for teens.

Consumer Math (<u>Bob Jones University Press</u>).

Applied Math (<u>A Beka</u>). More challenging than a consumer math program, focuses on business math and finance.

For All Practical Purposes: Introduction to Contemporary Mathematics (<u>W. H. Freeman and Co</u>). Emphasizes the practical applications of mathematics but at a higher level than most consumer math programs. A good choice for the college-bound.

Software:

Mathematica, Student Version, Wolfram Research (800-441-6284). This powerful tool is the leading software program at the university level. Beginning with algebra, your child will make use of this program right through graduate school and then for a small fee, be able to convert it for business applications. It will also eliminate your need to purchase a graphing calculator.

For fun:

The Joy of Mathematics and *More Joy of Mathematics* by Theoni Pappas.* Integrate these wonderful problems and anecdotes into your weekly program to help foster a love and fascination for mathematics in your teens.

Science

It is tragic that the discipline designed by God to demonstrate His existence and character is avoided by Christians and worshiped by man. God has given us mathematics as a tool to reason rightly, and He has given us science to apprehend truth. It is the discipline whereby we discover natural law. And it all points to Him. As creation mirrors the Creator, so natural law is intended to mirror spiritual law.

As a young Christian I viewed science as a threat to my fledgling faith and avoided those courses in college, but as a mature believer who has pursued a better understanding of science with my children, it has become a powerful validation of our faith. When my kids and I study the intricate microcosm of the atom and then see that same intelligent design magnified in the structure of the universe, it defies all logic to conclude there is no Designer.

Instead of Christians retreating from these disciplines, they should be flooding these fields of study and using their discoveries to point folks homeward.

Where Are We Headed?

To serve us in our adult lives, what do we need to glean now from science? If we teach science with an emphasis on memorizing facts, then it's pretty difficult to make a list of essentials relevant for all of us. But if we teach science *as a process,* then we can use science to give our kids the skills they need to *analyze, synthesize,* and *evaluate* information—in any discipline.

Analysis is the process we use to take things apart—subdivide, if you will, into components and categories. *Synthesis* is the process we use to put things together *in a new way*—it is the creative process that leads to new ideas, new products, new procedures. And *evaluation* is the skill we use to draw conclusions and make judgments about all the choices we have.

In life, we use analysis, synthesis, and evaluation for three things:

- ✔ problem-solving
- ✔ decision-making
- ✔ invention

Are these necessary skills we want our children to have as adults? If so, then there is no better vehicle than science as a concrete model for practicing these processes with your kids.

How Do We Get There?

> Good science education is always discovered
> and never force fed.
> —B. K. Hixson

My approach to science has been influenced by Bryce Hixson, science educator and developer of some of the coolest science labs I've seen. I was first exposed to Bryce's philosophy through the lab books he's produced for **Wild Goose Press,** a pretty off-the-wall science education company he founded. When the **Young Writers' Institute** decided to develop a **Young Scientists' Institute,** we tracked down Bryce and asked if he'd like the part of the "mad scientist." So he and some of his colleagues are now offering these two-day workshops of hands-on labs for homeschooled kids. They're pretty awesome if you like dissecting cow eyeballs, mapping the trajectory path of a soda bottle launched 150 feet into the air by an eight-year old, or creating artificial phlegm.

Here's Bryce's advice for teaching science:

1. **It's got to be hands-on.** What we perform we remember, Bryce asserts, backing up his theory with neurological research that has mapped the human mind. Information kids learn through memorization shows up stored in one tiny depository. But information acquired while performing a task is found stored in

numerous interconnected areas, creating, Bryce says, a 3-D hologram picture in our mind. Which approach enables us to retrieve and apply what we've learned to a variety of situations? Obviously, the one where kids get to *do*.

2. **It's got to be question-driven.** By the kids, that is. Your job is to ask open-ended questions. The kids' job is to find the answer. The criteria for the questions are:

    ✔ The student is in charge of determining if her answer is correct.

    ✔ Creativity, exploration, and inquisitiveness are required to answer the question.

    ✔ Failure is viewed as positive feedback.

3. **It's got to be fun.** Or, to quote Bryce more accurately, *funny*. He's also collected a pile of research on the benefits of learning while laughing. Among other things, our bodies release a stimulus while laughing, making us more alert, and our pupils dilate, enabling us to process more visual stimuli. If you see Bryce's stuff, you may suspect he merely went in search of the research he needed to validate his personality. But I can't argue with the enthusiasm I saw in my kids after the Young Scientists' Institute.

My reason for teaching science this way—or rather *facilitating* science opportunities for my kids with this kind of format—is the sense of wonder and discovery it evokes in kids. And that instills in them a reverence and awe for the One who is Creator.

We Now Interrupt Your Reading for This Theological Moment

Why did God create the universe? Have you ever answered that question for your kids? Another favorite proverb of mine:

> **It is the glory of God to conceal a matter;**
> **It is the glory of man to search it out.**
> **—Prov. 25:2**

When Mike first started having quiet times a few years ago, he came downstairs quite frustrated one morning. "Why does God make the Bible so hard to understand?" he demanded.

I shared this proverb with him. "Mike, this is what life is all about. God is not easy to know. He says He will only reveal Himself to those who diligently seek Him with all their hearts. But that's what makes life interesting. He deliberately conceals Himself and intends the pursuit of the knowledge of who He truly is to be a blessing in your life. It gives us purpose." (To quote Oswald Chambers one more time: "What we call the process, God calls the end.")

I love the mystery of life. I love the discovery. That God made the world such a fascinating place and gave us the intelligence to apprehend it is evidence of His great love for us. That's the point of science: To give testimony to the nature of God.

And that's my beef with science textbooks—even Christian ones. They take all the discovery out of it for the kids, settling rather for force-fed facts that defy the very reasons God created the universe in the first place—for our exploration.

Don't rob your kids of the opportunities to solve the mysteries of science themselves. There are eternal purposes at work in it.

What to Teach When in Science

The topics you introduce and the order in which you do so can really be driven by your child's interests. The goal is to use the area of exploration as a vehicle for developing process skills. Here are those listed by Bryce in *How to Turn Kids on to Science* (<u>**Wild Goose Press**</u>).

- ✔ creating
- ✔ classifying (grouping things according to their similarities and differences)
- ✔ experimenting (testing the hypothesis using the scientific method)
- ✔ following directions
- ✔ graphing
- ✔ hypothesizing
- ✔ inferring (drawing conclusions based on data collected)
- ✔ measuring
- ✔ observing
- ✔ sequencing (placing things in logical order)

And what is the scientific method? Here is the official criteria we used for entry in a regional science and engineering fair. This procedure, of course, would be simplified for younger children.

1. The student poses a question that can be answered through experimentation.

2. He formulates a hypothesis predicting the results.

3. He sets up an experiment for testing the hypothesis and records the results.

4. He draws conclusions from these and then formulates a new hypothesis if necessary. Example: "How does heat from below affect root development in house plants?"

5. He repeats the experiment to validate the conclusions.

Primary:

During the first few years of school, build a base of knowledge for your children to draw upon for more formal experimentation and laboratory work later on. The natural world, especially animals, and how things work are often of greatest interest to young children.

Strategies:

- 🐛 Read to your child from science books. *A Closer Look* series published by Dorling Kindersley, *The Magic School Bus** series by Joanne Cole and those by Ruth Heller, Aliki, and others listed on page 116–117 are recommended.

- 🐛 Collect things: insects, leaves, rocks, pictures of animals, etc.

- 🐛 Grow things.

- 🐛 Visit zoos, nature centers, aquariums.

- 🐛 Explore different ecosystems: a pond, a swamp, a forest, a meadow, the ocean.

- 🐛 Set up your own ecosystem: a backyard habitat, an aquarium, a terrarium.

- 🐛 Make recipes together; concoct your own.

- 🐛 Observe birds, insects, changing seasons, weather patterns.

- 🐛 Play with construction toys: blocks, Legos, Erector sets, etc.

Recommendations:

My Big Backyard science magazine published by the National Wildlife Federation (800-588-1650).

1-2-3 Science, Jean Warren (Frank Shaffer Publications).* Hands-on readiness activities for young children.

Science-Arts, MaryAnn Kohl (Bright Ring, 1993).* Fun art projects that illustrate a science concept.

Elementary:

The following units of study are usually explored informally before kids move into the more technical aspects of science on the high school level:

✔ Rocks, minerals, and fossils	✔ Machines and motion
✔ Solar system	✔ Energy
✔ Human body, nutrition, and health	✔ Heat, light, and sound
✔ Weather	✔ Kitchen chemistry
✔ Nature and environment	✔ Creation
✔ Electricity and magnets	

Strategies:

- 🐛 Have your child categorize his collections of rocks, plants, leaves, animals, etc.

- 🐛 Begin acquiring lab equipment.

- 🐛 Require your children to keep a lab notebook where questions, observations, experiments, data, conclusions, etc., are recorded.

- Using the list on page 221, design units of study around experimentation and demonstrations.
- Participate in <u>Science-By-Mail</u>, a terrific program that allows kids in grades four through nine to solve exciting science challenges and to correspond with a real scientist. See "Academic Competitions" in the Resource Guide.

Recommendations:

Organizing a day of science experiments does not come naturally to me. I'd rather administrate the group and find someone else to pull it off—hence the Young Scientists' Institute—so what I have here are those titles and sources I've found easy enough for me to pull off by my lonesome:

Biology for Every Kid, and scores of other titles by Janice Van Cleave (Wiley).* Van Cleave's books are filled with simple home-based experiments you can do with your kids, and titles are organized neatly into subject area, such as *Oceans, Human Body, Chemistry, Physics,* etc. Van Cleave expresses her Christian faith in the foreword of a number of her titles, and I have not found any positions that conflict with our beliefs.

Messing Around with Drinking Straw Construction, and other titles by Bernie Zobrowski (Little, Brown, 1981).

Blood and Guts, Linda Allison (Little, Brown, 1976).* Every title in this Brown Paper School series is a winner, but this is their best-seller.

<u>Tops Learning Systems</u>* are the resource of choice for creating appropriate laboratory experiences at home during high school. They have labs for children as young as third grade as well. They provide just the instructional manuals; you have to gather the supplies, but it's usually not too difficult.

Dorling Kindersley's *Eyewitness* books* and multimedia, such as David Macaulay's *The Way Things Work* CD-ROM* are attractively priced and eye-boggling.

<u>Usborne</u> books are also wildly popular with homeschoolers and their kids. You'll find many at the library or from the distributors listed in the Resource Guide.

For Creation Science:

It Couldn't Just Happen, Lawrence Richards (Word, 1994).* This is the very best resource available on the topic for elementary reading.

Science and the Creation Week (<u>Noble Publishing Associates</u>).* This is an elementary science curriculum that teaches the physics of light, the chemistry of basic elements, astronomy, and plant and animal biology through the Genesis record.

Order more creationism materials from:

Master Books
P. O. Box 26060
Colorado Springs, CO 80936
800-999-3777

Creation Resource Foundation
P. O. Box 570
El Dorado, CA 95623
916-626-4447

Especially recommended: *Unlocking the Mysteries of Creation*, Dennis Petersen from Creation Resource Foundation.

Order home lab kits, supplies, and books from:

Wild Goose Company
375 W. Witney Avenue
Salt Lake City, UT 84115
800-373-1498

Carolina Biological Supply Co.
2600 York Road
Burlington, NC 27215
919-584-0381

Delta Education
P. O. Box 3000
Nashua, NH 03061-3000
800-442-5444
(*Hands-On Science Catalog*)

Nature's Workshop
22777 State Road 119
Goshen, IN 46526-9375
219-534-2245
(Mennonite publication
   with reasonable pricing.)

Sargent Welch Scientific Company
911 Commerce Court
Buffalo Grove, IL 60089
800-SARGENT

Tobin's Lab
P. O. Box 6503
Glendale, AZ 85312-6503
800-522-4776

Tobin's Lab is a homeschool family business with a very helpful catalog organized in the order of creation and offering all the small quantities you need for lab science.

Secondary:

It's now time to acquire a rudimentary understanding of scientific formulas and the molecular structure of the universe without trying to kill all that science interest you cultivated in grade school. If I tell you the typical sequence of courses often studied on this level, will you promise not to be legalistic about it? It's a springboard, folks, please!

seventh—life sciences
eighth—earth sciences
ninth—biology

tenth—chemistry
eleventh—physics
twelfth—study hall (or an elective for the more serious student)

The laboratory experience is important at the high school level but perhaps the most challenging to facilitate at home—especially for the student headed toward a college major in this area. To maintain perspective, though, keep in mind that many public high schools have reduced their laboratory sciences to lectures because they can't trust the kids with the equipment. So the challenge of providing laboratory experience is not a reason to give up homeschooling in high school.

Strategies:

- At least once, participate in a science fair that follows the **International Science and Engineering Fair** guidelines. It's a lot of work, and I did myself in by organizing one on the elementary level that all my kids entered projects in. You may want to try this with smaller numbers.

- If you want to try laboratory science at home, use the **Tops Learning Systems***, **Wild Goose Press** MegaLabs*, or **Castle Heights Press** material and supplement with grade level science reading.

- To keep my kids interested in scientific knowledge, I am using the table of contents in a basic textbook to compile a reading list from the library of more interesting and better written trade books. I intend to make this alternative reading available through our next catalog.

- Here is where a course at the local community college or as part of a family school like CHESS really makes sense. Mike and Gabe took life sciences last year. They hated the textbook, but they did thirty labs, including those with microscopes and dissection—not something I have the money or desire to complete in my kitchen.

- If those options are not available, consider a video course or software program. (See recommended sources on pages 247 and 250.)

- Finally, there is a vast body of information available on the Internet. Many Web sites are run by innovative college students and feature engaging graphical design and interactive capabilities that are ideal for high school. You can even find simulated labs to download. If you can afford the technology, there is unprecedented opportunity here. See Web sites listed in chapter 28.

Recommendations:

The Soul of Science, Nancy Pearcey and Charles Thaxton (Crossway, 1994)*, and *Of Pandas and People: The Central Question of Biological Origins*, Charles Thaxton, et al. (Haughton [God's World Publications], 1989). These are science texts written from a Christian view.

Student Science Opportunities by Gail Grand (Wiley, 1994) is a sourcebook of national programs, competitions, internships, and scholarships in science for high school students.

History

If language arts prepares us to communicate our faith, math teaches us to reason rightly, and science helps us apprehend truth, then what do we study history for? To learn lessons from the past.

That's why God continuously reminded the nation of Israel to record events, make a memorial, observe a feast. These are still methods we need to use to ensure that the lessons are not forgotten.

To benefit from the study of history, we must teach it from this perspective.

Where Are We Headed?

Experience is the best teacher, the saying goes, but it's foolish to assume those experiences must always be our own and never gleaned from the experiences of others. I tell my kids stories from my childhood in the hopes that they will learn from my mistakes and be spared the consequences of repeating them themselves.

As adults, we must make decisions that direct our family life, our business life, our church life, and our civic life. Believing that God is calling us to raise leaders, I want to equip my kids to govern wisely the arenas of influence God opens up for them. And much of that equipping can be gleaned from studying people, civilizations, and events of the past.

How Do We Get There?

1. **Focus on Individuals and Principles.** We want to look to history for role models to emulate. We don't need to sanitize their lives or Christianize them to draw inspiration from them. The Bible is our guide here and it does neither.

Rather, we can use books to prepare our children for the moral choices they may face in the future. I find historical fiction and biography to be ideal for this purpose.

The recommended resources that follow will help you focus on principles, but you can easily do this yourself by choosing to talk with your children about the cause and effect of events in history, the character qualities of the main characters, and the biblical framework for making our choices in the same situation.

Though the books we read didn't intend this, we found much to discuss about the sovereignty of God in our study of Squanto. Captured and sold into slavery in Europe, there he was converted to Christianity. Upon his return to the New World, he found every member of his tribe had been wiped out by disease. Now bilingual, he became an interpreter and friend to the pilgrims at Plymouth—teaching them to plant corn and smoothing relations between them and neighboring tribes.

We also saw the dramatic repercussion from missed opportunities. During another unit of study, we learned that the emperor of China had asked Marco Polo to bring priests to explain Christianity to him on Polo's return visit. But the missionaries who began the journey were frightened away by tales of marauders and Muslim Turks lying in wait along the Mid Eastern trading trail. Polo returned to China alone. Shortly after that Buddhism appeared, the emperor converted, and the religion spread throughout the continent.

2. **Tell History As Story.** This is what makes Ken Burns's documentaries so captivating. He researches the lives of representative individuals and then lets them tell their stories in their own words, drawing upon diaries, letters, and articles from the time. The Old Testament records history predominantly through story, and Jesus taught His followers through story. I think there's a pretty obvious principle here—we want to share our own recorded history with our children through a story format. Then they can identify with the characters and draw lessons from their lives.

What to Teach When in History

Primary:

Working outward from your child's own history, begin to explore the past in greater and greater concentric circles. Storytelling is a powerful family tradition and one that should be recovered to give our children a greater sense of identity and purpose.

During this time our children acquire the fundamentals of our faith through the Bible stories we tell, as well. Make sure you focus on the moral lessons of the stories in the retelling. (Most Sunday school curricula do not.)

And finally, our primary-age children begin to acquire a base of understanding of our national history, primarily through the observance of holidays throughout the year.

Strategies:

- Make a family history book. We've collected stories from grandparents, and this is a wonderful way to make them a part of your homeschool program—and maybe soften their concerns about your choice as well.
- Focus on biography. Read books and use resources that create a sense of character by coloring in the details of the studied individuals' lives.
- Dramatize stories from history.
- Make recipes and crafts from different time periods.

Recommendations:

Your Story Hour tapes (<u>Library and Educational Services</u>) are very well produced and dramatize the lives of Bible characters, missionaries, and historical figures.

Uncle Arthur's Storytime: Children's True Adventures (Wolgemuth & Hyatt, 1989) is a reprinting of these classic tales of virtue, many drawn from history. This book is out of print but may be available through a church library.

A Children's Book of Virtues, William Bennett (Simon and Schuster, 1995). Character is now back in fashion in some corners, and Bill Bennett and others are doing us a great service by compiling readings for our children's moral education.

The Childhood of Famous Americans biographies (MacMillan)* are very popular books with emerging readers. These titles were first published in the 1940s, and many have now been reissued but not revised. Use interlibrary loan to find available copies of the more than two hundred titles in the original line. Augusta Stevenson is the best author of the series.

Cooking Up U.S. History: Recipes and Research to Share with Children, Suzanne Barchers and Patricia Marden (Teacher Ideas Press, 1991).*

Early Settler Activity Guide, Elizabeth Stenson (Crabtree Publishing,1992).*

Elementary:

You have a decision to make. Will you study American history or world history on the elementary level? It's a philosophical choice. The folks at <u>Greenleaf Press</u> make a compelling case for teaching American history only after students have acquired a basic understanding of the roots of Western civilization. Their curriculum starts with the Old Testament, then ancient Egypt, ancient Greece, and so forth. It's the best tool to use on the elementary level if you want this approach.

While I appreciate their perspective in theory, I find in practice it is easier to present American history on this level and then move into world history and cultures at a higher level. Why? It's difficult for a young child to conceptualize "ancient Egypt"—where it is and when it happened. It's a lot easier to build a concrete base for understanding American history—a family trip to Independence Mall in Philadelphia; Washington, D.C.; Plimoth Plantation; or opportunities in your locale will help kids acquire a framework on which to hang these stories.

By high school they don't necessarily need these hands-on experiences to conceptualize ancient events.

Strategies:

🐾 Use time lines, maps, and charts to help children see the relationship between people, places, and events.

- Read historical fiction to better visualize the human drama and culture of the times.

- Use history as the focal point of unit studies that incorporate the sciences, music, art, and literature. This will help children better understand the cause and effect of historic events.

- Visit sites with interpreters and artisans. Draw them out to glean the stories from them.

- To avoid a revisionist view of history, use primary source material in your program. This includes journals, diaries, and documents from the time period. The use of primary sources is being emphasized currently in the teaching of history, so more and more is being reprinted and made available. **Jackdaws,** available from **The Elijah Company,** is one example.

- Read **Using Primary Sources: A Guide for Teachers and Parents,** available from **Primary Source Media** (800-444-0799).

- Subscribe to *Cobblestone: The History Magazine for Young People* and *Calliope: World History for Young People* (800-821-0115).

- For current events from a Christian perspective, subscribe to **God's World Publications** (800-951-5437). These are biweekly newspapers geared to specific grade levels.

Recommendations:

The History of Us by Joy Hakim* is the best resource available to tell American history as a story. You won't agree with Hakim's biases at all times, but they certainly aren't enough to disregard these wonderful books.

Rea Berg's **History through Literature** study guides (**Beautiful Feet Books**)* will help you build a Christian framework around great historical fiction and children's trade books. Beautiful Feet has published units for world and American history as well as geography. This is a highly recommended company.

Use Dorling Kindersley's *Eyewitness* books and multimedia such as *The History of the World* CD-ROM.*

Use **Usborne** history titles as well.

For hands-on history activities:

Steven Caney's Kids' America, Steven Caney (Workman, 1978).*

KONOS, Jessica Hulcy and Carole Thaxton. This is an elementary curriculum that integrates the core subjects around a character quality. Each of the three volumes covers activities and reading for two years of study.

American Girl Study Guides (Pleasant Company) offer an activity-based thematic unit in history that corresponds with each of the American Girl series. These are very well-designed and remarkably inexpensive ($7.95). The **American Girl Study Guides** are available through us.

More Than Moccasins, and other activity books from Laurie Carlson (Chicago Review Press, 1994).*

Craft Topics: Greeks, and others in the series (Franklin Watts, 1992).*

Early Settler Activity Guide, Elizabeth Stenson (Crabtree, 1983).*

For cultural studies that build a heart for missions in your family, the following are recommended courses of study:

Sunlight Curriculum
8121 South Grant Way
Littleton, CO 80122-2701
303-730-6292
e-mail: 76702.2764@compuserve.com

Teaching with God's Heart for the World
Family Mission/Vision Enterprises, Inc.
P. O. Box 7198
Bend, OR 97708-7198
800-201-1668

Teaching Your Child God's Love for the World
Food for the Hungry
7729 East Greenway Road
Scottsdale, AZ 85260
800-2-HUNGER
http://www.fh.org

For geography:

Rea Berg's **Geography Through Literature** (<u>Beautiful Feet Books</u>)* uses four popular books by Holling C. Hollings to present four major regions of the United States and the history of each.

Geography for Life (<u>National Council for Geography Education</u>) is an elaboration of the new national standards for geography, K–12. With a current refocusing on the importance of this subject, you will find this handbook the best resource for integrating all aspects of geography into your curriculum.

Secondary:

At this level, you'll either focus in on American history or zoom out to cover world history and cultures. There are so many, many well-written books and fascinating videos out there, it would be a real shame to disintegrate to the textbook level for your studies here.

Strategies:

- Focus on building a Christian world view in your teens. Cathy Duffy outlines an excellent course of study in her *Christian Home Educators' Curriculum Manual: Junior/Senior High* (Home Run Enterprises, 1995).*

- David Quine of **The Cornerstone Curriculum Project** is also just finishing his three-year integrated high school course of study, entitled **World Views of the Western World** and based upon the works of Francis Schaeffer. Subjects covered include philosophy, art, music, government, economics, science, and literature.

- **Worldview Academy Leadership Camp**, recommended by Dr. James Dobson and Josh Harris, is a week-long course of study designed to equip teens with a Christian world view. The camp focuses on three spheres: world views, apologetics (defense of the faith) and evangelism, and leadership. Mike and Gabe recently attended this camp, and they both had a significant experience. I had to force them into the car to come home. We will definitely be participating again. Highly recommended.

Worldview Academy
Lifebuilders
P. O. Box 5032
Bryan, TX 77805
800-241-1123

http://www.cy-net.net/corp/wvacad/

- Participate in **The National History Day** academic competition. Students may enter individually or as a team and may present a project or research paper. This is a very well designed program.

Recommendations:

The creators of the **KONOS** integrated elementary curriculum are just beginning to publish their four-year course of study in world history that integrates history, English, and art. Years one and two are completed; they cover from Abraham to pre-Rome (year one) and Rome to pre-Renaissance (year two). This is a creative, well-organized, and independent study program for your teens that will continue the love for learning you inspired during the elementary years.

For providential history that has not been sanitized or overly Christianized:

The Story of Liberty (1987) and *Sweet Land of Liberty* (1992) by Charles Coffin (reprinted by Maranatha Publications)* were first authored in the early 1800s and are written as a very engaging narrative of the spread of democracy, beginning with the battle of Hastings and culminating with the founding of the thirteen colonies. Reprints of Coffin's other titles are also planned.

A New World in View, Gary DeMar and Fred Douglas Young (<u>American Vision</u>, 1996) is the first volume in a new series, *To Pledge Allegiance*, that has the look and feel of Joy Hakim's *History of Us*, only from a Christian perspective. This volume gives the Old World background of the age of discovery and exploration. This organization's catalog features many other resources you should consider for high school.

For economics and civics:

Whatever Happened to Penny Candy? (Bluestocking Press, 1993), ***Whatever Happened to Justice?*** (Bluestocking Press, 1993), and others by Richard Maybury, a libertarian, uses a fictionalized letter exchange between a young man and his Uncle Eric to simplify economics, civics, and government. Very lucid style.

Primary source documents:

In Their Own Words series by Milton Meltzer, for example, ***The Black Americans: A History in Their Own Words*** (HarperCollins, 1984)*.

Cobblestone Publishing (800-821-0115) has several volumes of primary source documents with teaching activities, grouped according to historic period.

For Christian history: I know no better source than **Christian History Institute**, publisher of *Christian History* magazine. The staff has uploaded all the past issues of *Glimpses* bulletin inserts at the magazine's website, and this is a terrific research center for teens. The contributors know how to make history interesting, with a very engaging writing style and "human interest" format. http://www.chinstitute.org

Leaders in Action is a new line of biographies edited by George Grant that focuses on the moral leadership of great men of history. Recommended titles include:

Never Give In: The Extraordinary Character of Winston Churchill, Stephen Mansfield (<u>Highland Books</u>, 1996).*

Carry a Big Stick: The Uncommon Heroism of Theodore Roosevelt, George Grant (<u>Highland Books</u>, 1996).*

Art and Music

Though not considered core subjects, it's important that we not neglect study in these areas. Music and art as they are expressed through human history are the best ways for our children to understand the impact of philosophical ideas. These are concrete expressions of the abstract forces that shape a culture.

Further, it is important that our children learn to express themselves creatively. Our ability to create is a part of "being made in the image of God," and it is a reflection of the divine nature within us. God intends us to create for His glory and for our own enjoyment in life.

Integrate art and music appreciation into your study of history and cultures, and cultivate your child's creative expression through art and music opportunities.

Recommended Resources: Elementary

Marsalis on Music, a video series from Sony and a TV show on PBS.

Music Masters* recordings integrate the lives of composers with excerpts of their most famous compositions.

History Alive! Through Music (<u>God's World Publications</u>) is a quality production of American folk songs grouped chronologically with helpful historic notes.

Music Education for the Christian Home, Dr. Mary Ann Froehlich (<u>Noble Publishing</u>).*

The Gift of Music, Jane Stuart Smith and Betty Carlson (Crossway, 1995).*

Art Adventures at Home, vols. 1 and 2, Jean Soyke.* These two volumes offer three years each of art activities for the elementary level.

Adventures in Art, Susan Milord (Williamson, 1990).*

Mudworks, Mary Ann Kohl (Bright Ideas Press, 1996).*

Drawing with Children, Mona Brooks (Putnam, 1996).*

Children of a Greater God, Terry Glaspey (Harvest House, 1995).*

Recommended Resources: Secondary

How Should We Then Live? The Rise and Decline of Western Thought and Culture, Francis A. Schaeffer (Crossway, 1983).*

Music and Moments with the Masters, David Quine (<u>Cornerstone Curriculum Project</u>).

Adventures in Art, David Quine (<u>Cornerstone Curriculum Project</u>).

Final Note

The U.S. Department of Education has published a collection of booklets for parents on helping elementary children learn various school subjects. They are well worth your time. Write to:

Consumer Information Center
Pueblo, CO 81009
http://www.pueblo.gsa.gov/

> Education is what you have left over when you've forgotten everything that you've learned.
>
> —Oscar Wilde

PART 6

Homeschooling Teens

In This Section

- Should You Do It?
- Planning a Course of Study
- Navigating College Admissions Channels
- College-at-Home

22

Should You Do It?

The day I got the contract for this book, my sons, for the first time ever, also announced they were thinking about going to school—public school! *Great timing, guys,* I thought as my euphoria over the contract evaporated. And furthermore, their reasons were incredulous: They wanted to be with their friends.

What had happened to their convictions! Where had Kermit and I gone wrong!

And this wasn't a momentary blip on the radar screen. They started bringing up the issue frequently.

It threw me into an emotional tailspin. I'd always been open to their participation in the decision—in theory—but I assumed this tactic would guarantee they'd always agree with me. I was outmaneuvered.

My first response was to begin forcefully going over all the reasons we had chosen to home-educate them, cutting off their points, wildly gesticulating in the center of the living room while foolishly believing we were having a discussion. Michael would roll his eyes and mumble, "another long lecture."

Katie shrewdly played the tension to her advantage. She'd angelically slip through the room announcing, "I love being homeschooled, Mom," give me a hug, and return to her work.

Kermit, who had once been very lukewarm to the whole idea of homeschooling, would simply say, "They're not going!" then roll over and go to sleep. End of discussion. (How do men do that?)

I, of course, even debated telling you this. But I'm committed to writing from the reality of our experience—no revisionist history allowed. Once I finally got the bright idea I might want to turn to the Lord on this one, I realized our experience is right where many families choosing to homeschool teens live.

Homeschooling through high school feels like making that initial decision all over again. And in many ways it is. Only the stakes are now higher. High school is the gateway to our children's future, and we're determining what resume they'll be taking with them. Choosing a private/public school route means they'll have all the traditional documentation college admissions offices and employers are used to seeing. Home-educating means we'll have a lot of explaining to do to get some of those future doors to open. And if we quit midstream, local school districts are not obligated to count the homeschooling years toward their high school graduation. We better be sure we're ready to go the distance before we bite off ninth grade!

The other issue is that our kids should now be more involved in the decision-making process. I still fall squarely in the "this is not a democracy" camp of family government, but I also know if teens don't have a personal conviction about home-educating, they'll know how to make us miserable.

Wow. How do we decide? Biggies like this make me want to lie down and go to sleep. Wake me when it's over, but don't ask me to make the call.

Aren't you glad you're a Christian? Aren't decisions like this just why we know we weren't designed to figure life out by ourselves? We need a heavenly Father we can count on for the future. No matter how you educate your teenagers, it's a decision of faith.

At Cindy's House

 I've only just arrived at the high school years, but I've watched Cindy and Marie walk this out. Every summer between Nate's four years of high school, Cindy struggled with the decision to continue homeschooling him. Nate's interest in medicine and a need for higher-level math and sciences really undermined her confidence. Cindy said repeatedly there wasn't a perfect choice; she and Cliff just needed to make the *best* choice—and then work quite hard to make that choice work as well as possible.

What that has meant is a continuous stretching on Cindy's part to match each program to each child:

Nate took classes his senior year at a community college as well as a distance education course through Penn State. His real passion in life is emergency medicine, so Cindy did the research necessary to find Nate an EMT course, which he passed at age sixteen. He then began riding regularly with the local ambulance crew and went on to get additional credits in rescue work and sports injuries before finishing high school.

Cindy's role model as a facilitator has worn off on Nate. Even though Nate received quite a bit of scholarship money and financial aid for college, he has still had to pay for a substantial part of his education. He has done this by joining the Army National Guard. Last summer he completed his medic specialist training, graduating with a number of honors. He's also found time to occupy many leadership positions at school, including class president. So much for concerns about homeschoolers integrating well on campus!

Cindy's next son, Daniel, will graduate from high school this spring, and his interest is in film. Daniel and Marie's son, Tom, hopes to pursue a degree in this area; Tom is planning to enter Ithaca College next fall. After three years of saving, Daniel bought his first video camera in junior high. Since then his and Tom's annual evaluation always includes a private screening of their latest avant-garde video clips. All their spare change goes toward more equipment. And what they don't have, they improvise. I don't know what the neighbors thought the day they repeatedly dropped a dummy from their third-story window.

Once again, Cindy set about facilitating opportunities for her son in his expressed area. She called a friend from college who now owns his own video production company in the Washington, D.C. Area. This friend not only agreed to set up an internship for Daniel and Tom but also invited them to spend the summer on location with his video crews. This opportunity gave Tom and Daniel valuable video experience and insight into the ups and downs of running a company.

Cindy's youngest son, Joey, is now in tenth grade. After seeing his older brothers pursue unique areas, he decided he needed to set goals at an early age as well. But rather than have me tell you about his high school life, Joey wants to speak for himself. (When you see how he flatters his English teacher, you'll know why I gave him the space.) Remember, this is the kid I talked about on page 26.

Okay, Joey, Here's Your Chance

"AAAAAAgh."

The time was three years ago, and I was sitting at my dining room table attempting to use the Pythagorean theorem to determine the amount of time a train had been traveling. My hands furiously flew through my dark blond hair in frustration. I let out a low moan and let my forehead rest on the table.

My mom, sitting across from me instructing my younger sister, Christi, looked up with sympathy. She tilted her head to one side, thinking. It was then she said something to me that would change my attitude toward school forever.

"Joey," she began, "there is one thing I really regret about my school experience when I was your age."

"Really? What's that?" I was mildly curious.

"I wish I would have taken my studies more seriously and not wasted my last few years of school. Now I realize how important they were, and I can't go back and change it."

The word "wasted" rang through my head all day, and the next and the next. I realized I wanted my life to be meaningful for myself, for others, and above all, for God. Would I be looking back five years from now, frustrated that I had wasted time that should have been spent more wisely? I realized I wanted to look back on a life that had been productive, relevant, and filled with good memories.

I made a promise to myself and God. I would make the most of these important years, disciplining myself to perform my best in my studies. I would strive for excellence and give everything my best shot. I would find joy in learning by knowing it would help me now and later in life. I would develop better relationships with my family and friends. My attitude, which had only been defeating me, changed by God's divine power and grace.

Now I am in tenth grade. I have a beautiful wife, three lovely kids, a dog, just paid off our new home, and bought a new car . . . just kidding. Two years later, I no longer see schoolwork as daily torture I have to go through. I am involved in a life-long enjoyable pursuit of knowledge that I have chosen for myself. High school is more than four inconsequential years of my life. It is a training ground, and I must treat it that way.

Studying still isn't always fun. I still get math problems wrong, science still confuses me, and my attitude stinks once in a while. I still have a lot of manicuring to do on myself, too. I still double-dip chips, leave the toilet seat up (an unpardonable sin in my mom's eyes), and burp at the dinner table. I'm not perfect, but I try to give it all I've got.

Last summer, I asked my friend Jeff, a fellow homeschooler, what subjects he would be studying this year. He laughed. "I don't know. My mom will tell me whenever I start."

I laughed with him, but I felt sorry for him because he is missing out on what I treasure most about homeschooling (drumroll, please): FREEDOM! (wild clapping, general hoopla). I value the chance to have an active role in determining my studies. I love that I can pick my subjects, my books, how I want to learn, when I want to learn, why I want to learn. My education is resting on my shoulders. The day-to-day operation of my school work is my responsibility. I love it!

I have always admired people who can capture the emotions, actions, and speech of characters in a story. This is why I want to become a writer: to express a story with all the details of life, to make the reader visualize and feel the thoughts of my characters, their joys and sadness, laughter and tears (sniff, sniff). Okay, I just want to write well.

Which is why I am taking a writing class from the talented (and beautiful) Mrs. Bell. Last year I took a literature class from her, and I was turned on more than ever to the classics and writing. This year I've enrolled in her composition class at CHESS [Creative Home Educators' Support Services], and I hope this will be a turning point in my writing.

At 4:30 in the afternoon on a cool, fall day, Mom and I drive past the local high school where the soccer team is playing a game. My face pressed against the cold window, I see the biggest disadvantage to homeschooling: organized sports. Those two words bring back frustrating memories. All through elementary school I took soccer seriously. When I reached junior high, the community soccer clubs became a place where kids would fool around after their regular school practice. I wanted to practice harder with guys who were more competitive. I figured the coaches for the school team would be more strict and skilled. But my district wouldn't permit me to play.

My mom, God bless her, allowed me to consider going to school so I could play. But homeschooling has too many advantages for me to dismiss it. The soccer situation, though, was a big frustration until I found a small Christian school that would let me play. So far it has been a good experience. The attitudes of the guys are great, and they want to be there.

My future plans include women, living in the Bahamas eleven months out of the year (just kidding!), and some sort of writing—journalist, novelist, freelancer. I think college seems to be the best bet for my writing career. I am looking at Hillsdale College in Michigan and at St. John's in Annapolis, Maryland. Currently, my goal is to get published. Published and paid, that is. I am planning to enter a number of competitions.

Politics also interests me, and I am currently interning at Pennsylvania Family Institute, an affiliate of Focus on the Family. Here I hope to merge my interests in journalism and public policy—though right now I am stuffing envelopes.

God's plans for my future seem to be pressed against the pane of writing. I desire an open heart for whatever God has for me, as long as it doesn't involve mathematics.

—Joseph (Joey) McKeown, fifteen

Back on the Home Front

I'm sure you're wondering what happened at our house as well. I relaxed enough to listen to Mike and Gabe talk about their consideration of public school. I think they needed to know they could express their feelings and the lacks they sometimes feel in homeschooling without us overreacting. They have never been in a traditional setting (with the exception of a one-day field trip to a Christian school), and of course they are curious. It's easy to imagine a better life on the other side.

Through a series of events not orchestrated by Mom (believe it or not) they realized (1) the popularity they thought was awaiting them there could very well be fleeting (i.e., kids are fickle), (2) they would often be asked to compromise their faith to fit in, and (3) they have more opportunities through homeschooling.

Kermit and I, of course, never thought social life was a valid reason to send our kids to school—but I understood their growing desire to interact more with their age-mates. I do think it is healthy for teenagers to move in wider and wider social circles. I desire my children to be leaders and influencers in their generation, and if I won't let them leave the nest their impact will be nil. However, until Mike and Gabe's faith is more mature, I want those social circles to be ones that support our family values. They aren't ready yet, I believe.

But I am a great believer in creative solutions. I don't want my children to view Christianity as limiting (my misconception that kept me from seriously exploring the claims of Christ for years). I asked God to give us a plan.

Checkmate

As a result of the tension Cindy and I felt between providing rigorous academic standards during high school and giving our children wider social contacts, Cindy started Creative Home Educators' Support Services (CHESS), a family school that meets every Tuesday for thirty weeks during the school year. We rent the facilities of a church that once housed a Christian school. Classes are available for students in third through twelfth grades. Instructors are qualified more by their passion for teaching kids and love of their subject matter than by their credentials, though several have the accompanying piece of paper as well. Most instructors are homeschooling also, so they understand what parents are looking for.

Our goal, especially on the secondary level, is to provide a framework for a complete course of study. Parents are welcome to sit in on classes and are responsible for overseeing the completion of their children's work during the week. Cindy is deeply committed to retaining the foundational principles of home education:

- parental authority
- child-centered learning

Even though CHESS had to organize as a private school to satisfy state regulations, the last thing Cindy wants to create is a traditional setting where parents have little input or control. We describe CHESS as a family school in order to better convey the level of parental involvement.

We've found CHESS supports our homeschooling families by providing:

- ✔ challenges for academic excellence and achievement
- ✔ outside evaluation and accountability
- ✔ deadlines
- ✔ group interaction and activities

In addition to the classes, CHESS hosts many events for the teens, including open gym twice a month, a volleyball tournament, graduation ceremony, and a yearbook. Enrollment doubled the second year, and many classes now have a waiting list. Focus on the Family ran a story last year on a similar hybrid of home and private education, and I believe family schools are the wave of the future.

If you'd like to know more about how we've pulled this off, you can request a packet of information from Cindy at the following address:

CHESS
35 E. Main Street
Middletown, PA 17057

Enclose $5 (made payable to CHESS) for copying and postage, please.

Advantages and Disadvantages of Homeschooling Teens

Drawbacks

1. It costs more money. To do it right, you're going to be spending money for video instruction, tutors, correspondence courses, textbooks, lab equipment, and technology. It does add up. Now's a good time to start expecting your kids to help pay for their education.

2. It will take more of your time. Not because you're teaching (they better be learning independently if you hope to survive), but because you are going to be facilitating all the opportunities they need, like apprenticeships and mentors. If they are headed for college, that can be a pretty big deal depending upon how broad a scope you want to explore. Cindy spent hundreds of hours working on Nate's college admissions. Now we hope to save you some of that time by telling you what we've learned (notice how I take credit for Cindy's work). But still, you are the guidance counselor in the homeschool equation. You will have lots of forms to fill out and lots of phone calls to make.

3. Loss of opportunities. By choosing to homeschool through high school, there are valid and worthwhile activities your child cannot participate in—sports, journalism clubs, dramatic productions, a band or orchestra. Unless you have the time to find alternative sources for these opportunities, this needs to be part of counting the cost in making your decision.

My friend Susan Farrell has a daughter graduating from homeschooling and a son graduating from a private school. She recently commented that it has been a challenge to demonstrate her daughter's leadership skills on college and scholarship applications; but for her son, it's been no problem. His involvement in many clubs and activities has been possible without much inconvenience to the family. Her daughter, on the other hand, hasn't had access to those conventional activities.

4. Loss of opportunities to influence others. It's debatable how much impact our elementary-level children might have on other kids. But our teens have the potential to make a real difference in other kids' lives—if they themselves are ready to withstand the peer pressure. I've seen many Christian kids do very poorly in high school, but I've also seen Christian kids who've been a tremendous influence, not just on other kids, but on faculty and the entire school atmosphere as well. When I taught public school, a very large youth group met at my house. The kids came, not because of the adults involved, but because of the Christian kids who invited them.

If I thought my kids were called and ready to make that kind of impact, they'd be there tomorrow. In fact, I pray for it. I don't want to push my kids out of the nest prematurely, but I don't want to hold them back either. I believe our lives are solely for the sake of others. We are called to build strong families that demonstrate our faith with integrity to attract others to the gospel of Jesus Christ. Some of our most influential years as Christians are often during our teens and twenties. That's because those are the years our peers are most open to the gospel. They aren't set in their ways but rather are searching for answers and making decisions themselves. At least at our house, this has been the biggest factor to weigh in deciding to continue on through high school.

Benefits

1. Your relationship with your teens. Kermit and I are jealous for the relationship we have seen between many, many parents and their home-educated teenagers. It's hard not to conclude that homeschooling is a big factor in the trust and camaraderie evidenced there.

A good friend took her three boys out of Christian school several years ago and began to homeschool. When I asked her what benefits she had found in homeschooling, she nodded toward her fourteen-year-old son and said, "Debby, he talks to me." With young children at the time, I didn't understand her amazement. But it was clear to me that that was reason enough to her to stick with homeschooling.

Now with fourteen-year-olds of my own, I know what she meant. I am deeply grateful that my guys share their hearts with Kermit and me. We know what is going on in their lives. They covet our opinions and care deeply about our approval of them. They enjoy their friends a lot, too; but their peer group isn't their primary source of recognition and identity.

2. More opportunities. Homeschooling may close some doors of opportunities for our children, but it also opens other ones that may be more beneficial in the long run. Because of the flexibility of your schedule, your high-schooler can get a headstart on the job market or make his high school resume more attractive to colleges: College-at-home, courses online, apprenticeships, entrepreneurial ventures, travel, missions, etc., are all more easily facilitated.

3. When you're done homeschooling through high school, you can go on Jeopardy!
Yes, you can win thousands of dollars or turn your knowledge and life experiences into a
college degree of your own. With a little ingenuity, you can broker all the mountains of
knowledge you are accumulating into more profitable ventures. The homeschool moms
I know are deadly in games of Trivial Pursuit. It's only one short step from there to a
career on game shows, I'm sure. Check out the chapter on college-at-home. All those
strategies for your kids you can easily use yourself to complete a college degree or earn a
new one.

Here's insight into two families who've chosen to continue to homeschool through high
school:

_I'm convinced that the successful schooling of our children is directly related to successful
parenting. And obviously, relationship is the core of that. One of our desires is to see our
relationship with our children transition from parenting and coaching them to guiding them
as they begin to walk on their own. I can't imagine doing that with them not home. Right
now we—and their brothers and sisters—are the ones with whom they are developing their
best friendships. And that positively influences their learning._

_As far as pros and cons, I don't see any cons at this stage. Our children have always been
homeschooled, so they haven't left an environment that they feel they are missing out on. As
our son Tim will testify to anyone who'll listen, he loves the freedom homeschooling has afforded
him. There are many experiences that he's been able to have because of the flexibility he's had
in scheduling. And Jennifer, who is very involved as an athlete, also appreciates this freedom,
too. Although I apply plenty of pressure to meet deadlines and require a good amount of work,
she realizes her life is much less stressful than her friends' with whom she is competing._

_We've been involved in work experiences and mission trips because the time constraint of
school is removed. We've been able to focus on character and developing a work ethic because
our goals are different from those of standard education. And we've been able to accelerate our
children's learning because of the individualized attention they have. It's amazing how quickly
our children can get things done. The older siblings are helping younger siblings. Our
fourteen-year-old has almost completed high school. It was not our goal; it just happened._

—Karen, mother of ten

_We have seven children, and our two oldest are grown. We've homeschooled off and on since
1979. This is our eleventh year of steady homeschooling. Our oldest son went to public high
school, and our second son went to a Christian high school, which we'd hope would be much
better. To be honest, we were not at all satisfied with either._

_The relationship that had been so important between us basically deteriorated as the boys were
away. It happened with both of them. They were away all day, then they got involved with_

activities. And being teenagers, they ended up getting jobs. Pretty soon we were not seeing our children at all; at least that was our experience. We could have limited the school activities, but that was an important part of what we sent them to high school for.

We've been so satisfied with the results from homeschooling the rest of our children. We have a daughter who graduated last year, and we've been so blessed with her. We also have one son we had expected to have a lot of trouble with. He's always been very active and likes to get out around people. He is always running from one thing to another. He's a very high-energy person. But he has not been at all the problem we thought he would be. He's been a real blessing. He works. He raises exotic animals. He's usually doing some variety of home business, but in the midst of that we've seen a lot of growth in his character. He's still very active. He tends to grow into our family's beliefs a little more slowly than the girls, but he does grow into them. That hasn't happened with the ones who went to school.

I really don't see a downside to homeschooling in high school. All the reasons that apply in the early years apply just as much, if not more, in the older years. Peer pressure in school settings becomes so intense and so important. Quite honestly, a lot of the adults your children run across in a school situation tend to reinforce that idea. They believe all teenagers are supposed to be rebellious, questioning everything, dressing funny, seeking their own paths in a variety of ways. They don't expect to guide them—we learned that through a painful experience. So our children are left at the mercy of the influence of the other young people around them, an influence that may or may not be good.

—Vickie, mother of seven

23

Planning a Course of Study

As with every other decision we've discussed in this book, planning a course of study for your high-schooler begins with listing the future targets he is aiming to hit:

- college
- trade or business school
- apprenticeship
- direct entrance into the job market

The avenues he might pursue in providing for himself and future family must be foremost in determining the courses he takes. Along with this, his targets may include preparation for marriage, leadership in the church or ministry, community service, and self-reliance skills. As he enters ninth grade, script out with your teen all the options you want to keep open. Plan your four-year curriculum so he is qualified to exercise any of these options upon leaving high school. As he narrows down his choices, you can more finely tune his program.

Traditional Courses of Study

For students planning to follow high school with job training or college, here is an overview of the traditionally expected courses of study.

Trade and Technical School

A high school transcript that qualifies a student for a technical, trade, or business school includes:

- ✔ four years of English
- ✔ two to four years of mathematics
- ✔ one to three years of science
- ✔ two to four years of history and social sciences

✔ zero to two years of a foreign language
✔ coursework in technical areas of interest

Four-Year Degree

At the other end of the scale, a high school transcript that qualifies a student for admissions at a four-year university will minimally include:

✔ four years of English
✔ two to four years of advanced mathematics (algebra, geometry, trigonometry, and calculus)
✔ two to four years of history and social science
✔ two to four years of laboratory science (biology, chemistry, physics)
✔ two to four years of the same foreign language
✔ one to two years of music and art
✔ computer skills

Direct Entry into the Job Market

If your teen's goals (such as self-employment) don't depend upon a traditional high school transcript, then the course of study you follow during high school can be much more flexible and fine-tuned with that end in mind. But don't be short-sighted. We don't want to close any doors that our children might need open in the future.

Kermit and I certainly want our daughters to see marriage and motherhood as noble callings and as highly desirable. But studies show women, on average, must be self-supporting seven years of their lives either through singleness, widowhood, or late marriage. I don't want our daughters to be left stranded and unskilled should that situation be in their futures.

You Still Have Room to Maneuver

Keep in mind that the above are merely the names of the courses your child is expected to take. You still have a great deal of flexibility in terms of the time devoted to each course and its content. Just because you use a traditional title does not mean you must use a traditional textbook or follow a traditional method of teaching. You can adapt the program to each child's readiness, interests, and learning style. For example, the introductory physics course Cindy designed for Joey focused on engineering—an interest of his—and used the Legos Dacta-Technic set to give him the hands-on activities he preferred.

My plan still includes lots of field experiences and projects. I assume once my kids get to college, their learning will be predominantly lecture and textbook studies. This is my last chance to have them delve into material on a visceral level.

How to Do the Hard Stuff

Okay, you're saying, let's get to the bone of the matter when we're talking high school. What about physics, calculus, and foreign languages? How am I going to provide this on a high school level, especially a college preparatory one?

You Facilitate

You pool your resources within the homeschool community or seek out new ones. But you don't teach—unless you have the time and really want to learn the subject, too. Pick the areas you do have an interest or background in and take responsibility there, but everything else you outsource. Here are your options:

#1. Video Courses

Say what you may about television, but when done correctly this medium can convey material better than any other. You just have to hunt pretty hard to find the few sources that have maximized the educational potential of video. The most dynamic science teacher cannot compete against *Newton's Apple* or *Bill Nye, the Science Guy.* She just wouldn't have the budget to pull together the models, real-life examples, experts, and experiments these shows use to illustrate scientific principles.

There are a growing number of companies providing complete courses of study on video. Here are three of the better produced sources:

> **PBS Video:** This catalog offers not only PBS documentaries, like Ken Burns's *Civil War,* but also those from other top producers. And they do have a price schedule for home use that makes these resources affordable for most families. (The home-use rights are extended to a face-to-face teaching situation that is part of a systematic educational program. That means you can set up a class at your co-op and use them.)

> Better, these are often stocked by a good public library. Be bold. Find out which librarian does the ordering, and ask her to consider purchasing the series of most interest to homeschoolers. There is, of course, lots of leftist-leaning fare, but *The American Experience, The Great War, Eyes on the Prize,* as well as all of Ken Burns's documentaries make for excellent resources in the high school curriculum.

PBS Video
1320 Braddock Place
Alexandria, VA 22314-1698
800-344-3337

Annenberg Collection: Founded by *TV Guide* magnet Walter Annenberg, the Annenberg School is one of the leading schools of communication and technology in the country. Its video courses are expensive but offer a superb integration of instruction and visual illustration. It has produced courses in physics, French, Spanish, algebra, statistics, the Western tradition, literature, ancient history, and more. It does have a price schedule for home use, but with the necessary texts and workbooks you still will have quite an investment. Some of these are available at a good library or can be recorded during special broadcasts on PBS if you have paid for recording rights (call your local PBS affiliate to see if homeschoolers may register for early morning broadcast rights offered to schools—ours does for seventy dollars a year, and it is well worth the video library that can be built during that time.)

These videos can also be rented from **Pennsylvania Homeschooler**. Their program allows you to rent each tape, which contains several lessons, for only six dollars, and the tape may be kept as long as needed. They can even provide you with some of the course materials in used condition when in stock.

Annenberg/CPB Collection
P. O. Box 2345
S. Burlington, VT 05407-2345
800-532-7637

http://www.learner.org

The Teaching Company: This is a relatively new company with a big vision. It has recruited the best classroom and college professors across the country and recorded their lectures on video and audiotape. The material is affordable (it even has a rental program), but is not as captivating as the big-budget productions from Annenberg and PBS. The academically minded student will find these lectures fascinating. The teachers know their stuff and can explain it well. However, the kid who needs to be entertained will not be able to sit still for the direct lecture presentation.

Of special note for high schoolers-at-home are the algebra 2, chemistry, and geometry lectures—which are well presented and can be used as a support to any basic text. You will want to order the videos. Many of the other courses, though, are just as effective on audio, which is less expensive and can be conveniently listened to while traveling.

When you see the universities from which these professors have been recruited, you will probably be concerned about the compatibility of their world view with Christian thinking. In an ideal world, a Christian publisher would produce a comparable program, but with that not being a choice, I have to say the presentations I reviewed were much more objective than expected.

The Teaching Company recently started Mirus University, which will award college credit to students completing its video course at home. The program will not receive accreditation for at least two years, but those credits can be grandfathered once accreditation is received.

The Teaching Company
7405 Alban Station Court
Suite A107
Springfield, VA 22150-2318
800-832-2412

Maximizing Video Instruction

The best way to use a video course is to view it as a family or group and follow up with discussion. One ambitious mom gathered a group of teens weekly at her home to watch the <u>A Beka</u> biology video course. She followed this up with simple labs, discussions, and tests. The videos, themselves, weren't that terrific; but in the larger context of discussion and interaction, the kids were motivated and the mom was able to cover a subject she knew little about beforehand.

Sure-Fire Way to Do Your Kids In

Video is a great solution for one or two courses, but video schools are the pits. I've worked with several families who tried this route, and they all eventually varied their strategies to include more reading and field experiences. Nothing but video day in and day out will sap your kids of motivation, pronto.

#2. Tutors and Mentors

You will probably find a professional tutoring service a very expensive route. But you can find a qualified tutor or mentor for much less in many other ways. Tutors don't need degrees, they just need to know and love the subject. Perhaps a member of your church who uses the subject matter as part of his or her occupation is available. One gentleman in our church who does research in artificial intelligence mentored a homeschool student in computer programming (using C++, an advanced language). That student, later a National Merit Scholar, turned around and mentored a younger homeschooled student in the same area.

A member of Cindy and Marie's church has tutored all of their children in advanced mathematics for several years, gratis. The kids find thoughtful ways to serve his family in return for his time. He isn't a trained math teacher, but he loves mathematics and attends math conventions for fun. The kids have not only learned the material well, but have often commented on how interesting this gentleman makes their weekly tutoring sessions.

Another homeschool family found a senior math major at a local college to tutor their children. The student charged half the going hourly rate for the sessions. Elsewhere, a group of homeschoolers went together and hired a furloughed missionary to teach a summer French course to their kids.

A local college has requested that their student teachers be used at our co-op as part of fulfilling their practicum requirements. This is an absolutely free opportunity. Your homeschool group could initiate this suggestion and would likely find local colleges very receptive to the idea. They need a variety of teaching situations for their students.

You can also check with folks who routinely provide services to school students during the evening hours; they will likely be very interested in providing services to homeschoolers during the day. In our area, piano teachers, gymnastics clubs, and an ice skating rink all created special daytime classes for homeschoolers at reduced rates. They were eager to extend their services—their facilities were otherwise idle during these hours.

If your child's test scores identify him or her as academically talented, you may be interested in a program sponsored by Duke University. You must first find a qualified local mentor for your child and then register for the program. Duke supplies the text and course outline.

Learn on Your Own
Duke University Talent Identification Program
P. O. Box 40077
Durham, NC 27706-0077
919-684-3847

One last idea is to approach the continuing-education department of a local college. They need to find new markets, and daytime classes are difficult to fill. A college-for-kids concept that traditionally runs only during the summer could be created during the school year for homeschool students.

#3. Software Programs

Most software courses have been developed to supplement a course of study, but there are a few that can be used as the core resource. Here are suggested titles to look into:

- **Syracuse Language Systems Triple Play*** program (800-797-5264). Titles include French, Spanish, German, and Hebrew, with new ones being developed. This program provides an oral language immersion course. You will need to supplement the software with written work.
- **A.D.A.M: The Inside Story*** (800-755-ADAM) is a multi-award-winning program suitable for an anatomy unit.
- **Mathematica** (800-441-6284) is a problem-solving program for math, science, and engineering.
- **Exploring Chemistry** (603-764-5788) is an expensive but complete program. I've included it because the company, **Falcon Software**, will be marketing lower-priced home versions sometime soon, so get on their mailing list.

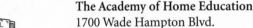

- **License to Drive** (800-766-0835) is a very nicely done interactive driver education program that can be used for your classroom instruction component.

Just like video courses, this method can be overdone. Complete curriculum software packages are typically very heavy on text and very low on visual and interactive capabilities. One or two courses a day via technology will maximize their use; anything more and you'll soon have a diminishing return.

#4. Distance and Online Learning

Another possible solution for a difficult course is high school courses via correspondence or over the Internet. Because many courses completed through this method can also be converted to college credit, I'll devote a section to that in the next chapter. For now, here are several institutions that provide high school courses via correspondence or online learning:

The Academy of Home Education
1700 Wade Hampton Blvd.
Greenville, SC 29614
803-242-5100
Note: This is the Bob Jones University correspondence school.

American School
850 East 58th Street
Chicago, IL 60637
312-947-3300
Secular, accredited, widely accepted diploma by correspondence.

Cambridge Academy
1111 S. W. 17th Street
Ocala, FL 34474
800-252-3777
Secular, accredited diploma by correspondence.

Christian Liberty Academy
502 W. Euclid Avenue
Arlington Heights, IL 60004
800-348-0899
Christian correspondence school.

Clonlara School Home Based Education Program
1289 Jewett
Ann Arbor, MI 48104
313-769-4515
Nonsectarian, student programs are individually designed and offered through correspondence and online classes.

Escondido Tutorial Service
2634 Bernardo Avenue
Escondido, CA 92029
619-746-0980

http://www.gbt.org

Online tutoring in core subjects from a classical persuasion.

Scholars Online Academy (SOLA)
3 Nellis Terrace
Bedford, MA 01731
617-274-0004

http://www.islas.org

Online classes in the classical tradition.

University of Nebraska-Lincoln
Department of Distance Education
Division of Continuing Studies
33rd and Holdrege Streets
Lincoln, NE 68583-9800
402-472-4321

http://www.unl.edu/cwis.html

Secular, accredited, correspondence.

Other options for high school correspondences courses are listed in Cathy Duffy's *Christian Home Educators' Curriculum Manual: Junior/Senior High**. And online learning is growing exponentially. To keep up with the latest opportunities here, subscribe to <u>Homeschool PC</u>.

Recommended sources of information on planning a high school course of study:

The Big Book of Home Learning, vol. 3, Mary Pride (Crossway, 1996).*

Christian Home Educators' Curriculum Manual: Junior/Senior High, Cathy Duffy. (<u>Home Run Enterprises</u>, 1997).*

The High School Handbook, Mary Schofield (<u>Christian Home Educators Press</u>, 1996).

Homeschooling the High Schooler, Diana McAlister and Candice Oneschak (<u>Family Academy Publications</u>, 1993).

Navigating College Admissions Channels

· ·

L et's look now at the teen who plans to go directly from homeschooling to a four-year institution. His high school record is what you will use to gain that college admission. This chapter shows you what you may be asked to produce and how to go about doing that.

Preparing in High School for College Entrance

To prepare for college, you (and your child) can start taking steps when he or she is in eighth grade.

The Good News

Let me begin by putting your mind at ease. Homeschooled students are not having difficulties getting into college. It's a buyer's market, and colleges are pursuing nontraditional students in droves. **Home School Legal Defense Association** (HSLDA) publishes a list of more than three hundred colleges and universities that have accepted homeschoolers. Further, homeschooled students already on campus have earned a reputation as highly motivated, responsible, and independent learners.

A study of 212 home-educated students at Oral Roberts University (ORU) found that while they had virtually the same average ACT/SAT scores as the student body, they had a statistically higher cumulative ORU grade point averages. Of these students, 88 percent were involved in one or more outreach ministries, 80 percent were involved in one or more campus clubs and organizations, and 90 percent were involved in the intramural sports program. As a result of the study, ORU instituted a six-thousand-dollar scholarship for home-educated graduates.

Boston University wrote in a letter sent to homeschool leaders in Massachusetts, "Boston University welcomes applications from home-schooled students. We believe students educated at home possess the passion for knowledge, the independence, and the self-reliance that enable them to excel in our intellectually challenging programs of study."

A survey of more than sixty colleges and universities by the <u>National Center for Home Education</u> collected the following responses:

- Harvard University, which accepts approximately ten home-educated students per year reported "home-educated students have done very well. They usually are very motivated in what they do."

- Commenting on the fifty home-educated students at the University of Montana, officials responded, "The homeschoolers in this state seem to be up to date and well organized. We even have homeschoolers in the honors program . . . one [female student] . . . is one of our top students."

- "These homeschoolers write fabulous essays!" wrote Emory University. "Very creative!"

- "Our homeschoolers (about fifty) tend to be very bright, and have scored very high on standardized tests," responded the University of Kentucky.

- A Dartmouth College respondent said, "The [portfolio] applications I've come across are outstanding. Homeschoolers have a distinct advantage because of the individualized instruction they have received."

- Hillsdale College wrote of the seventy-five to ninety home-educated students there, "Homeschoolers are consistently among our top students; in fact, homeschoolers have won our distinct Honors Program the last three years in a row. We tend to look very favorably upon homeschoolers applying to our college."[1]

College reps, especially from Christian colleges, are now attending homeschool conventions and advertising in the homeschool marketplace. Homeschooled students applying to Liberty University and Oral Roberts University automatically qualify for scholarship money. We are being courted, folks. You aren't going to have to bang down any doors.

On the Other Hand

Now the other side of the coin. You certainly will be able to find *a* college to admit your child, but there are several things you need to do to facilitate your child's getting into the college of his *choice*—especially if it is a competitive school.

Repeatedly, college admissions officers have told me their dilemma is with homeschooled applicants who lack traditional documentation. They are used to seeing a diploma, a transcript, a grade point average, and a class rank along with college board scores. Some admissions departments are adapting to homeschoolers and setting up alternative methods of evaluation. I'm sure more will follow, but in the meantime it is not unreasonable of them to ask us to package our child's nontraditional education in traditional terms.

Start Talking to Admissions Departments Early

Before you finalize the course of study your teen will follow in high school, you need to talk with admissions officers at the colleges he or she may potentially attend. I realize that is difficult to anticipate in ninth grade, but you should at least know whether you will consider a public university, private institution, or Bible college. Talking to representatives from any of these that might be considered should give you a pretty good idea of what other schools in the same category will want to see.

Tell the admissions office you anticipate home-educating your child through high school, and ask what documentation and coursework the college will need in order to be considered for admissions. In many cases you will need to indicate the child's areas of interest. In Cindy's case, Nate was interested in English and medicine. She focused on admissions requirements for the more competitive premed programs. Should Nate change his mind, the course of study he had followed in high school to qualify for premed acceptance would certainly be ample qualification for a humanities department as well.

Once you know what admissions offices will look for, you can either design a program that will meet their requirements or use the time between ninth and twelfth grade to negotiate for consideration of alternative documentation.

Diplomas, You Gotta Love 'Em

A diploma is still a pretty important piece of paper for our graduates to have. When I spoke to a group of fifty admissions directors last summer, the diploma was the crux of the issue for them. Most did not have an admissions policy that allowed for students without one.

It is also a requirement for more than just college. At numerous times throughout their lives, our kids are going to be asked to produce this piece of paper. Folks will make judgments about them based upon it. I want to give my kids one that properly represents their education, not misconstrues it.

GED

Currently a GED is the only option for a diploma most homeschoolers have. This, to me, is an unsatisfactory state of affairs. A GED is designed to be passed with only a tenth-grade general education. In fact, GED stands for "general educational development," not "graduation equivalency diploma," as many people assume. Institutions and employers that require a GED from a home-educated student cheapen the quality of the education this student has likely received.

Secondly, many states do not allow students to take the GED exam until they are seventeen, eighteen, or even nineteen years of age. This may mean delayed acceptance at institutions that require one. Further, some institutions place all GED candidates in one category. At one time, the armed forces had a maximum number of GED candidates it would accept in certain categories. This put homeschool applicants at a disadvantage until HSLDA stepped in to force fairer standards of evaluation.

If I find that a college we are considering for one of our kids will require the GED regardless of all other documentation, that will be one requirement I will work ardently to change during their high school years.

Local School District Diplomas

I am always surprised to find that many homeschoolers believe their local school district is obligated to issue a diploma to their children. That is not true, unless your homeschool is functioning under the umbrella of your local district. (This is possible in California, but the school district then sets the curriculum, too.) A diploma signifies that you have met the requirements set for graduation by the institution issuing it. If you aren't meeting the requirements of its program, it is unreasonable to the school district to give you its diploma.

Satellite Programs and Correspondence Schools

Another avenue that leads to a traditional-looking diploma from an accredited school is enrollment in a satellite program or correspondence school for the high school years.

Locally

There may be a local church or private school in your locale that is offering this service to homeschoolers through an umbrella program. However, this can mean paying close to full enrollment fees, following its course of study, using required materials, and submitting to student evaluations by its staff. The school may believe this is necessary to control the quality of its graduates. But in the process you may find yourself compromising the fundamental reasons you've chosen to home-educate.

Further, while the school may issue a diploma, if its program is not accredited by the state department of education, a GED may still be necessary for its graduates to qualify for college acceptance.

Numerous Christian schools have contacted me about services they wish to offer to the homeschool community. While their intentions are good, they often misunderstand what kinds of services homeschoolers are looking for. One solution is to set up an advisory board of homeschool parents who can help private schools and churches design a program and fee structure to match the homeschool community's needs.

Nationally

There are quite a few correspondence schools and satellite programs now offering a high-school-at-home program with a diploma upon graduation. But when considering this avenue, you need to know if the program is *accredited* and *by whom.* There are a lot of accrediting agencies, and their beauty is only in the eyes of the beholder. You must find out if the institutions you want your child to be admitted to after high school *recognize* these diplomas. Many correspondence schools advertising in the homeschool market are *not* recognized and do *not* qualify your child for state and federal financial aid programs. Again, working backward needs to be an essential part of your planning.

These programs still have many advantages to offer, but for the purposes of our discussion here, if you choose this route primarily to obtain a diploma, then you need to make sure upfront the school's diploma will open all the doors you want it to.

The correspondence schools listed on page 251 that have widely recognized, accredited diploma programs are the **American School** and the **University of Nebraska-Lincoln.**

Homeschool Diploma Programs

Many state homeschool organizations issue their own diplomas and hold annual graduation ceremonies. This is an important service to offer its members. But in most cases, again, these diplomas are not recognized by colleges and do not qualify the student for federal and state financial aid. A GED (which does qualify a student for aid) is still necessary.

There are, however, a few places (South Carolina and Pennsylvania) where homeschool diploma programs approved by the state department of education are in place. And these do qualify the student for financial aid programs. This is the kind of situation homeschoolers should work toward. The homeschool diploma is as recognized as any received from a public school, but parents have maintained control and flexibility in their programs.

A Model Program

Here in Pennsylvania, <u>Pennsylvania Homeschoolers</u> set up such a diploma program, PHAA (Pennsylvania Homeschoolers Accreditation Agency), in 1992. It is recognized by the Pennsylvania Department of Education and qualifies students for federal and state financial aid programs. The requirements for graduation are stringent enough to be respected by outside institutions but flexible enough to allow parents to adapt their program to every child's need. Parents award credits, and the evaluator of the program approves them. In 1997, 250-some students will be awarded this diploma.

PHAA also holds graduation services, publishes a newsletter for its students and alumni, and collects and publicizes statistical research about its graduates. (For instance, one in twenty-five graduates is a National Merit Semi-Finalist. The national norm is one in two hundred.)

PHAA has engendered great respect for its diploma program in just a few short years. Colleges and universities in Pennsylvania are familiar with it and have confidence in applicants who have earned one.

If you'd like to encourage the same type of program in your state, information about PHAA is available at Pennsylvania Homeschoolers' Web site or by writing:

Pennsylvania Homeschoolers
R.D. 2, Box 117
Kittanning, PA 16201
http://www.pahomeschoolers.com

Transcripts

A transcript is a record of your child's coursework and activities in high school. Traditionally it includes credits awarded, individual course grades, cumulative grade point average, and class rank. This is another important document you need to prepare for your child if you homeschool through high school. The purpose, once again, is to communicate his nontraditional education in the traditional terms outsiders will understand.

Reproducible transcript forms can be found in several homeschool publications, including Cathy Duffy's *Christian Home Educators' Curriculum Manual: Junior/Senior High**. The one I prefer is published by the National Association of Secondary School Principals. It is two-sided and includes an area to record not only academic history but also interests, activities, and achievements. These pre-printed forms are available from the Home School Resource Center for one dollar each. You may want several in case of errors.

Computing Credits

There are various ways to award credits for your teen's coursework. Here are some choices; choose the one that will be most meaningful to you and your child:

Most schools award 1 credit for completion of a full-year course and 1/2 credit for a one-semester course. Sometimes honors and advanced placement courses are weighted to provide extra credits—usually 1.25 or 1.50. I suggest you check with your local school district and follow its general guidelines. The system you choose should be carefully explained in an addendum to the transcript.

In a traditional setting, core courses meet every day for thirty-six weeks for forty-minute classes. This is roughly equivalent to 120 hours of classroom instruction (120 hours of instruction is traditionally called one Carnegie unit) and does not reflect outside assignment time. (The Carnegie unit of measuring credits is falling out of vogue currently, but you can impress the powers-that-be by knowing the term.) The college-bound student is expected to graduate with more than twenty credits.

The Pennsylvania Homeschoolers diploma program allows parents to award credit a number of different ways, one of which is for 120 hours of course work. But given the amount of time so often wasted in a traditional classroom, your home-educated student will easily complete the same amount of work in far less time.

Other options for awarding credit can include number of days logged, completion of predetermined coursework, a score of 3 or higher on the appropriate advanced placement exam, or passage of a College-Level Examination Program (CLEP) test. We'll talk about the last two later. For the purposes of college admissions, you should be consistent in how you determine credit, though, and include an explanation of your criteria in an addendum to your transcript.

Credit by Contract

I prefer contracts. Predetermine with your child what work he must accomplish for a course to be considered complete, and base his grade upon the level of his success in completing that work. Here is what I require to earn an A in my senior high American literature course at Creative Home Educators' Support Services (CHESS):

- ✔ Read the entire Bob Jones University eleventh-grade American literature anthology.
- ✔ Average 90 percent or higher on midterm and final exams as well as class quizzes.
- ✔ Score 90 percent or higher on ten-page (typed) research paper.
- ✔ Score 90 percent or higher on ten-minute speech.
- ✔ Score 90 percent or higher on three typed compositions, minimum length three pages.
- ✔ Read fifteen novels, three of which are deemed classics, and respond in writing to ten of these.
- ✔ Contribute consistently and thoughtfully to class discussion and activities.

The reading requirements for this class are very ambitious, and I would support a parent's decision to treat this as an honors English course and award 1.25 credits for completion (especially to the five freshman I had last year in this course).

Grades

Awarding grades to your high-schooler for the purpose of the transcript is also the best way to communicate his or her level of success in understandable terms. As with credits, I suggest contracting with your child what work he or she must complete to receive an A, B, or C from you. Pass/fail grades in nonacademic courses are acceptable but detrimental for core subjects.

A cumulative grade point average can be computed by averaging all the grades for high school. Use the scale below (I'm assuming you aren't going to accept less than a C in a course):

$$
\begin{array}{r}
4 \times \text{ number of A grades} \\
3 \times \text{ number of B grades} \\
+ \; 2 \times \text{ number of C grades} \\
\hline
\end{array}
$$

Total ÷ by number of courses = GPA

Typically, advanced placement and honors courses are awarded five points for an A grade, four points for a B grade, and three points for a C grade.

College Board Scores

While SAT and ACT scores have become less critical to a traditional student's acceptance at a four-year college, they are the most heavily factored documentation a homeschooled applicant will present. If your child scores exceptionally high on his boards (what that number is will vary for each program and school, but generally above 1,200 on the SAT or 30 on the ACT is considered a high score) you will only need to provide minimal additional documentation (i.e., you don't have to worry about all the paperwork I just covered). If his scores, however, place him smack-dab in the middle of the pack of other applicants (1000–1,200 on the SAT or 26 on the ACT) then your documentation needs to be designed to distinguish him from the competition.

Strategies to Maximize Board Scores

#1. Read

Students who score well on their college entrance exams are avid readers. The high school program you design should allow for ample opportunity to read widely across the curriculum and for pleasure. *Reading Lists for College-Bound Students* (Arco, 1990)* is a helpful resource that will give you an idea of the level of reading your teen should be reaching toward. This book compiles the freshman reading lists from more than one hundred private and public colleges and universities.

#2. Study Vocabulary

Starting in junior high, use a vocabulary-builder program that focuses on the Greek and Latin roots of words. In addition, get your kids involved with the study of words. In my composition class, I ask students to create a vocabulary section in their writing portfolio consisting of words they like and words they've learned. Each entry includes the definition, part of speech, origin, source where they originally found the word (dictionary,

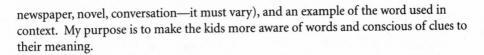

newspaper, novel, conversation—it must vary), and an example of the word used in context. My purpose is to make the kids more aware of words and conscious of clues to their meaning.

Fun vocabulary builders:

> *Word Smart Jr.* and *Word Smart* (Princeton Review, 1995).*
>
> *Tooth & Nail: A Novel Approach to the SAT* (Harcourt Brace, 1994). Uses vocabulary from the SATs in the context of a mystery novel.
>
> **WordSmart** software line (Smartek) (800-858-9673).
>
> http://www.wordsmart.com

#3. Complete Algebra 1 and Geometry

This is the level of math tested on the college boards. This may be overkill on my part, but I supplemented our algebra 1 text with video courses from the Annenberg School and the Teaching Company. And I continuously impress upon my kids the importance of not moving on to the next lesson in math if they do not understand conceptually what is going on. We don't want to sacrifice understanding for the sake of completing a course in a year's time. Mike and Gabe worked on elementary algebra most of sixth through eighth grade. I expect later advanced-math courses to take far less time because we have laid a thorough understanding. (It will have to if we expect to complete high school on time.)

Another point to weigh: <u>Saxon Math</u>, the most popular program among homeschoolers, does not provide a separate course in geometry. Rather, it is integrated throughout the program. I have had feedback from a number of kids who felt they were not sufficiently prepared for the geometry on the college boards as a result.

Geometry by Harold Jacobs (<u>W. H. Freeman</u>)* and *Discovering Geometry,* available from <u>Key Curriculum Press</u>, have been used by college-bound students desiring concentrated study in this area. Most kids can cover what they need to know in less than a year.

#4. Prepare

Test-preparation programs do result in higher scores. **Inside the SAT and PSAT** is an award-winning software program from **Princeton Review** (800-2-REVIEW). Study aids are also published by Princeton Review, Barron's, Gruber, and IDG Books' Dummies Guides. One student I evaluated who scored 1590 before the test was recentered (read that: "dumbed down") reviewed them all and recommends the Gruber guide. Nate McKeown liked *Cracking the System** from **Princeton Review**—it has a more entertaining presentation than the others.

The ACT for Dummies and *The SAT I for Dummies, 2nd edition,* both by Suzee Vlk, give practice work but focus more on strategies for improving your score.

#5. Practice

Taking tests is like learning to play baseball. The more you practice, the better you get. I don't like standardized tests as an evaluation tool, but because they are critical to college acceptance and academic scholarships, I have had my kids take all they can. I've even given them and other academically talented kids out-of-level tests (a standardized test one to four grade levels above their grade level) to sharpen their skills with a greater challenge. For students who typically score at the very top of the chart on a grade-level test, this strategy will give you a more accurate picture of your child's strengths and weaknesses.

There are also a number of talent searches that administer the SATs to seventh- and eighth-graders who score in the top 2 percent nationally on a standardized test. Johns Hopkins's **Institute for the Academic Advancement of Youth** is the most widely recognized. We weren't interested in (read that: "couldn't afford") the three-week summer residency program qualifiers may participate in, but I wanted Mike and Gabe to have the experience—one they were pretty grumpy about ("Mom, it's our only day to sleep in!").

Incidentally, Mike and Gabe typically score within a few points of each other on a standardized test, but in this situation the one who read through the test booklet and did the practice exercises did significantly better than the one who walked in cold. That was enough to convince me we would be using study aids to prepare when it really counts.

As an aside, participating in an academic talent search does look good on your child's resume, and it gets your name on a lot of mailing lists for other worthwhile opportunities. So take advantage of the opportunity if your child qualifies. I've listed talent searches in the Resource Guide under Academic Competitions.

#6. Take the PSAT

Minimally, your college-bound student should take the PSAT (Preliminary Scholastic Aptitude Test) in tenth grade. The eleventh-grade PSAT score is used to qualify for National Merit selection and is the score you will be using most frequently with colleges. The tenth-grade practice round will let you know how your child is predicted to do on the SATs and give you direction in preparing to improve his score.

The list below will help you find out more about the ACT, SAT, PSAT, and National Merit program. (Contact these organizations early so you have time to make the accommodations that may be necessary for a homeschool registrant.)

ACT Registration
P. O. Box 414
Iowa City, IA 52243-0414
319-337-1270

SAT Program
Educational Testing Services
P. O. Box 6200
Princeton, NJ 08541-6200
609-771-7600
http://www.ets.org

PSAT/NMSQT
P. O. Box 6720
Princeton, NJ 08541-6720
609-771-7070
http://www. collegeboard.org/psat/html/ready001.html

National Merit Scholarship Corp.
1560 Sherman Ave, Suite 200
Evanston, IL 60201-4897
847-866-5100

The College Board
45 Columbus Avenue
New York, NY 10023-6992
212-713-8165
http://www.collegeboard.org
Many test-preparation materials are available here.

Online **Princeton Review** runs a very informative Web site: http://www.review.com

Your local school district's guidance department will also have information on all these tests.

Learning to Improve PSAT Scores

I took my first PSAT as a sophomore. My score was 1270 (560 verbal, 710 math). I then began efforts to raise my score—especially my verbal—by working through some PSAT/SAT study books. I saw no improvement as I worked through the texts, so I disbanded the project.

When I took the test again in October 1994, my score was 1580 (780 verbal, 800 math). Even though I had not done a lot of work specifically aimed at raising my score, it had gone up. Without even considering my PSAT scores, I had decided that I wanted to become as knowledgeable as I possibly could on a wide range of subjects.

Between the two tests, I took a little over half of a year of Latin. This helped my vocabulary skills somewhat, but the largest contribution made by the Latin was that by doing it I became interested in reading about ancient Rome and the Roman poets featured in the program.

Eventually, I began reading the works of other poets as well as continuing to read classic novels. In between the two tests, I covered many different types and styles of literature that I really had not read a lot of before. I also read through a set of encyclopedias, taking notes on important items in history, science, literature, and other academic areas. This gave me a lot of experience at grasping new facts and restating information in a more concise way. Also, due to the sheer volume of reading involved in my study, my vocabulary increased and my ability to interpret a word's meaning in context sharpened. With so much reading, it is easy to see why I also became faster at reading.

When I took the PSAT a second time, I was able to read through the comprehension sections more quickly and with a greater understanding of the author's point than I had the first time. The result was a 120-point rise in my verbal score.

My math score was already pretty good at 710, but I knew I could do better. I did a few math tests in an SAT practice book, and then I examined where my problems were. I found that some of the time I missed a problem simply by not thinking hard enough or by making a careless error that I should not have made. These were the same reasons I missed problems in my regular math class in homeschool (Saxon). I realized that if I eliminated these problems, I would be almost 100 percent accurate. I completely changed the way I did math. Instead of doing an entire problem set then checking my answers and trying to remember what I did wrong that caused me to miss a certain point, I began checking every problem immediately after doing it. This worked out very well because it enabled me to see where my problems were so that I could remedy them. I reached a point where I rarely missed a problem and was then able to return to the usual way of doing math. On my second PSAT, my math score improved to a perfect score of 800.

My advice to someone wanting to raise his or her PSAT/SAT score:

1. *Stop wasting time and take responsibility for your education.*
2. *Pinpoint your problems and work to solve them.*
3. *Read, read, read your way to success.*

—Rhett Smith, Pennsylvania

More from Rhett's Mom

Rhett makes many study aids for himself, including posters and wall charts of things like the periodic table for chemistry and formulas in calculus. He has over a thousand flashcards on author/written work, Latin/English translations, chemical structures/names. Some of the flashcards are stapled together into books now. In a loose-leaf notebook he also made an encyclopedia of his own about anything and everything he thought important. Rhett has done all this and become very organized on his own. His involvement in Quiz Bowls, an academic team program, encouraged him greatly.[2]

—Audrey Smith, Rhett's mom

My Two Cents

Audrey coaches a homeschool Quiz Bowl team close to where my parents live. My dad regularly sends me features from the city papers about this team's success. They upset a local Catholic high school with a national reputation and made it to the nationals. I point this out to illustrate the level of motivation kids can achieve when their studies are purposeful and immediate. (Play ball!)

Additional Documentation That Looks Good on College Applications

#1. Advanced Placement or Other Advanced Courses

Advanced Placement (AP) courses are college-level studies completed in high school. Each May, then, students take an AP exam in the area of study. A score of 3 or higher (with 5 being the top) is considered a passing grade. Most colleges award credit to incoming freshmen for the AP tests passed in high school, though some may require higher than a 3 to qualify. It is possible to earn enough AP credits in high school to qualify for sophomore standing at leading universities (and save thousands of dollars in tuition).

Currently, twenty-eight courses in fifteen fields are available. The method of preparing for the test, though, is at your discretion. Barron's publishes AP test preparation books, and this is a good place to find help in designing a course.

The Advanced Placement Program also has booklets available outlining the recommended course of study.

Advanced Placement Program
The College Board
45 Columbus Avenue
New York, New York 10023-6992
212-713-8000

Pennsylvania Homeschoolers began offering AP courses via the Internet in 1996. Visit their Web site for more information.

http://www.pahomeschoolers.com

#2. Outside Evaluations

College admissions offices will weigh heavily any recommendations or evaluations from non-family members who can give a knowledgeable assessment of your child's academic aptitude and achievement. Include with your application these written recommendations from tutors, mentors, evaluators, or a teacher at a family school. These folks don't need to be credentialed as much as they need to be articulate. So be on the lookout for someone who can write a good letter, and get your kid under his or her tutelage for a season.

Many academic programs and scholarships require an outsider's evaluation in order for an applicant even to be considered for acceptance.

#3. Activities and Academic Honors

As erroneous as this is, many admissions offices will assume your kid has been living an isolated life and may not transition into the college experience well. (As a surprise, have Junior wear shoes to the interview.) They are wondering: *How will this kid handle the social life? How will he perform in a competitive environment?*

You can diffuse this issue quickly by including on the transcript the clubs, athletics, and organizations your teen has participated in during high school. Highlight any leadership, informal or formal, he has shown.

Involvement and achievement in academic competitions is another real plus on the transcript. The Resource Guide includes a list of scholastic competitions homeschoolers are welcome to participate in. Your child does not need to win, place, or show in any of these. It is the involvement that will count in the admissions officer's mind.

#4. Junior or Community College Transcript

Many community colleges and two-year institutions have open enrollment. You don't need a diploma, a transcript, or college board scores. Many also allow students to take courses while in high school. These can often be transferred to a four-year university as college credit. (If you intend to do this, make sure you talk to the college you wish to transfer credits to first.)

After Cindy McKeown worked with the admissions office at our local community college, they became very eager to accommodate homeschooolers, even to the point of accepting students as young as tenth grade. Quite a few homeschoolers in our area are now completing many of their higher-level courses through this route.

The transcript record from a community college and the recommendations your child gathers from instructors may be all he will need to be considered for acceptance at a four-year institution.

And if cost-cutting is a goal, there is no better deal than completing the first two years of college at a community college and then transferring to a four-year institution. Your child's diploma will look the same as the one given to kids who paid a great deal more.

Financial Aid

Most families, no matter how well off, are looking for financial aid for college. This is also an area, then, you should start looking into early. There is plenty of financial aid out there, folks. Nobody pays full price for college, cars, or a night in a motel. However, there are always criteria your child must meet to qualify—and one is typically a recognized high school diploma (remember, this can be a GED). That's why you need to have a plan in ninth grade that results in the right documentation at the end of the road.

The best source of information will be the financial aid offices of the colleges you are considering. Or perhaps a friendly guidance counselor at the local high school will be willing to help you.

First select the colleges you want to pursue based upon merit. Then work on the financial-aid package with their offices. Expensive private schools typically have big endowments, and it is not unusual to end up with a financial-aid package that actually comes in at less than the cost of a state-run institution.

What your child needs to qualify for competitive programs and scholarships:

✔ High SAT/ACT scores
✔ Honors and AP courses
✔ Strong written-communication skills
✔ Heavy course load in senior year—even if credits for graduation are already met
✔ Academic and avocational pursuits outside of school
✔ Leadership skills
✔ A *schtick*—be charming, unforgettable, and distinctive

For more info:

The Christian College Handbook/Homeschool Edition
Berry Publishing Service, Inc.
701 Main Street
Evanston, IL 60202
847-869-1573

This is an annual publication with helpful articles on choosing a college and financial aid as well as a guide to more than one hundred Christian liberal arts and Bible colleges. You will also want to request its *Great Commission Handbook,* a guide to short-term and career missions.

College Planning for Dummies, Pat Ordovensky (IDG Books, 1995).

The National Review College Guide, Charles Sykes and Brad Miner (Simon & Schuster, 1993).* This is an incisive and informative review of small liberal arts colleges that still have a core curriculum that is academically rigorous and hasn't succumbed to political correctness.

Summit Ministries Guide to Choosing a College, Ronald Nash and J. F. Baldwin (<u>Summit</u>, 1995).

Online there is a vast ocean of information. Make these stops first:

Goshen Internet Christian Resource Directory to Christian Colleges and Universities

http://www.goshen.net

FinAid provides free searches through massive databases for financial aid.

http://www.finaid.com

Peterson's Online College and Careers Center

http://www.petersons.com

25

College-at-Home

. . . .

There wouldn't be a hassle-free, dirt-cheap route through college, now, would there?

Funny you should ask. Yes, Virginia, there is.

It's called distance learning, and it's another rapidly growing segment of the education market—along with homeschooling. We Americans may have big government, but we're still encoded with the independent spirit of our forefathers—rapscallions and ruffians that they were. Any system they invent, we'll find a way to subvert.

How do you earn college credits or even a degree (called an external degree) without leaving home? Better, how can you maximize the high school years by earning dual credits with the same course? Through a number of strategies:

- ✔ Credit by examination
- ✔ Correspondence courses
- ✔ Online courses
- ✔ Life experience
- ✔ Independent study
- ✔ Portfolio assessment

Why Do I Want to Do This?

1. **Your child gains the academic knowledge and skips the indoctrination.** Again, my evolving opinions are Cindy's fault. After all that hard work she went through getting Nate

269

into college, she's now gnashing her teeth over a lot of the twaddle and PC indoctrination he's receiving. (Of course, spending his summers in the military does tend to offset the damages.) Cindy got me reading *The National Review College Guide** by Charles Sykes and Brad Miner (Simon and Schuster, 1993). I know it's from a very conservative camp to begin with, but this review's criteria for recommendation has nothing to do with political leanings. This is a guide to "the few and the brave" institutions still offering a core curriculum in the Western tradition. (If you need a persuasive defense for studying the Western tradition—no matter what your ethnic background—read E. D. Hirsch's *Cultural Literacy** [Houghton Mifflin, 1987].)

Sykes and Miner's research uncovered it is now possible to graduate from:

78% of the nation's colleges and universities without taking one course in the history of Western civilization

38% without taking any history course at all

45% without taking any course in American or English literature

41% without taking any mathematics

33% without studying natural or physical science[1]

You'll want to read *Illiberal Education* by Dinesh D'Souza (Vintage Books, 1992) as well. This impeccably researched but controversial book chronicles the massive revisionism of curricula taking place on most campuses today as well as the oppressive steps university administrations feel pressured to take to enforce political correctness.

Before you start shelling out tens of thousands of dollars on the presumption of giving your child an education, find out if the campus you're considering still upholds free speech and includes a few of the dead white guys—at least Shakespeare, Milton, or Homer. Keep in mind that 137 American universities have instituted restrictions on public speech, and at least one college, the University of Connecticut, has enacted rules that say a student can be suspended, among other things, for "conspicuous exclusion (of another student) from conversation."[2]

2. To save megabucks and complete a course of study at one's convenience. The opportunities in distance education first evolved to accommodate working adults seeking a degree for advancement but unable to afford to leave work to become traditional students for a season. This still makes up the bulk of the students using these strategies, but at the second tier are homeschoolers. And institutions are beginning to heavily pitch their services directly to us—which means they are better fine-tuning their programs to meet our needs every day.

3. To maximize your child's time and efforts in high school. The credits earned through the following strategies can be used to fulfill credits for high school graduation and converted into college credit as well.

In all cases, remember, it is the college to which you are applying that determines what credits, if any, it will award for these nontraditional strategies. However, the stigma once attached to correspondence courses and other distance learning options no longer holds true. Most universities and colleges accept credits earned through one or more of these methods.

Strategy #1: Equivalency Exams

Advanced placement tests mentioned earlier are the most prestigious equivalency exams, but they only allow students to opt out of freshman-level courses. Credit for more advanced levels, as well as freshman courses, can be earned through other equivalency exam programs.

The most widely accepted are the CLEP (College-Level Examination Program) tests, available from the makers of Advanced Placement exams and the SAT, and the PEP tests (Proficiency Examination Program), available from the maker of the ACT.

After independent study, the student takes an equivalency exam that is representative of the knowledge typically acquired in that college-level course. More than three thousand universities and colleges award credit for CLEP and PEP exams, though each institution sets its own standards for what constitutes a passing grade. These exams cost less than fifty dollars and are often worth three to six college credits—not a bad exchange for the price.

A fourteen-year-old young lady in our co-op has already passed the biology 1, American history 1, and American history 2 CLEP exams after preparing with Bob Jones University's high school level texts.

Here's an example of how I am considering using the CLEP exams to maximize our high school program. Mike and Gabe are now completing French 1 and algebra 1 in eighth grade. But I can't start accumulating credits for their high school diploma until next year. So they will need four more courses of advanced math and at least two more credits in a foreign language. If their French tutor returns to the mission field, it may not be easy to complete that requirement, and given their lack of interest in learning a foreign language, it just may not be worth the devotion of time. If they pass the CLEP test for French 1 and possibly, after short concentrated study, even the test for French 2, they can convert their junior high studies into high school and possibly college credit. They can also take a CLEP test for algebra 1 and then count that as one of their four math credits for high school if we so desire.

For information on CLEP exams:

College-Level Examination Program
P. O. Box 6600
Princeton, NJ 08540-6600
609-951-1026

Study guides for the exams are available from the CLEP program. Also see:

> *Barron's How to Prepare for the CLEP* (Barron's, 1995)

For information on the PEP exams:

> **American College Testing PEP**
> P. O. Box 4014
> Iowa City, IA 52243-4014
> 319-337-1387

In New York state, write:

> **Regents College Examinations**
> 7 Columbia Circle
> Albany, NY 12203
> 518-464-8500

Strategy #2: Correspondence Courses

These differ from the ones listed in Chapter 23 in that they award college credit for completion. And most of the ones you will find listed in the guides I recommend accept students while in high school. (Public schools are using university correspondence courses as an option for their gifted and talented tract.) If you take advantage of this route, here's what I most recommend:

- Take a correspondence course affiliated with a nationally recognized university. These will be the most widely accepted. In many cases there will be no indication on your transcript from that college that the credits were earned via correspondence.

- Look for those that require more than fill-in-the blank assignments and multiple-choice tests. The courses we are considering from Penn State University's distance learning program require extensive writing and essay tests. Credits earned through correspondence really save a lot of money, but I don't want to compromise our main target of raising kids who love to learn. Much of the correspondence material out there is dry and academically under-challenging. Don't settle for just the credits; get an education.

Where to find listings of reputable correspondence courses that award college credit:

> *Bears' Guide to Earning College Degrees Nontraditionally,* John and Mariah Bear (Ten Speed Press, 1996).*
>
> **Peterson's Independent Study Catalog** (Peterson's, 1995).

For a great story of how one homeschooled student earned a master's degree via correspondence by age sixteen, read:

> *No Regrets* by Alexandra Swann (<u>**Cygnet Press**</u>, 1989).*

Earn an External Degree from Two Big-Ten Schools

Penn State University and the University of Iowa entered into a cooperative agreement in 1996 that enables students to earn a diploma in combination from these two highly regarded schools without leaving home and for less than twelve thousand dollars. Students who complete an associate degree through PSU's distance learning program are automatically accepted into Iowa's Bachelor of Liberal Arts distance learning program. The University of Iowa has found that 83 percent of its distance learning graduates are accepted at the graduate school of their choice. And Penn State is very open to accepting homeschoolers still in high school into its distance learning program.

Contact: **LionHawk Program**
Department of Distance Education
207 Mitchell Building
University Park, PA 16802-3601
800-252-3592

Strategy #3: Online Courses

There are now hundreds of courses available over the Internet, with new ones cropping up every day. Plus, most correspondence schools and distance learning departments of universities are converting to online delivery faster than you can say "Bill Gates."

This technology will bring about revolutionary change to education, and in the not-too-distant future, every traditional method of delivery—classroom, independent study, correspondence, etc.,—will have an electronic component to it or be left in the dust. (I'm calling it right here, folks.)

Right now, the technology is in flux, and you can find all kinds of variations online. Some courses are conducted via e-mail, some are conducted real time, some are set up to allow live interaction back and forth between students and instructor. Technology that even allows for video and audio feed is now moving into the mainstream. You'll have to experiment to find which setup works best for your family. (If you can't type fast, forget about the live interaction format.)

You can get a sampling of what's available here:

The Electronic University: A Guide to Distance Learning Programs (Peterson's, 1993).

But online learning is growing exponentially. You will also find more options by searching your online service and the Internet under keyword "Distance Learning" and subscribing to <u>Homeschool PC</u>.

The Internet University

http://www.caso.com/iuhome.html

A listing of courses delivered online by major universities. A great place to shop price.

Yahoo's Links for Distance Learning

http://www.yahoo.com/Education/Distance_Learning/

Links to distance learning opportunities K–college.

Strategy #4: Life Experience, Independent Study, Portfolio Assessment

Has your child been overseas on a mission trip? Has he set up an extensive research project or completed substantial work in a particular subject area? These experiences can potentially be converted to college credit at a reputable institution.

You will find guidelines for doing so and the institutions that accept this in *Bears' Guide to Earning College Degrees Nontraditionally** and *How to Earn a College Degree without Going to College* by James Duffy (Wiley, 1994).

College-at-Home Counseling Service

If you want help in developing a plan for earning college credits and a degree at home, Dr. Douglas Batson of Essential Education offers such a service to homeschoolers. You can check out his Web page for more information or write to him at:

Essential Education
4 Regis Circle
Sterling, VA 20164
e-mail: dbatson@dgs.dgsys.com
Homepage: http://www2.dgsys.com/~dbatson

Apprenticeships and Careers

Just as homeschooling is an old idea making a big comeback, so are apprenticeships. For many careers, work experience and training are much more valuable than a college degree. Kermit recently found the graduate-level courses in computer science around our area a generation behind in technology. He realized he'd have to find another source of training. Institutions are just not equipped to adapt fast enough to the rapidly changing market place.

Finding a mentor who will train your child in his trade in exchange for the low-cost labor is an attractive opportunity for both parties.

If you pursue an apprenticeship, it is a good idea to talk through your expectations and those of the mentor before the apprenticeship begins. Then draw up a contract and a list of objectives that should be met during the experience. A written review from the mentor should be expected at the end of the program so you have the formal documentation to show. He will probably appreciate any evaluation forms you can provide him with as well.

Inge Cannon has fostered the resurgent interest in apprenticeships among the homeschool community. She conducts seminars on apprenticeships and career planning and has a helpful product available:

Education Plus
Apprenticeship Plus: Preparing Lives unto Service
P. O. Box 1029
Mauldin, SC 29662
864-281-9316

And for guidance in helping your child choose a career or course of study, I recommend this service from Larry Burkett's ministry:

Career Pathways
P. O. Box 1476
Gainesville, GA 30503-1476
770-534-1000

PART 7

Computers in the Homeschool

In This Section

- ❦ What Hardware Should I Buy?
- ❦ What Software Should I Buy?
- ❦ Navigating the Net

26

What Hardware Should I Buy?

· ·

If the last 275 pages aren't enough possibilities to wade through, you've done gone and chosen to homeschool during the technological revolution, for pity's sake! Now you must grapple with all those choices as well.

It's a Great Time to Be Alive!

If you have my temperament style—easily bored—you'll love it. (On the other hand, if you still believe the computer is the mark of the beast, prepare to be terrorized.) I know our society is in decay and the economy is due to collapse. Yes, there's so much to be distressed about. But none of this pending disaster dampens my enthusiasm for the times in which we live. I find all this technology absolutely fascinating.

It wasn't always so—when we first married, my husband would rattle on and on about microprocessors, kilobytes, RAM, etc., and break into a cold sweat of anticipation every time IBM announced its latest PC. Me? I'd only feign interest if I couldn't fall asleep. "Honey, talk to me about computers," I'd say. Five minutes later my insomnia would be cured.

He watched me type my 150-page master's thesis on an old typewriter and clucked his tongue in pity. I couldn't see what word processing could buy me that *Wite-Out* didn't already do. Such vision!

When the twins were five, Kermit bought me my first computer, a 286 AT. My response—I felt the same about the set of screwdrivers he gave me once for Christmas. Six months later, I was furious with him for not buying one sooner.

We've bought two new cars in the last sixteen years of marriage and six computers.

What You Need

So, being forewarned that I'm now a sitting duck for the latest technology, here's what you ought to buy. If you can't afford this, then wait till you can. Anything less is already meaningless. This is the current ideal "package" of up-to-date hardware. Many of the newest models will come "bundled" with most of these components; those that aren't included can be added at the time of purchase.

Pentium, or "586," chip
Quad-speed CD-ROM drive
16 bit sound card
1000 MB+ hard drive
16 MB RAM memory
1 MB of video RAM
28.8 baud or faster internal modem
Windows 95

Now, wasn't that simple?

Where to Get It

Here are some great mail-order sources:

Gateway 2000 (800-846-2000)
http://www.gw2k.com

Dell (800-613-3355)
http://www.dell.com/

Micron Electronics (800-223-6571)
http://www.mei.micron.com

For peripherals:

PC Connection (800-800-0003)
Great service and competitive pricing!

Computer Discount Warehouse (800-509-4239)
http://www.cdw.com

PC Zone (800-258-2088)

MicroWarehouse (800-367-7080)
http://www.microwarehouse.com

And Why

All right. I hear those conceptual-specific folks talking. They always want to do the research themselves. Since you insist. Here are the reasons:

1.   I read or interviewed a dozen techies who rambled on and on about various platforms, RAMs, thresholds, mergers, market share, etc., and in the end when I studied my notes they all said I needed the same thing (the list of what you ought to buy on page 20). (And yes, they all agree the Mac is still the easier machine to operate.)

2.   I have assumed that if you are going to take advice about buying a computer from someone (moi) who believes computer science should count toward a foreign language requirement then you are—how shall we say it politely?—technologically challenged.

3.   Therefore, I need to tell you to buy what everyone else has so you can easily find **HELP.** Which you are going to need. So make friends with that small cluster of techies at church. (I know they are barely shaving, but they will be more than happy to put your hardware together.) Better yet, schmooz your way into their group—you won't benefit from eaves-dropping on the fantasy baseball league crowd, but the techies have news you can use.

A Concession to the Rowdy "The Mac Will Rise Again" Crowd

Yes, the Mac is the easier machine to navigate and Windows 95 is close but no banana. But, what a country! That hasn't prevented Microsoft from capturing the larger market share, and software developers are putting out products for this platform first. If you don't go mainstream with a PC, be ready to live with fewer choices—and be ready to pay more. (If you aren't convinced, go to your closest megacomputer store and compare the PC software selection to the Mac selection.)

Why You Need the Power

4.   If you are buying a machine to run business applications, you don't really need the latest technology (though I'd hate to give up Microsoft Office). Educational software, however, makes use of the latest graphics and sound potential. Buy enough machine to run this stuff. Otherwise, you'll get irritating messages in the middle of a program that say you don't have enough memory or some other picky thing and eventually your Christian witness will be jeopardized. To avoid backsliding, get enough under the hood up front.

Why Mail Order?

5.   We've found buying mail order to be the right mix of consumer protection, price, and service. All three are very important. You can get some fantastic deals at computer shows, but these are often from fly-by-night organizations—don't expect any technical support after the sale or even a thirty-day return policy. It may be more convenient to shop locally, but it's sometimes difficult to find highly trained technical support at that level, especially in the discount stores.

6.   We've bought all our computers from Gateway. I love their boxes! (I have impressive decision-making powers, don't you think?) But we always shop comparatively at the other catalogers.

7.   While buying through mail order has worked for us, if you have access to a dependable computer retailer such as Comp USA, I certainly encourage you to at least go for a visit to get some hands-on experience and some face-to-face sales help.

8.   One other option is to find a local source of custom-built computers (ask friends for recommendations and check the Yellow Pages). The advantage of going this route is that the price is usually quite competitive, repairs are simple to arrange, help is just a local phone call away, and when the hardware becomes outdated, you can easily upgrade rather than having to buy a whole new system.

Do I Absolutely Need Technology?

No. But you're giving up a lot without it. Go back to that list of targets you're aiming to hit. Can you achieve them without technology? We can't. My kids are headed for the future job market, and technical skills are essential. Even kids headed for Christian service will be equipped to make a greater impact with computer know-how.

Though a computer is not a replacement for you as teacher of your kids, there's no more powerful tool to aid you in your responsibilities.

27

What Software Should I Buy?

Enter Multimedia

It wasn't until the advent of CD-ROM that I became such an enthusiast for computers in our homeschool; prior educational software was pretty hokey and of limited value. Our greatest benefit came from word processing. (Don't expect your kids to do a lot of original writing without it.) We moved to CD-ROM when I realized we no longer had time for lots of runs to the library. I wanted my older kids involved in lots of research projects and papers, but without a set of encyclopedia, it was time consuming trying to find information in other sources.

What a deal—for less than a hundred dollars we got an entire set of encyclopedia on disk, plus sound and video enhancements, PLUS we can store it all in a small desktop case with scores of other research software. I would have spent more on just the set of bookshelves to hold a traditional set of encyclopedia!

That was before Internet access. Now my kids not only have encyclopedia at their fingertips, they've got equivalent to the Library of Congress sitting on our desktop.

What to Look for in Software Packages

I'm going to name names in a minute, even though that's pretty risky. The software industry reinvents itself, it seems, every six months. What I mention here today may be woefully left in the dust by the time this book makes it into print (though the companies with cutting-edge programs today will most likely be the ones on the edge tomorrow). So, guarding against that inevitability, here are guidelines for evaluating software programs for your homeschool.

#1. How Much Educational Value Does It Have?

Unfortunately this can be hard to find. Most stuff designed to sell on the mass market focuses on the game format, cartoon-like characters, frills, and thrills. Developers throw in just enough content to get away with slapping "educational" on the packaging to attract parents.

As a rule of thumb, software marked "edutainment" is probably twaddle. I've had a few programs, such as early versions of **Carmen SanDiego** and **Algeblasters**, that didn't require any problem-solving or reading of information to play the game. Later versions became much more interactive and dependent upon the player acquiring knowledge.

Home versions of software initially designed for schools has a much higher chance of matching your needs.

Reviewers of software in the homeschool community are much more likely to evaluate programs for their educational value than their more mainstream counterparts are. See **Home Computer Market** and **Homeschool PC** to stay on top.

#2. Does It Maximize the Technology?

Conversely, the designers who jam-pack their programs with educational substance often do a poor job of using the available technology. It's not unusual to find that an educational program (especially one for high school or college) is no more than the reading material for a course poured onto your hard drive. It's bad enough reading through a hard copy of a textbook; it's far worse trying to read all that information on screen.

I want sound, video, interaction, and entertainment. Otherwise, I can get it from a book at a much cheaper price. The goal here is for Junior to use the software fairly independently of Mom. It's going to have to have some razzle-dazzle to do that.

Read the system requirements on the side of the packaging. Is a sound card required? Does the program feature full-color photos, video clips, and animation? Are there links to Internet sites, a reference library, or interactive modules? Any games and quizzes? These all indicate a multisensory experience awaits you.

If it's boring packaging, it's a boring program. If they don't feature sample screens on the box, they've got nothing impressive to show you inside.

Here's an Example of What You Want

A.D.A.M.: The Inside Story (800-775-ADAM)* will blow your socks off: 3-D fly-through animations right through the brain, down the spinal cord, into the heart. Voice pronunciation of more than twelve hundred anatomical structure names. One-button Internet access to top medical sites. Interactive quizzes. Animation. Dissection of over one hundred layers of human anatomy. Identification of more than four thousand structures. Online Video Doctor. The ability to rotate and zoom in on visuals. Do I sound like I'm in sales? (You can get this from us, by the way.) This is the kind of cool stuff I think will leave institutionalized learning in the dust. Once schools get wired, the days of boring lectures are over.

Recommendations

Here is a sample list of software that's popular at our house and with other homeschoolers. These programs are available from the software companies listed at the end of this section. These are all elementary programs. Software with an (S) can be used with ages twelve and above as well.

ART: **Kid Pix Studio** (Broderbund), **Fine Artist** (Microsoft), **With Open Eyes** (S)(Voyager).

READING: **PhonicsTutor** (<u>4:20 Communications</u>), **WordMunchers** (Learning Company).

LANGUAGE ARTS: **Ace Reading Series** (MindPlay), **Wordsmart** (S)(Smartek), **Creative Writer** (Microsoft), **The Student Writing and Research Center** (S) (The Learning Company).

LOGIC AND PROBLEM-SOLVING: **Lost Mind of Dr. Brain**(S) (Sierra On-Line), **Thinkin' Things** (Edmark).

MATH: **Math Munchers Deluxe** (MECC), **The Quarter Mile Math Game Series**(S) (Barnum), **Super Solvers: Outnumbered** (The Learning Company), **Mighty Math** (Edmark).

MUSIC: **Julliard Music Adventure** (Theatrix), **Making Music** (Voyager).

SCIENCE: **The Animals** (Mindscape), **Explorapedia** (Microsoft), **Magic School Bus series** (Microsoft), **Sammy's Science House** (Edmark), **What's the Secret?** (3-M), **Science Sleuths** (S)(Videodiscovery), **The Way Things Work** (S) (DK Multimedia), **Eyewitness Encyclopedia of Science** (S) (DK Multimedia), **A.D.A.M.: The Inside Story** (S) (A.D.A.M. Software), **Invention Studio** (S) (Discovery Channel).

HISTORY: **Eyewitness History of the World** (S) (DK Multimedia), **Nile: Passage to Egypt** (S) (Discovery Channel), **Oregon Trail II** (MECC), **SkyTrip America** (S) (Discovery Channel), **American History Explorer** (S) (Parsons Technology).

GEOGRAPHY: **World Discovery Deluxe** (S) (Great Wave), **GeoSafari Multimedia** (S) (Educational Insights), **Cartopedia**(S) (DK Multimedia), **SkyTrip America** (S) (Discovery Channel).

ENCYCLOPEDIA: **Encarta '97** (Microsoft).

INTEGRATED: **Microsoft Works** (spreadsheets, data base, word processing), **Claris Works** (Claris).

Word Processing

Microsoft's Word has lured us away from WordPerfect. The version in Microsoft Office is even designed to accommodate WordPerfect users who convert over. (If I use a WP keystroke, a window pops up with the correct Word keystroke—that's aggressive marketing.) If you use the same word processing package as others in your network of support, you'll find it easier to work on projects together and exchange information on disk. I've done quite a few newspapers with our co-op students, and everyone was at the time using WordPerfect. It was simple for me to just dump all the articles into my system and format the material.

Word processing packages designed for kids are engaging, but we haven't found it necessary. My girls enjoy **Creative Writer** (Microsoft) and I think the **Student Writing and Research Center** (the Learning Company) would get quite a few years of use, but my kids have the features for WordPerfect mastered now, and the boys are converting over to Word easily.

If you can't afford a big enough computer just yet to run the latest software or support the fastest Internet connect, then at least buy a word processor (a kind of glorified electronic typewriter) for your kids. It's a must if you want them to be writing prolifically.

Where to Buy Educational Software

You'll find best buys for popular programs at Sam's Club, PC Connection, and other vendors advertising in *PC World* and other computer magazines. For a wider selection and specialized attention:

Educational Resources
1550 Executive Drive
Elgin, IL 60123-9330
800-624-2926
Discount pricing.

The Edutainment Company
P. O. Box 21330
Boulder, CO 80308
800-338-3844

Fast Track
130 Burrer Dr
Sunbury, OH 43074
800-927-3936

Home Computer Market
P. O. Box 385377
Bloomington, MN 55438
800-827-7420 (catalog requests and orders)
612-891-8184 (technical advice)
This is a Christian, homebased, homeschooling family.

Home School Resource Center
1425 E. Chocolate Avenue
Hershey, PA 17033
717-533-1669
800-937-6311

Learning Services
11 School Street
North Chelmsford, MA 01863
800-877-3278 (east coast)
800-877-9378 (west coast)

MindPlay
P. O. Box 36491
Tucson, AZ 85740
800-221-7911

Online Shopping

Software can also be purchased and sometimes downloaded to your PC via the Internet.
You'll find an amazing selection at these online cyberstores:

Cyberian Outpost
http://cybout.com/cyberian.html

Egghead Software
http://www.egghead.com

Internet Shopping Network
http://www.isn.com

Software.net
http://www.software.net

28

Navigating the Net

. . . .

This Exit: Information Highway

The real fun and education begin when you venture beyond your desktop PC into cyberspace. This is where the education revolution is occurring and where home-educated kids have the opportunity to pioneer a world class education online.

Wires, You Need More Wires

I'll know the future has arrived when all the techies creating software and hardware take the time to figure out how to eliminate the cords. My house is a spider web of wiring, cords, and plugs. It's the price I guess I must pay to have the technology I want. (But as I tell Kermit, I bet Bill Gates doesn't have a nest of wires in the corner of every room—and I think he has a tad more techno-power than we do.)

Anyway, if you get serious about online education, you need to know up front it's going to lead to a second phone line and the fastest modem on the market. Why? Because your modem—a little gizmo in your computer with a screeching voice—dials up your online service over your phone line. And the slower modems take longer to get anywhere; you can perk a cup of coffee while you're waiting to connect with your destined Web site. And once you're there, you can read a book on the subject you're investigating while navigating hyperspace. While you are doing this, no one can call you on that line.

Now just add to this equation a few teenagers in the house, and we have Tension City.

Plus, if you don't have a local connect number for the online service you choose, your long distance charges will be incredible. And this is when "the Dad" usually gets involved.

So for family peace:

- ✔ get a second phone line
- ✔ get the fastest modem you can afford
- ✔ get a service with a local connect number

Choosing an Online Service

We, as well as our relatives and friends, have been using America Online for several years now, and I think the choice for online beginners has got to be **AOL** (800-827-6364) or **Compuserve** (800-943-8969). They are very user-friendly and have their corner of cyberspace neatly organized. Thus, the intimidation factor is very low. And it's the best place to get an education in using technology effectively.

Help is always a click away. The bulletin boards are easy to read through, and it's also easy to post your own questions and comments—this isn't true out on the Net. Step-by-step instructions for finding what you want online and out on the Net makes this a painless way to learn how to navigate the furthest recesses of cyberspace. Can't afford a math tutor? Your kids can post their questions and have an answer in less than forty-eight hours.

Areas are carefully monitored, and child-safety mechanisms are available for you. This is the best place for you and your kids to get acclimated.

Here are features we enjoy on AOL:

Christianity Online. Bulletin boards and some of our favorite Christian magazines.

Homework Tutors. Teachers from around the world are available for the elementary, high school, and college level. My kids have used this feature a lot. We typically get a response from an expert by the next day.

Reference Library. The Bible, dictionaries, encyclopedias, thesauruses, *The Dictionary of Cultural Literacy* by E. D. Hirsch, phone books, addresses, whatever you'd find in the reference section of the largest city library is right here.

Magazines. All the money you can save on subscription prices is enough to justify an online service. Kids' magazines, newsmagazines, special-interest magazines, educational journals. They're all here, or soon will be.

E-mail. AOL is still my favorite place to collect and send electronic mail. However, what I don't like is the junk mail that is increasingly cluttering up my mailbox. I'd support anti-pollution laws if they would extend to online solicitations.

News and Information. When Mike and Gabe were in a stock market competition (see Resource Guide) they found AOL to be the best place for up-to-the-minute prices and a lot less expensive than the *Wall Street Journal*. Likewise, weather tracking and other breaking events are as current as CNN.

Because of how quickly these online features will become integral to your daily life, the online service you ultimately settle on should offer the following features.

What You Want Is Unlimited Access

This means that you want to find a server with a *local* connect number that provides *unlimited access* to the Internet for a *flat monthly fee* and uses **Netscape Navigator** or **Microsoft Explorer** as a browser (that's your viewing "window" for the Internet). If your kids will be doing a lot of research online or taking a course via the Internet, this route is a must. The local service we've been using, in addition to America Online, provides unlimited access to the Internet plus a home page for $19.95 per month.

But what we don't have here is organization, pretty icons to click on, or the online help. At first, finding your way around feels like walking in the dark. Now that AOL is also offering the same terms, other major players will surely follow suit, and terms and service will improve across the board.

The Internet

What I Don't Like about the Internet

Just to give some balance to things, there are definitely disadvantages to cyberspace. More and more of these problems will be eliminated as the technology evolves, but right now here's the downside:

It is time consuming. Even with the fastest equipment and latest software to search for and retrieve information on the Internet, it's so vast and unregulated it's difficult to find the Web site to best suit your needs. I still find it easier to flip through a hardcopy of a book and more comfortable to channel surf on my couch.

Virtual versus Reality

I also think learning is better facilitated by group interaction and hands-on manipulation of material. Online learning is a great alternative when these options are not available or too expensive.

When I talked with Cindy about the advantages and disadvantages of distance learning, she mentioned all the leadership skills college has brought to the surface in Nate. She hadn't really seen this in him before because he had never been in a situation that created the opportunity. I think online courses are a serious option, but as with software and video instruction as well, I wouldn't want to use this for more than one or two courses at a time.

What I Do Like about the Internet

I like the incredible wealth of information conveniently available for practically nothing.

We use the Internet primarily to search for information on every topic imaginable and to get it at the earliest possible moment. We had prime seats at the most recent Christian concerts we went to because we had the schedules via the Internet much sooner than they were advertized locally.

I also shop on the Net. I've always been a mail-order shopper—I hate to "go shopping." I don't like the time consumed. I don't like traffic, long checkout lines, or incompetent salespersons—I have a pretty long list of gripes. This method is even more convenient than mail, stores are always open, and the selection is vast.

And we use the Internet to get connected to the virtual community beyond our locale. Homeschoolers across the country, friends in other states, penpals in other countries. We may all be cocooning, but virtually we're connected like never before.

Incredible Web Sites to Get You Started

I've tried to make your venture out into cyberspace less frustrating by scouring the Web for the past six months for the best sites for virtual homeschooling. Most of these have links embedded in their site that will automatically transfer you to their recommended sites of related interest. Just click on icons or any words highlighted or underlined in the text and you'll zoom right there.

General: Too Many Links to Categorize

ASK AN EXPERT
http://www.askanexpert.com
Links to Web sites where kids can find an expert on any topic.

B. J. PINCHBECK'S HOMEWORK HELPER
http://tristate.pgh.net/~pinch13
All the links you need for reference material in any subject.

DISCOVERY CHANNEL
http://www.discovery.com

GLOBAL SCHOOLNET FOUNDATION
http://www.gsn.org/
Working to create a worldwide educational community for kids online.

PBS ONLINE
http://www.pbs.org
Lots of teacher support for programming.

Fun

CRAYOLA
http://www.crayola.com

AMERICAN GIRL
http://www.pleasantco.com

History

AMERICAN HISTORY
http://grid.let.rug.nl/~welling/usa/

ANCIENT WORLD WEB: MAIN INDEX
http://atlantic.evsc.virginia.edu/julia/AncientWorld.html

HISTORY CHANNEL
http://www.historychannel.com
Oh, I wish I could get this channel!

PERSEUS PROJECT
http://www.perseus.tufts.edu
Major corporate funding makes this *the* place to connect to the ancient world
of Greece and Rome on the Web, designed by Tufts University's classics
department.

Homeschooling

The best sites with links of interest and help to homeschoolers have been designed by
members of the homeschool community. Visit these sites, and e-mail a thank you for all
the hard work and service.

HOMEFRONT EDUCATION
http://www.ebicom.net/~rileyafr/

KEVIN MCKAY'S HOME PAGE
http://integralink.com

THE MAY FAMILY HOME EDUCATION PAGE
http://www.cyberstation.net/~may/

MISSOURI HOME PAGE
http://www.win.org/library/staff/kmcmulle/mohome.htm
A librarian and homeschool dad has amassed an impressive list of links in all areas—especially of interest to the Reformed among us.

OREGON HOME EDUCATION NETWORK WEBSITES
http://www.teleport.com/~ohen/Web sites.html

Math

MATHCOUNTS
http://mathcounts.org
Click on POW for the challenging "problem of the week."

THE MATH FORUM and DR. MATH
http://forum.swarthmore.edu
Students at Swarthmore College operate this site for schoolchildren. Lots of recommended math resources and activities.

Museums

WORLD WIDE WEB VIRTUAL LIBRARY: MUSEUMS
http://www.icom.org/vlmp
Links to hundreds of museums around the world.

Music

MARSALIS ON MUSIC
http://www.wnet.org:80/mom/
I spent far too long here playing "Name that Tune."

Science

BILL NYE THE SCIENCE GUY
http://nyelabs.kcts.org
Why am I not surprised? This is a one-of-a-kind site.

DR. BOB'S INTERESTING SCIENCE STUFF
http://ny.frontiercomm.net/~bjenkin/science.htm

FROG DISSECTION
http://curry.edschool.Virginia.EDU/go/frog/home.html
Virtual dissection here.

HANDS-ON ACTIVITIES FROM NATIONAL ENGINEERS WEEK
http://www.sme.org/memb/neweek/Comm.hpact.htm

LAWRENCE HALL OF SCIENCE HOTLINKS PAGE
http://equals.lhs.berkeley.edu

NASA
http://www.nasa.gov/

OAKLAND ZOO ANIMALS A–Z
http://www.oaklandzoo.org
Great pictures.

SCIED: SCIENCE AND MATH EDUCATION RESOURCES
http://www-hpcc.astro.washington.edu/scied/science.html
Recommended resources.

HOMESCHOOLING and SCIENCE RESOURCES and LINKS
http://www.eskimo.com/~billb/
A homeschooler and amateur scientist.

Search Engine

METACRAWLER
http://metacrawler.com
This is a nifty site that allows you to use all the major search engines at once.

Find more help in:

The Internet Kids Yellow Pages, Jean Armour Polly (Osborne, 1996).*

The Internet for Teachers, Bard Williams (IDG Books, 1995).

How to Stay on the Edge of Technology

These sources will help you acquire and maintain a cutting-edge understanding of technology.

Books

For Dummies series, i.e., *PCs for Dummies, The Internet for Dummies,* etc. (IDG Books).

Netstudy: Your Guide to Getting Better Grades Using the Internet and Online Services, Michael Wolff, editor (Wolff New Media, 1996).

Visual 3D series, for example, *Computers Simplified, Windows 95* (MaranGraphics).

Magazines

These are the best magazines about surfing the Net and about technology in general—or at least these are the ones Kermit has piled around the bedroom that I am able to decipher.

PC World (800-825-7595)
http://www.pcworld.com

PC Magazine (800-335-1195)
http://www.pcmag.com

FamilyPC (800-413-9749)
http://www.familypc.com

Homeschool PC (800-346-6322)
http://www.home-school.com

PART 8

Creative Solutions

In This Section

- Winning Over Public Officials and Relatives
- Toddlers and Other Blessed Challenges
- Transitioning from School to Home
- Motivating the Reluctant Learner

29

Winning Over
Public Officials and Relatives

. . . .

T his is a chapter about your homeschool witness. There isn't uniform agreement on this topic amongst homeschoolers and leaders, but I'd like to take my best shot at making the case for a voluntary public relations campaign by every homeschool family out there.

I'm looking to create opportunities for my kids and to get doors to open for them. I'm sure you don't mind opportunities and open doors either. It's still our choice to take advantage of them.

Good relations with school officials, the public-at-large, and *our family members* will mean more doors, more choices, more opportunities. Poor relations with school officials, the public-at-large, and Grandma will mean fewer doors, fewer choices, fewer opportunities, fewer gifts at Christmas—not just for your family, but for other homeschoolers who come after you as well.

My Personal Testimony

Having tackled more than my share of legislators, school officials, traffic cops, baseball umpires, and other authority figures, including my father and husband, I'd like to draw from my extensive firsthand experience—which pretty much involves years of butting my head against a wall, offending nearly everyone I was trying to influence, and in general never getting my way—as righteous as it may have been.

In my recent past it occurred to me that a different strategy was worth a shot. I mean, given my impressive results, what did I have to lose?

I tried being pleasant, respectful, and overwhelmingly charming as a novel approach. Guess what? People still said no—but not quite so emphatically. I took this as an invitation to go another round. And eventually, in some cases they agreed with me.

The Terrain

Homeschooling is now legal in all fifty states, but that certainly doesn't mean it is hassle-free. Despite overwhelming research to support homeschool success, many school officials still show little respect for the rights of parents to direct their children's education. Teachers' unions, state school board associations, the national PTA, and other groups *with a vested interest in maintaining the status quo*, often disregard evidence to the contrary and issue categorical statements against homeschooling—amusingly, not about the quality of the education homeschool students might be receiving but almost always about their supposed lack of socialization.

Our culture is enamored with "experts" who are conditioned to believe the credentials they hold grant them authority and rights in children's lives that were once unequivocally the domain of parents.

It is a subtle and insidious attitude—I know because I possessed it. The college training I received and the culture in which I taught supported the belief that school officials know what is best for children—and not just in educating them but in determining the entire domain of their social, emotional, and intellectual development.

A condescending attitude toward parents is pervasive. It wasn't until I left the system that I could see this bias.

How Are We Gonna Win?

With that said, it may surprise you that I believe homeschoolers should do all we can to meet our legal requirements with excellence and treat school officials with respect.

I further think it is in our best interest to not lambast public education or public-educated kids. When we categorically question any product of the current system or advocate its demise we engender the same prejudicial attitudes in our own children that are directed toward us. A haughty attitude will only close doors of opportunity and create another destructive current of divisiveness in our churches and community.

Comply with Excellence

Having labored long in the pro-life and homeschool arenas, I have been faced with the decision to participate in civil disobedience on numerous occasions and sharply criticized when I did not. My husband would never let me, and I am grateful for his restraint. Instead we channeled our outrage into starting a pregnancy care center that now ministers to more than twelve hundred women annually. I also reported in to my school district when homeschooling was underground in Pennsylvania. I've met a number of times with my school administration and invited the superintendent to visit our home.

 My mentors in choosing these courses of action have been Francis Schaeffer and Chuck Colson. (See *A Christian Manifesto* [Crossway, 1981] and *Kingdoms in Conflict* [Zondervan, 1987].)

At the time, I was uncertain whether I was choosing the coward's way out or the righteous one. I realize others have sincerely held beliefs that have led them to other conclusions. But here are the benefits we have realized from choosing to respect the authority God has placed in our lives, even when we did not agree with that authority's policies:

#1. Excellence and Cooperation Are Good PR for the Homeschool Movement

I don't want my kids going through life constantly dealing with people's misconceptions about homeschooling or explaining their education to skeptics. A few years ago folks routinely responded negatively when they heard we homeschooled. Our family doctor, chosen because he was a Christian and pro-life, lectured me on homeschooling while I fumed. Others—even chance acquaintances—let us know right away they thought we were sheltering our kids and jeopardizing their future. My children were young at the time, and they did not like this reaction at all. They were worried we were going to get into trouble. (I have very compliant kids—which has always surprised my mother.)

This grousing rarely happens anymore. Why? The press on homeschooling has been overwhelmingly positive, and the undeniable results are impressive. Almost everyone knows someone who homeschools and often thinks highly of their results. Because most people now respond with high interest and respect, my children are proud to be homeschooled. I want them to feel homeschooling makes them unique, not suspect.

Responsibly complying with the homeschool regulations governing your state, even those you do not agree with, will engender respect for the homeschool movement at large. Doing an excellent job will raise public opinion of homeschooling and open doors to more opportunities for your kids and for those who come after them.

 Several years ago I was asked to evaluate a high school student at the end of his first homeschool year. His parents had desperately tried homeschooling to keep him from dropping out. When I found out his folks were both working full-time during the day, I became concerned. When I saw how little he had to show for his entire year, I was disturbed. I had heard something in the wind about this situation, and when I questioned the child at least he was truthful: He was not only *not* doing his work, he often spent his day at a park in the center of town with another "supposedly" homeschooled student—and smoking, to boot! I let him have it. His actions not only jeopardized his own future but the freedom of those who worked hard for a favorable law in Pennsylvania. The vast majority of homeschooling families are responsible. But it only takes one situation of abuse profiled in the media to start the erosion of our freedoms and public opinion.

Now here's someone we should be proud to call our own:

Last summer I sat on a panel that addressed more than forty college admissions officers. These folks had concerns about homeschooled kids' diplomas, transcripts, quality of education, and social adjustment to college. On the panel were three adults and one student—Jesse Richman, a graduate of homeschooling who now attends the Honors College at Pitt University on a full academic scholarship. Jesse entered Pitt with nineteen credits already to his name through Advanced Placement exams, correspondence courses, and summer studies. He spoke about what he had done during high school to prepare for college and his adjustment to college life. He was funny, articulate, and poised. He smashed every stereotypical concern those admissions officers held. You could feel the room buzz with interest. Several of the directors cornered us afterward—to talk not just about admitting homeschooled students but about the possibility of homeschooling their own kids! Jesse did a great deal that day to open doors for future homeschool applicants at some of the best schools in our state.

#2. Excellence and Respect Bring Honor to the Gospel

I was a very lackluster undergraduate. Even after I became a Christian, I attended no more than 50 percent of my classes—often cutting class to watch The 700 Club—and was satisfied with a low B average when I could have done far better. I didn't understand at the time why my professors were unmoved by my eloquent defense of my newfound faith.

Between graduation and graduate school, friends gave me *How Should We Then Live?** by Francis Schaeffer (Crossway, 1983). I can credit that book with awakening in my heart a love for learning and a deep desire to cultivate the intellectual abilities God has given me.

I set (and realized) a goal to achieve a 4.0 in a competitive graduate program. I attacked my studies with zeal, often going far beyond what was required because I was interested in learning, not just trying to get a grade. I hung around the English department and took full advantage of academic life. I became a graduate assistant and got to know my professors well. I can't report any conversions—but I can say my professors came to respect me enough as a student to take seriously my contribution to discussions on faith and morality. I learned a life lesson.

We are ambassadors for Christ. Your interaction with school officials, legislators, and others you seek to influence will attract them to or repeal them away from the gospel you seek to represent. How we conduct ourselves in these moments *where we have the greatest personal interest in the outcome* is the true indication of our character (a fact recently brought home to me by the Holy Spirit while yelling at an ump's bad call against my son). That's where the rubber meets the road, and others know it.

Are you attracting people to Christ? Are there some folks you don't particularly *care* to attract? Is that a bad attitude? (Just checking.)

#3. Others Will Go to Bat for You

I want homeschooling to open doors of opportunity for my kids, not shut them. And that has meant I've needed others to help me accomplish that. My word alone on the outstanding merits of my kids' achievements, their good looks, and terrific teacher doesn't seem to be enough. It's the rare scenario indeed that opens the doors to a child's future without others helping him or her get there.

We all benefit when others *outside the movement* speak well on our behalf. Don't be naive. Public education is not going to "go gently into that good night." As the ranks of homeschoolers swell and alternative educational choices abound, the status quo will dig in its heels and do all it can to stop these movements. We would be well-served to have respected researchers, educators, and professionals outside the movement speak up on our behalf. It's our job to be people they want to stick their necks out for.

The same superintendent whom I allowed to visit our home later helped me win open access to sports participation for Mike and Gabe.

One university professor was so impressed with homeschool portfolios he reviewed he launched a research project into homeschooling. His results have triggered interest at Penn State University, where quite a few studies are under way, all showing impressive findings. This is the kind of defense that will win battles in legislatures and the press.

Be the kind of person folks want to go out of their way for, and teach your children the same principle. Colleges are going to ask for letters of recommendation and references. Admissions officers and employers are inclined to call local school officials for their input on a homeschool applicant. Poor relations between yourself and those who hold the legal authority over you hurt you far more than they hurt them.

Bringing about Change When Change Is Necessary

Okay, so now that we've adjusted our attitude, let's talk about a practical strategy for disarming opposition. Be it your mother-in-law or truancy officer.

If the issues are legal, **Home School Legal Defense Association** (HSLDA) is who you want at bat. They provide an immeasurable service through their legal aid to homeschool families in conflict with authorities and its lobbying efforts on Capitol Hill.

Following their recommended guidelines for legal compliance in your state while they legally fight to change or relax regulations is the best way to see change brought about. We will not effect this by acting as individuals. We must work in concert with one another and follow recognized leadership. States with splintered homeschool groups would do well to form alliances for the purpose of exacting legislative change. Homeschoolers who are not unified will not be taken seriously by lawmakers and public school officials.

Getting the Job Done at Ground Zero

While HSLDA works, here's what you can do at the grassroots to cultivate a climate conducive for change:

It's a Public Relations Game

All politics is local, and PR is how it is played. This is why I run a homeschool program that is heavy on communication skills. I want to train my kids to persuasively articulate their convictions. Being well-spoken, with a life of integrity to back it up, is a powerful influencer.

How We Gained Access to Scholastic Sports

Everywhere I speak, parents ask me for help in gaining access to sports participation for their kids. It is the current flashpoint for the homeschool community, earning articles in the *New York Times*,[1] *USA Today*,[2] and *U.S. News & World Report*[3] this past year within a few weeks of each other.

While many homeschool families will not be interested in this kind of opportunity for their children, my heart goes out to those kids who love athletic competition and are unnecessarily denied the opportunity to participate if they continue to homeschool during high school.

I share the following story specifically to help families in this situation and at the same time to illustrate strategies that will help us successfully influence those in authority in other arenas.

#1. Be Involved in Your Community

To be an influencer, you can't afford a narrow identity. If folks know you only as a homeschooler, it's easy to ignore your plight and write you off as someone only concerned with his or her own interests. If folks in power see you as one of them because they know you from church, boy scouts, the paper drive, or the community recreational program, they will at least give your request a hearing.

Prior to homeschooling, Kermit and I had a relationship with our superintendent and several board members. All the board members knew we were involved in the community—especially in their reelection campaigns. When we approached them about our kids playing on the sports teams, all but one were opposed. But because they had favorable knowledge of us, they listened thoughtfully to our request. (See the box on "How to Build a Bridge" on page 307 for more suggestions along these lines.)

#2.   Establish Rapport Between Yourself and Those in Authority

Besides being involved, be personable. In many states, little personal interaction between school officials and homeschoolers is needed to fulfill legal requirements. Nevertheless, going out of your way to interact with those in authority will smash the stereotype that we are isolationists.

Introduce yourself to your legislator; take a field trip to his or her state office. Hold a legislative breakfast or homeschooling fair annually at the capital. Do all these things before you start making specific requests.

#3.   Have a Spirit of Inquiry

This has probably been the most valuable teaching I've ever received in terms of resolving difficulties in human relationships. A spirit of inquiry means you pose the issues in the form of a question. "Honey, how do you feel about our financial situation?" "Do you think we should come up with better strategies for staying on budget?" Not, "You are overspending again." "You aren't sticking to the budget we agreed to."

Whenever you are appealing to someone in authority, pose your appeal in the form of a question.

After my first meeting with the school board where I realized I was in for a resounding defeat, I decided to find out exactly what I was up against. Another homeschool father and I called every school board member personally. All I asked was, "What are your concerns about homeschool students' participation in extracurricular activities?"

My only goal was to listen, not lobby. I drew out every member until I felt I understood what his or her stumbling blocks were. In one case, we never even talked about the issue. The board member just went on and on about how difficult her job was and how unappreciated and misunderstood she was by the community. I realized she needed a sympathetic ear, so I listened and encouraged her. We never got to the issue. But I had the strong sense that God wanted me to table my concerns and focus on her needs.

#4.   Show Why Your Request Benefits Everyone Involved

I know those in authority are not primarily concerned with my interests, so I want to show them how granting my appeal will benefit them or the constituents they serve. In this particular situation, I didn't want the board to feel politically pressured to make a favorable decision (that is a last resort); I wanted to convince them this was the right decision for our school district. I took the list of concerns that I heard them express:

✔ The academic quality of homeschooling
✔ Fairness to other students
✔ Eligibility and attendance requirements
✔ Insurance
✔ Their lack of obligation to provide services to homeschoolers

I believed if our position was just, God would give me compelling reasons why it was the right decision for the district. I prepared an information packet that I distributed to every board member before their meeting (I was later told this was the most impressive packet they'd ever received from a constituent—another case for the benefits of excellence). This contained research on home education from the **National Home Education Research Institute** (NHERI) and **HSLDA**, an eligibility and attendance form I created, and proposed solutions for preventing abuse of the privilege as well as all the benefits to the district. (Among those benefits was the opportunity for the homeschooled community and the public-schooled community to better understand one another—a politically popular theme these days.)

#5.   Give the Political Process Time to Work

In all the cases I know of that have led to an open-access policy, the homeschoolers making the appeal gave themselves plenty of time to work with the school board or state legislature.

In the cases that have failed, homeschoolers waited until the last board meeting before the beginning of the sport they wanted their child to participate in. Then they naively thought they could present their case and get a victorious vote that night.

Authority figures, I've learned the hard way, do not vote for change under pressure. They always feel "no" is the safer bet.

In one case in Pennsylvania, a homeschool mom was ill-advised by her lawyer to sue her district in federal court. No public relations work, no negotiations, no political process— straight to court, where she lost resoundingly in twenty minutes. And in the process, she jeopardized every other family who had already won access should the judge's decision have been broadly worded. She has absolutely no recourse now. That administration and board are never going to change their minds about offering access to a family that sued them as the opening salvo of the appeal.

In our case, I approached the board two years before my sons would be affected. Along with a few other parents, I went to numerous meetings. When it looked like an unfavorable vote was imminent, we would ask them to postpone their decision one more meeting to allow us time to address their concerns. When the vote was finally taken, it was unanimously in favor—and the board even applauded![4]

I knew then the board had been convinced this was the right decision, and they were happy they could make one that gave them satisfaction.

Since then, the makeup of our board and administration has drastically changed, but the policy is firmly in place because we took the time to lay a solid foundation for it.

How to Build a Bridge

Things you can do on the local level to open the door to participation:

1. Comply promptly and with excellence with the homeschool laws.
2. Establish rapport between yourself and the administration. Ask what concerns the administrators have about participation. Listen.
3. Make sure your kids demonstrate leadership and respectful attitudes on their teams.
4. Get to know your school board members. Call them and ask what concerns they have. Work to positively address those concerns.
5. Call the local media to cover homeschool events or the accomplishments of homeschool students. If you can show the board feature stories about homeschool athletes participating in a neighboring district, that would be helpful. But be careful. If the media takes over and foments the situation to create controversy, you'll lose the battle. Know the reporter.
6. Work to build community-wide understanding about homeschooling. Participate as a support group in community events. Set up an informational booth for the purpose of education (not recruitment) at fairs and bazaars.
7. Choose a homeschool spokesperson who is articulate and respected.
8. Call your state and local representatives and ask them to write a letter on your behalf.
9. Collect signatures from registered voters who support homeschool students' participation.
10. Get coaches and other respected individuals to speak up on your kids' behalf. (Make sure your kids have done their job in earning respect.)
11. Be respectful and charming. Don't come across as someone demanding his or her rights. Ask for the privilege of participating. Request the opportunity for the homeschool community to show themselves responsible.
12. Show appreciation to your school board and administration for their work and consideration. Children who do participate should send thank you notes at the end of the sports season to the board and administration.
13. Diplomacy takes longer but in the end it works!

Yes, But What about My Mother-in-Law?

Give her the benefit of the doubt. She only wants to tell her friends all about her wonderful grandchildren. If you do all we've covered above—homeschool with excellence and maintain a respectful attitude toward her concerns—she'll eventually change her views.

I've spoken to many fretful moms, worried because a relative is threatening to turn them in for child abuse or some other trumped-up charge if they homeschool.

I don't know of a single case where this has occurred or where grandparents continued the barrage once they saw their grandkids turning out all right. Put yourself in their shoes. Will you feel threatened if your kids don't parent the way you do?

We started off with no support from either side. My poor parents—my dad, an administrator; my mom, a teacher—had to explain THIS in the faculty room, and my mother-in-law just couldn't believe what we were doing was legal. (That's because it wasn't at first.) Kermit's mom had been looking forward to all the special school events with her grandkids she had enjoyed with her own children. I understood her disappointment.

But nine years later, everyone is acclimated to the situation. And they all know other grandparents in the same boat—so they can commiserate together or share successes. I think they've all been real troopers.

Toddlers and Other Blessed Challenges

In a world that despises large families and routinely abuses or ignores little ones, the homeschool community should be a haven of welcome and adoration for our toddlers and babies. We need to make room for them in our lives as well as support and revere parents of large families.

But that doesn't mean we let them run the show.

Toddlers are in desperate need of training if they are to grow up to bow their knee to the Lordship of Jesus Christ.

If you have toddlers, your homeschool program has to be designed with their needs in mind. Otherwise, you are going to be frustrated, and they will feel ignored. And the two-year-olds I know don't take being ignored lying down. They make you pay for it.

Case in point: The day we moved into our new house, my daughter Kristen, just two, ate my contact lenses while I was consumed with unpacking. Fortunately, they were soft.

Despite all the challenges, it's possible for your older kids to get the education they need in an environment populated with assorted-size siblings. It may take an attitude adjustment though.

Tips:

1. **Raise independent learners.** Here's where the strategies in chapter 15 become essential. It is very easy to let our older kids drive the curriculum. But our younger children need our focus and attention to a greater extent. If we have designed a program that expects independence and self-government from our kids, our older kids should be able to complete their studies while we work in a more concentrated way with our young ones. Field trips, reading aloud, and hands-on experiences are essential building blocks for future academic success. You can't afford to shortchange them.

2. **Maximize naptime.** If you have maintained a consistent routine and schedule for your kids, then you should have an afternoon nap to take advantage of regularly. This is when you haul out the science experiments and art projects that can't accommodate your toddlers' involvement. Katie was never a nap-taker, but we still expected her to remain quietly in her room for an hour or more on weekday afternoons playing with her stuffed animals while I worked with the boys.

3. **Allow older kids to teach younger siblings.** While you tutor one child in algebra, assign another to complete an art project or read aloud to your toddlers. Give your older child responsibility for designing the lesson. This will give her valuable experience and reinforce her understanding of the material.

4. **Purchase special materials just for school time.** Like the Velveteen Rabbit, your toddlers want to be real. Set up a school area for them and place special items in a box that may only be used during "school time." I used to rotate toys to extend my kids' interest in them. If Legos are always available and spewed everywhere, they are taken for granted. But if kept in a sealed container and only permitted out at certain times of the day, they keep most toddlers transfixed. Puzzles, quality art supplies, a colorful workbook, a tube of paste, construction paper, a pop-up book, construction tools, etc., that are available on a limited basis will keep many kids occupied for the time you need to teach a brief lesson in history or grammar to other children.

5. **Limit their range.** Just as my kids did not have free access to all of their toys, they did not have free access to all of the house. I turned an unused pantry off the kitchen into a playroom. When they were toddlers, my kids spent their mornings there behind a safety gate while I did my chores or later taught school to the boys.

Had they been there all day, they surely would have rebelled. But I periodically rotated their play area to other sections of the house. In a Montessori preschool, kids move from station to station throughout the day. The same principle, in a more informal way, can be practiced here with success. (At the Learning Center homeschool co-op, even though not necessary, I have the toddlers change classrooms throughout the morning just to keep them moving.)

More from moms who know:

- Have lots of hands-on items for your toddlers to do while you do lessons, for example, Play-Doh, felt books, erasable crayons, preschool workpages.
- Invest in one or two large, fun play sets such as Legos, a Fisher Price farm set, a tool set, or Erector sets.
- Spend time with your toddler ten to fifteen minutes of every hour. If toddlers are with a sibling too long, they get fussy.
- Use a hands-on curriculum, such as KONOS, with older ones so toddlers can participate as well.

31

Transitioning from School to Home

. . . .

The largest growth in the homeschool ranks is coming from families who are withdrawing children from a public or private school. If this is you, then you have a greater challenge than those of us whose children have never known anything else.

Your children have a very strong picture of what school is supposed to look like, plus they are conditioned to be with their peers for the better part of their day. Functioning apart from the crowd requires learning a whole new set of skills and cultivating new avenues of interest.

In some cases, it is the child who is asking to be homeschooled. He recognizes that he is becoming a casualty of the system and is asking for relief. These kids make the transition much easier than those whose parents decide to homeschool without their kids' full cooperation.

Setting Realistic Expectations

To give homeschooling in this situation the best shot, you'll need these strategies:

#1. The Older the Child Is, the More Time It Will Take to Acclimate Him to Homeschooling

I've known several families who've homeschooled their younger children but have left their teenagers in school. They realized their teens were too entrenched to accept the decision well. In some cases, the older kids have asked to be homeschooled after seeing the benefits of homeschooling in their younger siblings.

If you decide to homeschool resistant children (and I would if I believed God was calling me to), invest significant time prior to the change into building faith for the venture in their hearts.

311

While I believe Kermit and I have full authority in our teenagers' lives, we also are willing to talk through with them time and again our reasons for the limitations we place upon them. I want an open air of communication between us. I much prefer that they feel free to disagree (respectfully) with us than to create an authoritarian environment that provokes them into putting on an appearance of compliance while hiding the true intentions of their hearts.

Give your kids time to adjust. Look for small steps forward and thank God for them. As I've said earlier, parenting is a risk. There are no guarantees that we will always make the right decisions. But that's not what we put our faith in. We put our faith in God's commitment to work all things for the good. With that kind of promise, we have to go with our best instincts in a given situation and trust that nothing we do subverts God's will in our kids' lives.

#2. You Need Involvement in a Support Group or Co-op

Your kids are going to miss their friends at school—even feel as though they have lost their identity (which is probably something you want to replace anyway). They need a new network of friends. Start networking with the homeschool community right away—attend activities before your kids are even withdrawn.

#3. Maximize the Opportunities Homeschooling Offers

If you merely re-create school at home, minus all the fun, your kids will likely be resentful. They need to see the benefits of homeschooling in a tangible way. One reason my sons have concluded homeschooling is the best place for them right now is because of the opportunities they have.

If your kids only see the limitations, not the benefits (freedom to control their day, apprenticeships, field trips, travel, etc.), don't expect them to be grateful for your sacrifices here.

You may find that family schools or co-ops require families to complete one year of homeschooling before being considered for membership. This doesn't make the transition any easier for you, but many groups have found it is best that parents have fully assumed the responsibility for their children's education before supplementing with other sources.

#4. Be Confident; Be a Leader—Even If It Is a Bluff!

Having worked with and observed kids, including juvenile delinquents, in thousands of situations, I am convinced that strong leadership always brings out their best behavior. Once they perceive a lack of confidence, control quickly deteriorates.

The most humiliating job I've ever had was that of a substitute teacher. You have _no power_ and _no penalty_ to impose. There isn't a lot of backup for you, either. The administration is just hoping you survive the day, not teach.

I took this a little longer than my father would have—two days. Rather than let them mock and humiliate me for one more minute, I decided to call these brawny seventeen-year-olds' bluff—or die trying. Without any weapon but my tongue, I threw kids out of class, buzzed for the principal (who was not happy about that), or sent them to the office. I left detailed notes for the regular teacher. My husband even called some parents for me.

Instead of accepting the standard "Give them a study hall" instructions left by absent teachers, I brought in my own lesson plans, taught poetry, taught algebra (I was clueless—but they didn't know the difference), and generally acted like I was someone they wouldn't dare mess with. Pretty soon I didn't have any problems, and worse, I had far too many calls to substitute.

Now, I sneak that story in just to say that if I can get high school seniors to treat a substitute teacher with respect (and you know what _you_ did to substitutes when you were a senior) then you can get your own disgruntled teenagers to cooperate with you. You _have_ power— you've got the food! Just act like you have no doubt they will do anything different.

Motivating the Reluctant Learner

My first three children are intrinsically motivated to learn. I took this characteristic for granted until Kristen came along. When they were younger, Mike, Gabe, and Katie were easily preoccupied for hours with games they invented, imaginative play, and being out of doors. They could hardly wait to begin our homeschool, to learn to read, to mess around with numbers, to get on the computer. For the most part, they've maintained that enthusiasm throughout the years.

Because of that, I assumed all kids were born with this inner motivation to learn. All parents need do is fill their homes with wonderful books, art supplies, musical instruments, and watch the magic unfold—à la Marie Montessori.

Then came Kristen, who couldn't have cared less about all this invited learning stuff—she wanted the TV.

Unlike the others, she was never anxious for me to begin homeschooling her. And when we did start, most of my day was spent calling her back to the kitchen table, lecturing her on staying focused, prodding her to initiate her own studies. I overreacted at first and zealously set out to change this kid. *I'm going to MAKE you love to learn,* I'd think angrily. Kristen won this battle of the wills.

Finally, the Holy Spirit got my attention, and I began seeking the Lord for some wisdom. I believe He gave us insight and a plan, and we have seen significant change in Kristen's motivation to learn as she has grown. Her situation also made me more observant of other children in the same boat. Here are my conclusions:

Why Kids Can Be Reluctant

There are two possible explanations for children who are reluctant to learn, and these usually appear in combination:

1. Their attitudes
2. Their abilities

Both can be hampering their success. Let's look at them now and talk about possible creative solutions.

Character Flaws

"Foolishness is bound up in the heart of a child" (Prov. 22:15). Not an honored premise of modern psychology but, nevertheless, an unchanging truth of the universe. Any honest parent will have to conclude its reality from experience.

God's job description for us includes helping our kids replace that foolishness with wisdom. That's pretty difficult to do if we don't hold a biblical view of children or follow a biblical pattern of training them during their early years. But if you haven't, I can guarantee your homeschooling goals will soon be derailed by bad attitudes, rebellion, disrespect, slothfulness, disorganization, etc.

It's beyond the purpose of this book to cover parenting skills, but often the heartaches we face with our reluctant learners are rooted in the undealt-with sin in their lives.

When I discern that sin is the root of resistance in one of our kids, I don't sugarcoat the truth by dreaming up fun and games to entice them into cooperating. I want them to clearly understand the heart of the matter and know they are responsible for recognizing it, repenting, and demonstrating a change of heart. My goal is to motivate by grace; my heart wants to see them do well.

One evening I poured out my concerns about Kristen to Kermit. I went to pains to elaborate on all the areas of difficulty I was facing with her and my fears. When I was through, Kermit said simply, "The problem is laziness." I had been expecting a more complicated explanation, but his succinctness had the piercing point of truth to it.

Kristen is very tender-hearted, and she responded attentively to my discussion with her the next day. She wants to please us and please the Lord. She also knew we would follow through with discipline if she continued to disregard her schoolwork. We saw immediate change, and I am confident Kermit discerned the situation rightly.

Prayerfully examine the areas of difficulty your child is having in school. What character flaws might be contributing to this? Kermit knew sin was a root problem for Kristen because he saw her "reluctance" as a pervasive characteristic of her life. It wasn't just math that lost her interest; it was disinterest across the board in anything requiring exertion: piano, reading, chores, getting up.

Ability to Learn

A child's ability to learn can be hampered. There are two factors to look at here:

1. Your child can be *internally* stalled because his learning style, readiness, or interests are not being respected.

2. He may be *externally* hampered by his learning environment. The lack of structure or routine, the resources you are using, or the approach you choose can all affect your child's ability to learn the material successfully.

In Kristen's case I was also not honoring her internal timetable. Despite knowing better, I was comparing Kristen to the time line followed by the twins and Katie. I did expect her to read by age six as they had and to match their temperament and motivation as well. When she didn't, I used my frustration and expectations to try and drive her forward. As strong-willed as her mother, Kristen would dig in and prepare for a fight. She *is* gifted in debate!

Cultivating Their Motivation

I always want to get to the heart of a matter. And for reluctant learners, the root is almost always a lack of motivation. This lack can be caused by their attitudes and their abilities, as described above. Step one is to discern what factors in each of these categories may be a drain on their drive.

Once discerned, my focus is not, "How do I *teach* this child this stuff?" It is always, "How do I *motivate* this child to learn this stuff?"

When motivated, human beings can overcome tremendous obstacles. Think of the endurance and accomplishments of musicians Itzhak Perlman and Ray Charles; Miss America, Heather Whitestone; and Olympic gymnast Kerri Strug. All of them overcame great challenges but still managed to excel. They should inspire you to believe in your child's potential *once he is motivated,* even if he has been diagnosed as learning disabled.

So, as you work with your reluctant learner, keep focused on the sole goal of motivating your child. Then let him take responsibility for his actual progress.

Ten Motivating Strategies

#1. Build Faith in Your Child to Learn—Get Everyone on Board

Your child needs to believe he can learn. That confidence is engendered at an early age by what he hears his parents say about him.

You're the coach; tell him what to believe: "You are a learner." "God has given you the ability to learn this." "You are a reader." "You are making progress." "Look how much farther you are than last week."

I'm very attuned to our children's self-concept. I want to stay on top of what they believe to be true about themselves. I cringe when I hear parents introduce a toddler as "my little monster" or the kid "who drives me crazy." Those children are going to fulfill their parents' expectations.

When my toddlers disobeyed me, I would frequently say, "I know you want to obey Mommy. You just need help again in this one area. I know you want to please me." I said this over and over again to imprint that message on their brains: *I obey Mommy. Yes, I want to please my mommy. That's who I am.*

 Even now that the twins are teens, I frequently tell them how trustworthy they are, how I *NEVER* even worry about them doing *ANYTHING* behind my back. I know it just *ISN'T* in their hearts to do *SUCH A THING.*

Some of you may think I stretch the truth a bit in these proclamations—I prefer to think that I have faith to believe in things yet unseen (see Hebrews 11) and a mother's love to believe the best of my kids (see 1 Corinthians 13).

Anyway, it appears to work.

Protect your child from the hurtful comments of others. As your child grows older, he'll take more seriously the comments of his peers and siblings. I have been adamant that my older kids treat Kristen with respect and not discourage her progress. I've talked with them about verbally encouraging her and taking an interest in her life.

 It's very natural for young children to memorize a favorite story and say they are reading it. When Katie began to do this with *Goodnight Moon,* her six-year-old brothers would insist, "You're not really reading that." I nipped that in the bud immediately. To read, a child needs to believe he can read. If your little one calls what Katie was doing reading, support him in that. Do all you can to show your confidence in him.

#2.   Adapt to His Learning Style

Go back to Part 2 and review the material on learning styles. Do you have an actual-spontaneous learner you are expecting to do seatwork five hours a day? If your total program isn't designed around an understanding of how your child learns best, you are asking him to swim upstream from the get-go.

 Since birth, Kristen has loved music and listening to audiotapes. We have the entire *Odyssey* collection from Focus on the Family, and Kristen has many of the dramas memorized. She could probably start her own Odyssey version of *trekkies.*

Audiotapes were the only thing that interested her more than the television. And as with TV, it was frustrating me that that was all she was motivated to do with her time. It suddenly occurred to me one day (about six years and a hundred dollars in tapes later) that she was an *auditory* learner. I wondered if she would be willing to learn other material if it were presented on tape. I tried an experiment: I bought some American history stories on tape and some French tapes. She was just as happy to listen to those as well.

Since I was now investing more time in *observing* how my child learned best than in figuring out a way to make her adapt to my expectations, I also noticed how well she remembered material she had learned on tape. Our homeschool spent one field trip sailing the Chesapeake Bay on a replica Pungy Schooner. As we sailed past Fort McHenry, the guide asked the students what had happened there. I was astounded when Kristen, then in second grade, shot up her hand. (I had not covered this with her. How could she possibly know?) Do you know?

Kristen not only answered correctly that Francis Scott Key had written our national anthem there, but she went into great detail about the War of 1812 between the British and the United States over water rights and how Key had been held captive during the night on a British warship. On the way home I asked her how in the world she had known all that stuff. *"Mom,"* she said with a great deal of surprise. "Don't you remember? It was a story on Odyssey!"

Where does your reluctant learner give you the greatest resistance? The least? Is there a correlation between this and the points where your program honors his learning style to the greater degree? Use the suggested methods in Part 2 to better modify your program to his learning style.

#3. Reevaluate Your Methods

I am reminded of Tad, a fifth-grader I tested a few years ago. He didn't do as well as his parents had hoped, so I spent an evening discussing his scores with them. I mentioned that during the test their son had appeared stressed and hurried. From that comment, I learned that Tad gets very upset when he is being timed. This had been a favored technique in the private school he had previously attended. And his mom was now using a timer to keep Tad diligently focused on his schoolwork. Without this method, his parents felt Tad took excessive amounts of time on his work and often didn't even finish.

I suggested a compromise that now helps Tad to manage his time better and also gives him more control of his environment. His parents have given Tad the egg timer and allow him to set it. It has become a competition with himself to see if he can improve his score from day to day. It has worked. Now that he has control of the timer, he is not distracted or stressed by it. He can focus in on his studies.

I also retested Tad. Only this time I did not time the standardized test. I told him he could take as long as he liked. (I noted this deviation from the norms on the test report and the reason for doing so as well.) This time Tad scored above grade level in almost every area! I also noticed that he finished most tests in the allotted time. Removing this stressor from his environment freed Tad up to do his best.

#4.   Reevaluate Your Resources

My kids have hated or loved a subject solely because of the resources we've used. Once I started using the *History of Us** series with Mike, Gabe, and Katie, I didn't need to do anything else in that subject area. They love Joy Hakim's fascinating style and read her books even when school is out. That resource alone made Mike name history as his favorite subject.

I switched my sons out of Saxon math for the same reason. They repeatedly complained about math. I told them all homeschool kids love Saxon (I thought this was an inbred trait). It's a terrific program, and most kids I've tested who switch to Saxon math see a big jump in their standardized test scores. But I eventually accepted the fact that Mike and Gabe do not like the Saxon approach. We switched to *Elementary Algebra** by Harold Jacobs, and they like it much better. Jacobs's text has personality and creativity injected into the approach. He has challenging puzzlers at the end of each unit for extra credit. For me, Saxon is the easier program to use, requiring much less time on my part. But for Mike and Gabe's sake, I'm sticking with Jacobs because it motivates them.

(I tell parents who are faced with this decision, "If it ain't broke, don't fix it." If your kids are contented with Saxon's approach, stick to it. Saxon has solution manuals for algebra 1–2 and beyond. Jacobs's just has a teacher guide and answer key, which is definitely a disadvantage for the mathematically challenged mom.)

If you have a reluctant reader, make sure you are using books he or she is interested in reading. Mike and Gabe learned to read using sports biographies and the *Childhood of Famous Americans* series. Katie read through all the *Boxcar Children* books the year she achieved independence, and Kristen's motivation finally kicked in when I purchased *The Beginner's Bible* for her.

Use some common sense. Ask yourself, *Would I be motivated to learn and retain this information if I were taught in this way?*

#5.   Assess Your Learning Environment

Remember: Kids learn best where there are clear boundaries, structure, and expectations. The unschooling[1] approach only works when kids are intrinsically motivated. It's a disastrous decision for the reluctant learner. Make sure your child is clear about what he is expected to get done and when. Don't say, "Johnny, do your math." Better to say, "I want you to do ten problems and recheck your work before you break for lunch."

In his book *Help for Struggling Learners* (Exceptional Diagnostics, 1996)*, Dr. Joe Sutton tells of testing a young boy with learning difficulties. The evaluation showed that this young man needed a quiet, well-lighted place to learn as well as snacks for his high metabolism rate. An interview with the mom revealed that he was currently trying to do his studies at the kitchen table with his other siblings sharing the space. His mom also allowed no snacking in between meals. On Dr. Sutton's recommendation, she set up a private place in a separate room and supplied him with snacks she could live with: sliced vegetables and fruit. Her son was now ready to concentrate on his work.

#6.   Make Sure There Is Timely Accountability

There needs to be a "day of reckoning," a time when the project is due, the test is taken, or the paper is turned in. How high on your priority list are those things without deadlines or obligation to others? Not at the top, right? So too with kids. There needs to be a point at which an evaluation of the work is done.

Contracts are often helpful motivators with older children. I use these with the courses I teach for CHESS. I make it clear that I do not _give_ grades; the students _earn_ them. The first day of class, I pass out a syllabus detailing the due dates for all the major assignments. I also distribute a contract that states specifically what the student agrees to do to earn an A or a B. (I won't accept a student being satisfied with anything less.) Use this same strategy in your home on a weekly basis.

Give the student self-monitoring tools to mark his progress and keep him focused: a daily log, a checklist for marking off completed work, an evaluation sheet for self-checking and assessing his work. Give clear deadlines for major assignments and projects and then stick to them. If these deadlines are tied to something certain, such as a presentation at your writers club or a contest entry, you won't be tempted to change the deadline and your child will be more focused on getting things done.

#7.   Use Outside Influences: Another Teacher, a Co-op Class, Peers

This is the value of a family school such as Creative Home Educators' Support Services (CHESS). Enrolling your reluctant learner in a class or a cooperative activity will often provide the accountability factor he needs. Parents have consistently commented that their children produce far more with less nagging for their CHESS classes. Older children, especially, need the extra incentive of an outside evaluation. They are naturally looking beyond Mom and Dad's approval for recognition.

I've also seen positive peer influence work well with reluctant learners. Among the homeschooled kids I know, doing well is valued and admired. This positive peer influence motivates the reluctant learner to do better to earn their fellow homeschoolers' respect.

#8.   Introduce an Element of Competition

Competition is a powerful trigger for a child's motivation. Bring this element into play in your home program by using games or computer software that challenges him to continuously better his score. **GeoSafari** (<u>Educational Insights</u>)* is a popular electronic game that the child can play with another person or against himself. <u>Muggins</u> math games and <u>24</u> are kid-enticing. Software like <u>MathBlaster</u>, <u>WordMunchers</u>, <u>SpellIt Plus</u>, and <u>Dr. Brain</u> require mastery of skills and academic content to win.

On a larger scale, you can also participate in one of the numerous academic contests now open to homeschoolers. We've been involved in quite a few of these: <u>The National Geography Bee</u>, <u>Math Olympiad</u>, <u>MathCounts</u>, <u>Science-By-Mail</u>, and <u>Knowledge Open</u> are some of our favorites. Check out the Resource Guide for more information on these and other competitions.

We don't usually win, but that's not the point—at least for me. My kids invest lots of time they wouldn't have otherwise spent studying the subject areas for these contests. The weeks before the National Geography Bee, everyone is suddenly interested in the **GeoSafari**, following current events, or reading back issues of *National Geographic's World* magazine (800-647-5463). Katie read an entire atlas her first year of eligibility. The kids scour the maps on the wall and quiz each other at the dinner table—all things they don't do naturally.

<u>Math Olympiad</u> is a great competition for fifth- and sixth-graders. At each of five meets during the year, the students are given five problems to solve within thirty minutes, and all can be solved without using algebra.

The first time I saw a set of problems, I was stunned that elementary students could do these. Here is a set to try:

1. If 20 is added to one-third of a number, the result is the double of what number?

2. Suppose five days before the day after tomorrow was Wednesday. What day of the week was yesterday?

3. The product of two whole numbers is 10,000. If neither number contains a zero digit, what are the numbers?

4. A woman spent two-thirds of her money. She lost two-thirds of the remainder and then had $4 left. With how much money did she start?

5. A4273B is a six-digit number in which A and B are digits. If the number is divisible by 72 without a remainder, what values do A and B have?

Answers appear at the end of this chapter.

The first year our group worked cooperatively without setting the timer. With moms and kids all helping out, we often got a few of the problems solved—but not without a great deal of frustration, and certainty there had to be typos in the problems or answers!

But we kept chipping away at these challenges at our weekly meetings. We studied the solutions and strategies given by George Lechner, the founder and problem-designer. As our repertoire of strategies for solving mathematical problems grew, our scores improved.

The next year we participated competitively, and Michael won a gold pin (by scoring in the top 2 percent nationally), Gabe a silver (top 10 percent nationally), and Katie, as a fourth-grader, a patch (top 50 percent). I even competed informally and would have earned a silver.

The better news is this: All of their math work has dramatically improved. Math Olympiad has taught them how to tackle mathematical problems and to think things through logically. They all invest significant time in their math work—because they are motivated to do well in the mathematical competitions they are preparing for. (Mike and Gabe are now in **MathCounts** for seventh- and eighth-graders, and Katie is determined to earn a gold pin this year in Math Olympiad.) No math curriculum would have ever produced this commitment.

If you are concerned about the negative effects of competition, these can be minimized by the tone that's set by organizers of the event. At the beginning, give everyone a pep talk on the purpose of the competition. Don't over-promote the winner, and recognize every child who participates—tell them that alone takes courage. Look for events that give lots of kids an opportunity for success. For instance, anyone who meets the standard can earn a **Presidential Physical Fitness** award. The National Geography Bee only recognizes one winner, but we added prizes on our own for the top five scores and a junior winner at the elementary level. And I found the Knowledge Open competition when my sons asked for a team event they could do *with* their friends rather than one where they competed *against* each other.

You don't even need these formal contests to have a competitive motivator, either. Create a team atmosphere on your own. When my friend Sue Geer taught a current events class at the Learning Center homeschool co-op, she created teams and posted their cumulative scores on weekly quizzes. This got everyone reading news magazines and daily papers in preparation.

I wanted to give the students in my CHESS English classes one more reason to delve deeply into the material we had covered that year. I was first intending an essay test, but I wanted an extra element of fun. So I broke the kids into teams and challenged them to create a puzzle, challenge, or quiz based on the course content to give to the opposing team to solve. The losers bought lunch. The actual event was chaotic and needs refining, but according to the parents I achieved my goal: Those kids poured over their English notes all week and worked diligently together looking for a way to stump their opponents. In the process they thoroughly reviewed the course material.

#9. Use Rewards

Once again experience brought an adjustment to my strategies. I started out as a purist who wanted my children motivated to learn for learning's sake. No grades, no stickers, no hokey contests to get you to read or count or write a term paper.

The first concession came when I promised Katie a trip to Friendly's for ice cream if she read ten books. Then someone organized a **Pizza Hut Book-It** program at the Learning Center co-op. We've participated in that now for seven years, and I've noted how many kids become independent readers during the five months of the program. The simple recognition of their names on a chart, a sticker for every monthly goal achieved, plus the pizza and the big party at the end is an irresistible combination. I admit it now: Rewards work. And these incentive programs also motivate parents to consistently help their kids work toward their goals as well.

Just to let you know how far I've fallen, I now pay Kristen for correct work. One day Kristen was getting every problem wrong on her math work. She couldn't even solve $6 + 1 =$ _____ or $3 + 1 =$_____. I thought, *Wow, we may really have a problem here.*

I told her I'd pay her a nickel for every problem she got right and left her on her own. When I checked her work, she had nineteen out of twenty correct. The good news: She can do it when motivated. The bad news: She works for pay.

It has continued to be one of the few extrinsic rewards that motivates Kristen. I have a big jar labeled "Kristen's Jar," and the pile of coins inside is climbing. When I get it out, Kristen's success sharply increases. I'd rather not be paying her, but I want her to learn more and this is a concession I have learned to live with. To make the best of it, I've used the money to teach her to count by fives and tens. I use it as manipulatives as well to illustrate fractions and decimals.

#10. Use Discipline

Discipline is also a motivator—one God uses with us and one we as parents are commanded to apply if we love our children. When I have resistance from my kids in a given area, I first do a quick check of the list above. Am I honoring this child's learning style? Are the resources I'm using engaging? How about the methods? etc. If I'm making a reasonable effort to give this kid his best shot at learning the stuff, I then look at the child's attitude. If that is the root of the problem, I need to bring restraints into his life through discipline.

Okay, here comes a controversial paragraph. Read it slowly so you don't miss any of the fences I've carefully constructed:

When our kids were younger, Kermit and I applied biblical discipline (that's spelled: s-p-a-n-k) in situations where *the boundaries were clearly defined* and *the consequences understood.* Biblical discipline was not applied out of anger, and forgiveness and restoration immediately followed.

As maligned as that method is, I have seen the fruit borne out. Our children, and the many children I know from homes where biblical discipline is understood and properly applied, are not repressed or violent. They don't lash out, hit others, or even sneak around behind their parents' backs. Sure, they still have a serious case of sin in their hearts and the final verdict is not in, but I see in these kids self-control, focus, and a responsive heart toward the Lord. I'm betting on the method that produced it.

With older children, of course, this is no longer the proper route. The consequences that motivate my resistant kids to stay focused now are food (or lack thereof), chores, or some other loss of privilege. Fortunately, with Katie, Mike, and Gabe, a heart-to-heart conversation is often all it takes to bring about change. That is because we have always prized "obedience from the heart."

It is very important to us that our children understand the boundaries we have set and why they are God's boundaries, not just ones for our own convenience. This means our parenting involves a lot of discussion and a lot of drawing our children out. In *Shepherding a Child's Heart* (<u>Shepherd Press</u>, 1995)*, Tedd Tripp does the best job I know of explaining the proper role of parental authority.

<u>Answers to Math Olympiad Problems</u>
1. 12;   2. Friday;   3. 16,625;   4. $36;   5. A=5, B=6

PART 9

Measuring Your Success

In This Section

- Are We on Target?
- Methods of Assessment
- Report Card: The Standardized Test
- Pre-Game Pep Talk

33

Are We on Target?

Ｈow well is your home-education program faring? You can't really answer that question if you don't have a method for assessment in place.

And how do we define success?

At our house, any assessment we use must measure our progress in achieving the goals we've set for our family:

- a love for learning
- a marketable set of skills
- accurate understanding of the Christian faith
- a passion for reaching this generation with the gospel

The Annual Review

As I mentioned in chapter 14, I have an annual planning time each summer. Before I begin my planning, I first review and evaluate the previous year. I find it best to conduct this evaluation a couple months *after* we've concluded our schooling. I need some distance before I can objectively assess things.

My first step in assessing our progress has to be an evaluation of the big picture. I am always fighting against absorption with the little things, for example, *Has Kristen's handwriting improved?* versus neglect of the important things, such as *Has Kristen's love for learning deepened?* Or, *What is our superintendent going to say about these test scores?* versus *What is God going to say about our family focus?*

Prayerfully, I start by asking God to give me His perspective of our program and asking for the strategies for next year that will bring us closer to our targets.

Planning Retreats

On occasion Kermit and I have even gone away for the weekend in order to do this. It's very romantic. Kermit brings his briefcase and an agenda. We then work through a review of our marriage, family life, and homeschool program. He runs a great meeting and is very wise about setting realistic goals for improvement. I also find husbands more naturally look at the big picture and can keep the family focused on what really matters.

It's been difficult to keep this up in recent years because of everyone's schedule, but I think this is the most effective way to conduct an annual assessment of family life.

Christianity 101: Conviction versus Condemnation

Most of the homeschool moms I know have little problem with overrating their program. Rather, they labor frequently under the weight of condemnation. And because of this an annual review can seem intimidating. It's always helpful for me to remind myself of the following truths:

- Our family has an adversary working against our success. His most effective tool is condemnation.
- When the Holy Spirit convicts He is always *specific,* and He always gives a *solution.*

If it isn't specific and there isn't a strategy for improvement, then I don't give in to discouragement.

Wise Counsel

I also solicit input from others. I have so much personally invested in my children's education and spiritual growth, I know it's unlikely that I'm objective in my thinking. Seeking out wise counsel is a biblical principle that further helps us see God's perspective. But what constitutes "wise counsel"?

One Special Adviser

Cindy's at the top of my list. First, because she loves me and my family. She's demonstrated her commitment to our success in countless ways during the past sixteen years of friendship. Second, she loves the Lord and consistently demonstrates this in her life. I know her to be a woman of spiritual wisdom and maturity. And finally, there's fruit in her life and family that I desire to see in mine. Those three factors—her love for me, her love for the Lord, and the evidence of fruit—I believe, constitute the biblical definition of wise counsel.

A Circle of Friends

I have three other women as well—Marie, Colette, and Barb—whom I can count on to speak the truth in love and to challenge and encourage me and who are involved enough with my children to have a helpful perspective. Beyond them, I have my support network at the Learning Center homeschool co-op.

Extend an Invitation

Wise counsel doesn't happen naturally. I have to invite this into my life, and if I want honesty, I must receive others' perspective graciously, even when it illuminates a weakness or identifies sin. Humility doesn't come naturally to me, but I know it's a requirement for God's blessing in my life and my family.

I'm in faith that these steps—an annual review and regular input from others of spiritual maturity—is God's method for assessing our program.

The Comparison Trap

Before we move on, it is also helpful to review what God's method of assessment is *not*.

Want to take a shot at identifying the Enemy's method for evaluating your program? You got it. Measuring your success by comparing yourself to others.

 It's a constant challenge the moms at the Learning Center face. Remember the prayer meeting we held at the start of school? Everyone was already struggling with feelings of failure and regret. We had not done enough in one area or another, our day was chaotic and disorganized, our household responsibilities were never done, one child or another was not getting the attention he needed, and somewhere in all we were trying to do, the spiritual qualities we had set out to foster were frequently put on the back burner.

But what was really doing us in was the belief that *everyone else* was doing a terrific job— from the families featured in the homeschool magazines to our circle of friends at the co-op. *I'm the only one who is making a mess of things!* was in everyone's mind. And that kept us from speaking up.

Comparing ourselves to others as a measurement of our success is a deadly trap. Sure, we can be spurred on by other homeschool families, we can gather resourceful and creative ideas, we can pool our talents and give our children the broader benefits of the group. But we will burn out faster than a meteorite if we are constantly stacking our weaknesses up against others' perceived strengths.

That's why you need a family vision and a (short) list of targets from the Lord to measure your success against. Don't use someone else's measuring stick, especially when you can't see the whole picture of his or her life.

34

Methods of Assessment

• •

Let's look now at the ongoing methods of assessment we can use with our children to measure their success in the core subject areas.

You may want to use one or all of these options in combination at different times during your child's school career. The mix is up to you. But here are two ingredients that are essential:

#1. You Need a Method of Evaluation in Place if You Expect Your Child to Stay Motivated

How long do you work at full tilt without evaluation or reward? If you have a long list of things to do, to which do you give priority? Those with a deadline and outside accountability, right? The older your child is, the more a moment of evaluation is essential.

#2. Your Child Needs to Know What the Standard of Evaluation Will be Before Beginning His Work

The reason why grades, testing, and other traditional methods have fallen into disrepute is they are often subjective and arbitrary. Remember scoping out teachers ahead of time to find out their grading biases? Or the feeling of frustration when you were evaluated by a boss who never gave you a clue what qualities he had been judging your performance against?

Now compare this to the game of baseball, if you will indulge me once again. Aren't the standards of success clearly spelled out? Isn't that why rabid fans, such as Yours Truly, feel justified in jumping from their seats when the ump clearly violates the rule book? Kids are motivated and focused in a game of baseball because the objectives are clear. Everyone knows what spells success.

Whatever method of evaluation you use, make sure the standards are clear to your kids from the beginning.

To Grade or Not to Grade

Why do we grade a child's work in school? Most frequently because the classroom teacher cannot give every child as long as he or she may want or need to complete or revise an assignment.

Mastery learning, on the other hand, says a child can study a particular subject area or practice a skill until he achieves competency. But without deadlines, kids often under-achieve and procrastinate.

So we need to strike a balance in our homes.

Many homeschoolers do not give cumulative grades in a subject during the elementary years. Tests in arithmetic or spelling are certainly corrected and may be graded. But I find there is more benefit for my kids in reworking their problems or correcting their errors than in assigning a grade and moving on.

Self-Correcting

In fact, my kids use the teacher's book a lot to check their answers and figure out their own mistakes. In a traditional setting, this may be viewed as "cheating," but I find it to be a powerful learning strategy. Because my kids have a real purpose in their studies, they don't shortchange themselves by simply copying the answers. They understand why they need to master the material, and should they ever forget this noble cause, Mom's right there holding them accountable to their goals.

When Grades Work

Somewhere around junior high, though, many parents begin assigning grades to their children's work. If we have honored their learning styles and interests from the beginning, we should be pretty attuned to the amount of time they reasonably need to complete a project or paper well.

Create a Contract

If you grade, set objective standards of measurement ahead of time. This is why I use contracts with my students at Creative Home Educators' Support Services (CHESS). (See page 259 for a sample.) It's not possible for me to individualize these contracts in that setting; but at home, I suggest you *negotiate* the contract with your kids before beginning the course. Making your child a participant in setting expectations will give him or her greater ownership and thus motivation.

Testing

Traditionally, a test is used to measure success in a skill or content area. But tests are often poorly designed and merely measure how skilled a child is at taking a test. Guessing is too big a factor on a true/false, matching, or multiple choice test to give you an accurate picture of student achievement. A better test requires kids to recall the answers.

The Best Test

The best kind of test, as you know by now, is the essay test—especially if you wish to measure understanding and mastery in a content areas such as literature or history.

Essay tests, with well-designed questions, require kids to think more deeply about the material and draw conclusions, make judgments, hunt for similarities, or highlight differences.

Here's an example of an essay test I designed for a literature discussion group at the Learning Center homeschool co-op:

FINAL: *The Hawk That Dare Not Hunt by Day* by Scott O'Dell

Name _____ Grade_____ Date_____

Directions:
The following essay questions are asking for your opinion, but you must support your position with evidence from the book. Write in paragraph form and use examples that show you understand the things we talked about and the book you read.

1. What direction do you imagine Tom's life may have taken as a result of the events in this story? Include how you think knowing William Tyndale influenced the outcome of the rest of Tom's life.

2. Do you agree with Tom's actions when he finally finds the traitor, Henry Phillips, at the end? What reasons do you think he would give for taking the actions he did here? Were you surprised? Was it the right decision in your mind? What do you think you would have done?

3. If you had fifteen minutes to talk with Scott O'Dell about his book, what comments would you make? What did you like or dislike about his writing style, characters, plot, and setting? What questions would you like him to answer about this story?

4. Think about what you learned about life in Europe during the sixteenth century. What are some of the difficulties you think you would have faced if you had lived at that time? What are some aspects you think you would have enjoyed?

5. Choose a biblical figure that has similarities with each of these characters in Scott O'Dell's book. Give a short reason for your choices.

Tom Barton	Uncle Jack	Henry Phillips
William Tyndale	Herbert Belsey	King Henry VIII

The essay test has the extra benefit of being a learning tool as well. Kids can't write well if they can't think well about the material. This type of evaluation requires them to compose their thoughts and to practice articulating them coherently.

You can accomplish the same benefits with early elementary students by allowing them to give their answers orally or dictate them to you.

Alternative Methods of Evaluation

Even though I do give grades and tests to my sons and secondary students at CHESS, these are still not my primary methods of evaluation. Here are the three ways I find kids can best demonstrate their mastery of material, have fun doing so, and learn a great deal in the process:

Projects, Papers, and Performances

I want my kids to more than memorize their history facts or grammar rules for a test. They will forget nearly everything learned using that method. That's why we focus on projects, papers, or performances to demonstrate what we have learned.

 Here are some of the things we and other families have done that were not only learning experiences but doubled as a method of evaluation as well:

- An American history fair where every child displayed and explained the project he had made.

- Several science fairs where younger children created models and older students were required to follow the scientific process. These projects were then evaluated by outside judges. The criteria used was given to the kids before they began their work.

- A world cultures night where each family designed a booth representing a different country and had games, food, music, or other activities planned for visitors.

- Numerous research papers of varying length that were then presented orally to the group for the purpose of educating others (not securing a grade from the teacher).

- Historical fiction that was written and published in magazine form after studying *The Hawk That Dare Not Hunt by Day.*

- Skits and plays written and produced by the kids for a family night.

- Musical and dance recitals.

- A family newspaper with puzzles, cartoons, and articles about the American Revolution.

Our list could go on and on. Nearly every major area of interest or study has culminated in a project, performance, or written report of some kind. These have been ultimately presented to an authentic audience, not a teacher for a grade, and my kids and their friends have been highly motivated to do their best.

If there's a downside, it's where to store this stuff. After all the work that's gone into these projects, it would be viewed as a sacrilege if I threw them out—further indication of the meaningfulness of the activity. (The one advantage of tests: No one cares if they are pitched.)

Written Evaluations

Another meaningful evaluation for your children is a written report from you or a tutor or mentor. Take a few minutes at the beginning of the year to write up what you hope to accomplish in each subject area. Go over this with your kids so they know what you are expecting, and then at the end, write up your review of the progress they have made. Add this to the permanent school record you are accumulating from each year. This little bit of formalization will give your kids an extra push in taking their work seriously.

Ask others who work with your children to do the same thing. You'll find your kids will pour over what anyone writes about them. And this will contribute significantly to how they view themselves as a learner.

At CHESS, Cindy asks her teachers to give each student a written progress report several times a year. After playing around with the format a bit I came up with this form for my literature and composition class. It doesn't take long to complete and attempts to comment on the student's character, communication skills, and understanding of course material.

Final Evaluation English 301
(American Literature)

Name: Honoria Erudite   Grade: A

_4_ Leadership   _4_ Ability to Communicate in Writing

_3_ Preparedness   _3_ Ability to Communicate Orally

_5_ Comprehension of Material   _4_ Outside Reading List

_3_ Timely Completion of Assignments   _5_ Final Project

_4_ Participation   _4_ Thoroughness of Assignments

_5_ Enthusiasm   _3_ Ability to Analyze

Criteria: **5** (exceptional) **4** (above average) **3** (satisfactory) **2** (needs improvement) **1** (dismal)

Additional Comments:
I will always remember this first senior high CHESS class with a great deal of fondness. What a joy it is to have a student like Honoria who does her absolute best all the time

---

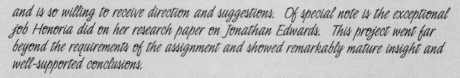

and is so willing to receive direction and suggestions. Of special note is the exceptional job Honoria did on her research paper on Jonathan Edwards. This project went far beyond the requirements of the assignment and showed remarkably mature insight and well-supported conclusions.

I look forward to seeing Honoria continue to grow as a writer and to gain confidence in her ability to express her ideas orally and in writing. I encourage Honoria to pursue wider audiences for her work as well.

Debra A. Bell, M.A.

You will probably be more successful in obtaining written evaluations from mentors and tutors if you create a similar form that is quick and easy to fill out. (As someone who is asked to write lots of evaluations and recommendations, I really appreciate forms.)

Portfolio Assessment

In our state, and a few others, home-educated students are required to present a portfolio of their progress at the end of the year to an evaluator who writes a progress report. Both are then submitted to the school district.

The portfolio is usually a three-ring binder (with a three- to five-inch spine) filled with pictures and work from the school year. I have a bookcase now filled with portfolios from every school year of each child's life. They were quite a time commitment to compile, but these are some of my children's most treasured possessions. Each is a scrapbook full of memories and a real pick-me-up when I am discouraged. I just pull one off the shelf and spend an afternoon reliving the special moments we've had learning together. It's hard *not* to see progress in our homeschool program with this tangible evidence in the house.

Even if you are not required to maintain a portfolio, you may wish to consider it as an invaluable assessment tool. My kids, except for Kristen, put together their own. It takes us about two weeks to pull them together—wiser women than I maintain theirs throughout the school year—but during that process my kids review their year's work in every subject area and often edit a story one more time, finish an art project, or rework some math problems. They know their work is now going to have an outside review, and they want to do their best. It's a great learning tool to reinforce our studies one more time.

The portfolio is divided into subject areas, and each is arranged chronologically so that it demonstrates academic progress. Here's a list of the kinds of documentation a family might include:

- ✔ written work from the student
- ✔ pictures of field trips and projects
- ✔ notes, outlines, rough drafts, and final papers

✔ tests and scores

✔ certificates from participation in National Geography Bee, Pizza Hut Book-It Program, etc.

✔ independent reading list with brief annotations; for example, award winner, nonfiction, biography, historical fiction, page length

✔ photocopied table of contents from text used, highlighting sections studied

✔ pamphlets from places visited

✔ list of resources referred to or read in each subject area

✔ list of objectives or units of study in each area

✔ pictures of learning environment, for example, computer, bookshelves, aquarium, educational video collection, outdoor gym equipment

✔ pictures of social experiences: favorite group of friends, co-op classes, volleyball tournament

✔ a narrative from Mom or older students explaining more about the pictures or projects included

Find an Audience Once Again

Once you've pulled your portfolios together, find an audience for your kids to share them with. My kids relish the opportunity to explain each page in detail to their evaluator, Grandma, or a reporter.

At our co-op, we had the students display theirs at the annual family night. I enjoy my role as an evaluator very much because I get to see all the great ideas and experiences other families have had. The same benefit can come from sharing our year's work through a display of projects, papers, and portfolios at a support group family night.

One-Subject Portfolio

If that sounds like too much work, you may want to compile a portfolio for just one subject. This would be an excellent way for a high-schooler to demonstrate the quality of his work to a college admissions office, for instance.

I am requiring a writing portfolio for my junior and senior high composition classes at CHESS this year. (I suggested a two-inch, three-ring binder.)

When I teach a content area, such as American literature, I need to assess the students' mastery of a set body of knowledge. I use essay tests, quizzes, and papers to determine the grade. But composition is a skill. My goal here is to evaluate student progress. I have sixty kids in seventh through twelfth grades, and they are all at different places in their development as writers. A lot of them have zero confidence in this area. I don't want my class to send that into the negative range. I want to encourage and inspire their growth as writers.

From the start I've made it clear that their grade is based upon their progress and the writing portfolio is how they will demonstrate this. The first day I took a writing sample. (I compared this to taking blood.) They chose from several topics and wrote cold for fifteen minutes. I also asked them to fill out a writer's inventory at the end. This assessed their attitude toward writing, their previous writing history, and the process they currently go through when composing a paper.

Everything they do for class is to be kept in chronological order in the writing portfolio. Throughout the course I will evaluate the progress demonstrated in the portfolio. I'll also take another writing sample in class and ask them to complete another writer's inventory at the end. I trust I will see improvement in skill and confidence.

35

Report Card: The Standardized Test

. . . .

In many places homeschoolers are required—or choose—to have their children tested periodically with a standardized test. They are necessary here in Pennsylvania, and each year I test more than two hundred homeschooled kids at various sites around the state. Despite my assurances, it's still a traumatic event—for the moms. The kids do just fine.

And once the scores are mailed back, it's the one time of the year I get lots of phone calls from dads. "My son scored at the 70th percentile in spelling. Now exactly what are we doing wrong?"

I can empathize. Despite all I know about the folly of standardized testing, when I'm opening my own children's return envelope, my palms are sweaty as well. Those numbers look so exacting, it's hard not to give them credence.

The intent of the requirement is to evaluate our children. But the truth is parents feel we're the ones being measured. When I open my test site with prayer, I ask the kids to pray for their moms as well. They're the ones who need the assurance.

Here's a primer to help you keep testing in perspective and also some tips for using those scores to better your program.

What Exactly Is a Standardized Test?

#1. Most Standardized Tests Are Achievement Tests

That means they are designed to measure how well a student has mastered the material he has presumably been taught. A standardized test is not an ability or an aptitude test, as is the college board's SAT (Scholastic Aptitude Test), which is attempting to predict a student's future scholastic success.

Low scores on an achievement test may indicate the student has not mastered that material yet, or it could also mean he has not been *presented* that material yet. If your child is required to take an achievement test, do your best to find out what skills will actually be measured. Does the third-grade test include division? Does the eighth-grade test measure knowledge of Latin roots? The test scores will mean nothing to you if you don't know what material the test-makers had anticipated would be covered.

#2. Most Only Test in Language Arts and Mathematics

While other skill areas may also be included, language arts and math form the core. On the Iowa Test of Basic Skills (ITBS), the test I prefer to use, the basic battery includes vocabulary, reading comprehension, spelling, mathematical concepts (terminology), mathematical problem-solving (word and number problems), and mathematical computation (speed and accuracy test).

The complete test, which I make optional, includes grammar, usage, punctuation, work study (library and map skills), science, and social studies. Those scores are not computed in the *Basic* Composite score but are part of the *Complete* Composite score.

If you are not giving the test yourself, ask the test administrator exactly what subtests will be given.

#3. Kids' Achievement Is Compared to a Sample Group

The scores your child receives are a comparison against the "norms" obtained from a sample group of children (usually tens of thousands) who took that same test at the same time of year. This is what is meant by "standardized." The average score of that sample group on each skill test translates into the 50th percentile. Your child's score at the 70th percentile in spelling means he did better on that test than 70 percent of the sample group of children who took that same test at that grade level.

The norms generated from this sample group are in use for several years. Test administrators can even choose between several sets of norms. The 1988 norms on the ITBS are higher than the 1985 norms. So student scores normed against the '85 sample group will be interpreted higher than the same achievement scores normed against the '88 ones. A slight upward or downward swing across the board in scores for your child can simply mean different norms were used.

Norms also vary from test to test. The Stanford Achievement Test (SAT) is the achievement test of choice in many private schools. Because those students are often part of the sample group, the norms for the Stanford are a bit higher than the norms on other tests.

Because of differences in norms and actual material tested, you get a more accurate picture of your child's achievement by using the same test year after year.

#4. Scores Are Reported a Number of Ways

Besides reporting your child's achievement in terms of percentile, the test report will probably include the following information:

- **Raw scores:** This is the actual number correct on a test. The percentile, grade equivalent, and stanine (explained below) are various ways of interpreting the meaning of this raw score when compared to the norms.

- **Grade equivalent:** This is usually the most misunderstood score. Your child's grade equivalent score of 79 on a fifth-grade reading test means he understood the reading material on that fifth-grade test the way we might expect an "average" seventh-grader in the ninth month of school to understand that same fifth-grade material. It does not mean you should advance him two grades or say he reads on a junior high level. You *can* accurately state that he is reading above grade level, which should have been already evident to you.

- **Stanine:** The stanine indicates which of nine groupings this child would fall into, with the fifth stanine representing the average group. The ninth stanine represents the group of children with the very highest achievement in this skill area, and the first stanine represents the group of children with the very lowest achievement in this skill area.

  I prefer to look at stanine when I am giving parents an interpretation of their child's test score. Stanines are a generalization of the child's achievement. And generalizations are all I believe you can accurately make when using a standardized test for evaluation. A lot of factors can affect a child's performance on the test. Given the same test several times, his grade equivalency and percentile rankings will fluctuate. But his stanine will likely be consistent.

- **Composite score:** Composite scores are calculated by averaging the individual scores on the battery of tests. Read the report carefully to note exactly which test scores were averaged. Sometimes the composite score includes all tests; sometimes it includes just the basic battery in language arts and mathematics. This composite score is then interpreted in terms of percentile, grade equivalency, and stanine as well.

How Much Weight Should Be Given to Scores?

#1. Your Own Observation Is More Accurate

In a traditional setting, individual assessments of every child's achievement in all subject areas is not possible. That's why we have standardized tests. They are a stab at helping the classroom teacher determine who is having problems, who is doing just fine, and who may be ready for acceleration. They are a helpful but imperfect tool.

Lots of factors, other than lack of skill in a subject area, can affect a child's score: He may not feel well, he may not be comfortable with the testing environment, he may have incorrectly filled out his answer sheet, he may not have effective test-taking strategies.

Your daily observation of your child's achievement at home is a *more accurate* assessment of his progress than the standardized test scores. In most cases, the test scores will affirm what you have already concluded from working with your child. When test scores are at odds with this, use caution in weighing them too heavily.

#2. There's a Growing Body of Research That Discredits Standardized Tests

The main problem with standardized tests is they report student achievement by comparing them to other students. That means the scoring always ensures some kids are not going to pass muster. A more helpful report would measure how much a child has learned, without making comparisons. Additional problems of standardized tests include cultural biases.

Standardized testing is especially unfair to the homeschool parent, who is not allowed to see the test ahead of time. If you don't know what skills or content will be tested, how can you ensure that the material has been presented to your child? You can't. If a standardized test covers material never presented to your child, then how helpful are the scores? Not much.

 If you want to read more about the problems with standardized tests, check out these sources:

Tests: Marked for Life?, S. Alan Cohen (Scholastic, 1988).
Standardized Tests and Our Children (Fair Test) (**John Holt Bookstore**).

How to Benefit from a Standardized Test

Since I'm already leading the charge on a number of other issues, I'll have to pass for now on taking up arms against standardized tests. I accept them as a fact of life and give them to my children every chance I get so they can do their best when the scores count most.

And I'll grudgingly admit that they have been assuring and helpful over the years. Here are ways to make them work for you:

#1. If Possible, *You* Should Administer the Test to Your Child at Least Once

The sources that allow parents to administer the test are indicated at the end of this section. If you do this, you will learn a lot about the nature of a standardized test and about your child's strengths and weaknesses in taking tests. Does he race through the material? Does he recheck his work? Does he lose his place easily? Does he read all the choices before deciding? Does he manage his time wisely? You are now better able to prepare him for a group testing situation.

You may find, as I did, that it's a real feat to refrain from coaching him during the test or sending nonverbal cues when he is about to make a mistake. So although I do test each of my kids once in my home, all subsequent tests are given at my group test site or by someone else.

If you cannot administer the test, ask permission to observe your child being tested as the next best way to gather this information.

#2.   If You Test, Test Annually with the Same Test

Because a child's performance on a test can be influenced by many different factors, it is more accurate to draw conclusions from the profile of your child's achievement that emerges over time. And this should be based upon the same test.

I frequently get calls from parents who have had their children tested with the CTBS (Comprehensive Test of Basic Skills) in the fall with another test service and who now wish to sign them up for the ITBS with me in the spring for the purpose of seeing if their child has improved. When I know this, I discourage them from doing so. There is such a big difference between the two tests that the results cannot be accurately compared.

#3.   Don't Put Much Stock in Early Test Results

The scores of early elementary children are very unreliable. My kids tested all over the board till fifth grade, when a consistent pattern began to emerge. I have seen this repeated time and time again with many children I have tested. I think states that require standardized tests of homeschool students before third grade are out to lunch. (Pardon my brashness.)

I've worked with kids who tested well below average during the early elementary years and who are now scoring well above average as teens. In the fall of fifth grade, my daughter Katie's scores took a big jump. I thought it was a fluke (what faith) till I retested her in the spring and got the same dramatic jump. Something had kicked in (it's that inner timetable again), and my daughter is currently a very motivated and determined learner. It's a new twist to her formerly nonchalant self.

Don't let a test determine how you view your child's academic potential. I told my sons time and again (and prayed I was right) that the kids who were the best athletes in elementary school were often not the best athletes in high school. It's the kids who work hardest who end up on top when it matters.

I'm also convinced that is equally true of academic success. Kids with academic motivation will test the best when in counts. So don't give up on your child. Focus your energies on *keeping your child motivated to learn* by designing a program that honors his learning style and cultivates a love for learning.

#4. Use a Test Service That Will Give You a Criterion-Referenced Report

Criterion-referenced sounds like a fancy word, but it's the information you need to really use the test scores. A criterion-reference report will tell you exactly what skills were tested, how many of those problems in that category your child attempted on the test and how many he got correct. <u>**Bob Jones University Testing Service,**</u> as well as my testing service, issues this kind of report.

When parents look at this report, they will be able to determine exactly where their child is having trouble and how to correct the problem.

Example 1:

Ellen scores at the 45 percentile on the fifth-grade math computation test. When we look at the report for this subtest, we see that she attempted all thirty-nine problems in this section. So we know she finished the test in the time allotted.

There were fifteen whole-number addition and subtraction problems, and she got thirteen correct. No problem there. But of the sixteen whole-number multiplication and division problems, she only got nine correct. Further practice in this area may be indicated. Plus, of the eight problems requiring addition and subtraction of decimals and fractions, she only got one correct. A discussion with Mom reveals that these types of problems have not yet been introduced in her math program. So her low score is understandable.

Let's look at another child.

Example 2:

William scored at the 53 percentile on the fifth-grade reading comprehension test. His parents are a bit surprised. His independent reading at home had seemed to be above grade level. He had picked up *The Call of the Wild* that summer and had recently finished reading it. With a criterion-referenced report we can find the explanation for this apparent discrepancy.

Of the fifty-four reading comprehension questions on the test, William had only completed thirty-two, all of which were correct.

William had not finished the test in the time allotted. He isn't having any difficulties with reading comprehension—his high score on the vocabulary section is further indication of this—but he is a slower reader than "average."

My recommendation to his parents is to just keep William reading. His speed will increase the more he reads.

It's Easy to Draw the Wrong Conclusions

Without this criterion-referenced report, can you see how a parent might jump to errone-ous conclusions? With just the percentile score, Ellen's mom may decide Ellen needs to go back through all her math lessons this year to make sure she is really getting it this time. Or William's parents might have concluded that he is obviously not understanding these hard books he is reading and insist that he choose easier ones. It would all be for naught.

If you cannot get a criterion-referenced report for the test administered, the test is useless to you as an evaluation tool.

Tips for Helping Your Child Do Well on a Standardized Test

1. **Use a Test-Preparation Program.** Test-preparation programs such as **Scoring High*** not only give practice with the content material typically found on the most widely used standardized tests but also teach your child test-taking strategies that prepare him to manage his time and make the best choices.

2. **If possible, arrange to have him tested in a familiar setting by someone he knows.**

3. **Make sure he is well-rested and has a nutritious breakfast high in protein and low in sugar the day of the test.**

4. **Send your child with a ruler to keep his place on the scoring sheet and a watch to manage his time wisely.**

5. **If it's allowed at the test site, he should also have a book to read if he finishes a test early and a high-protein snack for the breaks.**

6. **Don't drop your young child off at the test site; instead, be available at the breaks and lunchtime to encourage and affirm him.**

7. **Hide your own insecurities.** The proper use of a standardized test is to give you a tool to better tune your program to your child's needs. It will help you know what he

knows well and what he has not yet mastered. It should not be used to pass judgment on your homeschooling program.

National Testing Services

Bob Jones University
Greenville, SC 29614
800-845-5731
The administrator may be a parent but must have a four-year degree; criterion-referenced report; Iowa, Stanford, as well as many other types of tests.

Christian Liberty Academy
502 West Euclid Avenue
Arlington Heights, IL 60004
708-259-8736
The administrator may be a parent; California Achievement Test (CAT); grade equivalency report only.

McGuffey Testing Service
P. O. Box 109
Lakemont, GA 30552
706-782-7709
The administrator may be a parent in certain states; Stanford; detailed report.

Sycamore Tree
2179 Meyer Place
Costa Mesa, CA 92627
714-650-4466
The administrator may be a parent; Comprehensive Test of Basic Skills; detailed report.

Pre-Game Pep Talk

The Winning Strategies

1. Utterly rely upon the grace of God.
2. Keep a sharply focused vision in clear view.
3. Have faith in future fruit.
4. Give your kids control.
5. Give your kids a purpose that is immediate and relevant.
6. Enjoy the mystery of life.
7. Don't try this alone.
8. Be a learner.
9. Remember Oswald Chambers's comment:
   "What we call the *process*, God calls the *end*."
10. Play ball!

PART 10

Resource Guide

In This Section

- National and State Organizations and Publications
- Recommended Suppliers and Products
- Used-Curriculum Suppliers
- Academic Contests and Competitions
- Learning Center Homeschool Co-op Sample Information Packet

National and State Organizations and Publications

· ·

National

Home School Legal Defense Association
P. O. Box 159
Paeonian Springs, VA 20129
540-338-5600
Home School Court Report newsletter.

National Center For Home Education
P. O. Box 125
Paeonian Springs, VA 20129
540-338-7600

National Challenged Homeschoolers Associated Network
5383 Alpine Rd. SE
Olalla, WA 98359
206-857-4257
"Special needs" newsletter/catalog.

National Home Education Research Institute (NHERI)
P. O. Box 13939
Salem, OR 97309
503-364-1490
503-364-2827 (fax)
 http://www.nheri.org

Growing Without Schooling
Holt Associates
2269 Massachusetts Ave.
Cambridge, MA 02140
617-864-3100
Newsletter/catalog/secular

Homeschool PC
Home Life
P. O. Box 1250
Fenton, MO 63026-1850
800-346-6322

Homeschooling Today
P. O. Box 1425
Melrose, FL 32666
954-962-1930

Pennsylvania Homeschoolers Newsletter
R. D. 2 Box 117
Kittanning, PA 16201
412-783-6512

Practical Homeschooling
Home Life
P. O. Box 1250
Fenton, MO 63026
800-346-6322

http://www.home-school.com

The Teaching Home
P. O. Box 20219
Portland, OR 97294
800-395-7760

State

Alabama

Christian Home Education Fellowship (CHEF) of Alabama
816 Colonial Drive
Alabaster, AL 35007
205-664-2232

Alaska

Alaska Private Home Educators Association
P. O. Box 141764
Anchorage, AK 99514

Arizona

Arizona Families for Home Education
P. O. Box 4661
Scottsdale, AZ 85261-4661
800-929-3927

Arkansas

Arkansas Christian Home Education Association (ACHEA)
P. O. Box 4025
North Little Rock, AR 72190
501-758-9099

California

Christian Home Educators Association of California
P. O. Box 2009
Norwalk, CA 90651
800-564-2432

Colorado

Christian Home Educators of Colorado
3739 E. Fourth Avenue
Denver, CO 80206
303-388-1888

http://www.learnathome.com/chec/index.htm

Connecticut

The Education Association of Christian Homeschoolers
25 Field Stone Run
Farmington, CT 06032
860-677-4538
800-205-7844 (in Connecticut)

http://www.tiac.net/users/bobpers/teach

Delaware

Delaware Home Education Association
P. O. Box 1003
Dover, DE 19903
302-429-0515

Florida

Florida Parent Educators Association
P. O. Box 1372
Tallahassee, FL 32302-1372
904-224-7556
904-222-9513 (fax)

Georgia

Georgia Home Education Association
245 Buckeye Lane
Fayetteville, GA 30214
770-461-3657
770-461-9053 (fax)

Gwinnett Christian Home Educators
1981 Clinton Place
Lawrenceville, GA 30243
770-963-0713

Harvest Home Educators
P. O. Box 1756
Buford, GA 30518
770-455-0449

Hawaii

Christian Home Educators of Hawaii
91-824 Oama Street
Ewa Beach, HI 96706
808-689-6398
808-689-0878 (fax)

e-mail: CHOHALOHA@aol.com
http://www.maui.net/~madelein/chemnews.html.

Idaho

Idaho Home Educators
P. O. Box 1324
Meridian, ID 83680
208-323-0230

http://netnow.micron.net/~ihs

Illinois

Illinois Christian Home Educators
P. O. Box 261
Zion, IL 60099
847-328-7129

Indiana

Indiana Association of Home Educators
850 N. Madison Avenue
Greenwood, IN 46142
317-859-1202

Iowa

Network of Iowa Christian Home Educators
P. O. Box 158
Dexter, IA 50070
800-723-0438 (in Iowa)
515-830-1614

Kansas

Christian Home Educators Confederation of Kansas
P. O. Box 3968
Wichita, KS 67201
913-234-2927 information line
316-945-0810 newsletter

Kentucky

Christian Home Educators of Kentucky
691 Howardstown Road
Hodgensville, KY 42748
502-358-9270

Louisiana

Christian Home Educators Fellowship of Louisiana
P. O. Box 74292
Baton Rouge, LA 70874
504-775-9709

Maine

Homeschoolers of Maine
HC 62, Box 24
Hope, ME 04847
207-763-4251

Maryland

Christian Home Educators Network
P. O. Box 2010
Ellicott City, MD 21043
410-744-8919

Maryland Association of Christian Home Educators
P. O. Box 247
Point of Rock, MD 21777-0247
301-607-4284

Massachusetts

Massachusetts Homeschool Organization of Parent Educators
5 Atwood Road
Cherry Valley, MA 01611-3332
508-755-4754

Michigan

Christian Home Educators of Michigan
P. O. Box 2357
Farmington Hills, MI 48333
810-683-3395
810-978-2808 (fax)

Information Network for Christian Homes
4934 Cannonsburg Road
Belmont, MI 49306
616-874-5656

Minnesota

Minnesota Association of Christian Home Educators
P. O. Box 32308
Fridley, MN 55432-0308
612-717-9070

Mississippi

Mississippi Home Educators Association
109 Reagan Ranch Road
Laurel, MS 39440
601-649-6432

Missouri

Missouri Association of Teaching Christian Homes
307 East Ash Street #146
Columbia, MO 65201
573-443-8217
An online source of information for Missouri homeschoolers is:

http://www.win.org/library/staff/kmcmulle/mohome.htm

Montana

Montana Coalition of Home Educators
P. O. Box 43
Gallatin Gateway, MT 59730
406-587-6163

Nebraska

Nebraska Christian Home Educators Association
P. O. Box 57041
Lincoln, NE 68505-7041
402-423-4297

Nevada

Home Schools United/Vegas Valley
P. O. Box 93564
Las Vegas, NV 89193-3564
702-870-9566

Northern Nevada Home Schools
P. O. Box 21323
Reno, NV 89515
702-852-6647

New Hampshire

Christian Home Educators of New Hampshire
P. O. Box 961
Manchester, NH 03105
603-569-2343

New Jersey

Education Network of Christian Home Schoolers
65 Middlesex Road
Matawan, NJ 08817
908-583-7128

New Mexico

Christian Association of Parent Educators
P. O. Box 25046
Albuquerque, NM 87125
505-898-8548

New York

Loving Education at Home
P. O. Box 88
Cato, NY 13033
716-346-0939
http://www.leah.org

North Carolina

North Carolinians for Home Education
419 Boylan Avenue
Raleigh, NC 27603-1211
919-834-6243

North Dakota

North Dakota Home School Association
4007 N. State Street
Route 5, Box 9
Bismarck, ND 58501
701-223-4080

Ohio

Christian Home Educators of Ohio
P. O. Box 262
Columbus, OH 43216
614-474-3177

http://www.home-school.com/groups/OHIOCHEO. html

Oklahoma

Christian Home Educators Fellowship of Oklahoma
P. O. Box 471363
Tulsa, OK 74147
918-583-7323

Oklahoma Central Home Educators' Consociation
P. O. Box 270601
Oklahoma City, OK 73137
405-521-8439

Oregon

Oregon Christian Home Education Association Network
2815 Northeast 37th Avenue
Portland, OR 97212
508-288-1285
An Oregon Web site for homeschoolers is:

http://www.teleport.com/~ohen/index.html

Pennsylvania

Christian Home School Association of Pennsylvania
P. O. Box 3603
York, PA 17402
717-661-2428

Pennsylvania Homeschoolers
R. D. 2, Box 117
Kittanning, PA 16201
http://www.pahomeschoolers.com

Rhode Island

Rhode Island Guild of Home Teachers
P. O. Box 11
Hope, RI 02831
401-821-7700

South Carolina

South Carolina Home Education Association
P. O. Box 612
Lexington, SC 29071
803-951-8960

South Carolina Association of Independent Home Schools
P. O. Box 2104
Irmo, SC 29063-7104
803-551-1003

South Dakota

Western Dakota Christian Home Schools
P. O. Box 528
Black Hawk, SD 57718
605-923-1893

Tennessee

Tennessee Home Education Association
3677 Richbriar Court
Nashville, TN 37211
615-834-3529

Texas

Christian Home Education Association of Austin
P. O. Box 141998
Austin, TX 78714-1998
512-450-0070

Home-Oriented Private Education
P. O. Box 59876
Dallas, TX 75229
972-358-2221

Texas Home School Coalition
P. O. Box 6982
Lubbock, TX 79493
806-797-4927

Utah

Utah Christian Home Schoolers
P. O. Box 3942
Salt Lake City, UT 84110
801-255-4053

Vermont

Christian Home Education of Vermont
214 N. Prospect #105
Burlington, VT 05401
802-658-4561

Virginia

Home Educators Association of Virginia
1900 Byrd Avenue, Suite 201
P. O. Box 6745
Richmond, VA 23230-0745
804-288-1608

Washington

Washington Association of Teaching Christian Homes
N. 2904 Dora Road
Spokane, WA 992212
509-922-4811

West Virginia

Christian Home Educators of West Virginia
P. O. Box 8770
South Charleston, WV 25303
304-776-4664

Wisconsin

Wisconsin Christian Home Education Association
2307 Carmel Avenue
Racine, WI 53405
414-637-5127

Wyoming

Homeschoolers of Wyoming
339 Bicentennial Court
Powell, WY 82435
307-754-3271

Recommended
Suppliers and Products

· ·

HOME SCHOOL RESOURCE CENTER
1425 E. Chocolate Avenue
Hershey, PA 17033
717-533-1669
800-937-6311
717-533-0413 (fax)
http://www.hsrc.com
Discounts.

YOUNG WRITERS' INSTITUTE/YOUNG SCIENTISTS' INSTITUTE
1425 E. Chocolate Avenue
Hershey, PA 17033
717-520-1303
717-533-0413 (fax)
e-mail: YWIHERSHEY.aol.com

A BEKA BOOKS
P. O. Box 18000
Pensacola, FL 32532
800-874-2352

ADDISON-WESLEY
Jacob Way
Reading, MA 01867
800-552-2259
Source of Cuisenaire products.

ALPHAPHONICS
Paradigm
P. O. Box 45161
Boise, ID 83711
208-343-3790

for teresa

AMERICAN HOME-SCHOOL PUBLISHING
5310 Affinity Court
Centreville, VA 20120-4145
800-684-2121
800-557-0234 (fax)
http://www.doubled.com/ahsp
Great source of high school level and classical education resources.

AMERICAN VISION
P. O. Box 724088
Atlanta, GA 31139
404-988-0555
Source of the new Christian history series, I Pledge My Allegiance.

ANNENBERG SCHOOL/CPB
P. O. Box 2345
South Burlington, VT 05407-2345
800-532-7637

http://www.learner.org

BEAUTIFUL FEET BOOKS
139 Main Street
Sandwich, MA 02563
508-833-8626

BOB JONES UNIVERSITY PRESS
Greenville, SC 29614
800-845-5731

BRODERBUND
P. O. Box 6125
Novato, CA 94948-6125
800-474-8840
Source of Carmen SanDiego software.

CALLIOPE BOOKS
Route 3, Box 3395
Saylorsburg, PA 18353
610-381-2587
Foreign language resources.

CASTLE HEIGHTS PRESS
5866 Hunter Road
Enon, OH 45323
800-763-7148

CHALK DUST COMPANY
11 Sterling Court
Sugar Land, TX 77479
713-265-2495
Source of algebra video course.

CHRISTIAN BOOK DISTRIBUTORS (CBD)
P. O. Box 7000
Peabody, MA 01961-7000
508-977-5000
http://www.christianbook.com
Discounts.

CHRISTIAN FINANCIAL CONCEPTS
P. O. Box 1476
Gainesville, GA 30503
770-534-1000
Source of Larry Burkett's career guidance and money management course for teens.

CHRISTIAN HISTORY INSTITUTE
2030 Wentz Church Road
Worcester, PA 19490
610-584-1893
http://www.chinstitute.org

CHRISTIAN HOME EDUCATORS PRESS
P. O. Box 2009
Norwalk, CA 90651-2009
310-864-2432
e-mail: CHEAOFCA@aol.com
Source of the *High School Handbook*.

COBBLESTONE PUBLISHING
7 School Street
Peterborough, NH 03458-1454
800-821-0115

COMMON SENSE PRESS
P. O. Box 1365
8786 Highway 21
Melrose, FL 32666
904-475-5757

CORNERSTONE CURRICULUM PROJECT
2006 Flat Creek
Richardson, TX 75080
972-235-5149

CREATIVE KIDS LEARNING COMPANY
964 Holland Road
Holland, PA 18966
215-355-5834

CYGNET
HC 12, Box 7A
116 Highway 28
Anthony, NM 88021
505-874-3306

DALE SEYMOUR PUBLICATIONS
P. O. Box 10888
Palo Alto, CA 94303-0879
800-872-1100

DAVIDSON & ASSOCIATES, INC.
P. O. Box 2961
Torrance, CA 90509
800-556-6141

DELTA EDUCATION
P. O. Box 3000
Nashua, NH 03061
800-282-9560

DESIGN-A-STUDY
408 Victoria Avenue
Wilmington, DE 19804
302-998-3889

DORLING KINDERSLEY
95 Madison Avenue
New York, NY 10016
800-356-6575
http://www.dk.com

EDMARK CORPORATION
P. O. Box 97021
Redmond, WA 98073
800-362-2890
Good source of software.

EDUCATIONAL INSIGHTS
19560 S. Rancho Way
Dominguez Hills, CA 902202
800-933-3277

EDUCATORS PUBLISHING SERVICE
31 Smith Place
Cambridge, MA 02138-1000
800-225-5750

ELIJAH COMPANY
Route 2, Box 100-B
Crossville, TN 38555
615-456-6284
Very helpful catalog and source of literature-based curriculum.

EXCEPTIONAL DIAGNOSTICS (Dr. Joe Sutton)
220 Douglas Drive
Simpsonville, SC 29681
864-967-4729

FAMILY ACADEMY BOOKSTORE
146 Southwest 153rd
Box 289
Seattle, WA 98166
206-246-9227
Source of *Homeschooling the High Schooler, vols. 1 and 2.*

FAMILY CHRISTIAN ACADEMY
487 Myatt Drive
Madison, TN 37115
615-860-3000

FAMILY LEARNING SERVICES
P. O. Box 9596
Birmingham, AL 35220
205-854-6870
Discounts.

FARM COUNTRY GENERAL STORE
Route 1, Box 63
Metamora, IL 61548
800-551-3276
e-mail: fcgs@mtco.com

FEARON'S TEACHER AIDS
P. O. Box 2649
Columbus, OH 43216
800-321-3106

FERG N US SERVICES
P. O. Box 578-J
Richlandtown, PA 18955-0578
610-282-0401

4:20 COMMUNICATIONS
P. O. Box 421027
Minneapolis, MN 55442-0027
612-323-8257
Source of Alphaphonics Phonics Tutor software.

GOD'S WORLD PUBLICATIONS
P. O. Box 2330
Asheville, NC 28802-2330
800-951-5437
Biweekly current-events papers and book club.
Discounts.

GREAT CHRISTIAN BOOKS
P. O. Box 8000
229 S. Bridge Street
Elkton, MD 21922
800-775-5422
Extensive line of discounted materials.

GREENLEAF PRESS
1570 Old Laguardo Road
Lebanon, TN 37087
615-449-1617
http://www.greenleafpress.com

HEARTHSIDE HOMESCHOOL HELPS
74 Lynn Drive
Woodbury, NJ 08096
609-845-3681
This is a KONOS representative offering an extensive line of books used with this curriculum.

HIGHLAND BOOKS
GCB Publishing Group
P. O. Box 254
Elkton, MD 21922-0254
410-392-5554

HOME RUN ENTERPRISES
16172 Huxley Circle
Westminster, CA 92683
714-841-1220
Source of Cathy Duffy's *Christian Home Educator's Curriculum Manuals.*

INTERNATIONAL LEARNING SYSTEMS (ILS)
1000 112th Circle North, Suite 100
St. Petersburg, FL 33716
800-321-8322
Sing, Spell, Read and Write, and Winning reading programs

ISHA ENTERPRISES
5503 E. Beck Lane
Scottsdale, AZ 85254
602-482-1346

JOHN HOLT BOOKSTORE
2269 Massachusetts Avenue
Cambridge, MA 02140
617-864-3100

KEY CURRICULUM PRESS
P. O. Box 2304
Berkeley, CA 94702-0304
800-995-MATH

http://www.keypress.com

KONOS INC.
P. O. Box 250
Anna, TX 75409
972-924-2712
972-924-2733 (fax)

http://www.konos.com

LAWRENCE HALL OF SCIENCE
Equals
University of California
Berkeley, CA 94720

LEARNING COMPANY
6493 Kaiser Drive
Fremont, CA 94555
800-852-2255
Good source of educational software.

LIBRARY & EDUCATIONAL SERVICES
8784 Valley View Drive
Berrien Springs, MI 49103
616-471-1400
616-473-7323 (fax)
Source of *Your Story Hour*.
Discounts.

LIFETIME BOOKS AND GIFTS
3900 Chalet Suzanne Dr.
Lake Wales, FL 33853-7763
800-669-0724

MANCALA
Traditional African game available from **Hearthside**.

MATH-U-SEE
1378 River Road
Dunmore, PA 17518

MUGGINS
Old Fashion Products
Route 2, Box 2091
Ellijay, GA 30540
800-962-8849

NATIONAL COUNCIL FOR GEOGRAPHY EDUCATION
16A Leonard Hall
Indiana University of Pennsylvania
Indiana, PA 15705
412-357-6290
Geography for Life geography standards ($7, plus $2.50 shipping).

NOBLE PUBLISHING
P. O. Box 2250
Gresham, OR 97030
800-225-5259

PDI PUBLICATIONS
7881 Beechcraft Avenue, Suite B
Gaithersburg, MD 20879
800-736-2202
Books and video by Benny and Sheree Phillips.

PECCI EDUCATIONAL PUBLISHERS
440 Davis Covet #405
San Francisco, CA 94111
415-391-8579

PENNSYLVANIA HOMESCHOOLERS
R. D. 2, Box 117
Kittanning, PA 16201
412-783-6512

PROFESSOR PHONICS GIVES SOUND ADVICE
Attn: S.U.A.
1339 E. McMillan
Cincinnati, OH 45206
513-961-4877

PROGENY PRESS
200 Spring Street
Eau Claire, WI 54703-3225
715-833-5261
715-836-0105 (fax)

http://www.mgprogeny.com
Bible-based study guides for literature.

PROVIDENCE PROJECT
14566 NW 110th Street
Whitewater, KS 67154
316-799-2112

RAINBOW RE-SOURCE CENTER
P. O. Box 491
Kawanee, IL 61443
800-705-8809
e-mail: RAINBOWRES@aol.com
Discounts.

ROD AND STAFF PUBLISHERS
Route 172
Crockett, KY 41413
606-522-4348

SAXON PUBLISHERS
1320 West Lindsey
Norman, OK 73069
405-329-7071

SCHOLASTIC BOOK CLUBS
P. O. Box 7503
Jefferson City, MO 65102-9966
800-724-2424
Discounted software and children's books.

SHEPHERD PRESS
P. O. Box 24
Wapwallopen, PA 18660
800-338-1445

SHEKIHAH CURRICULUM CELLAR
101 Meador Road
Kilgore, TX 75662
903-643-2760
903-643-2796 (fax)

SING 'N' LEARN
2626 Club Meadow
Garland, TX 75043
800-460-1973
Lots of audiotapes for your auditory learner.

SONLIGHT CURRICULUM
8121 South Grant Way
Littleton, CO 80122-2701
303-730-6292
303-795-8668 (fax)
e-mail: 76702.2764@compuserve.com
Source of international homeschoolers curriculum.

SUMMIT MINISTRIES
P. O. Box 207
Manitou Springs, CO 80829
719-685-9103

TIMBERDOODLE
1510 E. Spencer Lake Road
Shelton, WA 98584
800-478-0672
360-427-5625 (fax)

http://www.timberdoodle.com

TOPS LEARNING SYSTEMS
10970 S. Mulino Road
Canby, OR 97013
503-263-2040

TWENTY-FOUR
See entry under Academic Competitions

USBORNE BOOKS AT HOME
Educational Development Co.
P. O. Box 470663
Tulsa, OK 74147
800-475-4522
or
Nancy Lotinsky
18800 Still Meadow Ct.
Gaithersburg, MD 20879
301-869-5827
Request "Teaching with Usborne Books."

W. H. FREEMAN/VHPS
175 Fifth Avenue
New York, NY 10010-7848
800-877-5351

WORLD BOOK EDUCATIONAL DIVISION
101 Northwest Point Boulevard
Elk Grove Village, IL 60007

Used-Curriculum Suppliers

Because inventory is always in flux, you must first send a list of what you are looking to buy, sell, or trade to these suppliers.

THE BACK PACK
P. O. Box 125
Ernul, NC 28527
919-244-0728

THE BOOK CELLAR
Granite Town Plaza
Milford, NH 03055
603-672-4333
603-672-0729 (fax)

EDUCATOR'S EXCHANGE
10755 Midlothian Pike
Richmond, VA 23236
804-794-6994
e-mail: jscgec@aol.com

HOME SCHOOL EXCHANGE
26 Colony Street
Saint Augustine, FL 32095
904-824-8247

MOORE EXPRESSIONS
750 Lord Dunmore Drive #105
Virginia Beach, VA 23464
757-474-2634

RAINBOW RE-SOURCE CENTER
P. O. Box 491
Kawanee, IL 61443
800-705-8809
e-mail: RAINBOWRES@aol.com
Send $2.50 for current used-curriculum list.

Academic Contests and Competitions

BOOK-IT! NATIONAL READING INCENTIVE PROGRAM
Pizza Hut, Inc.
P. O. Box 2999
Wichita, KS 67201
800-426-6548
Reading incentive program for grades K–6.

EDUCATION PROGRAM FOR GIFTED YOUTH (EPGY)
Ventura Hall, Stanford University
Stanford, CA 94305-4115
415-329-9924

http://www-epgy.stanford.edu/epgy/
Expensive but prestigious courses online.

FREEDOMS FOUNDATION'S NATIONAL AWARDS PROGRAM FOR YOUTH
Awards Department
Freedoms Foundation at Valley Forge
Route 23
P. O. Box 706
Valley Forge, PA 19482-0706

FUTURE PROBLEM-SOLVING PROGRAM
318 West Ann Street
Ann Arbor, MI 48104
313-998-7377

INSTITUTE FOR THE ACADEMIC ADVANCEMENT OF YOUTH
Center for Talented Youth Talent Search
The Johns Hopkins University
3400 North Charles Street
Baltimore, MD 21218
For fifth- through eighth-graders who score in the 98 percentile or above on standardized achievement test.

INTERNATIONAL SCIENCE AND ENGINEERING FAIR
Science Service, Inc.
1719 N. Street NW
Washington, D.C. 20036

INVENT AMERICA
U.S. Patent Model Foundation
Suite 420
510 King Street
Alexandria, VA 22314

KIDS AT HOME, INC.
P. O. Box 9148
Bend, OR 97708
541-389-8549
e-mail: kidshome@transport.com

KNOWLEDGE OPEN ACADEMIC COMPETITION
Academic Hallmarks
P. O. Box 998
Durango, CO 81302
800-321-9218
Competition comes on computer disk.

MAKE A DIFFERENCE DAY
USA WEEKEND/Make a Difference Day
1000 Wilson Boulevard
Arlington, VA 22229
For all ages. Group volunteer project.

MATHCOUNTS
National Society of Professional Engineers
1420 King Street
Alexandria, VA 22314

MATH OLYMPIAD
2154 Bellmore Avenue
Bellmore, NY 11710-5645
Deadline for registration: September 30.
Fees: $75 per team of up to thirty-five students.

NATIONAL ENERGY EDUCATION DEVELOPMENT PROJECT (NEED)
National Awards Program
P. O. Box 2518
Reston, VA 22090
K–12 group project.

NATIONAL HISTORY DAY
0119 Cecil Hall
University of Maryland
College Park, MD 20742
301-314-9739
e-mail: hstryday@aol.com

THE NATIONAL WRITTEN AND ILLUSTRATED BY . . . AWARD CONTEST FOR STUDENTS
Landmark Editions, Inc.
P. O. Box 4469
1402 Kansas Avenue
Kansas City, MO 64127
816-241-4919
For ages six through nineteen.

NATIONAL GEOGRAPHY BEE
National Geographic Society
1145 17th Street NW
Washington, DC 20036-4688

ODYSSEY OF THE MIND
P. O. Box 547
Glassboro, NJ 08028
609-881-1603

PRESIDENT'S CHALLENGE
President's Council of Physical Fitness and Sports
Poplars Research Center
400 E. Seventh Street
Bloomington, IN 47405
800-258-8146

QUILL & SCROLL SOCIETY
School of Journalism
University of Iowa
Iowa City, IA 52242-1528
Writing and photography contest.

SCHOLASTIC ART AND WRITING AWARDS
P. O. Box 517
New York, NY 10013

SCIENCE-BY-MAIL
Museum of Science
Science Park
Boston, MA 02114-1099
800-729-3300

SMG STOCK MARKET COMPETITION
Securities Industry Foundation for Economic Education
120 Broadway
New York, NY 10271-0080

STONE SOUP MAGAZINE
P. O. Box 83
Santa Cruz, CA 95063
800-447-4569

THINKQUEST
Advanced Network and Services, Inc.
200 Business Park Drive
Armonk, NY 10504

http://i. advanced.org/thinkquest
Academic competition on the Internet.

24 CHALLENGE MATH PROGRAM
First in Math
Suntex International Inc.
118 N. Third Street
Easton, PA 18042
610-253-5255
610-258-2180 (fax)

USA MATHEMATICAL TALENT SEARCH
Contact: George Berzsenyi
Department of Mathematics/Box 121
Rose-Hulman Institute of Technology
5500 Wabash Avenue
Terre Haute, IN 47803-3999
812-877-8474

YOUNG AMERICA HORTICULTURE CONTESTS
National Junior Horticultural Association
Joe Maxson
401 North Fourth
Durant, OK 74701
For ages eight through fourteen (group/individual projects).

Additional Sources of Academic Opportunities

These books list additional opportunities for academic competition and recognition:

All the Best Contests for Kids, Joan and Craig Bergstrom (Tricycle Press, 1996). Available from HSRC.

Free (and Almost Free) Adventures for Teenagers, Gail Grand (John Wiley and Sons, 1995).

NASSP Contests and Activities Advisory List, National Association of Secondary School Principals, 1904 Association Drive, Reston, VA 20191-1537.

Student Science Opportunities: Your Guide to Over 300 Exciting National Programs, Competitions, Internships, and Scholarships, Gail Grand (John Wiley and Sons, 1994).

Learning Center Homeschool Co-op
Sample Information Packet

· ·

This is an edited example of the 1996–97 packet mailed from the Learning Center Homeschool co-op in response to requests for information:

This is our ninth year organizing a homeschool co-op. The Learning Center was conceived and organized in 1988 by Beth and Ken Mellinger. Since then the number of home-educated children involved has grown dramatically, and we have needed to become increasingly more formally organized.

Currently the co-op is directed by myself (Debra Bell), Cindy McKeown (vice-president), and Nancy Mellinger (administrator), a.k.a. the Triumvirate. I do try to run the co-op as much by consensus as is possible. This is achieved through a summer meeting and through members' responses to questionnaires throughout the year.

We think things will run most smoothly if all families involved have a clear understanding of the purpose of the Learning Center and the responsibilities involvement with the co-op entails. We also think you need to know where we are coming from before you can make an informed decision about your involvement.

Please, then, read through this handout and bring any questions or comments you may have to our next organizational meeting.

1996–97 Membership

Interested families must apply for membership. (Request a form from the administrator.) Membership decisions are based upon the following:

- There is room.
- The oldest child in the family is at least seven.
- The teaching parent has gifts and talents that complement the Learning Center program and philosophy.
- The family is sponsored by a current Learning Center member family.

Educational Philosophy

Our educational goals include raising independent, life-long learners. To this end, we believe in emphasizing the learning "process over the product."

The activities at the Learning Center will be designed to give the children the opportunity to create, evaluate, experiment, make choices, and take risks. Whenever possible we would like the children (as opposed to the mothers) doing most of the "work," i.e., learning. Remember that in any given learning situation it is the teacher who learns the most. So let's allow the kids to have that opportunity. For example, in 1991 the older children had the opportunity to write, cast, design, and direct a scene from a play about the American Revolution.

Purpose of the Learning Center

The Learning Center, we believe, provides children with important experiences: The opportunity to interact in a group and to function under other adult leadership. Schools, of course, say they provide these experiences, but parents have no control over which group or teacher our children are placed with. The Learning Center gives us those important choices, and that should make all the difference.

Primarily, we believe the Learning Center is a social experience and that *that,* in itself, is good. If the children enjoy being together and have fun, we believe that is a worthwhile result.

However, we feel fun and social experiences can be integrated with academic endeavors without much effort. So every attempt will be made to provide academically challenging and meaningful projects for the children to collaborate on.

Second, major activities undertaken at the Learning Center should meet one of these standards:

1. The activity requires an audience (for example, play or science fair).
2. The activity requires a group (for example, choir or a soccer game).

We want to use the Learning Center to provide educational experiences we cannot create at home.

Responsibility

The Learning Center takes time to lead, organize, and administrate. We think it is a tremendous experience for our children, but we do not want to get burned out by the responsibility or see only a few moms carrying the load.

So we expect all mothers (and, to a lesser degree, fathers) whose children are involved to be willing to lead/assist in activities, care for little ones, administrate, and help clean up. Moms should expect to be in attendance at all Learning Center sessions. At the Learning Center, mothers should expect to be assigned to two out of three sessions as either a teacher or helper. Mothers without specific assignments should expect to fill in where needed.

A semester schedule will be put out well enough in advance that mothers will know what their major responsibilities are at the Learning Center and have adequate time to prepare for them.

Moms who are assigned to lead activities are also responsible to design that activity. In some cases I will provide some guidelines and help, but I need moms to shoulder the responsibility for planning. For example, the preschool program is intended to be semi-structured. The kids will do better if their time is planned. We would like to see a storytime, game time, puzzles, crafts, singing, etc., incorporated into their program. But it is the mothers who are assigned to the preschoolers for a particular center who will design that day's program.

Even when moms do not have a specific assignment on the schedule, they should still pitch in where they see a need during the Learning Center sessions. Because we want to run a creative, flexible co-op, the schedule is a general plan for the day. As things progress during a Learning Center session, other mothers will inevitably need to step in and lend assistance.

We also recognize that the Learning Center provides a social outlet for us mothers, and I do not want to set a rigid tone for our time together. We certainly can take time to converse with each other, just please don't wait to be asked before helping out.

We understand that some factors, like having a baby, will legitimately affect the level of a mom's involvement during a given year. Also, I see leadership as a seasonal responsibility. The level of responsibility shouldered by a given mom will ebb and flow. Typically, I do not look for a lot of leadership from a mother participating for the first time—but the second year is a different story! And moms who have been contributing heavily for several years should ideally have the opportunity to sit back and relax for a semester or so.

Learning Center Rules and Children's Behavior

The children will need to adjust to a lesser degree of freedom this year because we are such a large group. The leader of a group should adhere to the guidelines for bathroom privileges, drinks, and care of the facility, etc., and should not hesitate to address any misbehavior. Parents should discuss with their children why we need to establish certain routines (for example, younger children walking with a partner quietly to the gymnasium, drinks only at the break, ladies first) and address their children immediately if their behavior warrants that.

We will try to keep the "rules" to a minimum, and they will be clearly articulated and posted at the first Learning Center session.

Fees

The fees for involvement in the Learning Center this year are $10 per month per family (not per child). The co-op meets for nine months, so the total is $90. This can be paid in two installments. A minimum of $45 is due by the first co-op day in September. Then the balance is due by December 31. Fees are nonreturnable. We also raise money for the co-op with an annual hoagie sale in the spring.

Sample Electives and Activities Offered During the Past Few Years

Electives:
Economics
Civics
Pioneer days
Christian charm
Chemistry
Physics
Shakespeare
Pennsylvania History
Volleyball
Basketball
Square dancing
Aerobics
Weaving
Quilting
Cooking
Sewing
Medieval days
Poetry
Sign language
Drama/Mime
Sports history
Inventors and scientists
Chess

Activities:
Produced several plays
Made tin lanterns, dipped candles, carded wool
Christmas caroling
Packaged care packages for orphanage in Romania
International Christmas party
First aid classes
Fire prevention presentation
Writers' groups, published the *Learning Center Rag*
Juried science fair
Children's choir
National Geography Bee
Pizza Hut Book-It Program
Global challenge
Presidential Fitness Challenge
Overnight science camp
Arts festival/family night
End-of-the-year picnic
Participated in the Walk-for-Life
Sheep-shearing

1996–1997 Contract

In exchange for the benefits and opportunities membership in the Learning Center provides for my children, I agree to do my best to fulfill with excellence and joy the following minimum responsibilities:

1. I will lead or assist with two out of three sessions each Learning Center session.

2. I will be ready to serve as a substitute or assist with setup and clean-up on an as-needed basis.

3. Our family will pay promptly to the Learning Center treasurer the fee of $45 prior to the start of each semester.

4. Our family will sell a minimum of twenty hoagies for the spring fundraiser or make up the difference at one dollar per hoagie.

5. I will do my best to arrive promptly and ensure my children are prepared for their classes each Learning Center session.

6. If I have ideas for improving the Learning Center I will readily share them. If I am upset with Debby, I will come and tell her and not be afraid.

_____   _____

Signed   Date

I appreciate your willingness to commit yourself to the Learning Center for the sake of providing all our children with the best experience possible. In exchange, I promise to quickly extend *grace* for momentary lapses in fulfilling this commitment (provided that I have had my morning coffee first).

Notes

• •

Introduction

1. Pennsylvania law requires periodic testing and an annual review of a home-educated student's work by a certified teacher contracted by the parents. In providing this service, I've had close examination of scores of kids from a broad spectrum of backgrounds and abilities.

Chapter 1. Determining Your Destination

1. "Classical education" refers to a course of study that focuses on the "great books" of Western civilization, beginning with the Greek and Roman manuscripts. This is also referred to as a "liberal" education or "the grand conversation." A classical, Christian education is enjoying a resurgence of interest fueled by Douglas Wilson's book *Recovering the Lost Tools of Learning: An Approach to a Distinctively Christian Education* (Crossway, 1991).

Chapter 2. The Advantages of Homeschooling

1. *A Nation at Risk,* published by the National Commission on Excellence in Education, cited in Charles Sykes, *Dumbing Down Our Kids: Why American Children Feel Good About Themselves But Can't Read, Write, or Add* (New York: St. Martin's, 1995), 20.
2. Sykes, *Dumbing Down Our Kids,* 16.
3. Ibid.
4. Ibid.
5. Ibid., 17.
6. Ibid., 19.
7. Ibid., 11–12.
8. Theodore Sizer, *Horace's Compromise* (Houghton Mifflin, 1984) and *Horace's School* (Houghton Mifflin, 1992).

Chapter 5. Single Parents, Special Needs, Careers, and Other FAQs

1. While I've seen many try, I've yet to see a family succeed who thought they would homeschool in the evenings after putting in a full day at work. Both parent and child are usually too tired to care at that point.
2. *Fact Sheet III,* National Home Education Research Institute, 1995.
3. These conclusions are from National Home Education Research Institute's *Fact Sheet I,* 1994.

Chapter 8. How Do I Decide?

1. Scott Somerville, Home School Legal Defense Association attorney, speaking at the Maryland Christian Home Education Network Conference, June 1995.

Chapter 9. Determining Your Child's Learning Style

1. For more information on Keirsey's work, see David Keirsey and Marilyn Bates, *Please Understand Me: Character and Temperament Types* (Del Mar, CA: Prometheus Nemesis, 1982).
2. The following information about learning styles is adapted from the work of Dr. Keith Golay, *Learning Patterns and Temperament Styles* (Manas Systems), 714-870-1064.
3. Golay, *Learning Patterns and Temperament Styles,* 30.

Chapter 21. Subject-by-Subject Guidelines

1. *Newsweek,* Fall/Winter Special Edition: Education, 1990, 18.
2. Saxon also has a K–3 program that is well-designed and manipulative-based. However, it is fairly expensive and requires daily teacher-student tutorials. For this reason, I have not found it a practical choice for most families.
3. C. S. Lewis, *Mere Christianity* (New York: Macmillan, 1952), 56.

Chapter 24. Navigating College Admissions Channels

1. "Survey of Admissions Policies, 1996," National Center for Home Education.
2. This article, reprinted with permission from the author, first appeared in the *Pennsylvania Homeschoolers* newsletter, issue 50. Rhett is now attending college on a full academic scholarship.

Chapter 25. College-at-Home

1. Charles Sykes and Brad Miner, *The National Review College Guide* (New York: Simon & Schuster, 1993), 11–12.
2. Ibid., 16.

Chapter 29. Winning Over Public Officials and Relatives

1. *New York Times,* 12 December 1995.
2. *USA Today,* 8 January 1996.
3. *U.S. News & World Report,* 12 February 1996.
4. The same thing happened when the Pennsylvania Senate passed our homeschool bill into law. The entire assembly stood and gave a standing ovation to the hard-working homeschooling parents in the gallery—a first, the journalist covering the capitol beat reported. For a great story and an excellent example of how the political process is meant to work, read *The Story of a Bill* by Howard Richman (*Pennsylvania Homeschoolers*).

Chapter 32. Motivating the Reluctant Learner

1. The "unschooling" approach gives children complete autonomy in choosing what they will study, when, and for how long.

Index